Bradle
Peter Aitken
Dean Miller

Sams **Teach Yourself**

C Programming

in **One Hour a Day**

Seventh Edition

 | 800 East 96th Street, Indianapolis, Indiana 46240

Sams Teach Yourself C Programming in One Hour a Day, Seventh Edition

ISBN-10: 0-7897-5199-2

ISBN-13: 978-0-7897-5199-7

Library of Congress Control Number: 2013949045

Printed in the United States of America

First Printing: October 2013

Trademarks

All terms mentioned in this book that are known to be trademarks or service marks have been appropriately capitalized. Sams Publishing cannot attest to the accuracy of this information. Use of a term in this book should not be regarded as affecting the validity of any trademark or service mark.

Warning and Disclaimer

Every effort has been made to make this book as complete and as accurate as possible, but no warranty or fitness is implied. The information provided is on an "as is" basis. The authors and the publisher shall have neither liability nor responsibility to any person or entity with respect to any loss or damages arising from the information contained in this book.

Bulk Sales

Sams Publishing offers excellent discounts on this book when ordered in quantity for bulk purchases or special sales. For more information, please contact

U.S. Corporate and Government Sales
1-800-382-3419
corpsales@pearsontechgroup.com

For sales outside of the U.S., please contact

International Sales
international@pearsoned.com

Acquisitions Editor
Mark Taber

Managing Editor
Sandra Schroeder

Project Editor
Mandie Frank

Copy Editor
Apostrophe Editing Services

Indexer
Ken Johnson

Proofreader
Anne Goebel

Technical Editor
Siddhartha Singh

Team Coordinator
Vanessa Evans

Designer
Mark Shirar

Layout
Mary Sudul

Contents at a Glance

Table of Contents

PART II: Putting C to Work

About the Authors

Bradley L. Jones manages and directs the Developer.com Network, which includes sites such as Developer.com, CodeGuru, and DevX. He has developed systems using C, C#, C++, SQL Server, PowerBuilder, Visual Basic, HTML5, and more. His Twitter handle is @BradleyLJones.

Peter Aitken was on the faculty at Duke University Medical Center, where he cut his programming teeth developing computer programs for research. He is an experienced author in the IT field—on both applications and programming topics—with more than 70 magazine articles and 40 books to his credit. Aitken currently works as a consultant in the pharmaceutical industry.

Dean Miller is a writer and editor with more than 20 years of experience in both the publishing and licensed consumer product businesses. Over the years, he has created or helped shape a number of bestselling books and series, including *Teach Yourself in 21 Days*, *Teach Yourself in 24 Hours*, and the *Unleashed* series, all from Sams Publishing.

Acknowledgments

I'd like to thank Bradley Jones and Peter Aiken for creating an outstanding C programming tutorial that has stood strong for more than two decades, teaching hundreds of thousands how to program in the greatest language of all, C. I'd like to thank Mark Taber for the opportunity to take this book into a new format, and to Mandie Frank, San Dee Phillips, and Siddhartha Singh for taking the original text and my additions and molding it into a better product. On a personal level, thanks to my wife Fran, my kids John, Alice, and Margaret for their love and support. I'd like to dedicate my part of this edition to my two sisters, Sheryn and Rebecca, for their unparalleled strength through the adversity life throws them.

—Dean Miller

First and foremost, my thanks go to my coauthor, Brad Jones, for his hard work and dedication. I am also greatly indebted to all the people at Sams Publishing, unfortunately too many to mention by name, who helped bring this book from concept to completion.

—Peter Aitken

I'd first like to thank my wife for her continued understanding and patience as I take on such projects as the writing of books. A good book is the result of the symbiosis achieved by a number of people working together. I would like to acknowledge all the people—readers, editors, and others—who have taken the time to provide comments and feedback on previous editions of this book. By incorporating much of their feedback, I believe that we have made this the best book for easily learning to program C.

—Bradley L. Jones

We Want to Hear from You!

As the reader of this book, *you* are our most important critic and commentator. We value your opinion and want to know what we're doing right, what we could do better, what areas you'd like to see us publish in, and any other words of wisdom you're willing to pass our way.

We welcome your comments. You can email or write us to let us know what you did or didn't like about this book—as well as what we can do to make our books better.

Please note that we cannot help you with technical problems related to the topic of this book and may not be able to reply personally to every message we receive.

When you write, please be sure to include this book's title, edition number, and authors as well as your name and contact information. We will carefully review your comments and share them with the authors and editors who worked on the book.

Email: feedback@samspublishing.com

Mail: Sams Publishing
            201 West 103rd Street
            Indianapolis, IN 46290 USA

Reader Services

Visit our website and register this book at informit.com/register for convenient access to any updates, downloads, or errata that might be available for this book.

Introduction

As you can guess from the title, this book is set up so that you can teach yourself the C programming language in 22 one-hour lessons. Despite stiff competition from languages such as C++, Java, and C#, C remains the language of choice for people who are just learning programming. For reasons detailed in Lesson 1, "Getting Started with C," you can't go wrong in selecting C as your programming language.

You've made a wise decision selecting this book as your means of learning C. Although there are many books on C, this book presents C in the most logical and easy-to-learn sequence. The fact that the six previous editions have been on best-seller lists indicates that readers agree! This book is designed for you to work through the lessons in order on a daily basis. You don't need any previous programming experience; although experience with another language, such as BASIC, might help you learn faster. Also no assumptions are made about your computer or compiler; this book concentrates on teaching the C language, regardless of whether you use a PC, a Mac, or a UNIX system.

This Book's Special Features

This book contains some special features to aid you on your path to C enlightenment. Syntax boxes show you how to use specific C concepts. Each box provides concrete examples and a full explanation of the C command or concept. To get a feel for the style of the syntax boxes, look at the following example. (Don't try to understand the material; you haven't even reached Lesson 1!)

Syntax

```
#include <stdio.h>
 printf( format-string[,arguments,...]);
```

printf() is a function that accepts a series of *arguments*, each applying to a conversion specifier in the given format string. It prints the formatted information to the standard output device, usually the display screen. When using printf(), you need to include the standard input/output header file, stdio.h.

The *format-string* is required; however, *arguments* are optional. For each argument, there must be a conversion specifier. The format string can also contain escape sequences. The following are examples of calls to `printf()` and their output.

Example 1

```
#include <stdio.h>
int main( void )
{
    printf( "This is an example of something printed!");
}
```

Example 1 Output

```
This is an example of something printed!
```

Example 2

```
printf( "This prints a character, %c\na number, %d\na floating point,
%f", 'z', 123, 456.789 );
```

Example 2 Output

```
This prints a character, z
a number, 123
a floating point, 456.789
```

Another feature of this book is DO/DON'T boxes, which give you pointers on what to do and what not to do.

DO	**DON'T**
DO read the rest of this section. It explains the Workshop sections that appear at the end of each lesson.	**DON'T** skip any of the quiz questions or exercises. If you can finish the lesson's Workshop, you're ready to move on to new material.

You'll encounter Tip, Note, and Caution boxes as well. Tips provide useful shortcuts and techniques for working with C. Notes provide special details that enhance the explanations of C concepts. Cautions help you avoid potential problems.

Numerous sample programs illustrate C's features and concepts so that you can apply them in your own programs. Each program's discussion is divided into three components: the program itself, the input required and the output generated by it, and a line-by-line analysis of how the program works. These components are indicated by special icons.

Each lesson ends with a Q&A section containing answers to common questions relating to that lesson's material. There is also a Workshop at the end of each lesson. It contains quiz questions and exercises. The quiz tests your knowledge of the concepts presented in that lesson. If you want to check your answers, or if you're stumped, the answers are provided in Appendix D.

You won't learn C by just reading this book, however. If you want to be a programmer, you must write programs. Following each set of quiz questions is a set of exercises. You need to attempt each exercise. Writing C code is the best way to learn C.

The BUG BUSTER exercises are most beneficial. A bug is a program error in C. BUG BUSTER exercises are code listings that contain common problems (bugs). It's your job to locate and fix these errors. If you have trouble busting the bugs, these answers also are given in Appendix D.

As you progress through this book, some of the exercise answers tend to get long. Other exercises have a multitude of answers. As a result, later lessons don't always provide answers for all the exercises.

Conventions Used in This Book

This book uses different typefaces to help you differentiate between C code and regular English, and also to help you identify important concepts. Actual C code appears in a special `monospace` font. In the examples of a program's input and output, what the user types appears in **`bold monospace`**. Placeholders—terms that represent what you actually type within the code—appear in *`italic monospace`*. New or important terms appear in *italic*.

LESSON 1
Getting Started with C

Welcome to *Sams Teach Yourself C in One Hour a Day!* This lesson starts you toward becoming a proficient C programmer, as you learn:

- Why C is a great choice among programming languages

- The steps in the program development cycle

- How to write, compile, and run your first C program

- Error messages generated by the compiler and linker

A Brief History of the C Language

You might be wondering about the origin of the C language and where it got its name. C was created by Dennis Ritchie at the Bell Telephone Laboratories in 1972. The language was created for a specific purpose: to design the UNIX operating system (which is used on many computers). From the beginning, C was intended to be useful—to enable busy programmers to get things done.

Because C is such a powerful and flexible language, its use quickly spread beyond Bell Labs. Programmers everywhere began using it to write all sorts of programs. Soon, however, different organizations began utilizing their own versions of C, and subtle differences between implementations started to cause programmers headaches. In response to this problem, the American National Standards Institute (ANSI) formed a committee in 1983 to establish a standard definition of C, which became known as ANSI Standard C. With few exceptions, every modern C compiler has the capability to adhere to this standard.

NOTE

> Although C rarely changes, the most recent changes occurred in 2011 with the ANSI C11 Standard. This standard added a few new features to the language that this book covers. However, older compilers might not support these most recent standards.

Now, what about the name? The C language is so named because its predecessor was called B. The B language was developed by Ken Thompson of Bell Labs. You can guess why it was called B.

Why Use C?

In today's world of computer programming, you can choose from many high-level languages, such as C, Perl, BASIC, Java, PHP, and C#. These are all excellent languages suited for most programming tasks. Even so, several reasons exist why many computer professionals feel that C is at the top of the list:

- C is a powerful and flexible language. What you can accomplish with C is limited only by your imagination. The language places no constraints on you. C is used for projects as diverse as operating systems, word processors, graphics, spreadsheets, and even compilers for other languages.

- C is a popular language preferred by professional programmers. As a result, a wide variety of C compilers and helpful accessories are available.

- C is a portable language. *Portable* means that a C program written for one computer system (an IBM PC, for example) can be compiled and run on another system (a DEC VAX system, perhaps) with little or no modification. In addition, a program written with the Microsoft Windows operating system can be moved to a machine running Linux with little or no modification. Portability is enhanced by the ANSI Standard for C, the set of rules for C compilers.

- C is a language of few words, containing only a handful of terms, called *keywords,* which serve as the base on which the language's functionality is built. You might think that a language with more keywords (sometimes called *reserved words*) would be more powerful. This isn't true. As you program with C, you will find that it can be programmed to do any task.

- C is modular. C code can (and should) be written in routines called *functions.* These functions can be reused in other applications or programs. By passing pieces of information to the functions, you can create useful, reusable code.

As these features show, C is an excellent choice for your first programming language. What about C++? You might have heard about C++ and the programming technique called *object-oriented programming.* Perhaps you're wondering what the differences are between C and C++ and whether you should be teaching yourself C++ instead of C.

Not to worry! C++ is a superset of C, which means that C++ contains everything C does, plus new additions for object-oriented programming. If you do go on to learn C++, almost everything you learn about C will still apply to the C++ superset. In learning C, you are not only learning one of today's most powerful and popular programming languages, but you are also preparing yourself for object-oriented programming.

Another language that has gotten lots of attention is Java. Java, like C++, is based on C. If later you decide to learn Java, you will find that almost everything you learned about C can be applied.

The newest of these languages is C# (pronounced "See-Sharp"). Like C++ and Java, C# is an object-oriented language that is derived from C. Again, you will find that a lot of what you learn about C will directly apply to C# programming.

NOTE

> Many people who learn C later choose to learn C++, Java, or C#. Learning C first makes adding an additional language so much easier.

Preparing to Program

You should take certain steps when you solve a problem. First, you must define the problem. If you don't know what the problem is, you can't find a solution! When you know what the problem is, you can devise a plan to fix it. When you have a plan, you can usually implement it. After the plan is implemented, you must test the results to see whether the problem is solved. You can apply this same logic to many other areas, including programming.

When creating a program in C (or for that matter, a computer program in any language), you should follow a similar sequence of steps:

1. Determine the objective(s) of the program.
2. Determine the methods you want to use in writing the program.
3. Create the program to solve the problem.
4. Run the program to see the results.

An example of an objective (see step 1) might be to write a word processor or database program. A much simpler objective is to display your name on the screen. If you didn't have an objective, you wouldn't be writing a program, so you already have the first step done.

The second step is to determine the method you want to use to write the program. Do you need a computer program to solve the problem? What information should you track? What formulas should you use? During this step, you should try to determine what you need to know and in what order the solution should be implemented.

For example, assume that someone asks you to write a program to determine the area inside a circle. Step 1 is complete because you know your objective: Determine the area inside a circle. Step 2 is to determine what you need to know to ascertain the area. In this example, assume that the user of the program will provide the radius of the circle. Knowing this, you can apply the formula πr^2 to obtain the answer. Now you have the pieces you need, so you can continue to steps 3 and 4, which are called the Program Development Cycle.

The Program Development Cycle

The Program Development Cycle has its own steps. In the first step, you use an editor to create a disk file containing your source code. In the second step, you compile the source code to create an object file. In the third step, you link the compiled code to create an executable file. The fourth step is to run the program to see whether it works as originally planned.

Creating the Source Code

Source code is a series of statements or commands used to instruct the computer to perform your wanted tasks. As mentioned, the first step in the Program Development Cycle is to enter source code into an editor. For example, here is a line of C source code:

```
printf("Hello, Mom!");
```

This statement instructs the computer to display the message `Hello, Mom!` onscreen. (For now, don't worry about how this statement works.)

Using an Editor

Most C programming occurs in an Integrated Development Environment (IDE), which enables you to enter your programs in their editor and compile your programs, as well as debug and build your applications. (Although those concepts you tackle later.) You don't have to use the included editor, but it probably makes the most sense. However, most computer systems include a program that can be used as an editor. If you use a Linux or UNIX system, you can use such editors as ed, ex, edit, emacs, or vi. If you use Microsoft Windows, Notepad or WordPad is available.

Most word processors use special codes to format their documents. These codes can't be read correctly by other programs. The American Standard Code for Information Interchange (ASCII) has specified a standard text format that nearly any program, including C, can use. Many word processors, such as WordPerfect, Microsoft Word, WordPad, and WordStar can save source files in ASCII form (as a text file rather than a document file). When you want to save a word processor's file as an ASCII file, select the ASCII or text option when saving.

If none of these editors is what you want to use, you can always buy a different editor. There are packages, both commercial and shareware, that have been designed specifically for entering source code.

When you save a source file, you must give it a name. The name should describe what the program does. In addition, when you save C program source files, give the file a .c extension. Although you could give your source file any name and extension, .c is recognized as the appropriate extension to use.

Compiling the Source Code

Although you might understand C source code (at least after reading this book you will), your computer can't. A computer requires digital, or *binary*, instructions in *machine language*. Before your C program can run on a computer, it must be translated from source code to machine language. This translation, the second step in program development, is performed by a program called a *compiler*. The compiler takes your source code file as input and produces a disk file containing the machine language instructions that correspond to your source code statements. The machine language instructions created by the compiler are *object code,* and the disk file containing them is an *object file*.

NOTE
This book covers ANSI Standard C. This means that it doesn't matter which C compiler you use, as long as it follows the ANSI Standard. Not all compilers support the standards. The specific name of the current standard for C is ISO/IEC 9899:2011. Rather than using this complex name, this book refers to the standard as C11.

With your graphical IDE, compiling is simple. In most graphical environments, you can compile a program listing by selecting the compile icon or selecting something from a menu. After the code is compiled, selecting the run icon or selecting something from a menu executes the program. You should check your compiler's manuals for specifics on compiling and running a program. The Code::Blocks program that you can download for free is an example of a graphical development environment that has versions for most operating systems. There are other graphical development environments, both free and for sale, for almost every possible platform. Just pick your favorite.

After you compile, you have an object file. If you look at a list of the files in the directory or folder in which you compiled, you should find a file that has the same name as your source file, but with an .obj (rather than a .c) extension. The .obj extension is recognized as an object file and is used by the linker. On a Linux or UNIX system, the compiler creates object files with an extension of .o instead of .obj.

Linking to Create an Executable File

One more step is required before you can run your program. Part of the ANSI C language definition is a function library that contains *object code* (code that has already been compiled) for predefined functions. A *predefined function* contains C code that has already been written and is supplied in a ready-to-use form with your compiler package.

The printf() function used in the previous example is a *library function*. These library functions perform frequently needed tasks, such as displaying information onscreen and reading data from disk files. If your program uses any of these functions (and hardly a program exists that doesn't use at least one), the object file produced when your source code was compiled must be combined with object code from the function library to create the final executable program. (*Executable* means that the program can be run, or executed, on your computer.) This process is called *linking,* and it's performed by a program called (you guessed it) a *linker.*

Figure 1.1 shows the progression from source code to object code to executable program.

1

FIGURE 1.1
The C source code that you write is converted to object code by the compiler and then to an executable file by the linker.

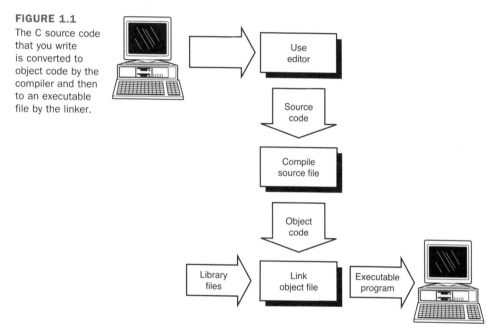

Completing the Development Cycle

When your program is compiled and linked to create an executable file, you can run it by clicking the run button (if you are still in your IDE) or double-clicking the program's icon (just like you would run any other program). If you run the program and receive results different from what you thought you would, you need to go back to the first step. You must identify what caused the problem and correct it in the source code. When you make a change to the source code, you need to recompile and relink the program to create a corrected version of the executable file. You keep following this cycle until you get the program to execute exactly as you intended.

One final note on compiling and linking: Although compiling and linking are mentioned as two separate steps, most compilers do both as one step. Graphical development environments generally give you the option of doing the compiling and linking together or separately. Regardless of the method by which compiling and linking are accomplished, understand that these two processes, even when done with one command, are two separate actions.

The C Development Cycle

Step 1   Use an editor to write your source code. By tradition, C source code files have the extension .c (for example, myprog.c, database.c, and so on).

Step 2   Compile the program using a compiler. If the compiler doesn't find any errors in the program, it produces an object file. The compiler produces object files with an .obj or .o extension and the same name as the source code file. (For example, myprog.c compiles to either myprog. obj or myprog.o.) If the compiler finds errors, it reports them. You must return to step 1 to make corrections in your source code.

Step 3   Link the program using a linker. If no errors occur, the linker produces an executable program located in a disk file with an .exe extension and the same name as the object file. (For example, myprog.obj is linked to create myprog.exe.)

Step 4   Execute the program. You should test to determine whether it functions properly. If not, start again with step 1 and make modifications and additions to your source code.

Figure 1.2 shows the program development steps. For all but the simplest programs, you might go through this sequence many times before finishing your program. Even the most experienced programmers can't sit down and write a complete, error-free program in just one step! Because you run through the edit-compile-link-test cycle many times, you must become familiar with your tools: the editor, compiler, and linker.

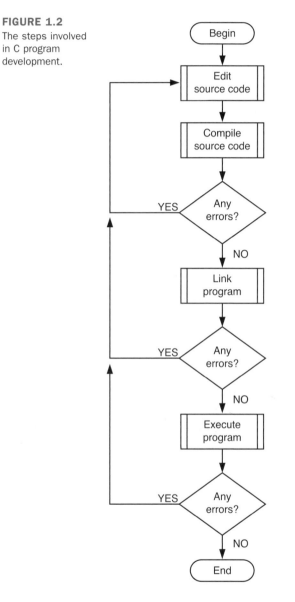

FIGURE 1.2
The steps involved
in C program
development.

1

Begin

Edit
source code

Compile
source code

YES ← Any
errors?

NO

Link
program

YES ← Any
errors?

NO

Execute
program

YES ← Any
errors?

NO

End

Your First C Program

You're probably eager to try your first program in C. To help you become familiar
with your compiler, Listing 1.1 contains a quick program for you to work through. You
might not understand everything at this point, but you should get a feel for the process of
writing, compiling, and running a real C program.

This demonstration uses a program named hello.c, which does nothing more than display the words Hello, World! onscreen. This program, a traditional introduction to C programming, is a good one for you to learn. The source code for hello.c is in Listing 1.1. When you type in this listing, do not include the line numbers on the left or the colons. Those numbers will be used throughout the book to analyze the programs you write.

LISTING 1.1   HELLO.C.

```
1:   #include <stdio.h>
2:
3:   int main(void)
4:   {
5:       printf("Hello, World!\n");
6:       return 0;
7:   }
```

Be sure that you have installed your compiler as specified in the installation instructions provided with the software. Whether you work with Linux, UNIX, MAC OS, Windows, or any other operating system, make sure you understand how to use the compiler and editor of your choice. When your compiler and editor are ready, follow these steps to enter, compile, and execute HELLO.C.

Entering and Compiling hello.c

To enter and compile the hello.c program, follow these steps:

1. Start your editor in the directory where your C program will be. As mentioned previously, you can use any text editor, but most C compilers come with an IDE that enables you to enter, compile, and link your programs in one convenient setting. Check your manuals to see whether your compiler has an IDE available.

2. Use the keyboard to type the hello.c source code exactly as shown in Listing 1.1. Press Enter at the end of each line.

NOTE   Don't enter the line numbers or colons. These are for reference only.

3. Save the source code. You should name the file **hello.c**.

4. Verify that hello.c is on disk by listing the files in the directory or folder. You should see hello.c within this listing.

5. Compile and link hello.c. Execute the appropriate command specified by your compiler's manuals. You should get a message stating that there were no errors or warnings.

6. Check the compiler messages. If you receive no errors or warnings, everything should be okay.

   If you made an error typing the program, the compiler will catch it and display an error message. For example, if you misspell the word `printf` as `prntf`, you would see a message similar to the following:

   ```
   Error: undefined symbols:_prntf in hello.c (hello.OBJ)
   ```

7. Go back to step 2 if this or any other error message displays. Open the hello.c file in your editor. Compare your file's contents carefully with Listing 1.1, make any necessary corrections, and continue with step 3.

8. Your first C program should now be compiled and ready to run. If you display a directory listing of all files named hello (with any extension), you should see the following:

   hello.c, the source code file you created with your editor

   hello.obj or hello.o, which contains the object code for hello.c

   hello.exe, the executable program created when you compiled and linked hello.c

9. To *execute*, or run, hello.exe, simply enter **hello**. The message `Hello, World!` displays onscreen.

Congratulations! You have just entered, compiled, and run your first C program. Admittedly, hello.c is a simple program that doesn't do anything useful, but it's a start. Actually, most of today's expert C programmers started learning C in this same way—by compiling hello.c—so you're in good company.

Compilation Errors

A compilation error occurs when the compiler finds something in the source code that it can't compile. A misspelling, typographical error, or any of a dozen other things can cause the compiler to choke. Fortunately, modern compilers don't just choke; they tell you what they're choking on and where the problem is! This makes it easier to find and correct errors in your source code.

This point can be illustrated by introducing a deliberate error into the hello.c program you entered earlier. If you worked through that example (and you should have), you now have a copy of hello.c on your disk. Using your editor, move the cursor to the end of the line containing the call to `printf()`, and erase the terminating semicolon. hello.c should now look like Listing 1.2.

LISTING 1.2 hello2.c - hello.c with an error.

```
1:   #include <stdio.h>
2:
3:   int main(void)
4:   {
5:       printf("Hello, World!")
6:       return 0;
7:   }
```

Next, save the file. You're now ready to compile it. Do so by entering the command for your compiler. Because of the error you introduced, the compilation is not completed. Rather, the compiler displays a message similar to the following:

```
hello.c(6) : Error: ';' expected
```

Looking at this line, you can see that it has three parts:

`hello.c`	The name of the file where the error was found
`(6) :`	The line number where the error was found
`Error: ';' expected`	A description of the error

This message is quite informative, telling you that in line 6 of hello.c the compiler expected to find a semicolon but didn't. However, you know that the semicolon was actually omitted from line 5, so there is a discrepancy. You're faced with the puzzle of why the compiler reports an error in line 6 when, actually, a semicolon was omitted from line 5. The answer lies in the fact that C doesn't care about things like breaks between lines. The semicolon that belongs after the `printf()` statement could have been placed on the next line. (Although doing so would look confusing and thus be a bad programming practice.) Only after encountering the next command (`return`) in line 6 is the compiler sure that the semicolon is missing. Therefore, the compiler reports that the error is in line 6.

This points out an undeniable fact about C compilers and error messages. Although the compiler is clever about detecting and localizing errors, it's no Einstein. Using your knowledge of the C language, you must interpret the compiler's messages and determine the actual location of any errors reported. You can often find them on the line reported by the compiler, but if not, they are almost always on the preceding line. You might have a bit of trouble finding errors at first, but you should soon get better at it.

NOTE	The errors reported might differ depending on the compiler. In most cases, the error message should give you an idea of what or where the problem is.

Before leaving this topic, look at another example of a compilation error. Load hello.c into your editor again and make the following changes:

1. Replace the semicolon at the end of line 5.
2. Delete the double quotation mark just before the word Hello.

Save the file to disk and compile the program again. This time, the compiler should display error messages similar to the following:

```
hello.c(5) : Error: undefined identifier 'Hello'
hello.c(7) : Lexical error: unterminated string
Lexical error: unterminated string
Lexical error: unterminated string

Fatal error: premature end of source file
```

The first error message finds the error correctly, locating it in line 5 at the word Hello. The error message undefined identifier means that the compiler doesn't know what to make of the word Hello because it is no longer enclosed in quotes. However, what about the other four errors reported? These errors, the meaning of which you don't need to worry about now, illustrate that a single error in a C program can sometimes cause multiple error messages.

The lesson to learn from all this is as follows: If the compiler reports multiple errors, and you can find only one, go ahead and fix that error and recompile. You might find that your single correction is all that's needed, and the program will compile without errors.

Linker Error Messages

Linker errors are relatively rare and usually result from misspelling the name of a C library function. In this case, you get an Error: undefined symbols: error message, followed by the misspelled name (preceded by an underscore). When you correct the spelling, the problem should go away.

Summary

After reading this lesson, you should feel confident that selecting C as your programming language is a wise choice. C offers an unparalleled combination of power, popularity, and portability. These factors, together with C's close relationship to the C++ object-oriented language as well as Java and C#, make C unbeatable.

This lesson explained the various steps involved in writing a C program—the process known as program development. You should have a clear grasp of the edit-compile-link-test cycle, as well as the tools to use for each step.

Errors are an unavoidable part of program development. Your C compiler detects errors in your source code and displays an error message, giving both the nature and the location of the error. Using this information, you can edit your source code to correct the error. Remember, however, that the compiler can't always accurately report the nature and location of an error. Sometimes you need to use your knowledge of C to track down exactly what causes a given error message.

Q&A

Q If I want to give someone a program I wrote, which files do I need to give him?

A One of the nice things about C is that it is a compiled language. This means that after the source code is compiled, you have an executable program. This executable program is a stand-alone program. If you wanted to give hello to all your friends with computers, you can. All you need to give them is the executable program, hello.exe. They don't need the source file, hello.c, or the object file, hello.obj. They don't need to own a C compiler, either. Your friends or those people you give the executable need to use the same type of machine as you—such as a PC, Macintosh, Linux machine, and so on.

Q After I create an executable file, do I need to keep the source file (.c) or object file (.obj)?

A If you get rid of the source file, you have no way to make changes to the program in the future, so you should keep this file. The object files are a different matter. There are reasons to keep object files, but they are beyond the scope of what you're doing now. For now, you can get rid of your object files after you have your executable file. If you need the object file, you can recompile the source file.

Most IDEs create files in addition to the source file (.c), the object file (.obj or .o), and the executable file. As long as you keep the source file (.c), you can always re-create the other files.

Q If my compiler came with an editor, do I have to use it?

A Definitely not. You can use any editor, as long as it saves the source code in text format. If the compiler came with an editor, you should try to use it. If you like a different editor better, use it. I use an editor that I purchased separately, even though all my compilers have their own editors. The editors that come with compilers are getting better. Some of them automatically format your C code. Others color-code different parts of your source file to make it easier to find errors.

Q What do I do if I have only a C++ compiler and not a C compiler?

A As mentioned in this lesson, C++ is a superset of C. This means that you can use a C++ compiler to compile C programs.

Q Can I ignore warning messages?

A Some warning messages don't affect how the program runs, and some do. If the compiler gives you a warning message, it's a signal that something isn't right. Most compilers let you set the warning level. By setting the warning level, you can get only the most serious warnings, or you can get all the warnings, including the most minute. Some compilers even offer various levels in-between. In your programs, you should look at each warning and make a determination. It's always best to try to write all your programs with absolutely no warnings or errors. (With an error, your compiler won't create the executable file.)

Workshop

The Workshop provides quiz questions to help you solidify your understanding of the material covered and exercises to provide you with experience in using what you've learned. Try to understand the quiz and exercise answers before continuing to the next lesson. Answers are provided in Appendix D, "Answers."

Quiz

1. Give three reasons why C is the best choice for a programming language.
2. What does the compiler do?
3. What are the steps in the Program Development Cycle?
4. What command do you need to enter to compile a program called program1.c with your compiler?
5. Does your compiler do both the linking and compiling with just one command, or do you have to enter separate commands?
6. What extension should you use for your C source files?

7. Is FILENAME.TXT a valid name for a C source file?

8. If you execute a program that you have compiled and it doesn't work as you expected, what should you do?

9. What is machine language?

10. What does the linker do?

Exercises

1. Use your text editor to look at the object file created by Listing 1.1. Does the object file look like the source file? (Don't save this file when you exit the editor.)

2. Enter the following program and compile it. What does this program do? (Don't include the line numbers or colons.)

```
1:   #include <stdio.h>
2:
3:   int radius, area;
4:
5:   int main( void )
6:   {
7:      printf( "Enter radius (i.e. 10): " );
8:      scanf( "%d", &radius );
9:      area = (int) (3.14159 * radius * radius);
10:     printf( "\n\nArea = %d\n", area );
11:     return 0;
12:  }
```

3. Enter and compile the following program. What does this program do?

```
1:   #include <stdio.h>
2:
3:   int x, y;
4:
5:   int main( void )
6:   {
7:      for ( x = 0; x < 10; x++, printf( "\n" ) )
8:          for ( y = 0; y < 10; y++ )
9:              printf( "X" );
10:
11:     return 0;
12:  }
```

4. **BUG BUSTER:** The following program has a problem. Enter it in your editor and compile it. Which lines generate error messages?

```
1:   #include <stdio.h>
2:
3:   int main( void );
```

```
4:   {
5:      printf( "Keep looking!" );
6:      printf( "You\'ll find it!\n" );
7:      return 0;
8:   }
```

5. **BUG BUSTER:** The following program has a problem. Enter it in your editor and compile it. Which lines generate problems?

```
1:   #include <stdio.h>
2:
3:   int main( void )
4:   {
5:      printf( "This is a program with a " );
6:      do_it( "problem!");
7:      return 0;
8:   }
```

6. Make the following change to the program in exercise 3. Recompile and rerun this program. What does the program do now?

```
9:   printf( "%c", 1 );
```

LESSON 2
The Components of a C Program

Every C program consists of several components combined in a specific way. Most of this book is devoted to explaining these various program components and how you use them. To help illustrate the overall picture, you should begin by reviewing a complete (though small) C program with all its components identified. In this lesson you learn:

- The components of a short C program
- The purpose of each program component
- How to compile and run a sample program

A Short C Program

Listing 2.1 presents the source code for bigyear.c. This is a simple program. All it does is accept a year of birth entered from the keyboard and calculate what year a person turns a specific age. At this stage, don't worry about understanding the details of how the program works. The point is for you to gain some familiarity with the parts of a C program so that you can better understand the listings presented later in this book.

Before looking at the sample program, you need to know what a function is because functions are central to C programming. A *function* is an independent section of program code that performs a certain task and has been assigned a name. By referencing a function's name, your program can execute the code in the function. The program also can send information, called *arguments,* to the function, and the function can return information to the main part of the program. The two types of C functions are *library functions,* which are a part of the C compiler package, and *user-defined functions,* which you, the programmer, create. You learn about both types of functions in this book.

Note that, as with all the listings in this book, the line numbers in Listing 2.1 are not part of the program. They are included only for identification purposes, so don't type them.

Input ▼

Listing 2.1   bigyear.c - A Program Calculates What Year a Person Turns a Specific Age

```
1:   /* Program to calculate what year someone will turn a specific age */
2:   #include <stdio.h>
3:   #define TARGET_AGE 88
4:
5:   int year1, year2;
6:
7:   int calcYear(int year1);
8:
9:   int main(void)
10:  {
11:      // Ask the user for the birth year
12:      printf("What year was the subject born? ");
13:      printf("Enter as a 4-digit year (YYYY): ");
14:      scanf(" %d", &year1);
15:
16:      // Calculate the future year and display it
17:      year2 = calcYear(year1);
18:
19:      printf("Someone born in %d will be %d in %d.",
20:              year1, TARGET_AGE, year2);
21:
22:      return 0;
23:  }
```

```
24:
25:   /* The function to get the future year */
26:   int calcYear(int year1)
27:   {
28:        return(year1+TARGET_AGE);
29:   }
```

Output ▼

```
What year was the subject born? 1963
Someone born in 1963 will be 88 in 2051.
```

2

The Program's Components

The following sections describe the various components of the preceding sample program. Line numbers are included so that you can easily identify the program parts discussed.

The `main()` Function (Lines 9 Through 23)

The only component required in every executable C program is the `main()` function. In its simplest form, the `main()` function consists of the name `main` followed by a pair of parentheses containing the word `void` (`(void)`) and a pair of braces (`{}`). You can leave the word `void` out and the program still works with most compilers. The ANSI Standard states that you should include the word `void` so that you know there is nothing sent to the `main` function.

Within the braces are statements that make up the main body of the program. Under normal circumstances, program execution starts at the first statement in `main()` and terminates at the last statement in `main()`. Per the ANSI Standard, the only statement that you need to include in this example is the `return` statement on line 22.

The `#include` and `#define` Directives (Lines 2 and 3)

The `#include` directive instructs the C compiler to add the contents of an include file into your program during compilation. An *include file* is a separate disk file that contains information that can be used by your program or the compiler. Several of these files (sometimes called *header files*) are supplied with your compiler. You rarely need to modify the information in these files; that's why they're kept separate from your source code. Include files should all have an .h extension (for example, stdio.h).

You use the `#include` directive to instruct the compiler to add a specific include file to your program during compilation. In Listing 2.1, the `#include` directive is interpreted to mean "Add the contents of the file stdio.h." You will almost always include one or more include files in your C programs. Lesson 22, "Advanced Compiler Use" presents more information about include files.

The `#define` directive instructs the C compiler to replace a specific term with its assigned value throughout your program. By setting a variable at the top of your program and then using the term throughout the code, you can more easily change a term if needed by changing the single `#define` line as opposed to every place throughout the code. For example, if you wrote a payroll program that used a specific deduction for health insurance and the insurance rate changed, tweaking a variable created with `#define` named `HEALTH_INSURANCE` at the top of your program (or in a header file) would be so much easier than searching through lines and lines of code looking for every instance that had the information. Lesson 3, "Storing Information: Variables and Constants" covers the `#define` directive.

The Variable Definition (Line 5)

A *variable* is a name assigned to a location in memory used to store information. Your program uses variables to store various kinds of information during program execution. In C, a variable must be defined before it can be used. A variable definition informs the compiler of the variable's name and the type of information the variable is to hold. In the sample program, the definition on line 4, `int year1, year2;`, defines two variables— named `year1` and `year2`—that each hold an integer value. Lesson 3 presents more information about variables and variable definitions.

The Function Prototype (Line 7)

A *function prototype* provides the C compiler with the name and arguments of the functions contained in the program. It appears before the function is used. A function prototype is distinct from a *function definition,* which contains the actual statements that make up the function. (Function definitions are discussed in more detail in "The Function Definition" section.)

Program Statements (Lines 12, 13, 14, 17, 19, 20, 22, and 28)

The real work of a C program is done by its statements. C statements display information onscreen, read keyboard input, perform mathematical operations, call functions, read disk files, and all the other operations that a program needs to perform. Most of this book is devoted to teaching you the various C statements. For now, remember that in your source code, C statements are generally written one per line and always end with a semicolon. The statements in bigyear.c are explained briefly in the following sections.

The `printf()` Statement

The `printf()` statement (lines 12, 13, 19, and 20) is a library function that displays information onscreen. The `printf()` statement can display a simple text message (as in lines 12 and 13) or a message mixed with the value of one or more program variables (as in lines 19-20).

The `scanf()` Statement

The `scanf()` statement (line 14) is another library function. It reads data from the keyboard and assigns that data to one or more program variables.

The program statement on line 17 calls the function named `calcYear()`. In other words, it executes the program statements contained in the function `calcYear()`. It also sends the argument `year1` to the function. After the statements in `calcYear()` are completed, `calcYear()` returns a value to the program. This value is stored in the variable named `year2`.

The `return` Statement

Lines 22 and 28 contain `return` statements. The `return` statement on line 28 is part of the function `calcYear()`. It calculates the year a person would be a specific age by adding the `#define` constant `TARGET_AGE` to the variable `year1` and returns the result to the program that called `calcYear()`. The `return` statement on line 22 returns a value of `0` to the operating system just before the program ends.

The Function Definition (Lines 26 Through 29)

When defining functions before presenting the program bigyear.c, two types of functions—library functions and user-defined functions—were mentioned. The `printf()` and `scanf()` statements are examples of the first category, and the function named `calcYear()`, on lines 26 through 29, is a user-defined function. As the name implies, user-defined functions are written by the programmer during program development. This function adds the value of a created constant to a year and returns the answer (a different year) to the program that called it. In Lesson 5, "Packaging Code in Functions," you learn that the proper use of functions is an important part of good C programming practice.

Note that in a real C program, you probably wouldn't use a function for a task as simple as adding two numbers. It has been done here for demonstration purposes only.

Program Comments (Lines 1, 11, 16, and 25)

Any part of your program that starts with `/*` and ends with `*/` or any single line that begins with `//` is called a *comment*. The compiler ignores all comments, so they have absolutely no effect on how a program works. You can put anything you want into a comment, and it won't modify the way your program operates. The first type of comment can span part of a line, an entire line, or multiple lines. Here are three examples:

```
/* A single-line comment */

int a,b,c; /* A partial-line comment */

/* a comment
spanning
multiple lines */
```

You should not use nested comments. A *nested* comment is a comment that has been put into another comment. Most compilers will not accept the following:

```
/*
/* Nested comment */
*/
```

Some compilers do allow nested comments. Although this feature might be tempting to use, you should avoid doing so. Because one of the benefits of C is portability, using a feature such as nested comments might limit the portability of your code. Nested comments also might lead to hard-to-find problems.

The second style of comment, the ones beginning with two consecutive forward slashes (//), are only for single-line comments. The two forward slashes tell the compiler to ignore everything that follows to the end of the line.

```
// This entire line is a comment
int x; // Comment starts with slashes
```

Many beginning programmers view program comments as unnecessary and a waste of time. This is a mistake! The operation of your program might be quite clear when you write the code; however, as your programs become larger and more complex, or when you need to modify a program you wrote 6 months ago, comments are invaluable. Now is the time to develop the habit of using comments liberally to document all your programming structures and operations. You can use either style of comments you prefer. Both are used throughout the programs in the book.

DO	DON'T

DO add abundant comments to your program's source code, especially near statements or functions that could be unclear to you or to someone who might have to modify it later.
 	
DO learn to develop a style that will be helpful. A style that's too lean or cryptic doesn't help. A style that is verbose may cause you to spend more time commenting than programming.
	DON'T add unnecessary comments to statements that are already clear. For example, entering
	
	`/* The following prints Hello`
	`World! on the screen */`
	`printf("Hello World!);`
	
	might be going a little too far, at least when you're completely comfortable with the `printf()` function and how it works.

Using Braces (Lines 10, 23, 27, and 29)

You use braces {} to enclose the program lines that make up every C function—including the `main()` function. A group of one or more statements enclosed within braces is called a *block*. As you see in later lessons, C has many uses for blocks.

Running the Program

Take the time to enter, compile, and run bigyear.c. It provides additional practice in using your editor and compiler. Recall these steps from Lesson 1, "Getting Started with C":

1. Make your programming directory current.
2. Start your editor.
3. Enter the source code for bigyear.c exactly as shown in Listing 2.1, but be sure to omit the line numbers and colons.
4. Save the program file.
5. Compile and link the program by entering the appropriate command(s) for your compiler. If no error messages display, you can run the program by clicking the appropriate button in your C environment.
6. If any error messages display, return to step 2 and correct the errors.

A Note on Accuracy

A computer is fast and accurate, but it also is completely literal. It doesn't know enough to correct your simplest mistake; it takes everything you enter exactly as you entered it, not as you meant it!

This goes for your C source code as well. A simple typographical error in your program can cause the C compiler to choke, gag, and collapse. Fortunately, although the compiler isn't smart enough to correct your errors (and you'll make errors—everyone does!), it *is* smart enough to recognize them as errors and report them to you. (You saw in Lesson 1 how the compiler reports error messages and how you interpret them.)

A Review of the Parts of a Program

Now that all the parts of a program have been described, you can look at any program and find some similarities. Look at Listing 2.2 and see whether you can identify the different parts.

Input ▼
Listing 2.2　list_it.c – A Program to List a Code Listing with Added Line Numbers

```
 1:   /* list_it.c__This program displays a listing with line numbers! */
 2:   #include <stdio.h>
 3:   #include <stdlib.h>
 4:   #define BUFF_SIZE 256
 5:   void display_usage(void);
 6:   int line;
 7:
 8:   int main( int argc, char *argv[] )
 9:   {
10:     char buffer[BUFF_SIZE];
11:     FILE *fp;
12:
13:     if( argc < 2 )
14:     {
15:        display_usage();
16:        return (1);
17:     }
18:
19:     if (( fp = fopen( argv[1], "r" )) == NULL )
20:     {
21:         fprintf( stderr, "Error opening file, %s!", argv[1] );
22:         return(1);
23:     }
24:
25:     line = (1);
26:
27:     while( fgets( buffer, BUFF_SIZE, fp ) != NULL )
28:         fprintf( stdout, "%4d:\t%s", line++, buffer );
29:
30:     fclose(fp);
31:     return 0;
32: }
```

```
33:
34: void display_usage(void)
35: {
36:         fprintf(stderr, "\nProper Usage is: " );
37:         fprintf(stderr, "\n\nlist_it filename.ext\n" );
38: }
```

Output ▼

```
C:\>list_it list_it.c
 1:    /* list_it.c - This program displays a listing with line numbers! */
 2:    #include <stdio.h>
 3:    #include <stdlib.h>
 4:    #define BUFF_SIZE 256
 5:    void display_usage(void);
 6:    int line;
 7:
 8:    int main( int argc, char *argv[] )
 9:    {
10:        char buffer[BUFF_SIZE];
11:        FILE *fp;
12:
13:        if( argc < 2 )
14:        {
15:            display_usage();
16:            return (1);
17:        }
18:
19:        if (( fp = fopen( argv[1], "r" )) == NULL )
20:        {
21:            fprintf( stderr, "Error opening file, %s!", argv[1] );
22:            return(1);
23:        }
24:
25:        line = 1;
26:
27:        while( fgets( buffer, BUFF_SIZE, fp ) != NULL )
28:            fprintf( stdout, "%4d:\t%s", line++, buffer );
29:
30:        fclose(fp);
31:        return (0);
32:    }
33:
34:    void display_usage(void)
35:    {
36:        fprintf(stderr, "\nProper Usage is: " );
37:        fprintf(stderr, "\n\nlist_it filename.ext\n" );
38:    }
```

2

Analysis ▼

The list_it.c program in Listing 2.2 displays C program listings that you have saved. These listings display on the screen with line numbers added.

Looking at this listing, you can summarize where the different parts are. The required `main()` function is in lines 8 through 32. Lines 2 and 3 have `#include` directives. Lines 6, 10, and 11 have variable definitions. Line 4 defines a constant BUFF_SIZE as 256, the stand size for buffers. The value to doing this is that if the buffer size changes, you only need to adjust this one line and all lines using this constant will automatically update. If you hardcode a number like 256, you'd have to search all your lines of code to make sure you caught all mentions.

A function prototype, `void display_usage(void)`, is in line 5. This program has many statements (lines 13, 15, 16, 19, 21, 22, 25, 27, 28, 30, 31, 36, and 37). A function definition for `display_usage()` fills lines 34 through 38. Braces enclose blocks throughout the program. Finally, only line 1 has a comment. In most programs, you should probably include more than one comment line.

list_it.c calls many functions. It calls only one user-defined function, `display_usage()`. The library functions that it uses are `fopen()` in line 19; `fprintf()` in lines 21, 28, 36, and 37; `fgets()` in line 27; and `fclose()` in line 30. These library functions are covered in more detail throughout this book.

Summary

This lesson was short, but it's important because it introduced you to the major components of a C program. You learned that the single required part of every C program is the `main()` function. You also learned that a program's real work is done by program statements that instruct the computer to perform your desired actions. You were also introduced to variables and variable definitions, and you learned how to use comments in your source code.

In addition to the `main()` function, a C program can use two types of subsidiary functions: library functions, supplied as part of the compiler package, and user-defined functions, created by the programmer. The next few lessons go into much more detail on many of the parts of a C program that you saw in this lesson.

Q&A

Q What effect do comments have on a program?

A Comments are for programmers. When the compiler converts the source code to object code, it throws the comments and the white space away. This means that they have no effect on the executable program. A program with a lot of comments executes just as fast as a program with few comments. Comments do make your source file bigger, but this is usually of little concern. To summarize, you should use comments and white space to make your source code as easy to understand and maintain as possible.

Q What is the difference between a statement and a block?

A A block is a group of statements enclosed in braces ({ }). A block can be used in most places that a statement can be used.

Q How can I find out what library functions are available?

A Many compilers come with online documentation dedicated specifically to documenting the library functions. They are usually in alphabetical order. Appendix C, "Common C Functions," lists many of the available functions. After you begin to understand more of C, it would be a good idea to read that appendix so that you don't rewrite a library function. (There's no use reinventing the wheel!)

Workshop

The Workshop provides quiz questions to help you solidify your understanding of the material covered and exercises to provide you with experience in using what you've learned.

Quiz

1. What is the term for a group of one or more C statements enclosed in braces?
2. What is the one component that must be present in every C program?
3. How do you add program comments, and why are they used?
4. What is a function?
5. C offers two types of functions. What are they, and how are they different?
6. What is the #include directive used for?
7. Can comments be nested?
8. Can comments be longer than one line?
9. What is another name for an include file?
10. What is an include file?

Exercises

1. Write the smallest program possible.

2. Consider the following program:

```
1:  /* ex02-02.c */
2:  #include <stdio.h>
3:
4:  void display_line(void);
5:
6:  int main(void)
7:  {
8:      display_line();
9:      printf("\n Teach Yourself C In One Hour a Day!\n");
10:     display_line();
11:
12:      return 0;
13: }
14:
15: /* print asterisk line */
16: void display_line(void)
17: {
18:     int counter;
19:
20:     for( counter = 0; counter < 30; counter++ )
21:         printf("*" );
22: }
23: /* end of program */
```

   a. What line(s) contain statements?

   b. What line(s) contain variable definitions?

   c. What line(s) contain function prototypes?

   d. What line(s) contain function definitions?

   e. What line(s) contain comments?

3. Write an example of a comment.

4. What does the following program do? (Enter, compile, and run it.)

```
1:  /* ex02-04.c */
2:  #include <stdio.h>
3:
4:  int main(void)
5:  {
6:      int ctr;
7:
8:      for( ctr = 65; ctr < 91; ctr++ )
9:          printf("%c", ctr );
10:
```

```
11:    printf("\n");
11:    return 0;
12: }
13: /* end of program */
```

5. What does the following program do? (Enter, compile, and run it.)

```
1:  /* ex02-05.c */
2:  #include <stdio.h>
3:  #include <string.h>
4:  int main(void)
5:  {
6:      char buffer[256];
7:
8:      printf( "Enter your name and press <Enter>:\n");
9:      fgets( buffer );
10:
11:      printf( "\nYour name has %d characters and spaces!",
12                        strlen( buffer ));
13:
14:      return 0;
15: }
```

2

LESSON 3

Storing Information: Variables and Constants

Computer programs usually work with different types of data and need a way to store the values being used. These values can be numbers or characters. C has two ways of storing number values—variables and constants—with many options for each. A variable is a data storage location that has a value that can change during program execution. In contrast, a constant has a fixed value that can't change. In this lesson you learn:

- How to store information using variables in C

- Ways to efficiently store different types of numeric values

- The differences and similarities between character and numeric values

- How to declare and initialize variables

- C's two types of numeric constants

Before you get to variables, however, you need to know a little about the operation of your computer's memory.

Understanding Your Computer's Memory

If you already know how a computer's memory operates, you can skip this section. If you're not sure, read on. Understanding your computer's memory and how it works can help you better understand certain aspects of C programming.

A computer uses random-access memory (RAM) to store information while it operates. RAM is generally located inside your computer. RAM is volatile, which means that it is erased and replaced with new information as often as needed. Being volatile also means that RAM "remembers" only while the computer is turned on and loses its information when you turn the computer off.

Each computer has a certain amount of RAM installed. The amount of RAM in a system is usually specified in gigabytes (GB), such as 1GB, 2GB, 4GB, 8GB, or more. One gigabyte of memory is 1,024 megabytes. One megabyte of memory is 1,024 kilobytes. One kilobyte of memory consists of 1,024 bytes. Thus, a system with 4GB of memory actually has 4×1,024 megabytes or 4×1,024×1,024 kilobytes, or 4,194,304 kilobytes of RAM. This would be 4,194,304KB×1,024 bytes for a total of 4,294,967,296 bytes of RAM.

A *byte* is the fundamental unit of computer data storage. Lesson 21, "Working with Memory," has more information about bytes. For now, Table 3.1 provides you with an idea of how many bytes it takes to store certain kinds of data.

TABLE 3.1 Memory Space Required to Store Data

Data	Bytes Required
The letter x	1
The number 500	2
The number 241.105	4
The phrase *Sams Teach Yourself C*	21
One typewritten page	Approximately 3,000

The RAM in your computer is organized sequentially, 1 byte following another. Each byte of memory has a unique address that can be used to identify it. This address can be used to distinguish the byte of memory from all other bytes. Addresses are assigned to memory locations in order, starting at zero and increasing to the system limit. For now, you don't need to worry about addresses; it's all handled automatically by the C compiler.

Your computer's RAM has several uses, but only data storage need concern you as a programmer. Data is the information with which your C program works. Whether your program maintains an address list, monitors the stock market, keeps a household budget, or tracks the price of hog bellies, the information (names, stock prices, expense amounts, or hog futures) is kept in your computer's RAM while the program runs.

Now that you understand a little about the nuts and bolts of memory storage, you can get back to C programming and how C uses memory to store information.

Storing Information with Variables

A *variable* is a named data storage location in your computer's memory. By using a variable's name in your program, you, in effect, refer to the data stored there.

Variable Names

To use variables in your C programs, you must know how to create variable names. In C, variable names must adhere to the following rules:

- The name can contain letters (a to z and A to Z), digits (0 to 9), and the underscore character (_).
- The first character of the name must be a letter. The underscore is also a legal first character, but its use is not recommended at the beginning of a name. A digit (0 to 9) cannot be used as the first character.
- Case matters (that is, upper- and lowercase letters). C is case-sensitive, thus, the names count and Count refer to two different variables.
- C keywords can't be used as variable names. A keyword is a word that is part of the C language. (A complete list of the C keywords can be found in Appendix B, "C/C++ Reserved Words.")

The following list contains some examples of legal and illegal C variable names:

Variable Name	Legality
Percent	Legal
y2x5__fg7h	Legal
annual_profit	Legal
_1990_tax	Legal but not advised
savings#account	Illegal: Contains the illegal character #
double	Illegal: Is a C keyword
4sale	Illegal: First character is a digit

Because C is case-sensitive, the names percent, PERCENT, and Percent would be considered three different variables. C programmers commonly use only lowercase letters in variable names, although this isn't required. Using all uppercase letters is usually reserved for the names of constants (which are covered later in this lesson).

For many compilers, a C variable name can be up to 31 characters long. (It can actually be longer than that, but the compiler looks at only the first 31 characters of the name.) With this flexibility, you can create variable names that reflect the data being stored. For example, a program that calculates loan payments could store the value of the prime interest rate in a variable named `interest_rate`. The variable name helps make its usage clear. You could also have created a variable named `x` or even `ozzy_osborne`; it doesn't matter to the C compiler. The use of the variable, however, wouldn't be nearly as clear to someone else looking at the source code. Although it might take a little more time to type descriptive variable names, the improvements in program clarity make it worthwhile.

Just because you can create variable names that are up to 31 characters, that doesn't mean you should. Longer variable names, although they might be clearer, increase the possibility of a typo, such as a misspelling or lowercase letter when it should be an uppercase letter or vice versa. Try to walk the line between descriptive and brief.

Many naming conventions are used for variable names created from multiple words. You've seen one style: `interest_rate`. Using an underscore to separate words in a variable name makes it easy to interpret. The second style is called *camel notation*. Instead of using spaces, the first letter of each word is capitalized. Instead of `interest_rate`, the variable would be named `InterestRate`. Camel notation is gaining popularity because it's easier to type a capital letter than an underscore. The underscore is used in this book because it's easier for most people to read. You should decide which style you want to adopt.

DO	**DON'T**
DO use variable names that are descriptive.	**DON'T** start your variable names with an underscore unnecessarily.
DO adopt and stick with a style for naming your variables.	**DON'T** name your variables with all uppercase letters unnecessarily.

Numeric Variable Types

C provides several different types of numeric variables. You need different types of variables because different numeric values have varying memory storage requirements and differ in the ease with which certain mathematical operations can be performed on them. Small integers (for example, 1, 199, and –8) require less memory to store, and your computer can perform mathematical operations (addition, multiplication, and so on) with such numbers quickly. In contrast, large integers and floating-point values (123,000,000, 3.14, or 0.000000871256, for example) require more storage space and more time for mathematical operations. By using the appropriate variable types, you ensure that your program runs as efficiently as possible.

C's numeric variables fall into the following two main categories:

- Integer variables hold values that have no fractional part (that is, whole numbers only). Integer variables come in two flavors: Signed integer variables can hold positive or negative values, whereas unsigned integer variables can hold only positive values (and 0).

- Floating-point variables hold values that have a fractional part (that is, real numbers).

Within each of these categories are two or more specific variable types. These are summarized in Table 3.2, which also shows the amount of memory, in bytes, generally required to hold a single variable of each type.

TABLE 3.2 C's Numeric Data Types

Variable Type	Keyword	Bytes Required	Range
Character	`char`	1	–128 to 127
Short integer	`short`	2	–32767 to 32767
Integer	`int`	4	–2,147,483,647 to 2,147,438,647
Long integer	`long`	4	–2,147,483,647 to 2,147,438,647
Long long integer	`long long`	8	–9,223,372,036,854,775,807 to 9,223,372,036,854,775,807
Unsigned character	`unsigned char`	1	0 to 255
Unsigned short integer	`unsigned short`	2	0 to 65535
Unsigned integer	`unsigned int`	4	0 to 4,294,967,295
Unsigned long integer	`unsigned long`	4	0 to 4,294,967,295
Unsigned long long integer	`unsigned long long`	8	0 to 18,446,744,073,709,551,615
Single-precision floating-point	`float`	4	1.2E–38 to 3.4E38[1]
Double-precision floating-point	`double`	8	2.2E–308 to 1.8E308[2]

[1]Approximate range; precision = 7 digits.
[2]Approximate range; precision = 19 digits.

> **NOTE**
>
> *Approximate range* means the highest and lowest values a given variable can hold. (Space limitations prohibit listing exact ranges for the values of these variables.) *Precision* is the accuracy with which a variable is stored. (For example, if you evaluate 1/3, the answer is 0.33333... with 3s going to infinity. A variable with a precision of 7 stores seven 3s.)

Referring to Table 3.2, you might notice that the variable types int and long are identical. Why are two different types necessary? The int and long variable type sizes listed are indeed identical on 64-bit Intel systems (PCs), but they might be different on other types of hardware. Remember that C is a flexible, portable language, so it provides different keywords for the two types. If you work on a PC, you can use int and long interchangeably.

No special keyword is needed to make an integer variable signed; integer variables are signed by default. You can, however, include the signed keyword if you want. The keywords shown in Table 3.2 are used in variable declarations, which are discussed in the next section.

Listing 3.1 helps you determine the size of variables on your particular computer. Don't be surprised if your output doesn't match the output presented after the listing.

Input ▼

LISTING 3.1   sizeof.c - A Program That Displays the Size of Variable Types

```
 1:    /* sizeof.c--Program to tell the size of the C variable */
 2:    /*            type in bytes */
 3:
 4:    #include <stdio.h>
 5:
 6:    int main(void)
 7:    {
 8:        printf( "\nA char      is %d bytes", sizeof( char ));
 9:        printf( "\nAn int      is %d bytes", sizeof( int ));
10:        printf( "\nA short     is %d bytes", sizeof( short ));
11:        printf( "\nA long      is %d bytes", sizeof( long ));
12:        printf( "\nA long long is %d bytes\n", sizeof( long long));
13:        printf( "\nAn unsigned char  is %d bytes", sizeof( unsigned char ));
14:        printf( "\nAn unsigned int   is %d bytes", sizeof( unsigned int ));
15:        printf( "\nAn unsigned short is %d bytes", sizeof( unsigned short ));
16:        printf( "\nAn unsigned long  is %d bytes", sizeof( unsigned long ));
17:        printf( "\nAn unsigned long long is %d bytes\n",
18:                                        sizeof( unsigned long long));
19:        printf( "\nA float     is %d bytes", sizeof( float ));
```

```
20:     printf( "\nA double    is %d bytes\n", sizeof( double ));
21:     printf( "\nA long double is %d bytes\n", sizeof( long double ));
22:
23:     return 0;
24:   }
```

Output ▼

```
A char      is 1 bytes
An int      is 4 bytes
A short     is 2 bytes
A long      is 4 bytes
A long long is 8 bytes

An unsigned char  is 1 bytes
An unsigned int   is 4 bytes
An unsigned short is 2 bytes
An unsigned long  is 4 bytes
An unsigned long long is 8 bytes

A float     is 4 bytes

A double    is 8 bytes

A long double is 12 bytes
```

Analysis ▼

As the preceding output shows, Listing 3.1 tells you exactly how many bytes each variable type on your computer takes. If you use a standard 64-bit PC (or an older 32-bit PC), your numbers should match those in Table 3.2.

Don't worry about trying to understand all the individual components of the program. Although some items are new, such as `sizeof`, others should look familiar. Lines 1 and 2 are comments about the name of the program and a brief description. Line 4 includes the standard input/output header file to help print the information onscreen. This is a simple program, in that it contains only a single function, `main()` (lines 7 through 24). Lines 8 through 21 are the bulk of the program. Each of these lines prints a textual description with the size of each of the variable types, which is done using the `sizeof` operator. Line 23 of the program returns the value 0 to the operating system before ending the program.

Although the size of the data types can vary depending on your computer platform, C does make some guarantees. There are five things you can count on:

- The size of a `char` is 1 byte.
- The size of a `short` is less than or equal to the size of an `int`.

3

- The size of an `int` is less than or equal to the size of a `long`.
- The size of an `unsigned` is equal to the size of an `int`.
- The size of a `float` is less than or equal to the size of a `double`.

NOTE

Table 3.2 listed the common keyword used to identify the different variable types. The following table (Table 3.3) lists the full name of each of the data types.

TABLE 3.3   Full Names of Data Types

Full Name	Commonly Used Keyword
char	signed char
short	signed short int
int	signed int
long	signed long int
long long	signed long long int
unsigned char	unsigned char
unsigned short	unsigned short int
unsigned int	unsigned int
unsigned long	unsigned long int
unsigned long long	unsigned long long int

As you can see from this table, `short` and `long` types are actually just variations on the `int` type. Most programmers don't use the full name of the variable types, rather, they use the shorter version.

Variable Declarations

Before you can use a variable in a C program, it must be declared. A variable declaration tells the compiler the name and type of a variable. The declaration may also initialize the variable to a specific value. If your program attempts to use a variable that hasn't been declared, the compiler generates an error message. A variable declaration has the following form:

```
typename varname;
```

typename specifies the variable type and must be one of the keywords listed in Table 3.2. *varname* is the variable name, which must follow the rules mentioned earlier. You can declare multiple variables of the same type on one line by separating the variable names with commas:

```
int count, number, start;    /* three integer variables */
float percent, total;        /* two float variables */
```

In Lesson 12, "Understanding Variable Scope," you learn that the location of variable declarations in the source code is important because it affects the ways in which your program can use the variables. For now, you can place all the variable declarations together just before the start of the `main()` function.

The `typedef` Keyword

The `typedef` keyword is used to create a new name for an existing data type. In effect, `typedef` creates a synonym. For example, the statement

```
typedef int integer;
```

3

creates `integer` as a synonym for `int`. You then can use `integer` to define variables of type `int`, as in this example:

```
integer count;
```

Note that `typedef` doesn't create a new data type; it enables you to use a different name for only a predefined data type. The most common use of `typedef` concerns aggregate data types, as explained in Lesson 11, "Implementing Structures, Unions, and TypeDefs." An aggregate data type consists of a combination of data types presented in this lesson. (I am sure you are a bit confused by this last sentence—don't worry about it; it just means that the `typedef` keyword will be much more valuable to you after you learn about structures.)

Initializing Variables

When you declare a variable, you instruct the compiler to set aside storage space for the variable. However, the value stored in that space—the value of the variable—isn't defined. It might be zero, or it might be some random "garbage" value. Before using a variable, you should always initialize it to a known value. You can do this independently of the variable definition by using an assignment statement, as in this example:

```
int count;   // Set aside storage space for count
count = 0;   // Store 0 in count
```

Note that this statement uses the equal sign (`=`), which is C's assignment operator and is discussed further in Lesson 4, "The Pieces of a C Program: Statements, Expressions, and

Operators." For now, you need to be aware that the equal sign in programming is not the same as the equal sign in algebra. If you write

```
x = 12
```

in an algebraic statement, you are stating a fact: "x equals 12." In C, however, it means something quite different. In C it means "Assign the value 12 to the variable named x."

You can also initialize a variable when it's declared. To do so, follow the variable name in the declaration statement with an equal sign and the wanted initial value:

```
int count = 0;
double percent = 0.01, taxrate = 28.5;
```

The first statement declares a variable called count as an integer and initializes it to 0. The second statement declares two variables as doubles and initializes them. The first, percent, is initialized to 0.01. The second, taxrate, is initialized to 28.5.

Be careful not to initialize a variable with a value outside the allowed range. Here are two examples of out-of-range initializations:

```
short weight = 100000;
unsigned int value = -2500;
```

The C compiler might not catch such errors. Your program might compile and link, but you might get unexpected results when the program runs.

DO	DON'T
DO understand the number of bytes that variable types take for your computer.	**DON'T** use a variable that hasn't been initialized. Results can be unpredictable.
DO use `typedef` to make your programs more readable.	**DON'T** use a `float` or `double` variable if you're storing only integers. Although they work, using them is inefficient.
DO initialize variables when you declare them whenever possible.	**DON'T** try to put numbers that are too big or too small into a variable if its type won't hold them.
	DON'T put negative numbers into variables with an `unsigned` type.

Constants

Like a variable, a *constant* is a data storage location used by your program. Unlike a variable, the value stored in a constant can't be changed during program execution. C has two types of constants, each with its own specific uses:

- Literal constants
- Symbolic constants

Literal Constants

A *literal constant* is a value that is typed directly into the source code wherever it is needed. Here are two examples:

```
int count = 20;
float tax_rate = 0.28;
```

The 20 and the 0.28 are literal constants. The preceding statements store these values in the variables count and tax_rate. Note that one of these constants contains a decimal point, whereas the other does not. The presence or absence of the decimal point distinguishes floating-point constants from integer constants.

A literal constant written with a decimal point is a floating-point constant and is represented by the C compiler as a double-precision number. Floating-point constants can be written in standard decimal notation, as shown in these examples:

```
123.456
0.019
100.
```

Note that the third constant, 100., is written with a decimal point even though it's an integer. (That is, it has no fractional part.) The decimal point causes the C compiler to treat the constant as a double-precision value. Without the decimal point, it is treated as an integer constant.

Floating-point constants also can be written in scientific notation. You might recall from high school math that scientific notation represents a number as a decimal part multiplied by 10 to a positive or negative power. Scientific notation is particularly useful for representing extremely large and extremely small values. In C, scientific notation is written as a decimal number followed immediately by an E or e and the exponent:

1.23E2	1.23 times 10 to the 2nd power, or 123
4.08e6	4.08 times 10 to the 6th power, or 4,080,000
0.85e-4	0.85 times 10 to the -4th power, or 0.000085

3

A constant written without a decimal point is represented by the compiler as an integer number. Integer constants can be written in three different notations:

- A constant starting with any digit other than 0 is interpreted as a decimal integer (that is, the standard base-10 number system). Decimal constants can contain the digits 0 through 9 and a leading minus or plus sign. (Without a leading minus or plus, a constant is assumed to be positive.)

- A constant starting with the digit 0 is interpreted as an octal integer (the base-8 number system). Octal constants can contain the digits 0 through 7 and a leading minus or plus sign.

- A constant starting with 0x or 0X is interpreted as a hexadecimal constant (the base-16 number system). Hexadecimal constants can contain the digits 0 through 9, the letters A through F, and a leading minus or plus sign.

Symbolic Constants

A *symbolic constant* is a constant represented by a name (symbol) in your program. Like a literal constant, a symbolic constant can't change. Whenever you need the constant's value in your program, you use its name as you would use a variable name. The actual value of the symbolic constant needs to be entered only once, when it is first defined.

Symbolic constants have two significant advantages over literal constants, as the following example shows. Suppose that you write a program that performs a variety of geometrical calculations. The program frequently needs the value π (3.14) for its calculations. (You might recall from geometry class that π is the ratio of a circle's circumference to its diameter.) For example, to calculate the circumference and area of a circle with a known radius, you could write

```
circumference = 3.14 * (2 * radius);
area = 3.14 * (radius)*(radius);
```

The asterisk (*) is C's multiplication operator and is covered in Lesson 4. Thus, the first of these statements means "Multiply 2 times the value stored in the variable radius, and then multiply the result by 3.14. Finally, assign the result to the variable named circumference."

If, however, you define a symbolic constant with the name PI and the value 3.14, you could write

```
circumference = PI * (2 * radius);
area = PI * (radius)*(radius);
```

The resulting code is clearer. Rather than puzzling over what the value 3.14 is for, you can see immediately that the constant PI is used.

The second advantage of symbolic constants becomes apparent when you need to change a constant. Continuing with the preceding example, you might decide that for greater accuracy your program needs to use a value of PI with more decimal places: 3.14159 rather than 3.14. If you had used literal constants for PI, you would have to go through your source code and change each occurrence of the value from 3.14 to 3.14159. With a symbolic constant, you need to make a change only in the place in which the constant is defined. The rest of your code would not need to be changed.

Defining Symbolic Constants

C has two methods for defining a symbolic constant: the #define directive and the const keyword. The #define directive is used as follows:

```
#define CONSTNAME literal
```

This creates a constant named CONSTNAME with the value of literal. literal represents a literal constant, as described earlier. CONSTNAME follows the same rules described earlier for variable names. By convention, the names of symbolic constants are uppercase. This makes them easy to distinguish from variable names, which by convention are lowercase. For the previous example, the required #define directive for a constant called PI would be

```
#define PI 3.14159
```

Note that #define lines don't end with a semicolon (;). #define statements can be placed anywhere in your source code, but the defined constant is in effect only for the portions of the source code that follow the #define directive. Most commonly, programmers group all #define statements together, near the beginning of the file and before the start of the main() function.

How a #define Works

The precise action of the #define directive is to instruct the compiler as follows: "In the source code, replace CONSTNAME with literal." The effect is exactly the same as if you had used your editor to go through the source code and make the changes manually. Note that #define doesn't replace instances of its target that occur as parts of longer names, within double quotes, or as part of a program comment. For example, in the following code, the instances of PI in the second and third lines would not get changed:

```
#define PI 3.14159
/* You have defined a constant for PI. */
#define PIPETTE 100
```

NOTE
The #define directive is one of C's preprocessor directives, and it is discussed more fully in Lesson 22, "Advanced Compiler Use."

Defining Constants with the const Keyword

The second way to define a symbolic constant is with the const keyword. const is a modifier that can be applied to any variable declaration. A variable declared to be const can't be modified when the program is executed. A value is initialized at the time of declaration and is then prohibited from being changed. Here are some examples:

```
const int count = 100;
const float pi = 3.14159;
const long debt = 12000000, float tax_rate = 0.21;
```

const affects all variables on the declaration line. In the last line, debt and tax_rate are symbolic constants. As a side note, in this example, debt was declared as a long and tax_rate was declared as a float.

If your program tries to modify a const variable, the compiler generates an error message. The following code would generate an error:

```
const int count = 100;
count = 200;          /* Does not compile! Cannot reassign or alter */
                      /* the value of a constant. */
```

What are the practical differences between symbolic constants created with the #define directive and those created with the const keyword? The differences have to do with pointers and variable scope. Pointers and variable scope are two important aspects of C programming, and you learn about them in Lesson 9, "Understanding Pointers," and Lesson 12.

Now take a look at a program that demonstrates variable declarations and the use of literal and symbolic constants. Listing 3.2 prompts you to enter a number of laps run and year of birth. It then calculates and displays the miles you covered and age this year. You can enter, compile, and run this program using the procedures explained in Lesson 1, "Getting Started with C."

NOTE
Most C programmers today use const instead of #define when declaring constants.

Input ▼

LISTING 3.2 const.c - A Program That Demonstrates the Use of Variables and Constants

```
1:     /* Demonstrates variables and constants */
2:     #include <stdio.h>
3:
4:     /* Define a constant to convert a number of laps to miles */
5:     #define LAPS_PER_MILE 4
6:
7:     /* Define a constant for the current year */
8:     const int CURRENT_YEAR = 2013;
9:
10:    /* Declare the needed variables */
11:    float miles_covered;
12:    int laps_run, year_of_birth, current_age;
13:
14:    int main( void )
15:    {
16:        /* Input data from user */
17:
18:        printf("How many laps did you run: ");
19:        scanf("%d", &laps_run);
20:        printf("Enter your year of birth: ");
21:        scanf("%d", &year_of_birth);
22:
23:        /* Perform conversions */
24:
25:        miles_covered = (float)laps_run/LAPS_PER_MILE;
26:        current_age = CURRENT_YEAR - year_of_birth;
27:
28:        /* Display results on the screen */
29:
30:        printf("\nYou ran %.2f miles.", miles_covered);
31:        printf("\nNot bad for someone turning %d this year!\n", current_age);
32:
33:        return 0;
34:    }
```

Output ▼

```
How many laps did you run: 7
Enter your year of birth: 1975

You ran 1.75 miles.
Not bad for someone turning 38 this year!
```

3

Analysis ▼

This program demonstrates the two methods you can use to declare symbolic constants. On line 5, the #define directive sets the value 4 to LAPS_PER_MILE. If you move to a place with a smaller or larger track, you can easily change the information in this one spot, and all code will be updated to calculate information using the new symbolic constant. Line 8 shows a second symbolic constant declaration, one using const int. A current year is another place a defined constant makes sense, as it is something you would need to change (you guessed it) only once a year.

Lines 11 and 12 contain the declarations you need for this program's calculations. You need to make miles_covered a floating-point variable because each lap is one-quarter of a mile (and could change to anything else) and you want to give your user an exact mileage based on how many laps they ran. Line 25 takes the laps entered by the user and calculates the total miles. Using the LAPS_PER_MILE makes the calculation clearer than just putting a 4 into the statement.

What may not be as clear is the (float) addition in front of laps_run. To understand why that little extra is needed, remove it, rerun the program, and make sure you enter a 7 as the number of laps. Surprised? Even though you declared miles_covered as a float, dividing two integers puts an integer answer into that variable, but the .00 might make you think otherwise. To make it worse, the value is truncated, and the .75 after the 1 is cut off and not rounded up, as 2.00 is a more accurate answer. So putting (float) in front of laps_run tells the compiler to treat it like a float instead of an int. Then you get a precise and correct answer.

Lines 18 and 20 print prompts onscreen. The printf() function is covered in greater detail later. To allow the user to respond to the prompts, lines 19 and 21 use another library function, scanf(), which is covered later. scanf() gets information from the screen. For now, accept that this works as shown in the listing. Later, you learn exactly how it works. Line 26 calculates what age the user will turn sometime in 2013. Obviously, you cannot answer with detail users' exact ages unless you get the day and month of their birthdays as well as today's day and month to calculate whether they've celebrated a birthday this year yet. For the purpose of this program, mentioning what age they will become this year is close enough. These statements and others are covered in detail in the next lesson. To finish the program, lines 30 and 31 display the results for the user.

DO	DON'T
DO use constants to make your programs easier to read.	**DON'T** try to assign a value to a constant after it has already been initialized.

Summary

This lesson explored numeric variables, which are used by a C program to store data during program execution. You've seen that there are two broad classes of numeric variables, integer and floating-point. Within each class are specific variable types. Which variable type—such as `int`, `long`, `float`, or `double`—you use for a specific application depends on the nature of the data to be stored in the variable. You've also seen that in a C program, you must declare a variable before it can be used. A variable declaration informs the compiler of the name and type of a variable.

You also learned about C's two constant types, literal and symbolic. Unlike variables, the value of a constant can't change during program execution. You type literal constants into your source code whenever the value is needed. Symbolic constants are assigned a name that is used wherever the constant value is needed. Symbolic constants can be created with the `#define` directive or with the `const` keyword.

Q&A

Q Why not always use the larger variables, such as `long int` and double instead of `int` and float variables so that you can hold bigger numbers?

A A `long int` variable takes up more RAM than the smaller `int`. In smaller programs, this doesn't pose a problem. As programs get bigger, however, you should try to be efficient with the memory you use. If you believe users will be entering numbers larger than the maximum size of an int or long, make the necessary adjustments, remembering that even if the numbers entered by the users fall into the range of the smaller variable size, any math you do, including addition or multiplication, could create an out-of-range number.

Q What happens if I assign a number with a decimal to an integer?

A You can assign a number with a decimal to an `int` variable. If you use a constant variable, your compiler probably will give you a warning. The value assigned will have the decimal portion truncated. For example, if you assign `3.14` to an integer variable called `pi`, `pi` will contain only `3`. The `.14` will be chopped off and thrown away.

Q What happens if I put a number into a type that isn't big enough to hold it?

A Many compilers allow this without signaling any errors. The number is wrapped to fit and therefore won't be correct. For example, if you assign 32768 to a 2-byte signed variable of type short, the variable would actually contain the value -32768. If you assign the value 65535 to this variable, it actually contains the value -1. Subtracting the maximum value that the field can hold generally gives you the value that will be stored.

Q What happens if I put a negative number into an unsigned variable?

A As the preceding answer indicated, your compiler might not signal any errors if you do this. The compiler does the same wrapping as if you assigned a number that was too big. For instance, if you assign -1 to an unsigned int variable that is 2 bytes long, the compiler puts the highest number possible in the variable (65535).

Q What are the practical differences between symbolic constants created with the #define directive and those created with the const keyword?

A The differences have to do with pointers and variable scope. Pointers and variable scope are two important aspects of C programming and are covered in Lessons 9 and 12.

Workshop

The Workshop provides quiz questions to help you solidify your understanding of the material covered and exercises to provide you with experience in using what you've learned.

Quiz

1. What's the difference between an integer variable and a floating-point variable?

2. Give two reasons for using a double-precision floating-point variable (type double) instead of a single-precision floating-point variable (type float).

3. What are five rules that you know are always true when allocating size for variables?

4. What are the two advantages of using a symbolic constant instead of a literal constant?

5. Show two methods for defining a symbolic constant named MAXIMUM that has a value of 100.

6. What characters are allowed in C variable names?

7. What guidelines should you follow in creating names for variables and constants?

8. What's the difference between a symbolic and a literal constant?

9. What's the minimum value that a type `int` variable can hold?

Exercises

1. In what variable type would you best store the following values?

    a. A person's age to the nearest year.

    b. The number of Facebook friends a person has.

    c. The radius of a circle.

    d. Your annual salary.

    e. The cost of an item.

    f. The highest grade on a test (assume it is always 100).

    g. A person's first initial.

    h. The temperature.

    i. A person's net worth.

    j. The distance to a star in miles.

2. Determine appropriate variable names for the values in exercise 1.

3. Write declarations for the variables in exercise 2.

4. Which of the following variable names are valid?

    a. `123variable`

    b. `x`

    c. `total_score`

    d. `Weight_in_#s`

    e. `one`

    f. `gross-cost`

    g. `RADIUS`

    h. `Radius`

    i. `radius`

    j. `this_is_a_variable_to_hold_the_width_of_a_box`

3

LESSON 4

The Pieces of a C Program: Statements, Expressions, and Operators

C programs consist of statements, and most statements are composed of expressions and operators. To write C programs, you need to understand statements, expressions, and operators. In this lesson you learn:

- What a statement is
- What an expression is
- How to use C's mathematical, relational, and logical operators
- What operator precedence is
- The `if` statement

Statements

A *statement* is a complete instruction that directs the computer to carry out some task. In C, statements are usually written one per line, although some statements span multiple lines. C statements always end with a semicolon (except for preprocessor directives such as `#define` and `#include`, which are discussed in Lesson 22, "Advanced Compiler Use"). You've already been introduced to some of C's statement types, for example:

```
x = 2 + 3;
```

is an assignment statement. It instructs the computer to add 3 to 2 and assign the result to the variable x. Other types of statements are introduced as needed throughout this book.

The Impact of White Space on Statements

The term *white space* refers to spaces, horizontal tabs, vertical tabs, and blank lines in your source code. The C compiler isn't sensitive to white space. When the compiler reads a statement in your source code, it looks for the characters in the statement and for the terminating semicolon, but it ignores white space. Thus, the statement

```
x=2+3;
```

is equivalent to this statement:

```
x = 2 + 3;
```

It is also equivalent to this:

```
x        =
2
     +
3   ;
```

This gives you a great deal of flexibility in formatting your source code. You shouldn't use formatting like the previous example. Statements should be entered one per line with a standardized scheme for spacing around variables and operators. If you follow the formatting conventions used in this book, you should be in good shape. As you become more experienced, you might discover that you prefer slight variations. The point is to keep your source code readable.

The rule that C doesn't care about white space has one exception. Within literal string constants, tabs and spaces aren't ignored; they are considered part of the string. A *string* is a series of characters. Literal string constants are strings that are enclosed within quotes and interpreted literally by the compiler, space for space. An example of a literal string is

```
"How now brown cow"
```

This literal string is different from the following:

```
"How    now    brown    cow"
```

The difference is a result of the additional spaces. With a literal string, C keeps track of the white space.

Although it's extremely bad form, the following is legal code in C:

```
printf(
"Hello, world!"
);
```

This, however, is not legal:

```
printf("Hello,
world!");
```

To break a literal string constant line, you must use the backslash character (\) just before the break. Thus, the following is legal:

```
printf("Hello,\
world!");
```

Creating a Null Statement

If you place a semicolon by itself on a line, you create a *null statement*. A null statement is one that doesn't perform any action. This is perfectly legal in C. Later in this book, you learn how the null statement can be useful.

Working with Compound Statements

A *compound statement*, also called a *block*, is a group of two or more C statements enclosed in braces. Here's an example of a block:

```
{
    printf("Hello, ");
    printf("world!");
}
```

In C, a block can be used anywhere a single statement can be used. Many examples of this appear throughout this book. Note that the enclosing braces can be positioned in different ways. The following is equivalent to the preceding example:

```
{printf("Hello, ");
printf("world!");}
```

It's a good idea to place braces on their own lines, making the beginning and ending of blocks clearly visible. Placing braces on their own lines also makes it easier to see whether you've left one out.

DO	DON'T
DO stay consistent with how you use white space in statements.	**DON'T** spread a single statement across multiple lines if there's no need to do so. Limit statements to one line if possible.
DO put block braces on their own lines. This makes the code easier to read.	**DON'T** forget to use a forward slash to continue a string of characters onto a second line.
DO line up block braces so that it's easy to find the beginning and ending of a block.	

Understanding Expressions

In C, an *expression* is anything that evaluates to a numeric value. C expressions come in all levels of complexity.

Simple Expressions

The simplest C expression consists of a single item: a simple variable, literal constant, or symbolic constant. Here are four expressions:

Expression	Description
PI	A symbolic constant (defined in the program)
20	A literal constant
rate	A variable
-1.25	Another literal constant

A *literal constant* evaluates to its own value. A *symbolic constant* evaluates to the value it was given when you created it using the `#define` directive. A variable evaluates to the current value assigned to it by the program.

Complex Expressions

Complex expressions consist of simpler expressions connected by operators, for example:

```
2 + 8
```

is an expression consisting of the subexpressions 2 and 8 and the addition operator +. The expression 2 + 8 evaluates, as you should know, to 10. You can write C expressions of great complexity:

```
1.25 / 8 + 5 * rate + rate * rate / cost
```

When an expression contains multiple operators, the evaluation of the expression depends on operator precedence. The concept of operator precedence is covered later in this lesson, as are details about all of C's operators.

C expressions can get more interesting. Look at the following assignment statement:

```
x = a + 10;
```

This statement evaluates the expression a + 10 and assigns the result to x. In addition, the entire statement x = a + 10 is an expression that evaluates to the value of the variable on the left side of the equal sign.

Thus, you can write statements such as the following, which assigns the value of the expression a + 10 to both variables, x and y:

```
y = x = a + 10;
```

You can also write statements such as this:

```
x = 6 + (y = 4 + 5);
```

The result of this statement is that y has the value 9 and x has the value 15. Note the parentheses, which are required for the statement to compile. The use of parentheses is covered later in this lesson.

4

NOTE	With just a few exceptions that are noted throughout this book, assignment statements should not be nested within other expressions.

Operators

An *operator* is a symbol that instructs C to perform some operation, or action, on one or more operands. An *operand* is something that an operator acts on. In C, all operands are expressions. C operators fall into several categories:

- Assignment operator
- Mathematical operators
- Relational operators
- Logical operators

The Assignment Operator

The *assignment operator* is the equal sign (=). Its use in programming is somewhat different from its use in regular math. If you write

```
x = y;
```

in a C program, it doesn't mean "x is equal to y." Instead, it means "Assign the value of y to x." In a C assignment statement, the right side can be any expression, and the left side must be a variable name. Thus, the form is as follows:

```
variable = expression;
```

When executed, `expression` is evaluated, and the resulting value is assigned to `variable`.

The Mathematical Operators

C's mathematical operators perform mathematical operations such as addition and subtraction. C has two unary mathematical operators and five binary mathematical operators.

The Unary Mathematical Operators

The *unary* mathematical operators are so named because they take a single operand. C has two unary mathematical operators, which are listed in Table 4.1.

TABLE 4.1 C's Unary Mathematical Operators

Operator	Symbol	Action	Examples
Increment	++	Increments the operand by one	++x, x++
Decrement	--	Decrements the operand by one	--x, x--

The increment and decrement operators can be used only with variables, not with constants. The operation performed is to add one to or subtract one from the operand. In other words, the statements

```
++x;
--y;
```

are the equivalent of these statements:

```
x = x + 1;
y = y - 1;
```

Referring to Table 4.1, you can see that either unary mathematical operator can be placed before its operand (*prefix* mode) or after its operand (*postfix* mode). These two modes are not equivalent. They differ in terms of when the increment or decrement is performed:

- When used in prefix mode, the increment and decrement operators modify their operand before the operand is used in the enclosing expression.
- When used in postfix mode, the increment and decrement operators modify their operand after the operand is used in the enclosing expression.

An example should make this clearer. Look at these two statements:

```
x = 10;
y = x++;
```

After these statements are executed, x has the value 11, and y has the value 10. The value of x was assigned to y, and then x was incremented. In contrast, the following statements result in both y and x having the value 11. x is incremented, and then its value is assigned to y:

```
x = 10;
y = ++x;
```

Remember that = is the assignment operator, not a statement of equality. As an analogy, think of = as the "photocopy" operator. The statement y = x means to copy x into y. Subsequent changes to x, after the copy has been made, have no effect on y.

The program in Listing 4.1 illustrates the difference between prefix mode and postfix mode.

Input ▼
LISTING 4.1   unary.c: Demonstrates Prefix and Postfix Modes

```
1:  /* Demonstrates unary operator prefix and postfix modes */
2:
3:  #include <stdio.h>
4:
5:  int a, b;
6:
7:  int main( void )
8:  {
9:      // Sets a and b to 0 to start
10:     a = b = 0;
11:
12:     // Start with the incremental operator
13:     // Print them, decrementing each time.
```

4

```
14:        // Use prefix mode for b, postfix mode for a
15:
16:        printf("Count up!\n");
17:        printf("Post     Pre\n");
18:        printf("%d       %d\n", a++, ++b);
19:        printf("%d       %d\n", a++, ++b);
20:        printf("%d       %d\n", a++, ++b);
21:        printf("%d       %d\n", a++, ++b);
22:        printf("%d       %d\n", a++, ++b);
23:
24:        printf("\nCurrent values of a and b:\n");
25:        printf("%d       %d\n\n", a, b);
26:
27:        printf("Count down!\n");
28:        printf("\nPost    Pre");
29:        printf("\n%d      %d", a--, --b);
30:        printf("\n%d      %d", a--, --b);
31:        printf("\n%d      %d", a--, --b);
32:        printf("\n%d      %d", a--, --b);
33:        printf("\n%d      %d\n", a--, --b);
34:
35:        return 0;
```

Output ▼

```
Count up!
Post    Pre
0       1
1       2
2       3
3       4
4       5

Current values of a and b;
5       5

Count Down!
Post    Pre
5       4
4       3
3       2
2       1
1       0
```

Analysis ▼

This program declares two variables, a and b, on line 5. On line 10, the variables are set to the value of 0. The first batch of printf statements (lines 18 through 22) are used to count up to 5 using the unary increment operators. For each line, a is printed and then incremented, whereas b is incremented before printing. After the last increment operator, an additional printf statement (line 25) demonstrates that both variables are equal to 5.

For the second batch of printf() statements (lines 29 through 33), both a and b are decremented by 1. After a is printed, it is decremented, whereas b is decremented before it is printed.

<table>
<tr><td>NOTE</td><td>In Lesson 2, "The Components of a C Program," you learned about another unary operator, sizeof. Although you might be inclined to think that operators should look like symbols, the sizeof keyword is actually considered an operator.</td></tr>
</table>

The Binary Mathematical Operators

C's binary operators take two operands. Table 4.2 lists the binary operators, which include the common mathematical operations found on a calculator.

TABLE 4.2 C's Binary Mathematical Operators

Operator	Symbol	Action	Example
Addition	+	Adds two operands	x + y
Subtraction	-	Subtracts the second operand from the first operand	x - y
Multiplication	*	Multiplies two operands	x * y
Division	/	Divides the first operand by the second operand	x / y
Modulus	%	Gives the remainder when the first operand is divided by the second operand	x % y

Referring to Table 4.2, the first four operators should be familiar to you, and you should have little trouble using them. The fifth operator, modulus, might be new. Modulus returns the remainder when the first operand is divided by the second operand. For example, 11 modulus 4 equals 3 (that is, 4 goes into 11 two times with 3 left over). Here are some more examples:

```
100 modulus 9 equals 1
10 modulus 5 equals 0
40 modulus 6 equals 4
```

4

Listing 4.2 illustrates how you can use the modulus operator to convert a large number of seconds into hours, minutes, and seconds.

Input ▼

LISTING 4.2   seconds.c: Demonstrates the Modulus Operator

```
1:   /* Illustrates the modulus operator. */
2:   /* Inputs a number of seconds, and converts to hours, */
3:   /* minutes, and seconds. */
4:
5:   #include <stdio.h>
6:
7:   /* Define constants */
8:
9:   #define SECS_PER_MIN 60
10:  #define SECS_PER_HOUR 3600
11:
12:  unsigned seconds, minutes, hours, secs_left, mins_left;
13:
14:  int main( void )
15:  {
16:      /* Input the number of seconds */
17:
18:      printf("Enter number of seconds (< 65000): ");
19:      scanf("%d", &seconds);
20:
21:      hours = seconds / SECS_PER_HOUR;
22:      minutes = seconds / SECS_PER_MIN;
23:      mins_left = minutes % SECS_PER_MIN;
24:      secs_left = seconds % SECS_PER_MIN;
25:
26:      printf("%u seconds is equal to ", seconds);
27:      printf("%u h, %u m, and %u s\n", hours, mins_left, secs_left);
28:
29:      return 0;
30:  }
```

Output ▼

```
Enter number of seconds (< 65000): 3666
3666 seconds is equal to 1 h, 1 m, and 6 s
```

Output ▼

```
Enter number of seconds (< 65000): 10000
10000 seconds is equal to 2 h, 46 m, and 40 s
```

Analysis ▼

The seconds.c program follows the same format that all the previous programs have followed. Lines 1 through 3 provide some comments to state what the program does. Line 4 is white space to make the program more readable. Just like the white space in statements and expressions, blank lines are ignored by the compiler. Line 5 includes the necessary header file for this program. Lines 9 and 10 define two constants, SECS_PER_MIN and SECS_PER_HOUR, used to make the statements in the program easier to read. Line 12 declares all the variables that will be used. Some people choose to declare each variable on a separate line rather than all on one. As with many elements of C, this is a matter of style. Either method is correct.

Line 14 is the main() function, which contains the bulk of the program. To convert seconds to hours and minutes, the program must first get the values it needs to work with. To do this, line 18 uses the printf() function to display a statement onscreen, followed by line 19, which uses the scanf() function to get the number that the user entered. The scanf() statement then stores the number of seconds to be converted into the variable seconds. The printf() and scanf() functions are covered in more detail in Lesson 7, "Fundamentals of Reading and Writing Information."

Line 21 contains an expression to determine the number of hours by dividing the number of seconds by the constant SECS_PER_HOUR. Because hours is an integer variable, the remainder value is ignored. Line 22 uses the same logic to determine the total number of minutes for the seconds entered. Because the total number of minutes figured in line 22 also contains minutes for the hours, line 23 uses the modulus operator to divide the hours and keep the remaining minutes. Line 24 carries out a similar calculation for determining the number of seconds that are left. Lines 26 and 27 are similar to what you have seen before. They take the values that have been calculated in the expressions and display them. Line 29 finishes the program by returning 0 to the operating system before exiting.

4

Operator Precedence and Parentheses

In an expression that contains more than one operator, what is the order in which operations are performed? The importance of this question is illustrated by the following assignment statement:

```
x = 4 + 5 * 3;
```

Performing the addition first results in the following, and x is assigned the value 27:

```
x = 9 * 3;
```

In contrast, if the multiplication is performed first, you have the following, and x is assigned the value 19:

```
x = 4 + 15;
```

Clearly, some rules are needed about the order in which operations are performed. This order, called *operator precedence,* is strictly spelled out in C. Each operator has a specific precedence. When an expression is evaluated, operators with higher precedence are performed first. Table 4.3 lists the precedence of C's mathematical operators. Number 1 is the highest precedence and thus is evaluated first.

TABLE 4.3   The Precedence of C's Mathematical Operators

Operators	Relative Precedence
++ --	1
* / %	2
+ -	3

Looking at Table 4.3, you can see that in any C expression, operations are performed in the following order:

- Unary increment and decrement
- Multiplication, division, and modulus
- Addition and subtraction

If an expression contains more than one operator with the same precedence level, the operators are generally performed in left-to-right order as they appear in the expression. For example, in the following expression, the % and * have the same precedence level, but the % is the leftmost operator, so it is performed first:

```
12 % 5 * 2
```

The expression evaluates to 4 (12 % 5 evaluates to 2; 2 times 2 is 4).

Returning to the previous example, you see that the statement x = 4 + 5 * 3; assigns the value 19 to x because the multiplication is performed before the addition.

What if the order of precedence doesn't evaluate your expression as needed? Using the previous example, what if you want to add 4 to 5 and then multiply the sum by 3? C uses parentheses to modify the evaluation order. A subexpression enclosed in parentheses is evaluated first, without regard to operator precedence. Thus, you could write

```
x = (4 + 5) * 3;
```

The expression 4 + 5 inside parentheses is evaluated first, so the value assigned to x is 27.

You can use multiple and nested parentheses in an expression. When parentheses are nested, evaluation proceeds from the innermost expression outward. Look at the following complex expression:

```
x = 25 - (2 * (10 + (8 / 2)));
```

The evaluation of this expression proceeds as follows:

1. The innermost expression, `8 / 2`, is evaluated first, yielding the value `4`:

   ```
   x = 25 - (2 * (10 + 4))
   ```

2. Moving outward, the next expression, `10 + 4`, is evaluated, yielding the value `14`:

   ```
   x = 25 - (2 * 14)
   ```

3. The last, or outermost, expression, `2 * 14`, is evaluated, yielding the value `28`:

   ```
   x = 25 - 28
   ```

4. The final expression, `25 - 28`, is evaluated, assigning the value –3 to the variable `x`:

   ```
   x = -3
   ```

You might want to use parentheses in some expressions for the sake of clarity, even when they aren't needed for modifying operator precedence. Parentheses must always be in pairs, or the compiler generates an error message.

Order of Subexpression Evaluation

As mentioned in the previous section, if C expressions contain more than one operator with the same precedence level, they are evaluated left to right. For example, in the expression

```
w * x / y * z
```

`w` is first multiplied by `x`, the result of the multiplication is then divided by `y`, and the result of the division is then multiplied by `z`.

Across precedence levels, however, there is no guarantee of left-to-right order. Look at this expression:

```
w * x / y + z / y
```

Because of precedence, the multiplication and division are performed before the addition. However, C doesn't specify whether the subexpression `w * x / y` is to be evaluated before or after `z / y`. It might not be clear to you why this matters. Look at another example:

```
w * x / ++y + z / y
```

4

If the left subexpression is evaluated first, y is incremented when the second expression is evaluated. If the right expression is evaluated first, y isn't incremented, and the result is different. Therefore, you should avoid this sort of indeterminate expression in your programming.

Near the end of this lesson, the section "Operator Precedence Revisited" lists the precedence of all C's operators.

DO	DON'T
DO use parentheses to make the order of expression evaluation clear.	**DON'T** overcomplicate an expression. It is often more clear to break an expression into two or more statements. This is especially true when you use the unary operators (--) or (++).

The Relational Operators

You can use C's relational operators to compare expressions, asking questions such as, "Is x greater than 100?" or "Is y equal to 0?" An expression containing a relational operator evaluates to either true (1) or false (0). Table 4.4 lists C's six relational operators.

Table 4.5 shows some examples of how relational operators might be used. These examples use literal constants, but the same principles hold with variables.

NOTE _____ | "True" is considered the same as "yes," which is also considered the same as 1. "False" is considered the same as "no," which is considered the same as 0.

TABLE 4.4 C's Relational Operators

Operator	Symbol	Question Asked	Example
Equal	==	Is operand 1 equal to operand 2?	x == y
Greater than	>	Is operand 1 greater than operand 2?	x > y
Less than	<	Is operand 1 less than operand 2?	x < y
Greater than or equal to	>=	Is operand 1 greater than or equal to operand 2?	x >= y
Less than or or equal to	<=	Is operand 1 less than or equal to operand 2?	x <= y
Not equal	!=	Is operand 1 not equal to operand 2?	x != y

TABLE 4.5 Relational Operators in Use

Expression	How It Reads	What It Evaluates To
5 == 1	Is 5 equal to 1?	0 (false)
5 > 1	Is 5 greater than 1?	1 (true)
5 != 1	Is 5 not equal to 1?	1 (true)
(5 + 10) == (3 * 5)	Is (5 + 10) equal to (3 * 5)?	1 (true)

DO	DON'T
DO learn how C interprets true and false. When working with relational operators, true is equal to 1, and false is equal to 0.	**DON'T** confuse ==, the relational operator, with =, the assignment operator. This is one of the most common errors that C programmers make.

The if **Statement**

Relational operators are used mainly to construct the relational expressions used in if and while statements, covered in detail in Lesson 6, "Basic Program Control." For now, you learn the basics of the if statement to show how relational operators are used to make *program control statements*.

You might wonder what a program control statement is. Statements in a C program normally execute from top to bottom, in the same order as they appear in your source code file. A program control statement modifies the order of statement execution. Program control statements can cause other program statements to execute multiple times or to not execute at all, depending on the circumstances. The if statement is one of C's program control statements. Others, such as do and while, are covered in Lesson 6.

In its basic form, the if statement evaluates an expression and directs program execution depending on the result of that evaluation. The form of an if statement is as follows:

```
if (expression)
{
    statement;


}
```

If *expression* evaluates to true, *statement* is executed. If *expression* evaluates to false, *statement* is not executed. In either case, execution then passes to whatever code follows the if statement. You can say that execution of *statement* depends on the result of *expression*. Note that both the line if (*expression*) and the line *statement*; are considered to make up the complete if statement; they are not separate statements.

An if statement can control the execution of multiple statements through the use of a compound statement, or block. As defined earlier in this lesson, a block is a group of two or more statements enclosed in braces. A block can be used anywhere a single statement can be used. Therefore, you could write an if statement as follows:

```
if (expression)
{
    statement1;
    statement2;
    /* additional code goes here */
    statementn;
}
```

DO	**DON'T**
DO remember that if you program too much in one day, you'll get C sick.	
DO indent statements within a block to make them easier to read. This includes the statements within a block in an if statement.	

CAUTION

Don't make the mistake of putting a semicolon at the end of an if statement's expression. An if statement should end with the conditional statement that follows it. In the following example, due to the semicolon, *statement1* executes whether or not x equals 2. The semicolon causes each line to be evaluated as a separate statement, not together as intended:

```
if( x == 2);          /* semicolon does not belong!  */
statement1;
```

The compiler generally does not produce an error for this mistake.

In your programming, if statements are used most often with relational expressions; in other words, "Execute the following statement(s) only if such-and-such a condition is true." Here's an example:

```
if (x > y)
    y = x;
```

This code assigns the value of x to y only if x is greater than y. If x is not greater than y, no assignment takes place. Listing 4.3 illustrates the use of if statements.

Input ▼
LISTING 4.3 agechecker.c: Demonstrates if Statements

```
1: // Demonstrates if statements and some of C's relational operators
2:
3:    #define CURRENTYEAR 2013
4:    #include <stdio.h>
5:
6:    int birth_year, age;
7:
8:    int main(void)
9:    {
10:       printf("Enter the year you were born: ");
11:       scanf("%d", &birth_year);
12:
13:       // Two tests to calculate whether the user was a leap year birth
14:
15:       if (birth_year % 4 == 0)
16:           printf("You were born in a leap year!\n");
17:       if (birth_year % 4 != 0)
18:           printf("You were not born in a leap year!\n");
19:
20:       age = CURRENTYEAR - birth_year;
21:
22:       // Can check on voting age as well as drinking age
23:
24:       if (age >= 18)
25:           printf("You can vote this year!\n");
26:       if (age <= 21)
27:           printf("It is illegal for you to drink alcohol!\n");
28:
29:       return(0);
30:
31:    }
```

Output ▼

```
Enter the year you were born: 1970
You were not born in a leap year!
You can vote this year!
```

Output ▼

```
Enter the year you were born: 1996
You were born in a leap year!
It is illegal for you to drink alcohol!
```

Output ▼

```
Enter the year you were born: 1994
You were not born in a leap year!
You can vote this year!
It is illegal for you to drink alcohol!
```

Analysis ▼

The ageChecker.c program shows four `if` statements in action (lines 15 through 27). Hopefully, with each new program in the book, key elements are becoming more familiar to you. Line 3 creates a CURRENTYEAR constant with the `#define` directive, and line 4 includes the stdio.h file that is needed whenever you use the `printf` and `scanf` functions. Line 6 defines two integer variables that will be used by the `if` statements.

The first two `if` statements are used to determine if the user was born in a leap year. This is the place in which the modulus operator (`%`) proves useful. Any leap year is divisible by 4, so testing whether the entered year has a remainder equal to 0 (again, remember to use `==` instead of `=` when testing equality) means the year is a leap year. The second `if` statement uses the not equal (`!=`) operator for all other years. This setup is far more efficient than testing whether the remainder is equal to 1, 2, or 3. Not equal is a great choice when you need to exclude one case.

The second pair of `if` statements test the user's current age against voting and drinking eligibility. The first, on line 24, uses greater than or equal to and tells eligible voters they should be good and do their civic duty. The second statement, on line 26, reminds users under the age of 21 that they cannot drink (legally).

Although most birth years entered can satisfy only one of those requirements, as the sample output demonstrates, there is a small section that hits both.

NOTE	The statements within an `if` clause are indented. This is a common practice to aid readability.

The `else` Clause

An `if` statement can optionally include an `else` clause. The `else` clause is included as follows:

```
if (expression)
    statement1;
else
    statement2;
```

If *expression* evaluates to true, *statement1* is executed. If *expression* evaluates to false, control goes to the else statement, *statement2*, which is then executed. Both *statement1* and *statement2* can be compound statements or blocks.

Listing 4.4 shows the program in Listing 4.3 rewritten to use an if statement with an else clause.

Input ▼

LISTING 4.4   agechecker2.c: An if Statement with an else Clause

```
1:  // Demonstrates if and else statements and some of C's relational operators
2:
3:      #define CURRENTYEAR 2013
4:      #include <stdio.h>
5:
6:      int birth_year, age;
7:
8:      int main(void)
9:      {
10:         printf("Enter the year you were born: ");
11:         scanf("%d", &birth_year);
12:
13:         // Two tests to calculate whether the user was a leap year birth
14:
15:         if (birth_year % 4 == 0)
16:             printf("You were born in a leap year!\n");
17:         else
18:             printf("You were not born in a leap year!\n");
19:
20:         age = CURRENTYEAR - birth_year;
21:
22:         // Can check on voting age as well as drinking age
23:
24:         if (age >= 18)
25:             printf("You can vote this year!\n");
26:         if (age <= 21)
27:             printf("It is illegal for you to drink alcohol!\n");;
28:
29:         return(0);
30:
31:      }
```

Output ▼

```
Enter the year you were born: 1975
You were not born in a leap year!
You can vote this year!
```

Output ▼

```
Enter the year you were born: 2000
You were born in a leap year!
It is illegal for you to drink alcohol!
```

Output ▼

```
Enter the year you were born: 1993
You were not born in a leap year!
You can vote this year!
It is illegal for you to drink alcohol!
```

Analysis ▼

Lines 15 through 18 are slightly different from the previous listing. Line 15 still checks to see whether `birth_year` is divisible by 4 without a remainder, which would make the year a leap year. Rather than also checking whether `birth_year` divided by 4 creates a remainder other than 0 (making the year a nonleap year), the `else` clause on line 17 kicks in. The second set of `if` statements are not an either-or situation, so `else` clauses would not make sense, unless you wanted to add "You cannot vote" and "You can legally drink" statements.

The `if` Statement

Form 1

```
if( expression )
{
    statement1;
}
next_statement;
```

This is the `if` statement in its simplest form. If *expression* is true, *statement1* is executed. If *expression* is not true, *statement1* is ignored.

Form 2

```
if( expression )
{
    statement1;
}
else
{
    statement2;
}
next_statement;
```

This is the most common form of the if statement. If *expression* is true, *statement1* is executed; otherwise, *statement2* is executed.

Form 3

```
if( expression1 )
    statement1;
else if( expression2 )
    statement2;
else
    statement3;
next_statement;
```

This is a nested if. If the first expression, *expression1*, is true, *statement1* is executed before the program continues with the *next_statement*. If the first expression is not true, the second expression, *expression2*, is checked. If the first expression is not true, and the second is true, *statement2* is executed. If both expressions are false, *statement3* is executed. Only one of the three statements is executed.

Example 1

```
if( salary > 450000 )
{
    tax = .30;
}
else
{
    tax = .25;
}
```

4

Example 2

```
if( age < 18 )
    printf("Minor");
else if( age < 65 )
    printf("Adult");
else
    printf( "Senior Citizen");
```

Evaluating Relational Expressions

Expressions using relational operators evaluate to a value of either false (0) or true (1). Although the most common use of relational expressions is within if statements and other conditional constructions, they can be used as purely numeric values. This is illustrated in Listing 4.5.

Input ▼

LISTING 4.5   Relational.c: Evaluating Relational Expressions

```
1:    /* Demonstrates the evaluation of relational expressions */
2:
3:    #include <stdio.h>
4:
5:    int a;
6:
7:    int main()
8:    {
9:        a = (5 == 5);              /* Evaluates to 1 */
10:       printf("\na = (5 == 5)\na = %d", a);
11:
12:       a = (5 != 5);              /* Evaluates to 0 */
13:       printf("\na = (5 != 5)\na = %d", a);
14:
15:       a = (12 == 12) + (5 != 1); /* Evaluates to 1 + 1 */
16:       printf("\na = (12 == 12) + (5 != 1)\na = %d\n", a);
17:       return 0;
18:   }
```

Output ▼

```
a = (5 == 5)
a = 1
a = (5 != 5)
a = 0
a = (12 == 12) + (5 != 1)
a = 2
```

Analysis ▼

The output from this listing might seem a little confusing at first. Remember, the most common mistake people make when using the relational operators is to use a single equal sign—the assignment operator—instead of a double equal sign. The following expression evaluates to 5 (and also assigns the value 5 to x):

```
x = 5
```

In contrast, the following expression evaluates to either 0 or 1 (depending on whether x is equal to 5) and doesn't change the value of x:

```
x == 5
```

If by mistake you write

```
if (x = 5)
   printf("x is equal to 5");
```

the message always prints because the expression tested by the `if` statement always evaluates to true, no matter what the original value of x happens to be.

Looking at Listing 4.5, you can begin to understand why a takes on the values that it does. In line 9, the value 5 does equal 5, so true (1) is assigned to a. In line 12, the statement "5 does not equal 5" is false, so 0 is assigned to a.

To reiterate, the relational operators are used to create relational expressions that ask questions about relationships between expressions. The answer returned by a relational expression is a numeric value of either 1 (representing true) or 0 (representing false).

The Precedence of Relational Operators

Like the mathematical operators discussed earlier in this lesson, the relational operators each have a precedence that determines the order in which they are performed in a multiple-operator expression. Similarly, you can use parentheses to modify precedence in expressions that use relational operators. The section "Operator Precedence Revisited" near the end of this lesson lists the precedence of all C's operators.

First, all the relational operators have a lower precedence than the mathematical operators. Thus, if you write the following, 2 is added to x, and the result is compared to y:

```
if (x + 2 > y)
```

This is the equivalent of the following line, which is a good example of using parentheses for the sake of clarity:

```
if ((x + 2) > y)
```

Although they aren't required by the C compiler, the parentheses surrounding `(x + 2)` make it clear that it is the sum of x and 2 that is to be compared with y.

There is also a two-level precedence within the relational operators, as shown in Table 4.6.

TABLE 4.6   The Order of Precedence of C's Relational Operators

Operators	Relative Precedence
< <= > >=	1
!= ==	2

Thus, if you write

```
x == y > z
```

4

it is the same as

```
x == (y > z)
```

because C first evaluates the expression `y > z`, resulting in a value of `0` or `1`. Next, C determines whether `x` is equal to the `1` or `0` obtained in the first step. You will rarely, if ever, use this sort of construction, but you should know about it.

DO	DON'T
	DON'T put assignment statements in the expression block of an `if` statement. This can confuse other people who look at your code. They might think it's a mistake and change your assignment to the logical equal statement.

	DON'T use the "not equal to" operator (`!=`) in an `if` statement containing an `else`. It's almost always clearer to use the "equal to" operator (`==`) with an `else`. For instance, the following code:
	
	```\nif (x != 5)\n statement1;\nelse\n statement2;\n```
	
	would be better written as this:
	
	```\nif (x == 5)\n statement2;\nelse\n statement1;\n```

The Logical Operators

Sometimes you might need to ask more than one relational question at once. For example, "If it's 7:00 a.m. and a weekday and not my vacation, then ring the alarm." C's logical operators let you combine two or more relational expressions into a single expression that evaluates to either true or false. Table 4.7 lists C's three logical operators.

TABLE 4.7 C's Logical Operators

Operator	Symbol	Example
AND	&&	*exp1* && *exp2*
OR	||	*exp1* || *exp2*
NOT	!	*!exp1*

Table 4.8 explains the way these logical operators work.

TABLE 4.8 C's Logical Operators in Use

Expression	What It Evaluates To
(exp1 && exp2)	True (1) only if both *exp1* and *exp2* are true; false (0) otherwise.
(exp1 || exp2)	True (1) if either *exp1* or *exp2* is true; false (0) only if both are false.
(!exp1)	False (0) if *exp1* is true; true (1) if *exp1* is false.

Expressions that use the logical operators evaluate to either true or false depending on the true/false value of their operand(s). Table 4.9 shows code examples.

TABLE 4.9 Code Examples of C's Logical Operators

Expression	What It Evaluates To
(5 == 5) && (6 != 2)	True (1), because both operands are true
(5 > 1) || (6 < 1)	True (1), because one operand is true
(2 == 1) && (5 == 5)	False (0), because one operand is false
!(5 == 4)	True (1), because the operand is false

You can create expressions that use multiple logical operators. For example, to ask the question "Is x equal to 2, 3, or 4?" you could write

```
(x == 2) || (x == 3) || (x == 4)
```

The logical operators often provide more than one way to ask a question. If x is an integer variable, the preceding question also could be written in either of the following ways:

```
(x > 1) && (x < 5)
(x >= 2) && (x <= 4)
```

More on True/False Values

You've seen that C's relational expressions evaluate to 0 to represent false and to 1 to represent true. It's important to be aware, however, that any numeric value is interpreted as either true or false when it is used in a C expression or statement that is expecting a logical value (that is, a true or false value). The rules for this are as follows:

- A value of zero represents false.
- Any nonzero value represents true.

This is illustrated by the following example, in which the value of x is printed:

```
x = 125;
if (x)
    printf("%d", x);
```

Because x has a nonzero value, the if statement interprets the expression (x) as true. You can further generalize this because, for any C expression, writing

(*expression*)

is equivalent to writing

(*expression* != 0)

Both evaluate to true if *expression* is nonzero and to false if *expression* is 0. Using the not (!) operator, you can also write

(!*expression*)

which is equivalent to

(*expression* == 0)

The Precedence of Operators

As you might have guessed, C's logical operators also have a precedence order, both among themselves and in relation to other operators. The ! operator has a precedence equal to the unary mathematical operators ++ and --. Thus, ! has a higher precedence than all the relational operators and all the binary mathematical operators.

In contrast, the && and || operators have much lower precedence, lower than all the mathematical and relational operators, although && has a higher precedence than ||. As with all C's operators, you can use parentheses to modify the evaluation order when using the logical operators. Consider the following example:

You want to write a logical expression that makes three individual comparisons:

1. Is a less than b?

2. Is a less than c?

3. Is c less than d?

You want the entire logical expression to evaluate to true if condition 3 is true and if either condition 1 or condition 2 is true. You might write

```
a < b || a < c && c < d
```

However, this won't do what you intended. Because the && operator has higher precedence than ||, the expression is equivalent to

```
a < b || (a < c && c < d)
```

and evaluates to true if (a < b) is true, whether or not the relationships (a < c) and (c < d) are true. You need to write

```
(a < b || a < c) && c < d
```

which forces the || to be evaluated before the &&. This is shown in Listing 4.6, which evaluates the expression written both ways. The variables are set so that, if written correctly, the expression should evaluate to false (0).

Input ▼

LISTING 4.6   LogicalOrder.c: Logical Operator Precedence

4

```
1:   #include <stdio.h>
2:
3:   /* Initialize variables. Note that c is not less than d, */
4:   /* which is one of the conditions to test for. */
5:   /* Therefore, the entire expression should evaluate as false.*/
6:
7:   int a = 5, b = 6, c = 5, d = 1;
8:   int x;
9:
10:  int main( void )
11:  {
12:      /* Evaluate the expression without parentheses */
13:
14:      x = a < b || a < c && c < d;
15:      printf("\nWithout parentheses the expression evaluates as %d", x);
16:
17:      /* Evaluate the expression with parentheses */
18:
19:      x = (a < b || a < c) && c < d;
20:      printf("\nWith parentheses the expression evaluates as %d\n", x);
21:      return 0;
22:  }
```

Output ▼

```
Without parentheses the expression evaluates as 1
With parentheses the expression evaluates as 0
```

Analysis ▼

Enter and run this listing. Note that the two values printed for the expression are different. This program initializes four variables, in line 7, with values to be used in the comparisons. Line 8 declares x to be used to store and print the results. Lines 14 and 19 use the logical operators. Line 14 doesn't use parentheses, so the results are determined by operator precedence. In this case, the results aren't what you wanted. Line 19 uses parentheses to change the order in which the expressions are evaluated.

Compound Assignment Operators

C's compound assignment operators provide a shorthand method for combining a binary mathematical operation with an assignment operation. For example, say you want to increase the value of x by 5, or, in other words, add 5 to x and assign the result to x. You could write

```
x = x + 5;
```

Using a compound assignment operator, which you can think of as a shorthand method of assignment, you would write

```
x += 5;
```

In more general notation, the compound assignment operators have the following syntax (where op represents a binary operator):

```
exp1 op= exp2
```

This is equivalent to writing

```
exp1 = exp1 op exp2;
```

You can create compound assignment operators using the five binary mathematical operators discussed earlier in this lesson. Table 4.10 lists some examples.

TABLE 4.10   Examples of Compound Assignment Operators

When You Write This	It Is Equivalent to This
x *= y	x = x * y
y -= z + 1	y = y - z + 1
a /= b	a = a / b
x += y / 8	x = x + y / 8
y %= 3	y = y % 3

The compound operators provide a convenient shorthand, the advantages of which are particularly evident when the variable on the left side of the assignment operator has a long name. As with all other assignment statements, a compound assignment statement is an expression and evaluates to the value assigned to the left side. Thus, executing the following statements results in both x and z having the value 14:

```
x = 12;
z = x += 2;
```

The Conditional Operator

The conditional operator is C's only *ternary* operator, meaning that it takes three operands. Its syntax is

```
exp1 ? exp2 : exp3;
```

If *exp1* evaluates to true (that is, nonzero), the entire expression evaluates to the value of *exp2*. If *exp1* evaluates to false (that is, zero), the entire expression evaluates as the value of *exp3*. For example, the following statement assigns the value 1 to x if y is true and assigns 100 to x if y is false:

```
x = y ? 1 : 100;
```

Likewise, to make z equal to the larger of x and y, you could write

```
z = (x > y) ? x : y;
```

Perhaps you've noticed that the conditional operator functions somewhat like an if statement. The preceding statement could also be written like this:

```
if (x > y)
z = x;
else
z = y;
```

The conditional operator can't be used in all situations in place of an if...else construction, but the conditional operator is more concise. The conditional operator can also be used in places you can't use an if statement, such as inside a call to another function such as a single printf() statement:

```
printf( "The larger value is %d", ((x > y) ? x : y) );
```

The Comma Operator

The comma is frequently used in C as a simple punctuation mark, serving to separate variable declarations, function arguments, and so on. In certain situations, the comma

4

acts as an operator rather than just as a separator. You can form an expression by separating two subexpressions with a comma. The result is as follows:

- Both expressions are evaluated, with the left expression being evaluated first.
- The entire expression evaluates to the value of the right expression.

For example, the following statement assigns the value of b to x, then increments a, and then increments b:

```
x = (a++ , b++);
```

Because the ++ operator is used in postfix mode, the value of b—before it is incremented—is assigned to x. Using parentheses is necessary because the comma operator has low precedence, even lower than the assignment operator.

As you learn in the next lesson, the most common use of the comma operator is in for statements.

DO	DON'T
DO use the logical operators && and || instead of nesting if statements.	**DON'T** confuse the assignment operator (=) with the equal to (==) operator.

Operator Precedence Revisited

Table 4.11 lists the C operators in order of decreasing precedence. Operators on the same line have the same precedence.

TABLE 4.11 C Operator Precedence

Level	Operators
1	() [] -> .
2	! ~ ++ -- * *(indirection)* & *(address of)* (type)
	sizeof + *(unary)* - *(unary)*
3	* *(multiplication)* / %
4	+ -
5	<< >>
6	< <= > >=
7	== !=
8	& *(bitwise* AND*)*
9	^

10	`|`
11	`&&`
12	`||`
13	`?:`
14	`= += -= *= /= %= &= ^= |= <<= >>=`
15	`,`

`()` is the function operator; `[]` is the array operator.

TIP

This is a good table to keep referring to until you become familiar with the order of precedence. You might find that you need it later.

Summary

This lesson covered a lot of material. You learned what a C statement is, that white space doesn't matter to a C compiler, and that statements always end with a semicolon. You also learned that a compound statement (or block), which consists of two or more statements enclosed in braces, can be used anywhere a single statement can be used.

Many statements are made up of some combination of expressions and operators. Remember that an expression is anything that evaluates to a numeric value. Complex expressions can contain many simpler expressions, which are called subexpressions.

Operators are C symbols that instruct the computer to perform an operation on one or more expressions. Some operators are unary, which means that they operate on a single operand. Most of C's operators are binary, however, operating on two operands. One operator, the conditional operator, is ternary. C's operators have a defined hierarchy of precedence that determines the order in which operations are performed in an expression that contains multiple operators.

The C operators covered in this lesson fall into three categories:

- Mathematical operators perform arithmetic operations on their operands (for example, addition).
- Relational operators perform comparisons between their operands (for example, greater than).

4

- Logical operators operate on true/false expressions. Remember that C uses 0 and 1 to represent false and true, respectively, and that any nonzero value is interpreted as being true.

You've also been introduced to C's if statement, which enables you to control program execution based on the evaluation of relational expressions.

Q&A

Q What effect do spaces and blank lines have on how a program runs?

A White space (lines, spaces, and tabs) makes the code listing more readable. When the program is compiled, white space is stripped and thus has no effect on the executable program. For this reason, you should use white space to make your program easier to read.

Q Is it better to code a compound if statement or to nest multiple if statements?

A You should make your code easy to understand. If you nest if statements, they are evaluated as shown in this lesson. If you use a single compound statement, the expressions are evaluated only until the entire statement evaluates to false.

Q What is the difference between unary and binary operators?

A As the names imply, unary operators work with one variable, and binary operators work with two.

Q Is the subtraction operator (-) binary or unary?

A It's both! The compiler is smart enough to know which one you're using. It knows which form to use based on the number of variables in the expression that is used. In the following statement, it is unary:

```
x = -y;
```

versus the following binary use:

```
x = a - b;
```

Q Are negative numbers considered true or false?

A Remember that 0 is false, and any other value is true. This includes negative numbers.

Workshop

The Workshop provides quiz questions to help you solidify your understanding of the material covered and exercises to provide you with experience in using what you've learned.

Quiz

1. What is the following C statement called, and what is its meaning?

```
x = 5 + 8;
```

2. What is an expression?

3. In an expression that contains multiple operators, what determines the order in which operations are performed?

4. If the variable x has the value 10, what are the values of x and a after each of the following statements is executed separately?

```
a = x++;
a = ++x;
```

5. To what value does the expression 10 % 3 evaluate?

6. To what value does the expression 5 + 3 * 8 / 2 + 2 evaluate?

7. Rewrite the expression in question 6, adding parentheses so that it evaluates to 16.

8. If an expression evaluates to false, what value does the expression have?

9. In the following list, which has higher precedence?

    a. == or <

    b. * or +

    c. != or ==

    d. >= or >

10. What are the compound assignment operators, and how are they useful?

Exercises

1. The following code is not well written. Enter and compile it to see whether it works.

```
#include <stdio.h>
int x,y;int main(){ printf(
"\nEnter two numbers");scanf(
"%d %d",&x,&y);printf(
"\n\n%d is bigger",(x>y)?x:y);return 0;}
```

2. Rewrite the code in exercise 1 to be more readable.

3. Change Listing 4.1 to count upward instead of downward.

4. Write an if statement that assigns the value of x to the variable y only if x is between 1 and 20. Leave y unchanged if x is not in that range.

5. Use the conditional operator to perform the same task as in exercise 4.

6. Rewrite the following nested `if` statements using a single `if` statement and logical operators:

```
if (x < 1)
    if ( x > 10 )
        statement;
```

7. To what value does each of the following expressions evaluate?

   a. `(1 + 2 * 3)`

   b. `10 % 3 * 3 - (1 + 2)`

   c. `((1 + 2) * 3)`

   d. `(5 == 5)`

   e. `(x = 5)`

8. If `x = 4`, `y = 6`, and `z = 2`, determine whether each of the following evaluates to true or false:

   a. `if( x == 4)`

   b. `if(x != y - z)`

   c. `if(z = 1)`

   d. `if(y)`

9. Write an `if` statement that determines whether someone is legally an adult (age 21) but not a senior citizen (age 65).

10. **BUG BUSTER:** Fix the following program so that it runs correctly:

```
/* a program with problems... */
#include <stdio.h>
int x = 1:
int main( void )
{
    if( x = 1);
        printf(" x equals 1" );
    otherwise
        printf(" x does not equal 1");
    return 0;
}
```

LESSON 5
Packaging Code in Functions

Functions are central to C programming and to the philosophy of C program design. You've already been introduced to some of C's library functions, which are complete functions supplied as part of your compiler. This lesson covers user-defined functions, which, as the name implies, are functions defined and created by you, the programmer. In this lesson you learn:

- What a function is and what its parts are

- The advantages of structured programming with functions

- How to create a function

- How to declare local variables in a function

- How to return a value from a function to the program

- How to pass arguments to a function

Understanding Functions

To understand functions, you need to understand both what functions are and how they are used.

A Function Defined

First the definition: A *function* is a named, independent section of C code that performs a specific task and optionally returns a value to the calling program. Now take a look at the parts of this definition:

- *A function is named.* Each function has a unique name. By using that name in another part of the program, you can execute the statements contained in the function. This is known as *calling* the function. A function can be called from within another function.

- *A function is independent.* A function can perform its task without interference from or interfering with other parts of the program.

- *A function performs a specific task.* This is the easy part of the definition. A task is a discrete job that your program must perform as part of its overall operation, such as sending a line of text to a printer, sorting an array into numerical order, or calculating a cube root.

- *A function can return a value to the calling program.* When your program calls a function, the statements it contains are executed. If you want them to, these statements can pass information back to the calling program.

That's all there is to define a function. Keep the previous definition in mind as you look at the next section.

A Function Illustrated

Listing 5.1 contains a user-defined function.

Input ▼

LISTING 5.1   cube.c: A Program That Uses a Function to Calculate the Cube of a Number

```
1:    // Demonstrates a simple function
2:    #include <stdio.h>
3:
4:    long cube(long x);
5:
6:    long input, answer;
7:
8:    int main( void )
9:    {
```

```
10:     printf("Enter an integer value: ");
11:     scanf("%ld", &input);
12:     answer = cube(input);
13:     /* Note: %ld is the conversion specifier for
14:         a long integer */
15:     printf("\nThe cube of %ld is %ld.\n", input, answer);
16:
17:     return 0;
18: }
19:
20: // Function: cube() - Calculates the cubed value of a variable
21: long cube(long x)
22: {
23:     long x_cubed;
24:
25:     x_cubed = x * x * x;
26:     return x_cubed;
27: }
```

Output ▼

Enter an integer value: **100**

The cube of 100 is 1000000.

Output ▼

Enter an integer value: **9**

The cube of 9 is 729.

Output ▼

Enter an integer value: **678**

The cube of 678 is 311665752.

NOTE The following analysis focuses on the components of the program that relate directly to the function rather than explaining the entire program.

5

Analysis ▼

Line 4 contains the *function prototype,* a model for a function that appears later in the program. A function's prototype contains the name of the function, a list and type of any variables that must be passed to it, and the type of variable it returns, if any. Looking at line 4, you can tell that the function is named `cube`, that it requires a variable of the type `long`, and that it will return a value of type `long`. The variables to be passed to the function are called *arguments,* and they are enclosed in parentheses following the function's name. In this example, the function has a single argument: `long x`. The keyword before the name of the function indicates the type of variable the function returns. In this case, a variable of type `long` is returned.

Line 12 calls the function `cube` and passes the variable `input` to it as the function's argument. The function's return value is assigned to the variable `answer`. Notice that both `input` and `answer` are declared on line 6 as variables of type `long`. This matches the types used in the function prototype on line 4.

The function itself is called the *function definition.* In this case, the function is called `cube` and is contained on lines 21 through 27. Like the prototype, the function definition has several parts. The function starts with a function header on line 21. The *function header* is at the start of a function and gives the function's name (in this case, the name is `cube`). The header also gives the function's return type and describes its arguments. Note that the function header is identical to the function prototype (minus the semicolon).

The body of the function, lines 22 through 27, is enclosed in braces. The body contains statements, such as on line 25, that are executed whenever the function is called. Line 23 is a variable declaration that looks like the declarations you have seen before, with one difference: it's local. *Local* variables are declared within a function body. (Local declarations are discussed further in Lesson 12, "Understanding Variable Scope.") Finally, the function concludes with a `return` statement on line 26, which signals the end of the function. A `return` statement also passes a value back to the calling program. In this case, the value of the variable `x_cubed` is returned.

If you compare the structure of the `cube()` function with that of the `main()` function, you can see that they are the same. `main()` is also a function. Other functions that you already have used are `printf()` and `scanf()`. Although `printf()` and `scanf()` are library functions (as opposed to user-defined functions), they are functions that can take arguments and return values just like the functions you create.

How a Function Works

A C program doesn't execute the statements in a function until the function is called by another part of the program. When a function is called, the program can send the function information in the form of one or more arguments. An *argument* is program data sent to the function. This data can be used by the function to perform its task. The statements in the function then execute, performing whatever task each was designed to do. When the function's statements finish, execution passes back to the same location in the program that called the function. Functions can send information back to the program in the form of a return value.

Figure 5.1 shows a program with three functions, each of which is called once. Each time a function is called, execution passes to that function. When the function finishes, execution passes back to the place from which the function was called. A function can be called as many times as needed, and functions can be called in any order.

FIGURE 5.1
When a program calls a function, execution passes to the function and then back to the calling program.

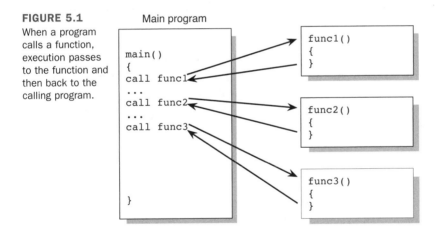

You now know what a function is and the importance of functions. Lessons on how to create and use your own functions follow.

Syntax

Functions

Function Prototype

```
return-type function_name( arg-type name-1,...,arg-type name-n);
```

Function Definition

```
return-type function_name( arg-type name-1,...,arg-type name-n)
{
    /* statements; */
}
```

A *function prototype* provides the compiler with a description of a function that will be defined at a later point in the program. The prototype includes a return type indicating the type of variable that the function will return. It also includes the function name, which should describe what the function does. The prototype also contains the variable types of the arguments (`arg-type`) that will be passed to the function. Optionally, it can contain the names of the variables that will be passed. A prototype should always end with a semicolon.

A *function definition* is the actual function. The definition contains the code that will be executed. If the prototype contains the names of the variables, the first line of a function definition, called the *function header,* should be identical to the function prototype, with the exception of the semicolon. A function header shouldn't end with a semicolon. In addition, although the argument variable names were optional in the prototype, they must be included in the function header. Following the header is the function body, containing the statements that the function will perform. The function body should start with an opening bracket and end with a closing bracket. If the function return type is anything other than `void`, a `return` statement should be included, returning a value matching the return type. If you want, you can always include a `return` statement without a value to return in your void function types. It does no harm, and is good practice for including `return` statements in all functions—better safe than sorry!

Function Prototype Examples

```
double squared( double number );
void print_report( int report_number );
int get_menu_choice( void );
```

Function Definition Examples

```
double squared( double number )          /* function header */
{                                         /* opening bracket */
    return(  number * number );           /* function body   */
}                                         /* closing bracket */
void print_report( int report_number )
{
    if( report_number == 1 )
        puts( "Printing Report 1" );
    else
        puts( "Not printing Report 1" );
    return;
}
```

Functions and Structured Programming

By using functions in your C programs, you can practice *structured programming,* in which individual program tasks are performed by independent sections of program code. "Independent sections of program code" sounds just like part of the definition of functions given earlier, doesn't it? Functions and structured programming are closely related.

The Advantages of Structured Programming

Why is structured programming so great? There are two important reasons:

- It's easier to write a structured program because complex programming problems are broken into a number of smaller, simpler tasks. Each task is performed by a function in which code and variables are isolated from the rest of the program. You can progress more quickly by dealing with these relatively simple tasks one at a time.

- It's easier to debug a structured program. If your program has a *bug* (something that causes it to work improperly), a structured design makes it easy to isolate the problem to a specific section of code (such as a specific function).

A related advantage of structured programming is the time you can save by reusing sections of code. If you write a function to perform a certain task in one program, you can quickly and easily use it in another program that needs to execute the same task. Even if the new program needs to accomplish a slightly different task, you'll often find that modifying a function you created earlier is easier than writing a new one from scratch. Consider how much you've used the two functions `printf()` and `scanf()` even though you probably haven't seen the code they contain. If your functions have been created to perform a single task, using them in other programs is much easier.

5

Planning a Structured Program

If you're going to write a structured program, you need to do some planning first. This planning should take place before you write a single line of code, and it usually can be done with nothing more than pencil and paper. Your plan should be a list of the specific tasks your program performs. Begin with a global idea of the program's function. If you were planning a program to manage your contacts (a list of names and addresses), what would you want the program to do? Here are some obvious things:

- Enter new names and addresses.
- Modify existing entries.
- Sort entries by last name.
- Print mailing labels.

With this list, you've divided the program into four main tasks, each of which can be assigned to a function. Now you can go a step further, dividing these tasks into subtasks. For example, the "Enter new names and addresses" task can be subdivided into these subtasks:

- Read the existing address list from disk.
- Prompt the user for one or more new entries.
- Add the new data to the list.
- Save the updated list to disk.

Likewise, the "Modify existing entries" task can be subdivided as follows:

- Read the existing address list from disk.
- Modify one or more entries.
- Save the updated list to disk.

You might have noticed that these two lists have two subtasks in common—the ones dealing with reading from and saving to disk. You can write one function to "Read the existing address list from disk," and that function can be called by both the "Enter new names and addresses" function and the "Modify existing entries" function. The same is true for "Save the updated list to disk."

Already you should see at least one advantage of structured programming. By carefully dividing the program into tasks, you can identify parts of the program that share common tasks. You can write "double-duty" disk access functions, saving yourself time and making your program smaller and more efficient.

This method of programming results in a *hierarchical,* or layered, program structure. Figure 5.2 illustrates hierarchical programming for the address list program.

FIGURE 5.2
A structured program is organized hierarchically.

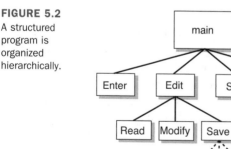

When you follow this planned approach, you quickly make a list of discrete tasks that your program needs to perform. Then you can tackle the tasks one at a time, giving all your attention to one relatively simple task. When that function is written and working properly, you can move on to the next task. Before you know it, your program starts to take shape.

The Top-Down Approach

By using structured programming, C programmers take the *top-down approach*. You saw this illustrated in Figure 5.2, where the program's structure resembles an inverted tree. Many times, most of the real work of the program is performed by the functions at the tips of the "branches." The functions closer to the "trunk" primarily direct program execution among these functions.

As a result, many C programs have a small amount of code in the main body of the program—that is, in `main()`. The bulk of the program's code is found in functions. In `main()`, all you might find are a few dozen lines of code that direct program execution among the functions. Often, a menu is presented to the person using the program. Program execution is branched according to the user's choices. Each branch of the menu uses a different function.

NOTE

> Using menus is a good approach to program design. Lesson 13, "Advanced Program Control," shows how you can use the `switch` statement to create a versatile menu-driven system.

5

Now that you know what functions are and why they're so important, the time has come for you to learn how to write your own.

DO	DON'T
DO plan before starting to code. By determining your program's structure ahead of time, you can save time writing the code and debugging it.	**DON'T** try to do everything in one function. A single function should perform a single task, such as reading information from a file.

Writing a Function

The first step in writing a function is to know what you want the function to do. When you know that, the actual mechanics of writing the function aren't particularly difficult.

The Function Header

The first line of every function is the function header, which has three components, each serving a specific function. They are shown in Figure 5.3 and explained in the following sections.

FIGURE 5.3
The three components of a function header.

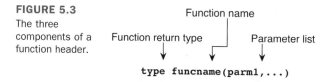

```
type funcname(parm1,...)
```

The Function Return Type

The return type of a function specifies the data type that the function returns to the calling program. The function return type can be any of C's data types. This includes `char`, `int`, `long`, `float`, or `double`. You can also define a function that doesn't return a value by using a return type of `void`. Here are some examples:

```
int func1(...)      /* Returns a type int.   */
float func2(...)    /* Returns a type float. */
void func3(...)     /* Returns nothing.      */
```

In these examples, you can see that *func1* returns an integer, *func2* returns a floating-point number, and *func3* doesn't return anything.

The Function Name

You can name a function anything you like, as long as you follow the rules for C variable names (given in Lesson 3, "Storing Data: Variables and Constants"). In C programs, a function name must be unique (not assigned to any other function or variable). It's a good idea to assign a name that reflects what the function does.

The Parameter List

Many functions use *arguments*, which are values passed to the function when they're called. A function needs to know what kinds of arguments to expect—the data type of each argument. You can pass to a function any of C's data types. Argument type information is provided in the function header by a parameter list.

For each argument that is passed to the function, the parameter list must contain one entry. This entry specifies the data type and the name of the parameter. For example, here's the header from the function in Listing 5.1:

```
long cube(long x)
```

The parameter list consists of `long x`, specifying that this function takes one type `long` argument, represented by the parameter `x`. If there is more than one parameter, each must be separated by a comma. The function header

```
void func1(int x, float y, char z)
```

specifies a function with three arguments: a type `int` named `x`, a type `float` named `y`, and a type `char` named `z`. Some functions take no arguments, in which case the parameter list should consist of `void`, like this:

```
int func2(void)
```

NOTE Do not place a semicolon at the end of a function header. If you mistakenly include one, the compiler generates an error message.

Sometimes confusion arises about the distinction between a parameter and an argument. A *parameter* is an entry in a function header; it serves as a "placeholder" for an argument. A function's parameters are fixed; they do not change during program execution.

An *argument* is an actual value passed to the function by the calling program. Each time a function is called, it can be passed different arguments. In C, a function must be passed the same number and type of arguments each time it's called, but the argument values can be different. In the function, the argument is accessed by using the corresponding parameter name.

An example will make this clearer. Listing 5.2 presents a simple program with one function that is called three times.

Input ▼
LISTING 5.2   halfof.c: The Difference Between Arguments and Parameters

```
1:    // Illustrates the difference between arguments and parameters.
2:
3:    #include <stdio.h>
4:
5:    float x = 3.5, y = 65.11, z;
6:
```

5

```
7:    float half_of(float k);
8:
9:    int main( void )
10:   {
11:       // In this call, x is the argument to half_of().
12:       z = half_of(x);
13:       printf("The value of z = %f\n", z);
14:
15:       // In this call, y is the argument to half_of().
16:       z = half_of(y);
17:       printf("The value of z = %f\n", z);
18:
19:       // In this third call, z is the argument to half_of().
20:       z = half_of(z);
21:       printf("The value of z = %f\n", z);
22:
23:       return 0;
24:   }
25:
26:   float half_of(float k)
27:   {
28:       /* k is the parameter. Each time half_of() is called, */
29:       /* k has the value that was passed as an argument. */
30:
31:       return (k/2);
32:   }
```

Output ▼

```
The value of z = 1.750000
The value of z = 32.555000
The value of z = 16.277500
```

Figure 5.4 shows the relationship between arguments and parameters.

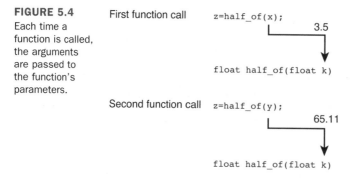

FIGURE 5.4
Each time a function is called, the arguments are passed to the function's parameters.

Analysis ▼

Looking at Listing 5.2, you can see that the `half_of()` function prototype is declared on line 7. Lines 12, 16, and 20 call `half_of()`, and lines 26 through 32 contain the actual function. Lines 12, 16, and 20 each send a different argument to `half_of()`. Line 12 sends x, which contains a value of `3.5`, and line 16 sends y, which contains a value of `65.11`. Line 20 sends z, which contains the value of 32.555 from the most recent function call. When the program runs, it prints the correct number for each. The values in x, y, and z are passed into the argument k of `half_of()`. This is like copying the values from x to k, y to k, and then from z to k. `half_of()` then returns this value after dividing it by 2 (line 31).

NOTE

> The last function call should make it clear that you can call a function passing the same variable that will then receive the new value. It can be a bit confusing until you are used to it.

DO	DON'T
DO use a function name that describes the purpose of the function.	**DON'T** pass values to a function that it doesn't need.
DO make sure that the data type of the arguments you pass to a function matches the data types of the parameters of the function.	**DON'T** try to pass fewer (or more) arguments to a function than there are parameters. In C programs, the number of arguments passed must match the number of parameters.

The Function Body

The *function body* is enclosed in braces and immediately follows the function header. It's in the function body that the real work is done. When a function is called, execution begins at the start of the body and terminates (returns to the calling program) when a `return` statement is encountered or when execution reaches the closing brace.

Local Variables

You can declare variables within the body of a function. Variables declared in a function are called *local variables*. The term *local* means that the variables are private to that particular function and are distinct from other variables of the same name declared elsewhere in the program. This will be explained shortly; for now, you should learn how to declare local variables.

A local variable is declared like any other variable, using the same variable types and rules for names that you learned in Lesson 3. Local variables can also be initialized when they are declared. You can declare any of C's variable types in a function. Here is an example of four local variables declared within a function:

```
int func1(int y)
{
    int a, b = 10;
    float rate;
    double cost = 12.55;
    /* function code goes here... */
}
```

The preceding declarations create the local variables a, b, rate, and cost, which can be used by the code in the function. Note that the function parameters are considered to be variable declarations, so the variables, if any, in the function's parameter list also are available.

When you declare and use a variable in a function, it is totally separate and distinct from any other variables declared elsewhere in the program. This is true even if the variables have the same name. Listing 5.3 demonstrates this independence.

Input ▼
LISTING 5.3   var.c: A Demonstration of Local Variables

```
1:    /* Demonstrates local variables. */
2:
3:    #include <stdio.h>
4:
5:    int x = 1, y = 2;
6:
7:    void demo(void);
8:
9:    int main( void )
10:   {
11:     printf("\nBefore calling demo(), x = %d and y = %d.", x, y);
12:     demo();
13:     printf("\nAfter calling demo(), x = %d and y = %d\n.", x, y);
14:
15:     return 0;
16:   }
17:
18:   void demo(void)
19:   {
20:       /* Declare and initialize two local variables. */
21:
22:       int x = 88, y = 99;
23:
```

```
24:        /* Display their values. */
25:
26:        printf("\nWithin demo(), x = %d and y = %d.", x, y);
27:  }
```

Output ▼

```
Before calling demo(), x = 1 and y = 2.
Within demo(), x = 88 and y = 99.
After calling demo(), x = 1 and y = 2.
```

Analysis ▼

Listing 5.3 is similar to the first two programs in this lesson. Line 5 declares variables x and y. These are declared outside of any functions and therefore are considered global. Line 7 contains the prototype for the demonstration function, named demo(). It doesn't take any parameters, so it has void in the prototype. It also doesn't return any values, giving it a return type of void. Line 9 starts the main() function, which is simple. First, printf() is called on line 11 to display the values of x and y, and then the demo() function is called. Notice that demo() declares its own local versions of x and y on line 22. Line 26 shows that the local variables take precedence over any others. After the demo function is called, line 13 again prints the values of x and y. Because you are no longer in demo(), the original global values are printed.

As you can see, local variables x and y in the function are totally independent from the global variables x and y declared outside the function. Three rules govern the use of variables in functions:

- To use a variable in a function, you must declare it in the function header or the function body (except for global variables, which are covered in Lesson 12).
- For a function to obtain a value from the calling program, the value must be passed as an argument.
- For a calling program to obtain a value from a function, the value must be explicitly returned from the function.

To be honest, these "rules" are not strictly applied because you'll learn how to get around them later in this book. However, follow these rules for now, and you should stay out of trouble.

Keeping the function's variables separate from other program variables is one way in which functions are independent. A function can perform any sort of data manipulation you want, using its own set of local variables. There's no worry that these manipulations

5

will have an unintended effect on another part of the program. In addition, if you use variables local to the function, it's easier to cut and paste that function into another program if you need to accomplish the same task in a new program.

Function Statements

There is essentially no limitation on the statements that can be included within a function. The only thing you can't do inside a function is to define another function. You can, however, use all other C statements, including loops (these are covered in Lesson 6, "Basic Program Control"), `if` statements, and assignment statements. You can call library functions and other user-defined functions.

What about function length? C places no length restriction on functions, but as a matter of practicality, you should keep your functions relatively short. Remember that in structured programming, each function is supposed to perform a somewhat simple task. If you find that a function is getting long, perhaps you're trying to perform a task too complex for one function alone. It probably can be broken into two or more smaller functions.

How long is too long? There's no definite answer to that question, but in practical experience it's rare to find a function longer than 25 or 30 lines of actual code. Functions with more lines of actual code will generally be doing more than one thing. You have to use your own judgment. Some programming tasks require longer functions, whereas many functions are only a few lines long. As you gain programming experience, you will become more adept at determining what should and shouldn't be broken into smaller functions.

Returning a Value

To return a value from a function, you use the `return` keyword, followed by a C expression. When execution reaches a `return` statement, the expression is evaluated, and execution passes the value back to the calling program. The return value of the function is the value of the expression. Consider this function:

```
int func1(int var)
{
    int x;
    /* Function code goes here... */
    return x;
}
```

When this function is called, the statements in the function body execute up to the `return` statement. The `return` terminates the function and returns the value of `x` to the calling program. The expression to the right of the `return` keyword can be any valid C expression.

A function can contain multiple `return` statements. The first `return` executed is the only one that has any effect. Multiple `return` statements can be an efficient way to return different values from a function, as demonstrated in Listing 5.4.

Input ▼

LISTING 5.4   roomassign.c: Using Multiple `return` Statements in a Function

```
 1:   /* Demonstrates using multiple return statements in a function. */
 2:
 3:   #include <stdio.h>
 4:
 5:   char last_init;
 6:   int room;
 7:
 8:   int room_assign( char last_init);
 9:
10:   int main( void )
11:   {
12:       puts("Enter the first initial of your last name: ");
13:       scanf("%c", &last_init);
14:
15:       room = room_assign(last_init);
16:
17:       printf("\nYou need to report to room %d.", room);
18:
19:       return 0;
20:   }
21:
22:   int room_assign( char li)
23:   {
24:       // This if statement tests whether the first initial is A-M or N-Z
25:       // with the first group being assigned room 1045 and the rest 1055
26:
27:       // The or part of the statement lets us check both lower and uppercase
28:
29:       if ((li >= 'a' && li <= 'm') || (li >= 'A' && li <= 'M'))
30:           return 1045;
31:       else
32:           return 1055;
33:   }
```

Output ▼

```
Enter the first initial of your last name:
d

You need to report to room 1045.
```

Output ▼

```
Enter the first initial of your last name:
R

You need to report to room 1055.
```

Analysis ▼

As in other examples, Listing 5.4 starts with a comment to describe what the program does (line 1). The `stdio.h` header file is included for the standard input/output functions that allow the program to display information to the screen and get user input. Line 8 is the function prototype for `room_assign()`. Notice that `room_assign()` takes one `char` variable for a parameter and returns an `int`. Line 15 calls `room_assign()` with `last_init`. This function contains the multiple `return` statements. Using an `if` statement, the function checks to see whether `li` (the `last_init` in `main()` is passed to `li` in the function) falls between "A" and "M" or "a" and "m". If it does, line 30 executes a `return` statement, and the function immediately ends. Lines 31 and 32 are ignored in this case. If the initial doesn't fall between "a" and "m" (the initial is between "n" and "z"), the `else` clause is instigated, and the `return` on line 32 executes. You should be able to see that, depending on the argument passed to the function `room_assign()`, either the first or the second `return` statement is executed, and the appropriate value is passed back to the calling function.

One final note on this program. Line 12 is a new function that you haven't seen before. `puts()`—meaning *put string*—is a simple function that displays a string to the standard output, usually the computer screen. (Strings are covered in Lesson 10, "Working with Characters and Strings." For now, know that they are just quoted text.)

Remember that a function's return value has a type that is specified in the function header and function prototype. The value returned by the function must be of the same type, or the compiler generates an error message.

NOTE

> Structured programming suggests that you have only one entry and one exit in a function. This means that you should try to have only one `return` statement within your function. At times, however, a program might be much easier to read and maintain with more than one `return` statement. In such cases, maintainability should take precedence.

The Function Prototype

A program should include a prototype for each function it uses. You saw an example of a function prototype on line 4 of Listing 5.1, and there have been function prototypes in the other listings as well. What is a function prototype, and why is it needed?

You can see from the earlier examples that the prototype for a function is identical to the function header, with a semicolon added at the end. Like the function header, the function prototype includes information about the function's return type, name, and parameters. The prototype's job is to tell the compiler about the function. By providing information on the function's return type, name, and parameters, the compiler can check every time your source code calls the function and verify that you're passing the correct number and type of arguments and using the return value correctly. If there's a mismatch, the compiler generates an error message.

Strictly speaking, a function prototype doesn't need to exactly match the function header. The parameter names can be different, as long as they are the same type and number, and in the same order. There's no reason for the header and prototype not to match; having them identical makes source code easier to understand. Matching the two also makes writing a program easier. When you complete a function definition, use your editor's cut-and-paste feature to copy the function header and create the prototype. Be sure to add a semicolon at the end of the prototype.

Where should function prototypes be placed in your source code? They should be placed before the start of the first function. For readability, it's best to group all prototypes in one location.

DO	DON'T
DO use local variables whenever possible.	**DON'T** try to return a value that has a type different from the function's type.
DO limit each function to a single task.	**DON'T** let functions get too long. If a function starts getting long, try to break it into separate, smaller tasks.
	DON'T have multiple `return` statements if they aren't needed. You should try to have one `return` when possible; however, sometimes having multiple `return` statements is easier and clearer.

5

Passing Arguments to a Function

To pass arguments to a function, you list them in parentheses following the function name. The number of arguments and the type of each argument must match the parameters in the function header and prototype. For example, if a function is defined to take two type `int` arguments, you must pass it exactly two `int` arguments—no more, no less—and no other type. If you try to pass a function an incorrect number and/or type of argument, the compiler can detect it, based on the information in the function prototype.

If the function takes multiple arguments, the arguments listed in the function call are assigned to the function parameters in order: the first argument to the first parameter, the second argument to the second parameter, and so on, as shown in Figure 5.5.

FIGURE 5.5
Multiple arguments are assigned to function parameters in order.

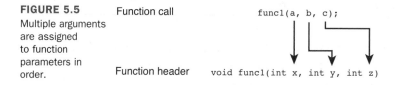

Each argument can be any valid C expression: a constant, a variable, a mathematical or logical expression, or even another function (one with a return value). For example, if `half()`, `square()`, and `third()` are all functions with return values, you could write

```
x = half(third(square(half(y))));
```

The program first calls `half()`, passing it `y` as an argument. When execution returns from `half()`, the program calls `square()`, passing `half()`'s return value as an argument. Next, `third()` is called with `square()`'s return value as the argument. Then, `half()` is called again, this time with `third()`'s return value as an argument. Finally, `half()`'s return value is assigned to the variable `x`. The following is an equivalent piece of code:

```
a = half(y);
b = square(a);
c = third(b);
x = half(c);
```

Calling Functions

There are two ways to call a function. Any function can be called by simply using its name and argument list alone in a statement, as in the following example. If the function has a return value, it is discarded.

```
wait(12);
```

The second method can be used only with functions that have a return value. Because these functions evaluate to a value (that is, their return value), they are valid C expressions and can be used anywhere a C expression can be used. You've already seen an expression with a return value used as the right side of an assignment statement. Here are some more examples.

In the following example, `half_of()` is a parameter of a function:

```
printf("Half of %d is %d.", x, half_of(x));
```

First, the function `half_of()` is called with the value of x, and then `printf()` is called using the values `"Half of %d is %d."`, x, and `half_of(x)`.

In this second example, multiple functions are used in an expression:

```
y = half_of(x) + half_of(z);
```

Although `half_of()` is used twice, the second call could have been any other function. The following code shows the same statement, but not all on one line:

```
a = half_of(x);
b = half_of(z);
y = a + b;
```

The following final two examples show effective ways to use the return values of functions. Here, a function is used with the `if` statement:

```
if ( half_of(x) > 10 )
{
    /* statements; */        /* these could be any statements! */
}
```

5

If the return value of the function meets the criteria (in this case, if `half_of()` returns a value greater than 10), the `if` statement is true, and its statements are executed. If the returned value doesn't meet the criteria, the statements in the `if` block are not executed.

The following example is even better:

```
if ( do_a_process() != OKAY )
{
    /* statements; */        /* do error routine */
}
```

Again, actual statements are not provided, nor is `do_a_process()` a real function; however, this is an important example. The return value of a process is checked to see whether it ran correctly. If it didn't, the statements take care of any error handling or cleanup. This is commonly used with accessing information in files, comparing values, and allocating memory.

CAUTION	If you try to use a function with a `void` return type as an expression, the compiler generates an error message.

DO	**DON'T**
DO pass parameters to functions to make the function generic and thus reusable.	**DON'T** make an individual statement confusing by putting a bunch of functions in it. You should put functions into your statements only if they don't make the code more confusing.
DO take advantage of the ability to put functions into expressions.	

Recursion

The term *recursion* refers to a situation in which a function calls itself either directly or indirectly. *Indirect recursion* occurs when one function calls another function that then calls the first function. C allows recursive functions, and they can be useful in some situations.

For example, recursion can be used to calculate the factorial of a number. The factorial of a number `x` is written `x!` and is calculated as follows:

```
x! = x * (x-1) * (x-2) * (x-3) * ... * (2) * 1
```

However, you can also calculate `x!` like this:

```
x! = x * (x-1)!
```

Going one step further, you can calculate `(x-1)!` using the same procedure:

```
(x-1)! = (x-1) * (x-2)!
```

You continue calculating recursively until you're down to a value of `1`, in which case you're finished. The program in Listing 5.5 uses a recursive function to calculate factorials. Because the program uses `unsigned` integers, it's limited to an input value of `8`; the factorial of `9` and larger values are outside the allowed range for integers.

Input ▼

LISTING 5.5   recurse.c: Using a Recursive Function to Calculate Factorials

```
1:   /* Demonstrates function recursion. Calculates the */
2:   /* factorial of a number. */
3:
4:   #include <stdio.h>
5:
6:   unsigned int f, x;
7:   unsigned int factorial(unsigned int a);
8:
9:   int main( void )
10:  {
11:      puts("Enter an integer value between 1 and 8: ");
12:      scanf("%d", &x);
13:
14:      if( x > 8 || x < 1)
15:      {
16:          printf("Only values from 1 to 8 are acceptable!");
17:      }
18:      else
19:      {
20:          f = factorial(x);
21:          printf("%u factorial equals %u\n", x, f);
22:      }
23:
24:      return 0;
25:  }
26:
27:  unsigned int factorial(unsigned int a)
28:  {
29:      if (a == 1)
30:          return 1;
31:      else
32:      {
33:          a *= factorial(a-1);
34:          return a;
35:      }
36:  }
```

Output ▼

```
Enter an integer value between 1 and 8:
6
6 factorial equals 720
```

5

Analysis ▼

The first half of this program is like many of the other programs you have worked with so far. It starts with comments on lines 1 and 2. On line 4, the appropriate header file is included for the input/output routines. Line 6 declares a couple of `unsigned` integer values. Line 7 is a function prototype for the factorial function. Notice that it takes an `unsigned int` as its parameter and returns an `unsigned int`. Lines 9 through 25 are the `main()` function. Lines 11 and 12 print a message asking for a value from 1 to 8 and then accept an entered value.

Lines 14 through 22 show an interesting `if` statement. Because a value greater than 8 causes a problem, this `if` statement checks the value. If it's greater than 8, an error message is printed; otherwise, the program figures the factorial on line 20 and prints the result on line 21. When you know there could be a problem, such as a limit on the size of a number, add code to detect the problem and prevent it.

The recursive function, `factorial()`, is located on lines 27 through 36. The value passed is assigned to a. On line 29, the value of a is checked. If it's 1, the program returns the value of 1. If the value isn't 1, a is set equal to itself times the value of `factorial(a-1)`. The program calls the factorial function again, but this time the value of a is `(a-1)`. If `(a-1)` isn't equal to 1, `factorial()` is called again with `((a-1)-1)`, which is the same as `(a-2)`. This process continues until the `if` statement on line 29 is true. If the value of the factorial is 3, the factorial is evaluated to the following:

```
3 * (3-1) * ((3-1)-1)
```

DO	DON'T
DO understand and work with recursion before you use it in a program you are going to distribute.	**DON'T** use recursion if there will be several iterations. (An iteration is the repetition of a program statement.) Recursion uses many resources because the function has to remember where it is.

Where the Functions Belong

You might be wondering where in your source code you should place your function definitions. For now, they should go in the same source code file as `main()` and after the end of `main()`.

You can keep your user-defined functions in a separate source-code file, apart from `main()`. This technique is useful with large programs and when you want to use the same set of functions in more than one program. This technique is discussed in Lesson 22, "Advanced Compiler Use."

Working with Inline Functions

There is a special type of function that can be created in C. These are inline functions. Inline functions are generally small functions. When the compiler executes, it tries to execute an inline function in the fastest manner possible. This may be done by copying the function's code into the calling function. Because execution of this code would be placed right into the calling function's code, it is called *inline*.

A function is made inline by using the `inline` keyword. The following declares an inline function called `toInches`:

```
inline int toInches( int Feet )
{
    return (Feet*12);
}
```

When the `toInches()` function is used, the compiler will do its best to optimize it to be fast. Be aware that although the general assumption is that the code will simply be moved into the calling function, this is not a guarantee. The only guarantee is that the compiler will do its best to optimize the use of the code in this function. You can use inline functions the same way as any other function.

5

Summary

This lesson introduced you to functions, an important part of C programming. Functions are independent sections of code that perform specific tasks. When your program needs a task performed, it calls the function that performs that task. The use of functions is essential for structured programming—a method of program design that emphasizes a modular, top-down approach. Structured programming creates more efficient programs and also is much easier for you, the programmer, to use.

You also learned that a function consists of a header and a body. The header includes information about the function's return type, name, and parameters. The body contains local variable declarations and the C statements that are executed when the function is called. Finally, you saw that local variables—those declared within a function—are totally independent of any other program variables declared elsewhere.

Q&A

Q **What if I need to return more than one value from a function?**

A Many times you will need to return more than one value from a function, or, more commonly, you will want to change a value you send to the function and keep the change after the function ends. This process is covered in Lesson 19, "Getting More from Functions."

Q **How do I know what a good function name is?**

A Effective function naming is similar to effective variable naming. A good function name describes as specifically as possible what the function does.

Q **When variables are declared at the top of the listing, before `main()`, they can be used anywhere, but local variables can be used only in the specific function. Why not just declare everything before `main()` as global?**

A Variable scope is discussed in more detail in Lesson 12. You will learn at that time why it is better to declare variables locally within functions instead of globally before `main()`.

Q **What other ways are there to use recursion?**

A The factorial function is a prime example of using recursion. The factorial number is needed in many statistical calculations. Recursion is just a loop; however, it has one difference from other loops. With recursion, each time a recursive function is called, a new set of variables is created. This is not true of the other loops that you learn about in the next lesson.

Q **Does `main()` have to be the first function in a program?**

A No. It is a standard in C that the `main()` function is the first function to execute; however, it can be placed anywhere in your source file. Most people place it either first or last so that it's easy to locate.

Workshop

The Workshop provides quiz questions to help you solidify your understanding of the material covered and exercises to provide you with experience in using what you've learned.

Quiz

1. Will you use structured programming when writing your C programs?
2. How does structured programming work?
3. How do C functions fit into structured programming?

4. What must be the first line of a function definition, and what information does it contain?

5. How many values can a function return?

6. If a function doesn't return a value, what type should it be declared?

7. What's the difference between a function definition and a function prototype?

8. What is a local variable?

9. How are local variables special?

10. Where should the `main()` function be placed?

Exercises

1. Write a header for a function named `do_it()` that takes three type `char` arguments and returns a type `float` to the calling program.

2. Write a header for a function named `print_a_number()` that takes a single type `int` argument and doesn't return anything to the calling program.

3. What type value do the following functions return?

   a. `int print_error( float err_nbr);`

   b. `long read_record( int rec_nbr, int size );`

4. **BUG BUSTER:** What's wrong with the following listing?

```
#include <stdio.h>
void print_msg( void );
int main( void )
{
    print_msg( "This is a message to print" );
    return 0;
}
void print_msg( void )
{
    puts( "This is a message to print" );
    return 0;
}
```

5. **BUG BUSTER:** What's wrong with the following function definition?

```
int twice(int y);
{
    return (2 * y);
}
```

6. Rewrite Listing 5.4 so that it needs only one `return` statement in the `larger_of()` function.

5

7. Write a function that receives two numbers as arguments and returns the value of their product.

8. Write a function that receives two numbers as arguments. The function should divide the first number by the second. Don't divide by the second number if it's zero. (Hint: Use an `if` statement.)

9. Write a function that calls the functions in exercises 7 and 8.

10. Write a program that uses a function to find the average of five type `float` values entered by the user.

11. Write a recursive function to take the value 3 to the power of another number. For example, if 4 is passed, the function will return 81.

LESSON 6
Basic Program Control

Lesson 4, "The Pieces of a C Program: Statements, Expressions, and Operators," covered the `if` statement, which gives you some control over the flow of your programs. Many times, though, you need more than just the ability to make true and false decisions. This lesson introduces three new ways to control the flow of the program. In this lesson you learn:

- How to use simple arrays

- How to use `for`, `while`, and `do...while` loops to execute statements multiple times

- How you can nest program control statements

This is not intended to be a complete treatment of these topics, but rather, this lesson provides enough information for you to start writing real programs. These topics are covered in greater detail in Lesson 13, "Advanced Program Control."

Arrays: The Basics

Before covering the `for` statement, you should take a short detour to learn about the basics of arrays. (Lesson 8, "Using Numeric Arrays," gives you a complete treatment of arrays.) The `for` statement and arrays are closely linked in C, so it's difficult to define one without explaining the other. To help you understand the arrays used in the `for` statement examples to come, a quick treatment of arrays follows.

An *array* is an indexed group of data storage locations that have the same name and are distinguished from each other by a *subscript,* or *index*—a number following the variable name, enclosed in brackets. (This will become clearer as you continue.) Like other C variables, arrays must be declared. An array declaration includes both the data type and the size of the array (the number of elements in the array). For example, the following statement declares an array named `data` that is type `int` and has 1,000 elements:

```
int data[1000];
```

The individual elements are referred to by subscript as `data[0]` through `data[999]`. The first element is `data[0]`, not `data[1]`.

NOTE

One way to look at the index number is as an offset. For the first item in the array, you want to be offset by nothing (or zero). For the second item, you are offset by one item, so the index is one.

Each element of this array is equivalent to a normal integer variable and can be used the same way. The subscript of an array can be another C variable, as in this example:

```
int data[1000];
int index;
index = 100;
data[index] = 12;      /* The same as data[100] = 12 */
```

This has been a quick introduction to arrays. However, you should now understand how arrays are used in the program examples later in this lesson. If every detail of arrays isn't clear to you, don't worry. You can learn more about arrays in Lesson 8.

DO	DON'T
	DON'T declare arrays with subscripts larger than you need. It wastes memory.
	DON'T forget that in C, arrays are referenced starting with subscript 0, not 1.

Controlling Program Execution

The default order of execution in a C program is top-down. Execution starts at the beginning of the `main()` function and progresses, statement by statement, until the end of `main()` is reached. However, this sequential order is rarely encountered in real C programs. The C language includes a variety of program control statements that enable you to control the order of program execution. You have already learned how to use C's fundamental decision operator, the `if` statement, so now it's time to explore three additional control statements you will find useful:

- The `for` statement
- The `while` statement
- The `do...while` statement

The `for` Statement

The `for` statement is a C programming construct that executes a block of one or more statements a certain number of times. It is sometimes called the `for` *loop* because program execution typically loops through the statement more than once. You've seen a few `for` statements used in programming examples earlier in this book. Now you're ready to see how the `for` statement works.

A `for` statement has the following structure:

```
for ( initial; condition; increment )
    statement;
```

initial, *condition*, and *increment* are all C expressions, and *statement* is a single or compound C statement. When a `for` statement is encountered during program execution, the following events occur:

1. The expression *initial* is evaluated. *initial* is usually an assignment statement that sets a variable to a particular value.

6

2. The expression `condition` is evaluated. `condition` is typically a relational expression.

3. If `condition` evaluates to false (that is, it is equal to zero), the `for` statement terminates and execution passes to the first statement following `statement`.

4. If `condition` evaluates to true (that is, it is equal to a nonzero value), the C statement(s) in `statement` are executed.

5. The expression `increment` is evaluated, and execution returns to step 2.

Figure 6.1 shows the operation of a `for` statement. Note that `statement` never executes if `condition` is false the first time it's evaluated.

FIGURE 6.1
A schematic representation of a `for` statement.

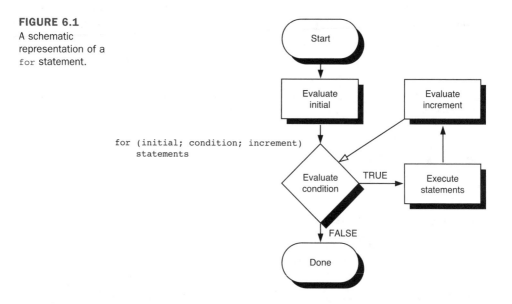

```
for (initial; condition; increment)
        statements
```

Listing 6.1 presents a simple example by using a `for` statement to print the numbers 1 through 20. You can see that the resulting code is much more compact than it would be if a separate `printf()` statement were used for each of the 20 values.

Input ▼

LISTING 6.1   forstate.c: A Simple `for` Statement

```c
1:    /* Demonstrates a simple for statement */
2:
3:    #include <stdio.h>
4:    #define MAXCOUNT 20
5:    int count;
6:
7:    int main( void )
8:    {
9:        /* Print the numbers 1 through 20 */
10:
11:       for (count = 1; count <= MAXCOUNT; count++)
12:           printf("%d\n", count);
13:
14:       return 0;
15:   }
```

Output ▼

```
1
2
3
4
5
6
7
8
9
10
11
12
13
14
15
16
17
18
19
20
```

Figure 6.2 illustrates the operation of the `for` loop in Listing 6.1.

6

FIGURE 6.2
How the `for` loop
in Listing 6.1
operates.

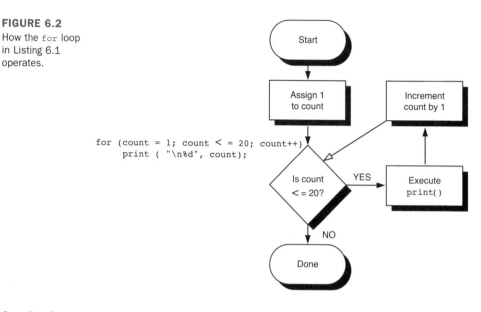

```
for (count = 1; count < = 20; count++)
        print ( "\n%d", count);
```

Analysis ▼

Line 3 includes the standard input/output header file. Line 5 declares a type `int` variable, named `count`, that will be used in the `for` loop. Lines 11 and 12 are the `for` loop. When the `for` statement is reached, the initial statement is executed first. In this listing, the initial statement is `count = 1`. This initializes `count` so that it can be used by the rest of the loop. The second step in executing this `for` statement is the evaluation of the condition `count <= 20`. Because `count` was just initialized to 1, you know that it is less than 20, so the statement in the `for` command, the `printf()`, is executed. After executing the printing function, the increment expression, `count++`, is evaluated. This adds 1 to `count`, making it 2. Now the program loops back and checks the condition again. If it is true, the `printf()` reexecutes, the increment adds to `count` (making it 3), and the condition is checked. This loop continues until the condition evaluates to false, at which point the program exits the loop and continues to the next line (line 14), which returns 0 before ending the program.

The `for` statement is frequently used, as in the previous example, to "count up," incrementing a counter from one value to another. You also can use it to "count down," decrementing (rather than incrementing) the counter variable:

```
for (count = 100; count > 0; count--)
```

You can also "count by" a value other than 1, as in this example which counts by 5:

```
for (count = 0; count < 1000; count += 5)
```

The `for` statement is quite flexible. For example, you can omit the initialization expression if the test variable has been initialized previously in your program. (You still must use the semicolon separator as shown, however.)

```
count = 1;
for ( ; count < 1000; count++)
```

The initialization expression doesn't need to be an actual initialization; it can be any valid C expression. Whatever it is, it is executed once when the `for` statement is first reached. For example, the following prints the statement `Now sorting the array...`:

```
count = 1;
for (printf("Now sorting the array...") ; count < 1000; count++)
    /* Sorting statements here */
```

You can also omit the increment expression, performing the updating in the body of the `for` statement. Again, the semicolon must be included. To print the numbers from 0 to 99, for example, you could write

```
for (count = 0; count < 100; )
    printf("%d", count++);
```

The test expression that terminates the loop can be any C expression. As long as it evaluates to true (nonzero), the `for` statement continues to execute. You can use C's logical operators to construct complex test expressions. For example, the following `for` statement prints the elements of an array named `array[]`, stopping when all elements have been printed or an element with a value of 0 is encountered:

```
for (count = 0; count < 1000 && array[count] != 0; count++)
    printf("%d", array[count]);
```

You could simplify this `for` loop even further by writing it as follows. (If you don't understand the change made to the test expression, you need to review Lesson 4.)

```
for (count = 0; count < 1000 && array[count]; )
    printf("%d", array[count++]);
```

6

You can follow the `for` statement with a null statement, allowing all the work to be done in the `for` statement itself. Remember, the null statement is a semicolon alone on a line. For example, to initialize all elements of a 1,000-element array to the value `50`, you could write

```
for (count = 0; count < 1000; array[count++] = 50)
    ;
```

In this `for` statement, `50` is assigned to each member of the array by the increment part of the statement. A better way to write this statement is

```
for (count = 0; count < 1000; array[count++] = 50)
{
    ;
}
```

Putting the semicolon into a block (the two brackets) makes it more obvious that there is no work being done in the body of the `for` statement.

Lesson 4 mentioned that C's comma operator is most often used in `for` statements. You can create an expression by separating two subexpressions with the comma operator. The two subexpressions are evaluated (in left-to-right order), and the entire expression evaluates to the value of the right subexpression. By using the comma operator, you can make each part of a `for` statement perform multiple duties.

Imagine that you have two 1,000-element arrays, `a[]` and `b[]`. You want to copy the contents of `a[]` to `b[]` in reverse order so that after the copy operation, `b[0]` = `a[999]`, `b[1]` = `a[998]`, and so on. The following `for` statement does the trick:

```
for (i = 0, j = 999; i < 1000; i++, j--)
    b[j] = a[i];
```

The comma operator is used to initialize two variables, `i` and `j`. It is also used to increment part of these two variables with each loop.

Syntax

The `for` Statement

```
for (initial; condition; increment)
    statement(s)
```

`initial` is any valid C expression. It is usually an assignment statement that sets a variable to a particular value.

`condition` is any valid C expression. It is usually a relational expression. When `condition` evaluates to false (zero), the `for` statement terminates, and execution passes to the first statement following `statement(s)`; otherwise, the C statement(s) in `statement(s)` are executed.

`increment` is any valid C expression. It is usually an expression that increments a variable initialized by the initial expression.

`statement(s)` are the C statements executed as long as the condition remains true.

A `for` statement is a looping statement. It can have an initialization, test condition, and increment as parts of its command. The `for` statement executes the initial expression first. It then checks the condition. If the condition is true, the statements execute. When the statements are completed, the increment expression is evaluated. The `for` statement then rechecks the condition and continues to loop until the condition is false.

Example 1

```
/* Prints the value of x as it counts from 0 to 9 */
int x;
for (x = 0; x <10; x++)
    printf( "\nThe value of x is %d", x );
```

Example 2

```
/* Obtains values from the user until 99 is entered */
int nbr = 0;
for ( ; nbr != 99; )
   scanf( "%d", &nbr );
```

Example 3

```
/* Lets user enter up to 10 integer values       */
/* Values are stored in an array named value. If 99 is */
/* entered, the loop stops                         */
int value[10];
int ctr,nbr=0;
for (ctr = 0; ctr < 10 && nbr != 99; ctr++)
{
    puts("Enter a number, 99 to quit ");
    scanf("%d", &nbr);
    value[ctr] = nbr;
}
```

Nesting `for` **Statements**

A `for` statement can be executed within another `for` statement. This is called *nesting*. (You saw nesting in Lesson 4 with `if` statements.) By nesting `for` statements, you can do some complex programming. Listing 6.2 is not a complex program, but it illustrates the nesting of two `for` statements.

6

Input ▼

LISTING 6.2   nestfor.c: Nested for Statements

```
1: // Program to demonstrate nesting for loops
2:
3: #include <stdio.h>
4: void print_ttable(int outer, int inner);
5:
6: main()
7: {
8:     int inner = 10;
9:     int outer = 10;
10:
11:     printf("The times table:\n");
12:     print_ttable(outer, inner);
13:     return(0);
14: }
15:
16: void print_ttable(int outer, int inner)
17: {
18:     int a, b;
19:     for (a = 1; a <= outer; a++)
20:     {
21:         for (b = 1; b <= inner; b++)
22:         {
23:             printf("%d\t", a*b);
24:         }
25:         printf("\n");
26:     }
27:     return;
27: }
```

Output ▼

```
The times table:
1    2    3    4    5    6    7    8    9    10
2    4    6    8    10   12   14   16   18   20
3    6    9    12   15   18   21   24   27   30
4    8    12   16   20   24   28   32   36   40
5    10   15   20   25   30   35   40   45   50
6    12   18   24   30   36   42   48   54   60
7    14   21   28   35   42   49   46   63   70
8    16   24   32   40   48   56   64   72   80
9    18   27   36   45   54   63   72   81   90
10   20   30   40   50   60   70   80   90   100
```

Analysis ▼

Remember in grade school when you had to memorize your times table? Now, thanks to C and nested loops, you can print one out. Initially, it is set to create a 10 by 10 table, but you can change those numbers to make the table smaller or bigger. (And the loops do not have to be the same size.) You could create a 10 by 5 or 12 by 9; but if you make it too big, each number could take up more than one line and ruin your perfect layout. However, now look at the details of the program.

In this listing, a function prototype for `print_ttable()` is declared on line 4. This function takes two type `int` variables, `outer` and `inner`, which contain the dimensions of the times table to be displayed. On line 12, `main()` calls `print_ttable()` and passes the variables of inner and outer, each of which was initialized to 10 as the arguments.

Looking closely at the `print_ttable()` function, you might see a couple things you don't readily understand. The first is why the local variables `a` and `b` were declared. The second is why the second `printf()` on line 25 was used. Both of these will become clearer after you look at the two `for` loops.

Line 19 starts the first `for` loop. The local variable `a` is initialized to 1 to begin the loop. Looking at the condition, you see that this `for` loop is executed until `a` is greater than the variable `outer`. On first executing line 19, `a`, set to 1, is less than `outer`, which is `10`; therefore, the program continues to line 19.

Line 21 contains the second `for` statement. Here the second local variable, `b`, is also initialized to 1, and compared to the second passed variable, inner. Because `b` is less than 10 (the value of `inner`), line 23 is executed, printing the value of `a` times `b` and a tab (`\t`, which is probably new to you, tells C to move over one tab). Adding these tabs moves the printing over an even number of spaces, which is nice when you are formatting a table, like this program is doing with a times table. Then `b` is incremented, and the loop continues. When `b` is `11`, the `for` loop ends, and control goes to line 25. Line 25 causes the onscreen printing to start on a new line. (Printing is covered in detail in Lesson 7, "Fundamentals of Reading and Writing Information.") After moving to a new line on the screen, control reaches the end of the first `for` loop's statements, thus executing the increment expression, which adds 1 to `a`, making it 2. This puts control back at line 21. Notice that the value of `b` is re-initialized to 1. If `b` kept its previous value, 11, it would fail the condition test, because it will never be less than or equal to 10. Only the first line of the times table would be printed.

6

DO	**DON'T**
DO remember the semicolon if you use a `for` with a null statement. Put the semicolon placeholder on a separate line, or place a space between it and the end of the `for` statement. It's clearer to put it on a separate line.	**DON'T** put too much processing in the `for` statement. Although you can use the comma separator, it is often clearer to put some of the functionality into the body of the loop.

```
for (count = 0; count < 1000;
array[count] += 50) ;
    /* note space! */
```

The `while` Statement

The `while` statement, also called the `while` *loop*, executes a block of statements as long as a specified condition is true. The `while` statement has the following form:

```
while (condition)
    statement
```

`condition` is any C expression, and `statement` is a single or compound C statement. When program execution reaches a `while` statement, the following events occur:

1. The expression `condition` is evaluated.

2. If `condition` evaluates to false (that is, zero), the `while` statement terminates, and execution passes to the first statement following `statement`.

3. If `condition` evaluates to true (that is, nonzero), the C statement(s) in `statement` are executed.

4. Execution returns to step 1.

The operation of a `while` statement is shown in Figure 6.3.

FIGURE 6.3
The operation of a
`while` statement.

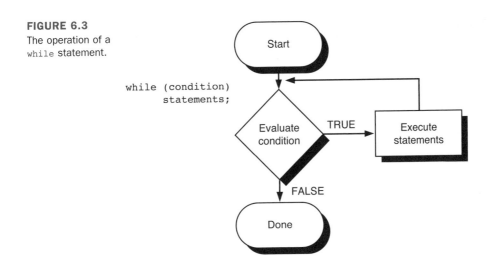

```
while (condition)
    statements;
```

Listing 6.3 is a simple program that uses a `while` statement to print the numbers 1 through 20. (This is the same task performed by a `for` statement in Listing 6.1.)

Input ▼

LISTING 6.3   whilest.c: A Simple `while` Statement

```
1:   // Demonstrates a simple while statement
2:
3:   #include <stdio.h>
4:   #define MAXCOUNT 20
5:   int count;
6:
7:   int main( void )
8:   {
9:       // Print the numbers 1 through 20
10:
11:      count = 1;
12:
13:      while (count <= MAXCOUNT)
14:      {
15:          printf("%d\n", count);
16:          count++;
17:      }
18:      return 0;
19:  }
```

6

Output ▼

```
1
2
3
4
5
6
7
8
9
10
11
12
13
14
15
16
17
18
19
20
```

Analysis ▼

Examine Listing 6.3 and compare it with Listing 6.1, which uses a `for` statement to perform the same task. In line 11, `count` is initialized to `1`. Because the `while` statement doesn't contain an initialization section, you must take care of initializing any variables before starting the `while` loop. Line 13 is the actual `while` statement, and it contains the same condition statement from Listing 6.1, `count <= 20`. In the `while` loop, line 16 takes care of incrementing `count`. What do you think would happen if you forgot to put line 16 in this program? Your program wouldn't know when to stop because `count` would always be 1, which is always less than 20.

You might have noticed that a `while` statement is essentially a `for` statement without the initialization and increment components. Thus,

```
for ( ; condition ; )
```

is equivalent to

```
while (condition)
```

Because of this equality, anything that can be done with a `for` statement can also be done with a `while` statement. When you use a `while` statement, any necessary initialization must first be performed in a separate statement, and the updating must be performed by a statement that is part of the `while` loop.

<table>
<tr><td>CAUTION</td><td>Remember to include something to change the value of your condition within the block of code inside the while loop, or you will create an infinite loop. This is a common error beginning programmers (and even seasoned veterans) often make.</td></tr>
</table>

When initialization and updating are required, most experienced C programmers prefer to use a `for` statement rather than a `while` statement. This preference is based primarily on source code readability. When you use a `for` statement, the initialization, test, and increment expressions are located together and are easy to find and modify. With a `while` statement, the initialization and update expressions are located separately and might be less obvious.

Syntax

The while Statement

```
while (condition)
    statement(s)
```

condition is any valid C expression, usually a relational expression. When *condition* evaluates to false (zero), the `while` statement terminates, and execution passes to the first statement following *statement(s)*; otherwise, the first C statement in *statement(s)* is executed.

statement(s) is the C statement(s) executed as long as *condition* remains true.

A `while` statement is a C looping statement. It enables repeated execution of a statement or block of statements as long as the condition remains true (nonzero). If the condition is not true when the `while` command is first executed, the *statement(s)* is never executed.

Example 1

```
int x = 0;
while (x < 10)
{
    printf("\nThe value of x is %d", x );
    x++;
}
```

Example 2

```
/* get numbers until you get one greater than 99 */
int nbr=0;
while (nbr <= 99)
    scanf("%d", &nbr );
```

6

Example 3

```
/* Lets user enter up to 10 integer values      */
/* Values are stored in an array named value. If 99 is */
/* entered, the loop stops                       */
int value[10];
int ctr = 0;
int nbr;
while (ctr < 10 && nbr != 99)
{
    puts("Enter a number, 99 to quit ");
    scanf("%d", &nbr);
    value[ctr] = nbr;
    ctr++;
}
```

Nesting while Statements

Just like the for and if statements, while statements can also be nested. Listing 6.4 shows an example of nested while statements. Although this isn't the best use of a while statement, the example does present some new ideas.

Input ▼

LISTING 6.4   nestwhile.c: Nested while Statements

```
1:    /* Demonstrates nested while statements */
2:
3:    #include <stdio.h>
4:
5:    int array[5];
6:
7:    int main( void )
8:    {
9:       int ctr = 0,
10:          nbr = 0;
11:
12:       printf("This program prompts you to enter 5 numbers\n");
13:       printf("Each number should be from 1 to 10\n");
14:
15:       while ( ctr < 5 )
16:       {
17:          nbr = 0;
18:          while (nbr < 1 || nbr > 10)
19:          {
20:             printf("\nEnter number %d of 5: ", ctr + 1 );
21:             scanf("%d", &nbr );
22:          }
23:
```

```
24:            array[ctr] = nbr;
25:            ctr++;
26:        }
27:
28:        for (ctr = 0; ctr < 5; ctr++)
29:            printf("Value %d is %d\n", ctr + 1, array[ctr] );
30:
31:        return 0;
32:    }
```

Output ▼

```
This program prompts you to enter 5 numbers
Each number should be from 1 to 10

Enter number 1 of 5: 3

Enter number 2 of 5: 6

Enter number 3 of 5: 3

Enter number 4 of 5: 9

Enter number 5 of 5: 2

Value 1 is 3
Value 2 is 6
Value 3 is 3
Value 4 is 9
Value 5 is 2
```

Analysis ▼

As in previous listings, line 1 contains a comment with a description of the program, and line 3 contains an #include statement for the standard input/output header file. Line 5 contains a declaration for an array (named array) that can hold five integer values. The function main() contains two additional local variables, ctr and nbr (lines 9 and 10). Notice that these variables are initialized to zero at the same time they are declared. Also notice that the comma operator is used as a separator at the end of line 9, allowing nbr to be declared as an int without restating the int type command. Stating declarations in this manner is a common practice for many C programmers. Lines 12 and 13 print messages stating what the program does and what is expected of the user. Lines 15 through 26 contain the first while command and its statements. Lines 18 through 22 also contain a nested while loop with its own statements that are all part of the outer while.

6

This outer loop continues to execute while `ctr` is less than `5` (line 15). As long as `ctr` is less than `5`, line 17 sets `nbr` to `0`, lines 18 through 22 (the nested `while` statement) gather a number in variable `nbr`, line 24 places the number in `array`, and line 25 increments `ctr`. Then the loop starts again. Therefore, the outer loop gathers five numbers and places each into `array`, indexed by `ctr`.

The inner loop is a good use of a `while` statement. Only the numbers from `1` to `10` are valid, so until the user enters a valid number, there is no point continuing the program. Lines 18 through 22 prevent continuation. This `while` statement states that while the number is less than `1` or greater than `10`, the program should print a message to enter a number, and then get the number.

Lines 28 and 29 print the values that are stored in `array`. Notice that because the `while` statements are done with the variable `ctr`, the `for` command can reuse it. Starting at zero and incrementing by one, the `for` loops five times, printing the value of `ctr` plus one (because the count started at zero) and printing the corresponding value in `array`.

For additional practice, there are two things you can change in this program. The first is the values that the program accepts. Instead of `1` to `10`, try making it accept from `1` to `100`. You can also change the number of values that it accepts. Currently, it allows for five numbers. Try making it accept 10.

DO	DON'T

DO use the `for` statement instead of the `while` statement if you need to initialize and increment within your loop. The `for` statement keeps the initialization, condition, and increment statements all together. The `while` statement does not.	**DON'T** use the following convention if it isn't necessary:
	
	`while (x)`
	
	Instead, use this convention:
	
	`while (x != 0)`
	
	Although both work, the second is clearer when you're debugging (trying to find problems in the code). When compiled, these produce virtually the same code.

The `do...while` Loop

C's third loop construct is the `do...while` loop, which executes a block of statements as long as a specified condition is true. The `do...while` loop tests the condition at the end of the loop rather than at the beginning, as is done by the `for` loop and the `while` loop.

The structure of the do...while loop is as follows:

```
do
    statement
while (condition);
```

condition is any C expression, and statement is a single or compound C statement. When program execution reaches a do...while statement, the following events occur:

1. The statements in statement are executed.

2. condition is evaluated. If it's true, execution returns to step 1. If it's false, the loop terminates.

The operation of a do...while loop is shown in Figure 6.4.

FIGURE 6.4
The operation of a
do...while loop.

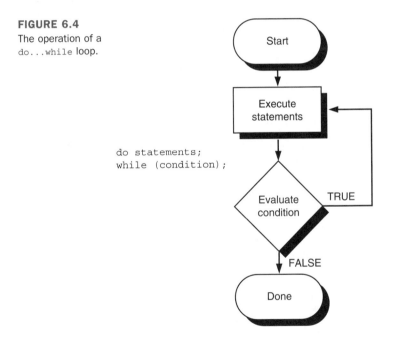

```
do statements;
while (condition);
```

The statements associated with a do...while loop are always executed at least once. This is because the test condition is evaluated at the end, instead of the beginning, of the loop. In contrast, for loops and while loops evaluate the test condition at the start of the loop, so the associated statements are not executed at all if the test condition is initially false.

The do...while loop is used less frequently than while and for loops. It is most appropriate when the statement(s) associated with the loop must be executed at least once. You could, of course, accomplish the same thing with a while loop by making sure

6

that the test condition is true when execution first reaches the loop. A do...while loop probably would be more straightforward, however.

Listing 6.5 shows an example of a do...while loop.

Input ▼

LISTING 6.5 dowhilestate.c: A Simple do...while Loop

```
1:   /* Demonstrates a simple do...while statement */
2:
3:   #include <stdio.h>
4:
5:   int get_menu_choice( void );
6:
7:   int main( void )
8:   {
9:       int choice;
10:
11:      choice = get_menu_choice();
12:
13:      printf("You chose Menu Option %d\n", choice );
14:
15:      return 0;
16:  }
17:
18:  int get_menu_choice( void )
19:  {
20:      int selection = 0;
21:
22:      do
23:      {
24:          printf("\n" );
25:          printf("\n1 - Add a Record" );
26:          printf("\n2 - Change a record");
27:          printf("\n3 - Delete a record");
28:          printf("\n4 - Quit");
29:          printf("\n" );
30:          printf("\nEnter a selection: " );
31:
32:          scanf("%d", &selection );
33:
34:      }while ( selection < 1 || selection > 4 );
35:
36:      return selection;
37:  }
```

Output ▼

```
1 - Add a Record
2 - Change a record
3 - Delete a record
4 - Quit

Enter a selection: 8

1 - Add a Record
2 - Change a record
3 - Delete a record
4 - Quit

Enter a selection: 4
You chose Menu Option 4
```

Analysis ▼

This program provides a menu with four choices. You can select one of the four choices. The program then prints the number selected. Programs later in this book use and expand on this concept. For now, you can follow most of the listing. The `main()` function (lines 7 through 16) adds nothing to what you already know.

NOTE

> The body of `main()` could have been written into one line, like this:
>
> ```
> printf( "You chose Menu Option %d", get_menu_option() );
> ```
>
> If you were to expand this program and act on the selection, you would need the value returned by `get_menu_choice()`, so it is wise to assign the value to a variable (such as `choice`).

Lines 18 through 37 contain `get_menu_choice()`. This function displays a menu onscreen (lines 24 through 30) and then gets a selection. Because you have to display a menu at least once to get an answer, it is appropriate to use a `do...while` loop. In the case of this program, the menu is displayed until a valid choice is entered. Line 34 contains the `while` part of the `do...while` statement and validates the value of the selection, appropriately named `selection`. If the value entered is not between `1` and `4`, the menu is redisplayed, and the user is prompted for a new value. When a valid selection is entered, the program continues to line 36, which returns the value in the variable selection.

6

Syntax

The do...while **Statement**

```
do
{
    statement(s)
}while (condition);
```

condition is any valid C expression, usually a relational expression. When *condition* evaluates to false (zero), the while statement terminates, and execution passes to the first statement following the while statement; otherwise, the program loops back to the do, and the C statement(s) in *statement(s)* is executed.

statement(s) is either a single C statement or a block of statements executed the first time through the loop and then as long as *condition* remains true.

A do...while statement is a C looping statement. It enables repeated execution of a statement or block of statements as long as the condition remains true (nonzero). Unlike the while statement, a do...while loop executes its statements at least once.

Example 1

```
/* prints even though condition fails! */
int x = 10;
do
{
    printf("\nThe value of x is %d", x );
}while (x != 10);
```

Example 2

```
/* gets numbers until the number is greater than 99 */
int nbr;
do
{
    scanf("%d", &nbr );
}while (nbr <= 99);
```

Example 3

```
/* Enables user to enter up to 10 integer values       */
/* Values are stored in an array named value. If 99 is */
/* entered, the loop stops                             */
int value[10];
int ctr = 0;
int nbr;
do
```

```
{
    puts("Enter a number, 99 to quit ");
    scanf( "%d", &nbr);
    value[ctr] = nbr;
    ctr++;
}while (ctr < 10 && nbr != 99);
```

Nested Loops

The term *nested loop* refers to a loop that is contained within another loop. You have seen examples of some nested statements. C places no limitations on the nesting of loops, except that each inner loop must be enclosed completely in the outer loop; you can't have overlapping loops. Thus, the following is not allowed:

```
for ( count = 1; count < 100; count++)
{
    do
    {
        /* the do...while loop */
} /* end of for loop */
    }while (x != 0);
```

If the `do...while` loop is placed entirely in the `for` loop, there is no problem:

```
for (count = 1; count < 100; count++)
{
    do
    {
        /* the do...while loop */
    }while (x != 0);
} /* end of for loop */
```

When you use nested loops, remember that changes made in the inner loop might affect the outer loop as well. Note, however, that the inner loop might be independent from any variables in the outer loop; in this example, they are not. In the previous example, if the inner `do...while` loop modifies the value of `count`, the number of times the outer `for` loop executes is affected.

Good indenting style makes code with nested loops easier to read. Each level of loop should be indented one step further than the last level. This clearly labels the code associated with each loop.

6

DO	DON'T
DO use the `do...while` loop when you know that a loop should be executed at least once.	**DON'T** try to overlap loops. You can nest them, but they must be entirely within each other.

Summary

After this lesson, you are almost ready to start writing real C programs on your own.

C has three loop statements that control program execution: `for`, `while`, and `do...while`. Each of these constructs lets your program execute a block of statements zero times, one time, or more than one time, based on the condition of certain program variables. Many programming tasks are well served by the repetitive execution allowed by these loop statements.

Although all three can be used to accomplish the same task, each is different. The `for` statement enables you to initialize, evaluate, and increment all in one command. The `while` statement operates as long as a condition is true. The `do...while` statement always executes its statements at least once and continues to execute them until a condition is false.

Nesting is the placing of one command within another. C enables the nesting of any of its commands. Nesting the `if` statement was demonstrated in Lesson 4. In this lesson, the `for`, `while`, and `do...while` statements were nested.

Q&A

Q **How do I know which programming control statement to use: `for`, `while`, or `do...while`?**

A If you look at the syntax boxes provided, you can see that any of the three can be used to solve a looping problem. Each has a small twist to what it can do, however. The `for` statement is best when you know that you need to initialize and increment in your loop. If you have a condition that you only want to meet, and you aren't dealing with a specific number of loops, `while` is a good choice. If you know that a set of statements needs to be executed at least once, a `do...while` might be best. Because all three can be used for most problems, the best course is to learn them all and then evaluate each programming situation to determine which is best.

Q How deep can I nest my loops?

A You can nest as many loops as you want. If your program requires you to nest more than two loops deep, consider using a function instead. You might find sorting through all those braces difficult, so perhaps a function would be easier to follow in code.

Q Can I nest different loop commands?

A You can nest `if`, `for`, `while`, `do...while`, or any other command. You will find that many of the programs you try to write require that you nest at least a few of these.

Workshop

The Workshop provides quiz questions to help you solidify your understanding of the material covered, and exercises to provide you with experience in using what you've learned.

Quiz

1. What is the index value of the first element in an array?
2. What is the difference between a `for` statement and a `while` statement?
3. What is the difference between a `while` statement and a `do...while` statement?
4. Is it true that a `while` statement can be used and still get the same results as coding a `for` statement?
5. Is there a limit to the number of statements you can nest?
6. Can a `while` statement be nested in a `do...while` statement?
7. What are the four parts of a `for` statement?
8. What are the two parts of a `while` statement?
9. What are the two parts of a `do...while` statement?

Exercises

1. Write a declaration for an array that can hold 50 type `long` values.
2. Show a statement that assigns the value of `123.456` to the 50th element in the array from exercise 1.
3. What is the value of x when the following statement is complete?

```
for (x = 0; x < 100, x++) ;
```

6

4. What is the value of `ctr` when the following statement is complete?

```
for (ctr = 2; ctr < 10; ctr += 3) ;
```

5. How many `x`'s does the following print?

```
for (x = 0; x < 10; x++)
    for (y = 5; y > 0; y--)
        puts("X");
```

6. Write a `for` statement to count from 1 to 100 by 3s.

7. Write a `while` statement to count from 1 to 100 by 3s.

8. Write a `do...while` statement to count from 1 to 100 by 3s.

9. BUG BUSTER: What is wrong with the following code fragment?

```
record = 0;
while (record < 100)
{
    printf( "\nRecord %d ", record );
    printf( "\nGetting next number..." );
}
```

10. BUG BUSTER: What is wrong with the following code fragment? (MAXVALUES is not the problem!)

```
for (counter = 1; counter < MAXVALUES; counter++);
    printf("\nCounter = %d", counter );
```

LESSON 7
Fundamentals of Reading and Writing Information

In most programs you create, you need to display information on the screen or receive input from the keyboard. Many of the programs presented in earlier lessons have performed these tasks, but you might not have understood exactly how. In this lesson you learn:

- The basics of C's input and output statements

- How to display information onscreen with the `printf()` and `puts()` library functions

- How to format the information that displays onscreen

- How to read data entered from the keyboard with the `scanf()` library function

This lesson isn't intended to be a complete treatment of these topics, but it provides enough information so that you can start writing real programs. These topics are covered in greater detail later in this book.

Displaying Information Onscreen

You will want most of your programs to display information onscreen. Two of the most frequently used ways to display information are with C's library functions `printf()` and `puts()`.

The `printf()` Function

The `printf()` function is part of the standard C library and is included as a part of the ANSI standard. It is perhaps the most versatile way for a program to display data on the screen. You've already seen `printf()` used in many of the examples in this book. Now you can see how `printf()` works.

Printing a text message on the screen is simple. You call the `printf()` function, passing the desired message enclosed in double quotation marks. For example, to display How Now Brown Cow! on the screen, you write

```
printf("How Now Brown Cow!");
```

In addition to text messages, however, you frequently need to display the value of program variables. This is a little more complicated than displaying only a message. For example, suppose you want to display the value of the numeric variable myNumber on the screen, along with some identifying text. Furthermore, you want the information to start at the beginning of a new line. You could use the `printf()` function as follows:

```
printf("\nThe value of myNumber is %d", myNumber);
```

The resulting screen display, assuming that the value of myNumber is 12, would be

```
The value of myNumber is 12
```

In this example, two arguments are passed to `printf()`. The first argument is enclosed in double quotation marks and is called the *format string*. The second argument is the name of the variable (myNumber) containing the value to be printed.

The `printf()` Format Strings

A `printf()` format string specifies how the output is to be formatted. Here are the three possible components of a format string:

- *Literal text* is displayed exactly as entered in the format string. In the preceding example, the characters starting with the T (in The) and up to, but not including, the % comprise a literal string.

- An *escape sequence* provides special formatting control. An escape sequence consists of a backslash (\) followed by a single character. In the preceding example, \n is an escape sequence. It is called the *newline character,* and it means "move to the start of the next line." A listing in the previous lesson used the `\t` character to print tabs and help format a table. Escape sequences are also used to print certain characters. Common escape sequences are listed in Table 7.1.

- A *conversion specifier* consists of the percent sign (`%`) followed by a character. In the example, the conversion specifier is `%d`. A conversion specifier tells the `printf()` function how to interpret the variable(s) being printed. The `%d` tells `printf()` to interpret the variable `myNumber` as a signed decimal integer.

TABLE 7.1   The Most Frequently Used Escape Sequences

Sequence	Meaning
\a	Bell (alert)
\b	Backspace
\f	Form feed
\n	Newline
\r	Carriage return
\t	Horizontal tab
\v	Vertical tab
\\	Backslash
\?	Question mark
\'	Single quotation
\"	Double quotation

The `printf()` Escape Sequences

Escape sequences are used to control the location of output by moving the screen cursor. They are also used to print characters that would otherwise have a special meaning to `printf()`. For example, to print a single backslash character, you include a double backslash (\\) in the format string. The first backslash tells `printf()` that the second backslash is to be interpreted as a literal character, not as the start of an escape sequence. In general, the backslash tells `printf()` to interpret the next character in a special manner. Here are some examples:

Sequence	Meaning
n	The character n
\n	Newline
\"	The double quotation character
"	The start or end of a string

7

Table 7.1 lists C's most commonly used escape sequences. Listing 7.1 demonstrates some of the frequently used escape sequences.

Input ▼

LISTING 7.1 escape.c: Using `printf()` Escape Sequences

```c
1:   /* Demonstration of frequently used escape sequences */
2:
3:   #include <stdio.h>
4:
5:   #define QUIT   3
6:
7:   int  get_menu_choice( void );
8:   void print_report( void );
9:
10:  int main( void )
11:  {
12:      int choice = 0;
13:
14:      printf("\"We\'d like to welcome you to the menu program\"\n");
15:      printf("Are you ready to make a choice\?\n");
16:      while (choice != QUIT)
17:      {
18:          choice = get_menu_choice();
19:
20:          if (choice == 1)
21:              printf("\nBeeping the computer\a\a\a" );
22:          else
23:          {
24:              if (choice == 2)
25:                  print_report();
26:          }
27:      }
28:      printf("You chose to quit!\n");
29:
30:      return 0;
31:  }
32:
33:  int get_menu_choice( void )
34:  {
35:      int selection = 0;
36:
37:      do
38:      {
39:          printf( "\n" );
40:          printf( "\n1 - Beep Computer" );
41:          printf( "\n2 - Display Report");
42:          printf( "\n3 - Quit");
43:          printf( "\n" );
```

```
44:            printf( "\nEnter a selection:" );
45:
46:            scanf( "%d", &selection );
47:
48:        }while ( selection < 1 || selection > 3 );
49:
50:        return selection;
51:  }
52:
53:  void print_report( void )
54:  {
55:        printf( "\nSAMPLE REPORT" );
56:        printf( "\n\nSequence\tMeaning" );
57:        printf( "\n=========\t=======" );
58:        printf( "\n\\a\t\tbell (alert)" );
59:        printf( "\n\\b\t\tbackspace" );
60:        printf( "\n...\t\t...");
61:  }
```

Output ▼

```
"We'd like to welcome you to the menu program"
Are you ready to make a choice?

1 - Beep Computer
2 - Display Report
3 - Quit

Enter a selection:1

Beeping the computer

1 - Beep Computer
2 - Display Report
3 - Quit

Enter a selection:2

SAMPLE REPORT

Sequence        Meaning
=========       =======
\a              bell (alert)
\b              backspace
...             ...

1 - Beep Computer
2 - Display Report
3 - Quit

Enter a selection:3
You chose to quit!
```

7

Analysis ▼

Listing 7.1 seems long compared with previous examples, but it offers some additions that are worth noting. The `stdio.h` header was included on line 3 because `printf()` is used in this listing. On line 5, a constant named `QUIT` is defined. From Lesson 3, "Storing Information: Variables and Constants," you know that `#define` makes using the constant `QUIT` equivalent to using the value `3`. Lines 7 and 8 are function prototypes. This program has two functions: `get_menu_choice()` and `print_report()`. The `get_menu_choice()` function is defined in lines 33 through 51. This is similar to the menu function in Listing 6.5. Lines 39 and 43 contain calls to `printf()` that print the newline escape sequence. Lines 40, 41, 42, and 44 also use the newline escape character, and they print text. Line 39 could have been eliminated by changing line 40 to the following:

```
printf( "\n\n1 - Beep Computer" );
```

However, leaving line 39 makes the program easier to read.

Looking at the `main()` function, lines 14 and 15 contain `printf()` statements that demonstrate the escape sequences needed to print the question mark and both the single and double quotation marks. You may not need to use those punctuation marks often, but forgetting the escape sequences when you do may not produce compiler errors, instead creating unintended printing sequences. A `while` loop starts on line 16. The `while` loop's statements can keep looping as long as `choice` is not equal to `QUIT`. Because `QUIT` is a constant, you could have replaced it with `3`; however, the program wouldn't be as clear. Line 18 gets the variable `choice`, which is then analyzed in lines 20 through 26 in an `if` statement. If the user chooses `1`, line 21 prints the newline character, a message, and then three beeps. If the user selects `2`, line 25 calls the function `print_report()`.

TIP

The `while` loop that controls the top menu on lines 16-27 will always run at least once, so a `do...while` loop might be a better choice, although it is always a matter of personal preference how to set your code. However, as a fun bonus assignment, consider tweaking this listing to change the loop to a `do...while` loop.

The `print_report()` function is defined on lines 53 through 61. This simple function shows the ease of using `printf()` and the escape sequences to print formatted information to the screen. You've already seen the newline character. Lines 56 through 60 also use the tab escape character, `\t`. As demonstrated in the last lesson, the tab character aligns the columns of the report vertically. Lines 58 and 59 might seem confusing at first, but if you start at the left and work to the right, they make sense. Line

58 prints a new line (\n), a backslash (\), the letter a, and then two tabs (\t\t). The line ends with some descriptive text, (bell (alert)). Line 59 follows the same format.

This program prints the first two lines of Table 7.1, along with a report title and column headings. In exercise 9 at the end of this lesson, you complete this program by making it print the rest of the table.

The `printf()` Conversion Specifiers

The format string must contain one conversion specifier for each printed variable. The `printf()` function then displays each variable as directed by its corresponding conversion specifier. You learn more about this process in Lesson 14, "Working with the Screen, Printer, and Keyboard." For now, be sure to use the conversion specifier that corresponds to the type of variable being printed.

Exactly what does this mean? If you print a variable that is a signed decimal integer (types `int` and `long`), use the `%d` conversion specifier. For an unsigned decimal integer (types `unsigned int` and `unsigned long`), use `%u`. For a floating-point variable (types `float` and `double`), use the `%f` specifier. The conversion specifiers you need most often are listed in Table 7.2.

TABLE 7.2 The Most Commonly Needed Conversion Specifiers

Specifier	Meaning	Types Converted
`%c`	Single character	`char`
`%d`	Signed decimal integer	`int, short`
`%ld`	Signed long decimal integer	`long`
`%f`	Decimal floating-point number	`float, double`
`%s`	Character string	`char` arrays
`%u`	Unsigned decimal integer	`unsigned int, unsigned short`
`%lu`	Unsigned long decimal integer	`unsigned_long`

> **NOTE**
>
> Any program that uses `printf()` should include the header file `stdio.h`.

The literal text of a format specifier is anything that doesn't qualify as either an escape sequence or a conversion specifier. Literal text is simply printed as is, including all spaces.

What about printing the values of more than one variable? A single `printf()` statement can print an unlimited number of variables, but the format string must contain one

7

conversion specifier for each variable. The conversion specifiers are paired with variables in left-to-right order. If you write

```
printf("Rate = %f, amount = %d", rate, amount);
```

the variable `rate` is paired with the `%f` specifier, and the variable `amount` is paired with the `%d` specifier. The positions of the conversion specifiers in the format string determine the position of the output. If there are more variables passed to `printf()` than there are conversion specifiers, the unmatched variables aren't printed. If there are more specifiers than variables, the unmatched specifiers print "garbage."

You aren't limited to printing the value of variables with `printf()`. The arguments can be any valid C expression. For example, to print the sum of `x` and `y`, you could write

```
total = x + y;
printf("%d", total);
```

You also could write

```
printf("%d", x + y);
```

Listing 7.2 demonstrates the use of `printf()`. Lesson 14 gives more details on `printf()`.

Input ▼
LISTING 7.2   nums.c: Using `printf()` to Display Numerical Values

```
1:    /* Demonstration using printf() to display numerical values. */
2:
3:    #include <stdio.h>
4:
5:    int a = 2, b = 10, c = 50;
6:    float f = 1.05, g = 25.5, h = -0.1;
7:
8:    int main( void )
9:    {
10:       printf("\nDecimal values without tabs: %d %d %d", a, b, c);
11:       printf("\nDecimal values with tabs: \t%d \t%d \t%d", a, b, c);
12:
13:       printf("\nThree floats on 1 line: \t%f\t%f\t%f", f, g, h);
14:       printf("\nThree floats on 3 lines: \n\t%f\n\t%f\n\t%f", f, g, h);
15:
16:       printf("\nThe rate is %f%%", f);
17:       printf("\nThe rate to 2 decimal places is %.2f%%", f);
18:       printf("\nThe rate to 1 decimal place is %.1f%%", f);
19:       printf("\nThe result of %f/%f = %f\n", g, f, g / f);
20:
21:       return 0;
22:    }
```

Output ▼

```
Decimal values without tabs: 2 10 50
Decimal values with tabs:      2        10       50
Three floats on 1 line:         1.050000       25.500000        -0.100000
Three floats on 3 lines:
        1.050000
        25.500000
        -0.100000
The rate is 1.050000%
The rate to 2 decimal places is 1.05%
The rate to 1 decimal place is 1.0%
The result of 25.500000/1.050000 = 24.285715
```

Analysis ▼

Listing 7.2 prints eight lines of information. Lines 10 and 11 each print three decimals: a, b, and c. Line 10 prints them without tabs, and line 11 prints them with tabs. Lines 13 and 14 each print three float variables: f, g, and h. Line 13 prints them on one line, and line 14 prints them on three lines. Line 16 prints a float variable, f, followed by a percent sign. Because a percent sign is normally a message to print a variable, you must place two in a row to print a single percent sign. This is exactly like the backslash escape character.

Lines 17 and 18 present a new concept. Whenever you print a floating-point variable, C prints it to six decimal places as a default. Even if you define a variable with one digit past the decimal, like 5.5, when C prints it using the %f conversion specifier, it prints as 5.500000. This often may not serve your purposes, so C has a simple method to reduce the number of decimal digits it prints. As you can see on lines 17 and 18, adding a period (.) and a number between the % and f in the specifier instructs the compiler to print only the number of decimal points you set. One warning, though: C truncates the number instead of rounding. So 1.05 becomes 1.0 and not 1.1. Line 19 shows one final concept. When printing values in conversion specifiers, you don't have to use variables. You can also use expressions such as g / f, or even constants.

DO	DON'T
DO remember to use the newline escape character when printing multiple lines of information in separate printf() statements.	**DON'T** try to put multiple lines of text into one printf() statement. In most instances, it's clearer to print multiple lines with multiple print statements than to use just one with several newline (\n) escape characters.
	DON'T misspell stdio.h. Many C programmers accidentally type studio.h; however, there is no u. It stands for STanDard I/O (Input/Output).

7

Syntax

The `printf()` Function

```
#include <stdio.h>
printf( format-string[,arguments,...]);
```

`printf()` is a function that accepts a series of *arguments*, each applying to a conversion specifier in the given format string. `printf()` prints the formatted information to the standard output device, usually the display screen. When using `printf()`, you need to include the standard input/output header file, `stdio.h`. The *format-string* is required; however, arguments are optional. For each argument, there must be a conversion specifier. Table 7.2 lists the most commonly used conversion specifiers.

The *format-string* can also contain escape sequences. Table 7.1 lists the most frequently used escape sequences.

The following are examples of calls to `printf()` and their output:

Example 1 Input

```
#include <stdio.h>
int main( void )
{
    printf("This is an example of something printed!");
    return 0;
}
```

Example 1 Output

```
This is an example of something printed!
```

Example 2 Input

```
printf("This prints a character, %c\na number, %d\na floating \
point, %f", 'z', 123, 456.789 );
```

Example 2 Output

```
This prints a character, z
a number, 123
a floating point, 456.789
```

TIP

You may notice in the second example, that the `printf()` function uses a string that wraps to a second line. At the end of the first line, a forward slash (\) indicates that the string continues to the next line. The compiler treats the two lines as one.

Displaying Messages with `puts()`

The `puts()` function can also be used to display text messages on the screen, but it can't display numeric variables. The `puts()` function takes a single string as its argument and displays it, automatically adding a newline at the end. For example, the statement

```
puts("Hello, world.");
```

performs the same action as

```
printf("Hello, world.\n");
```

You can include escape sequences (including \n) in a string passed to `puts()`. They have the same effect as when they are used with `printf()`. (See Table 7.1 for the most common escape sequences.)

Just like `printf()`, any program that uses `puts()` should include the header file `stdio.h`. Note that `stdio.h` should be included only once in a program.

DO	DON'T
DO use the `puts()` function instead of the `printf()` function whenever you want to print text but don't need to print any variables.	**DON'T** try to use conversion specifiers with the `puts()` statement.

Syntax

The `puts()` Function

```
#include <stdio.h>
puts( string );
```

`puts()` is a function that copies a string to the standard output device, usually the display screen. When you use `puts()`, include the standard input/output header file (`stdio.h`). `puts()` also appends a new line character to the end of the string that is printed. The format string can contain escape sequences. Table 7.1 lists the most frequently used escape sequences.

The following are examples of calls to `puts()` and their output:

Example 1 Input

```
puts("This is printed with the puts() function!");
```

Example 1 Output

```
This is printed with the puts() function!
```

7

Example 2 Input

```
puts("This prints on the first line. \nThis prints on the second line.");
puts("This prints on the third line.");
puts("If these were printf()s, all four lines would be on two lines!");
```

Example 2 Output

```
This prints on the first line.
This prints on the second line.
This prints on the third line.
If these were printf()s, all four lines would be on two lines!
```

Inputting Numeric Data with scanf()

Just as most programs need to output data to the screen, they also need to input data from the keyboard. The most flexible way your program can read numeric data from the keyboard is by using the scanf() library function.

The scanf() function reads data from the keyboard according to a specified format and assigns the input data to one or more program variables. Like printf(), scanf() uses a format string to describe the format of the input. The format string utilizes the same conversion specifiers as the printf() function. For example, the statement

```
scanf("%d", &x);
```

reads a decimal integer from the keyboard and assigns it to the integer variable x. Likewise, the following statement reads a floating-point value from the keyboard and assigns it to the variable rate:

```
scanf("%f", &rate);
```

What is that ampersand (&) before the variable's name? The & symbol is C's *address-of* operator, which is fully explained in Lesson 9, "Understanding Pointers." For now, all you need to remember is that scanf() requires the & symbol before each numeric variable name in its argument list.

A single scanf() can input more than one value if you include multiple conversion specifiers in the format string and variable names (again, each preceded by & in the argument list). The following statement inputs an integer value and a floating-point value and assigns them to the variables x and rate, respectively:

```
scanf("%d %f", &x, &rate);
```

When multiple variables are entered, scanf() uses white space to separate input into fields. White space can be spaces, tabs, or newlines. Each conversion specifier in the `scanf()` format string is matched with an input field; the end of each input field is identified by white space.

This gives you considerable flexibility. In response to the preceding `scanf()`, you could enter

```
10 12.45
```

You also could enter this:

```
10                  12.45
```

or this:

```
10
12.45
```

As long as there's some white space between values, `scanf()` can assign each value to its variable.

CAUTION   Be careful when setting up `scanf()`. If you are looking for a character and the user enters a number, or if you are looking for a number and the user enters a character, then your user might see unexpected results.

As with the other functions discussed in this lesson, programs that use `scanf()` must include the `stdio.h` header file. Although Listing 7.3 gives an example of using `scanf()`, a more complete description is presented in Lesson 14.

Input ▼
LISTING 7.3   scanit.c: Using `scanf()` to Obtain Numerical Values

```
1:    /* Demonstration of using scanf() */
2:
3:    #include <stdio.h>
4:
5:    #define QUIT 4
6:
7:    int get_menu_choice( void );
8:
9:    int main( void )
10:   {
11:       int   choice   = 0;
12:       int   int_var  = 0;
13:       float float_var = 0.0;
```

7

```
14:      unsigned unsigned_var = 0;
15:
16:      while (choice != QUIT)
17:      {
18:          choice = get_menu_choice();
19:
20:          if (choice == 1)
21:          {
22:              puts("\nEnter a signed decimal integer (i.e. -123)");
23:              scanf("%d", &int_var);
24:          }
25:          if (choice == 2)
26:          {
27:              puts("\nEnter a decimal floating-point number\
28:                  (e.g. 1.23)");
29:              scanf("%f", &float_var);
30:          }
31:          if (choice == 3)
32:          {
33:              puts("\nEnter an unsigned decimal integer \
34                  (e.g. 123)" );
35:              scanf( "%u", &unsigned_var );
36:          }
37:      }
38:      printf("\nYour values are: int: %d  float: %f  unsigned: %u \n",
39:                                  int_var, float_var, unsigned_var );
40:
41:      return 0;
42:  }
43:
44:  int get_menu_choice( void )
45:  {
46:      int selection = 0;
47:
48:      do
49:      {
50:          puts( "\n1 - Get a signed decimal integer" );
51:          puts( "2 - Get a decimal floating-point number" );
52:          puts( "3 - Get an unsigned decimal integer" );
53:          puts( "4 - Quit" );
54:          puts( "\nEnter a selection:" );
55:
56:          scanf( "%d", &selection );
57:
58:      }while ( selection < 1 || selection > 4 );
59:
60:      return selection;
61:  }
```

Output ▼

```
1 - Get a signed decimal integer
2 - Get a decimal floating-point number
3 - Get an unsigned decimal integer
4 - Quit

Enter a selection:
1

Enter a signed decimal integer (e.g. -123)
-123

1 - Get a signed decimal integer
2 - Get a decimal floating-point number
3 - Get an unsigned decimal integer
4 - Quit

Enter a selection:
3

Enter an unsigned decimal integer (e.g. 123)
321

1 - Get a signed decimal integer
2 - Get a decimal floating-point number
3 - Get an unsigned decimal integer
4 - Quit

Enter a selection:
2

Enter a decimal floating point number (e.g. 1.23)
1231.123

1 - Get a signed decimal integer
2 - Get a decimal floating-point number
3 - Get an unsigned decimal integer
4 - Quit

Enter a selection:
4

Your values are: int: -123   float: 1231.123047 unsigned: 321
```

Analysis ▼

Listing 7.3 uses the same menu concepts that were used in Listing 7.1. The differences in `get_menu_choice()` (lines 44 through 61) are minor but should be noted. First, `puts()` is used instead of `printf()`. Because no variables are printed, there is no need to use `printf()`. Because `puts()` is used, the newline escape characters have been removed from lines 51 through 53. Line 58 was also changed to allow values from 1 to 4 because there are now four menu options. Notice that line 56 has not changed; however, now it should make a little more sense. `scanf()` gets a decimal value and places it in the variable `selection`. The function returns `selection` to the calling program in line 60.

Listings 7.1 and 7.3 use the same `main()` structure. An `if` statement evaluates `choice`, the return value of `get_menu_choice()`. Based on `choice`'s value, the program prints a message, asks for a number to be entered, and reads the value using `scanf()`. Notice the difference between lines 23, 29, and 35. Each is set up to get a different type of variable. Lines 12 through 14 declare variables of the appropriate types.

When the user selects Quit, the program prints the last-entered number for all three types. If the user didn't enter a value, 0 is printed because lines 12, 13, and 14 initialized all three types. One final note on lines 20 through 36: The `if` statements used here are not structured well. If you think that an `if...else` structure would have been better, you're correct. Lesson 13, "Advanced Program Control," introduces a new control statement, `switch`. This statement offers a better option.

DO	DON'T
DO use `printf()` or `puts()` with `scanf()`. Use the printing functions to display a prompting message for the data you want `scanf()` to get.	**DON'T** forget to include the address-of operator (`&`) when using `scanf()` variables.

Syntax

The `scanf()` Function

```
#include <stdio.h>
scanf( format-string[,arguments,...]);
```

`scanf()` is a function that uses a conversion specifier in a given format-string to place values into variable arguments. The arguments should be the addresses of the variables rather than the actual variables themselves. For numeric variables, you can pass the address by putting the address-of (`&`) operator at the beginning of the variable name. When using `scanf()`, you should include the `stdio.h` header file.

`scanf()` reads input fields from the standard input stream, usually the keyboard. It places each of these read fields into an argument. When it places the information, it converts it to the format of the corresponding specifier in the format string. For each argument, there must be a conversion specifier. Table 7.2 lists the most commonly needed conversion specifiers.

Example 1

```
int x, y, z;
scanf( "%d %d %d", &x, &y, &z);
```

Example 2

```
#include <stdio.h>
int main( void )
{
    float y;
    int x;
    puts( "Enter a float, then an int" );
    scanf( "%f %d", &y, &x);
    printf( "\nYou entered %f and %d ", y, x );
    return 0;
}
```

Using Trigraph Sequences

You have now learned the basics of reading and writing information using functions such as `printf()` and `scanf()`. There is one additional topic that will be covered in this lesson. This is not about reading and writing information; rather, it is about special sequences of characters in your source file that will be interpreted to mean something else. These special sequences are called *trigraph sequences*.

NOTE

> You will most likely never use trigraph sequences. It is included here in case you inadvertently use a trigraph sequence in your code and find that it automatically gets converted as described here.

7

Trigraph sequences are similar to the escape sequences you learned about earlier. The biggest difference is that trigraph sequences are interpreted at the time the compiler looks at your source code. Anywhere in your source file that a trigraph sequence is found, it will be converted.

Trigraph sequences start with two question marks (?). Table 7.3 lists the trigraph sequences listed in the ANSI standard. Per the standards, no other trigraph sequences should exist.

TABLE 7.3 The Trigraph Sequences

Code	Character Equivalent
??=	#
??(	[
??/	\
??)	]
??'	^
??<	{
??!	|
??>	}
??-	~

If a trigraph sequence code—one of the values in Table 7.3—is present in your source file, it will be changed to the character equivalent. It will be changed even if it is part of a string, for example,

```
printf("??(WOW??)");
```

will be changed to

```
printf("[WOW]");
```

If extra question marks are included, they are not changed; for example,

```
printf("???-");
```

will be changed to

```
printf("?~");
```

Summary

With the completion of this lesson, you are ready to write your own C programs. By combining the printf(), puts(), and scanf() functions and the programming control statements you learned about in earlier lessons, you have the tools needed to write simple programs.

Screen display is performed with the printf() and puts() functions. The puts() function can display text messages only, whereas printf() can display text messages and variables. Both functions use escape sequences for special characters and printing controls.

The `scanf()` function reads one or more numeric values from the keyboard and interprets each one according to a conversion specifier. Each value is assigned to a program variable.

At the end of this lesson, you learned about the trigraph sequences. You learned that trigraph sequences are special codes that are converted to character equivalents.

Q&A

Q **Why should I use `puts()` if `printf()` does everything `puts()` does and more?**

A Because `printf()` does more, it has additional overhead. When you try to write a small, efficient program, or when your programs get big and resources are valuable, you should take advantage of the smaller overhead of `puts()`. In general, you should use the simplest available resource.

Q **Why do I need to include `stdio.h` when I use `printf()`, `puts()`, or `scanf()`?**

A `stdio.h` contains the prototypes for the standard input/output functions. `printf()`, `puts()`, and `scanf()` are three of these standard functions. Try running a program without the `stdio.h` header and see the errors and warnings.

Q **What happens if I leave the address-of operator (`&`) off a `scanf()` variable?**

A This is an easy mistake to make. Unpredictable results can occur if you forget the address-of operator. When you read about pointers in Lessons 9, 15, and 16, you will understand this better. For now, know that if you omit the address-of operator, `scanf()` doesn't place the entered information in your variable but in some other place in memory. This could do anything from apparently having no effect to locking up your computer so that you must reboot.

Workshop

The Workshop provides quiz questions to help you solidify your understanding of the material covered, and exercises to provide you with experience in using what you've learned.

7

Quiz

1. What is the difference between `puts()` and `printf()`?
2. What header file should you include when you use `printf()`?

3. What do the following escape sequences do?

    a. \\

    b. \b

    c. \n

    d. \t

    e. \a

4. What conversion specifiers should you use to print the following?

    a. Character string

    b. Signed decimal integer

    c. Decimal floating-point number

5. What is the difference between using each of the following in the literal text of puts()?

    a. b

    b. \b

    c. \

    d. \\

Exercises

NOTE

Starting with this lesson, some of the exercises ask you to write complete programs that perform a particular task. Because there is always more than one way to do things in C, the answers provided at the back of the book shouldn't be interpreted as the only correct ones. If you can write your own code that performs what's required, great! If you have trouble, refer to the answers for help. The answers are presented with minimal comments because it's good practice for you to figure out how they operate.

1. Write both a printf() and a puts() statement to start a newline.

2. Write a scanf() statement that could be used to get a character, an unsigned decimal integer, and another single character.

3. Write the statements to get an integer value and print it.

4. Modify exercise 3 so that it accepts only even values (2, 4, 6, and so on).

5. Modify exercise 4 so that it returns values until the number 99 is entered, or until six even values have been entered. Store the numbers in an array. (Hint: You need a loop.)

6. Turn exercise 5 into an executable program. Add a function that prints the values, separated by tabs, in the array on a single line. (Print only the values that were entered into the array.)

7. **BUG BUSTER:** Find the error(s) in the following code fragment:

```
printf( "Jack said, "Peter Piper picked a peck of pickled peppers."");
```

8. **BUG BUSTER:** Find the error(s) in the following program:

```
int get_1_or_2( void )
{
    int answer = 0;
    while (answer < 1 || answer > 2)
    {
        printf(Enter 1 for Yes, 2 for No);
        scanf( "%f", answer );
    }
    return answer;
}
```

9. Using Listing 7.1, complete the `print_report()` function so that it prints the rest of Table 7.1.

10. Write a program that inputs two floating-point values from the keyboard and then displays their product.

11. Write a program that inputs 10 integer values from the keyboard and then displays their sum.

12. Write a program that inputs integers from the keyboard, storing them in an array. Input should stop when a zero is entered or when the end of the array is reached. Then, find and display the array's largest and smallest values. (Note: This is a tough problem because arrays haven't been completely covered in this book yet. If you have difficulty, try solving this problem again after reading Lesson 8, "Using Numeric Arrays.")

7

LESSON 8
Using Numeric Arrays

Arrays are a type of data storage that you often use in C programs. You had a brief introduction to arrays in Lesson 6, "Basic Program Control." In this lesson you learn

- What an array is

- The definition of single-dimensional and multidimensional numeric arrays

- How to declare and initialize arrays

What Is an Array?

An *array* is a collection of data storage locations, each storing the same type of data and having the same name. Each storage location in an array is called an *array element*. Why do you need arrays in your programs? This question can be answered with an example.

If you're keeping track of your business expenses for 2014 and filing your receipts by month, you could have a separate folder for each month's receipts, but it would be more convenient to have a single folder with 12 compartments.

Extend this example to computer programming. Imagine that you're designing a program to keep track of your business expenses. The program could declare 12 separate variables, one for each month's expense total. This approach is analogous to having 12 separate folders for your receipts. Good programming practice, however, would utilize an array with 12 elements, storing each month's total in the corresponding array element. This approach is comparable to filing your receipts in a single folder with 12 compartments. Figure 8.1 illustrates the difference between using individual variables and an array.

FIGURE 8.1
Variables are like individual folders, whereas an array is like a single folder with many compartments.

Individual variables   An array

Using Single-Dimensional Arrays

A *single-dimensional array* has only a single subscript. A *subscript* is a number in brackets that follows an array's name. This number can identify the number of individual elements in the array. An example should make this clear. For the business expenses program, you could use the following line to declare an array of type `float`:

```
float expenses[12];
```

The array is named `expenses`, and contains 12 elements. Each of the 12 elements is the exact equivalent of a single `float` variable.

All of C's data types can be used for arrays. C array elements are always numbered starting at 0, so the 12 elements of expenses are numbered 0 through 11. In the preceding example, January's expense total would be stored in `expenses[0]`, February's in `expenses[1]`, and so on. The expense total for December would be in `expenses[11]`.

When you declare an array, the compiler sets aside a block of memory large enough to hold the entire array. Individual array elements are stored in sequential memory locations, as shown in Figure 8.2.

FIGURE 8.2
Array elements are stored in sequential memory locations.

```
int array[10];
```

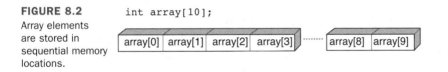

Where you declare an array in your source code is important. As with variables that are not a part of an array, the declaration's location affects how your program can use the array. The effect of a declaration's location is covered in more detail in Lesson 12, "Understanding Variable Scope." For now, place your array declarations with other variable declarations.

An array element can be used in your program anywhere a nonarray variable of the same type can be used. Individual elements of the array are accessed by using the array name followed by the element subscript enclosed in square brackets. For example, the following statement stores the value `89.95` in the second array element. (Remember, the first array element is `expenses[0]`, not `expenses[1]`):

```
expenses[1] = 89.95;
```

Likewise, the statement

```
expenses[10] = expenses[11];
```

assigns a copy of the value stored in array element `expenses[11]` into array element `expenses[10]`. When you refer to an array element, the array subscript can be a literal constant, as in these examples. However, your programs might often use a subscript that is a C integer variable or expression, or even another array element. Here are some examples:

```
float expenses[100];
int a[10];
/* additional statements go here */
expenses[i] = 100;          // i is an integer variable
expenses[2 + 3] = 100;      // equivalent to expenses[5]
expenses[a[2]] = 100;       // a[] is an integer array
```

That last example might need an explanation. If, for instance, you have an integer array named `a[]` and the value 8 is stored in element `a[2]`, writing

```
expenses[a[2]]
```

has the same effect as writing

```
expenses[8];
```

When you use arrays, keep the element numbering scheme in mind: In an array of n elements, the allowable subscripts range from 0 to $n-1$. If you use the subscript value n, you might get program errors. The C compiler doesn't recognize whether your program uses an array subscript that is out of bounds. Your program compiles and links, but out-of-range subscripts generally produce erroneous results.

CAUTION　　　Remember that array elements start with 0, not 1. Also remember that the last element is one less than the number of elements in the array. For example, an array with 10 elements contains elements 0 through 9.

Sometimes you might want to treat an array of n elements as if its elements were numbered 1 through n. For instance, in the previous example, a more natural method might be to store January's expense total in `expenses[1]`, February's in `expenses[2]`, and so on. The simplest way to do this is to declare the array with one more element than needed, and ignore element 0. In this case, you would declare the array as follows. You could also store some related data in element 0 (the yearly expense total, perhaps):

```
float expenses[13];
```

The program expenses.c in Listing 8.1 demonstrates the use of an array. This is a simple program with no real practical use.

Input ▼
LISTING 8.1   expenses.c: Using an Array

```
1:   /* expenses.c - Demonstrates use of an array */
2:
3:   #include <stdio.h>
4:
5:   /* Declare an array to hold expenses, and a counter variable */
6:
7:   float expenses[13];
8:   int count;
9:   float year_expenses = 0;
10:
11:  int main( void )
12:  {
13:      /* Input data from keyboard into array */
14:
15:      for (count = 1; count < 13; count++)
16:      {
17:          printf("Enter expenses for month %d: ", count);
18:          scanf("%f", &expenses[count]);
19:      }
20:
21:      /* Print array contents */
22:
23:      for (count = 1; count < 13; count++)
24:      {
25:          printf("Month %d = $%.2f\n", count, expenses[count]);
26:           year_expenses += expenses[count];
27:      }
28:      printf("Yearly expenses are $%.2f\n", year_expenses);
29:      return 0;
30:  }
```

Output ▼

```
Enter expenses for month 1: 45.67
Enter expenses for month 2: 100.65
Enter expenses for month 3: 3421.04
Enter expenses for month 4: 34.67
Enter expenses for month 5: 5.60
Enter expenses for month 6: 1267
Enter expenses for month 7: 200.00
Enter expenses for month 8: 45.21
Enter expenses for month 9: 23.12
Enter expenses for month 10: 187.90
Enter expenses for month 11: 12.54
Enter expenses for month 12: 3
Month 1 = $45.67
```

```
Month 2 = $100.65
Month 3 = $3421.04
Month 4 = $34.67
Month 5 = $5.60
Month 6 = $1267.00
Month 7 = $200.00
Month 8 = $45.21
Month 9 = $23.12
Month 10 = $187.90
Month 11 = $12.54
Month 12 = $3.00
Yearly expenses are $5346.40
```

Analysis ▼

When you run expenses.c, the program prompts you to enter expenses for months 1 through 12. The values you enter are stored in an array. You must enter a value for each month. After the 12th value is entered, the array contents display onscreen.

The flow of the program is similar to listings you've seen before. Line 1 starts with a comment that describes what the program does. Notice that the name of the program, expenses.c, is included. When the name of the program is included in a comment, you know which program you're viewing. This is helpful when you're reviewing printouts of a listing.

Line 5 contains an additional comment explaining the variables declared. In line 7, an array of 13 elements is declared. In this program, only 12 elements are needed, one for each month, but 13 have been declared. Line 9 declares a total variable that will be used after the array is filled. The `for` loop on lines 15 through 19 ignores element 0. This lets the program use elements 1 through 12, which relate directly to the 12 months. Going back to line 8, a variable, `count`, is declared and is used throughout the program as a counter and an array index.

The program's `main()` function begins on line 11. As stated earlier, this program uses a `for` loop to print a message and accept a value for each of the 12 months. Notice that on line 18, the `scanf()` function uses an array element. On line 7, the `expenses` array was declared as `float`, so `%f` is used. The address-of operator (`&`) also is placed before the array element, just as if it were a regular type `float` variable and not an array element.

Lines 23 through 27 contain a second `for` loop that prints the values just entered. As discussed in the last lesson, adding .2 between the percent sign and the `f` (`%.2f`) prints a floating number with two digits to the right of the decimal, a format that makes more sense when printing financial totals. Additional formatting commands are covered in more detail in Lesson 14, "Working with the Screen, Printer, and Keyboard."

DO	DON'T
DO use arrays instead of creating several variables that store the same thing. For example, if you want to store total sales for each month of the year, create an array with 12 elements to hold sales rather than creating a sales variable for each month.	**DON'T** forget that array subscripts start at element 0.

Using Multidimensional Arrays

A multidimensional array has more than one subscript. A two-dimensional array has two subscripts, a three-dimensional array has three subscripts, and so on. There is no limit to the number of dimensions a C array can have. (There *is* a limit on total array size, as discussed later in this lesson.)

For example, you might write a program that plays checkers. The checkerboard contains 64 squares arranged in eight rows and eight columns. Your program could represent the board as a two-dimensional array, as follows:

```
int checker[8][8];
```

The resulting array has 64 elements: `checker[0][0]`, `checker[0][1]`, `checker[0][2]`...`checker[7][6]`, `checker[7][7]`. The structure of this two-dimensional array is illustrated in Figure 8.3.

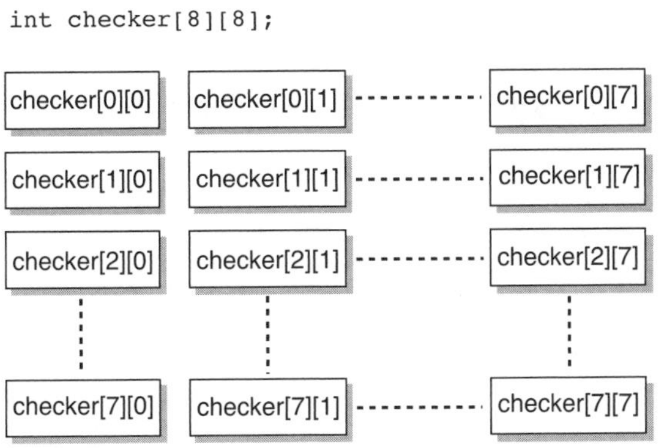

FIGURE 8.3
A two-dimensional array has a row-and-column structure.

`int checker[8][8];`

Similarly, a three-dimensional array could be thought of as a cube. Four-dimensional arrays (and higher) are probably best left to your imagination. All arrays, no matter how many dimensions they have, are stored sequentially in memory. More detail on array storage is presented in Lesson 15, "Pointers to Pointers and Arrays of Pointers."

Naming and Declaring Arrays

The rules for assigning names to arrays are the same as for variable names, covered in Lesson 3, "Storing Information: Variables and Constants." An array name must be unique. It can't be used for another array or for any other identifier (variable, constant, and so on). As you have probably realized, array declarations follow the same form as declarations of nonarray variables, except that the number of elements in the array must be enclosed in square brackets immediately following the array name.

When you declare an array, you can specify the number of elements with a literal constant (as was done in the earlier examples) or with a symbolic constant created with a #define directive. Thus, the following

```
#define MONTHS 12
int array[MONTHS];
```

is equivalent to this statement:

```
int array[12];
```

With most compilers, however, you can't declare an array's elements with a symbolic constant created with the const keyword:

```
const int MONTHS = 12;
int array[MONTHS];          /* Wrong! */
```

Listing 8.2, teamstats.c, demonstrates the use of a two-dimensional array. The program uses an array to store the scoring totals of five basketball players in four games.

Input ▼

LISTING 8.2 scoring.c: Storing the Point Totals of Five Players in Four Different Games in a Two-Dimensional Array

```
1: // scoring.c: Using a two-dimensional array to store basketball point totals
2:
3: #include <stdio.h>
4: #define PLAYERS 5
5: #define GAMES 4
6:
7: int scores[6][5];
8: float score_avg[6], best_avg;
9: int point_total, best_player;
10: int counter1, counter2;
11:
12: int main()
13: {
14:     // The outer loop is for each of the games
```

```
15:      for (counter2 = 1; counter2 <= GAMES; counter2++)
16:      {
17:          printf("\nGetting scoring totals for Game #%d.\n", counter2);
18:          // The inner loop is for each player in the specific game.
19:          for (counter1 = 1; counter1 <= PLAYERS; counter1++)
20:          {
21:              printf("What did player #%d score in the game\? ", counter1);
22:              scanf("%d", &scores[counter1][counter2]);
23:          }
24:      }
25:
26:      // Loop through the array to calculate scoring average per player
27:      for (counter1 = 1; counter1 <= PLAYERS; counter1++)
28:      {
29:          point_total = 0;
30:          for (counter2 = 1; counter2 <= GAMES; counter2++)
31:          {
32:              point_total += scores[counter1][counter2];
33:          }
34:          score_avg[counter1] = (float)point_total/GAMES;
35:      }
36:
37:      // Now loop through and store who has the best scoring average
38:      best_avg = 0;
39:      for (counter1 = 1; counter1 <= PLAYERS; counter1++)
40:      {
41:          if (score_avg[counter1] > best_avg)
42:          {
43:              best_avg = score_avg[counter1];
44:              best_player = counter1;
45:          }
46:      }
47:
48:      printf("\nPlayer #%d had the best scoring average,\n", best_player);
49:      printf("at %.2f points per game.\n", score_avg[best_player]);
50:
51:      return (0);
52: }
```

Output ▼

```
Getting scoring totals for Game #1

What did player #1 score in the game? 5
What did player #2 score in the game? 6
What did player #3 score in the game? 3
What did player #4 score in the game? 1
What did player #5 score in the game? 8
```

```
Getting scoring totals for Game #2

What did player #1 score in the game? 4
What did player #2 score in the game? 2
What did player #3 score in the game? 12
What did player #4 score in the game? 3
What did player #5 score in the game? 3

Getting scoring totals for Game #3

What did player #1 score in the game? 5
What did player #2 score in the game? 6
What did player #3 score in the game? 8
What did player #4 score in the game? 8
What did player #5 score in the game? 3

Getting scoring totals for Game #4

What did player #1 score in the game? 3
What did player #2 score in the game? 2
What did player #3 score in the game? 6
What did player #4 score in the game? 4
What did player #5 score in the game? 6

Player #3 had the best scoring average,
at 7.25 points per game.
```

Analysis ▼

Like expenses.c, this listing prompts the user to enter values. It prompts for the scoring totals of five players from four different games. After getting all the scores, the program calculates each player's scoring average and prints the number of the player with the best average, as well as the average.

As you learned earlier, arrays, whether one-, two-, or three-dimensional, are named like regular variables. On line 7, a two-dimensional array named scores is declared. The first dimension is set to 6, for the five players (so you can ignore the 0 element and fill 1 through 5) and the second dimension is set to 5 (for the four games plus one, again to ignore the 0 element). A second, single-dimension array named score_avg is declared on line 8. It is of type float because there's a good chance that a scoring average will not be an exact integer. On lines 4 and 5, two constants, PLAYERS and GAMES, are defined. If you want to change the number of players or games, these constants can be changed easily.

8

TIP

> As written, changing the constants would not be enough to change the entire program. Can you see why? The two arrays are declared with specific numbers. A better way to declare the two arrays would be
>
> ```
> int scores[PLAYERS + 1][GAMES + 1];
> float score_avg[PLAYERS + 1];
> ```
>
> With this format, any changes to the number of players or the number of games would result in a properly sized array.

Five other variables are declared: counter1, counter2, point_total, bestavg, and bestplayer. The first two are used in loops, point_total is used to calculate scoring averages for each player, and the last two variables are used to figure out what player had the best scoring average.

Lines 15 through 24 contain a for loop nested inside of another for loop, and the two loops are used to populate the two-dimensional scoring array. The outer loop cycles through each game and contains a printf() statement to let the user know which game the stats need to come from before passing control to the inner loop on line 19, which cycles through each of the players. When a game is complete, control passes back to the outer loop, which increases by one, prints a new message, and then starts the inner loop over.

After all the scores have been entered in the array, a new nested for loop begins on line 27. This loop flips the order from the previous pairing with the outer loop covering the players and then the inner loop, starting on line 30, looping through all the games, adding each score to an overall total on line 32. After this total variable is filled, that amount is divided by the number of games on line 34 to calculate a player's scoring average. This data is then stored in the score_avg array. When the outer loop increments and starts over, it is important to re-initialize the point_total variable to 0 on line 29; otherwise player #2's point total would also include all the points from player #1. This is another common error programmers make. Note that there is no interaction with the user via printf() or scanf() statements in this section of code. C is just doing what computers do best—taking your data and performing calculations and storing new data.

The final for loop, starting on line 39, walks through the score_avg array and determines which player had the highest scoring average. This is the job of the nested if code on lines 41–45. It takes each player's average and compares it against the current high average. If the player has scored more per game, that player's average becomes the new bestavg on line 43, and the player's number is set to the bestplayer variable on line 44. Lines 48 and 49 report the results of this data analysis.

DO	**DON'T**
DO use #define statements to create constants that can be used when declaring arrays. Then you can easily change the number of elements in the array. In grades.c, for example, you could change the number of students in the #define, and you wouldn't have to make any other changes in the program.	**DON'T** use multidimensional arrays with more than three dimensions if you can avoid them. Remember, multidimensional arrays can get very big very quickly.

Initializing Arrays

You can initialize all or part of an array when you first declare it. Follow the array declaration with an equal sign and a list of values enclosed in braces and separated by commas. The listed values are assigned in order to array elements starting at number 0.

Consider the following code:

```
int array[4] = { 100, 200, 300, 400 };
```

For this example, the value 100 is assigned to array[0], the value 200 is assigned to array[1], the value 300 is assigned to array[2], and the value 400 is assigned to array[3].

If you omit the array size, the compiler creates an array just large enough to hold the initialization values. Thus, the following statement would have exactly the same effect as the previous array declaration statement:

```
int array[] = { 100, 200, 300, 400 };
```

You can, however, include too few initialization values, as in this example:

```
int array[10] = { 1, 2, 3 };
```

If you don't explicitly initialize an array element, you can't be sure what value it holds when the program runs. If you include too many initializers (more initializers than array elements), the compiler detects an error. According to the ANSI standard, the elements that are not initialized will be set to zero.

TIP

Don't rely upon the compiler to automatically initialize values. It is best to make sure you know what a value is initialized to by setting it yourself.

Initializing Multidimensional Arrays

Multidimensional arrays can also be initialized. The list of initialization values is assigned to array elements in order, with the last array subscript changing first. For example:

```
int array[4][3] = { 1, 2, 3, 4, 5, 6, 7, 8, 9, 10, 11, 12 };
```

results in the following assignments:

```
array[0][0] is equal to 1
array[0][1] is equal to 2
array[0][2] is equal to 3
array[1][0] is equal to 4
array[1][1] is equal to 5
array[1][2] is equal to 6
array[2][0] is equal to 7
array[2][1] is equal to 8
array[2][2] is equal to 9
array[3][0] is equal to 10
array[3][1] is equal to 11
array[3][2] is equal to 12
```

When you initialize multidimensional arrays, you can make your source code clearer by using extra braces to group the initialization values and also by spreading them over several lines. The following initialization is equivalent to the one just given:

```
int array[4][3] = { { 1, 2, 3 } , { 4, 5, 6 } ,
{ 7, 8, 9 } , { 10, 11, 12 } };
```

Remember, initialization values must be separated by a comma—even when there is a brace between them. Also, be sure to use braces in pairs—a closing brace for every opening brace—or the compiler becomes confused.

Now look at an example that demonstrates the advantages of arrays. Listing 8.3, randomarray.c, creates a 1,000-element, three-dimensional array and fills it with random numbers. The program then displays the array elements onscreen. Imagine how many lines of source code you would need to perform the same task with nonarray variables.

You see a new library function, getchar(), in this program. The getchar() function reads a single character from the keyboard. In Listing 8.3, getchar() pauses the program until the user presses the Enter key. The getchar() function is covered in detail in Lesson 14.

Input ▼

LISTING 8.3   randomarray.c: Creating a Multidimensional Array

```
1:   /* randomarray.c - Demonstrates using a multidimensional array */
2:
3:   #include <stdio.h>
4:   #include <stdlib.h>
5:   /* Declare a three-dimensional array with 1000 elements */
6:
7:   int random_array[10][10][10];
8:   int a, b, c;
9:
10:  int main( void )
11:  {
12:      /* Fill the array with random numbers. The C library */
13:      /* function rand() returns a random number. Use one */
14:      /* for loop for each array subscript. */
15:
16:      for (a = 0; a < 10; a++)
17:      {
18:          for (b = 0; b < 10; b++)
19:          {
20:              for (c = 0; c < 10; c++)
21:              {
22:                  random_array[a][b][c] = rand();
23:              }
24:          }
25:      }
26:
27:      /* Now display the array elements 10 at a time */
28:
29:      for (a = 0; a < 10; a++)
30:      {
31:          for (b = 0; b < 10; b++)
32:          {
33:              for (c = 0; c < 10; c++)
34:              {
35:                  printf("\nrandom_array[%d][%d][%d] = ", a, b, c);
36:                  printf("%d", random_array[a][b][c]);
37:              }
38:              printf("\nPress Enter to continue, CTRL-C to quit.");
39:
40:              getchar();
41:          }
42:      }
43:      return 0;
44:  }   /* end of main() */
```

8

Output ▼

```
random_array[0][0][0] = 346
random_array[0][0][1] = 130
random_array[0][0][2] = 10982
random_array[0][0][3] = 1090
random_array[0][0][4] = 11656
random_array[0][0][5] = 7117
random_array[0][0][6] = 17595
random_array[0][0][7] = 6415
random_array[0][0][8] = 22948
random_array[0][0][9] = 31126
Press Enter to continue, CTRL-C to quit.

random_array[0][1][0] = 9004
random_array[0][1][1] = 14558
random_array[0][1][2] = 3571
random_array[0][1][3] = 22879
random_array[0][1][4] = 18492
random_array[0][1][5] = 1360
random_array[0][1][6] = 5412
random_array[0][1][7] = 26721
random_array[0][1][8] = 22463
random_array[0][1][9] = 25047
Press Enter to continue, CTRL-C to quit.
...        ...
random_array[9][8][0] = 6287
random_array[9][8][1] = 26957
random_array[9][8][2] = 1530
random_array[9][8][3] = 14171
random_array[9][8][4] = 6951
random_array[9][8][5] = 213
random_array[9][8][6] = 14003
random_array[9][8][7] = 29736
random_array[9][8][8] = 15028
random_array[9][8][9] = 18968
Press Enter to continue, CTRL-C to quit.

random_array[9][9][0] = 28559
random_array[9][9][1] = 5268
random_array[9][9][2] = 20182
random_array[9][9][3] = 3633
random_array[9][9][4] = 24779
random_array[9][9][5] = 3024
random_array[9][9][6] = 10853
random_array[9][9][7] = 28205
random_array[9][9][8] = 8930
random_array[9][9][9] = 2873
Press Enter to continue, CTRL-C to quit.
```

Analysis ▼

In Lesson 6, you saw a program that used a nested `for` statement; this program has two nested `for` loops. Before you look at the `for` statements in detail, note that lines 7 and 8 declare four variables. The first is an array named `random_array`, used to hold random numbers. `random_array` is a three-dimensional type `int` array that is 10-by-10-by-10, giving a total of 1,000 type `int` elements (10×10×10). Imagine coming up with 1,000 unique variable names if you couldn't use arrays! Line 8 then declares three variables, a, b, and c, used to control the `for` loops.

This program also includes the header file `stdlib.h` (for standard library) on line 4. It is included to provide the prototype for the `rand()` function used on line 22.

The bulk of the program is contained in two nests of `for` statements. The first is in lines 16 through 25, and the second is in lines 29 through 42. Both `for` nests have the same structure. They work just like the loops in Listing 6.2, but they go one level deeper. In the first set of `for` statements, line 22 is executed repeatedly. Line 22 assigns the return value of a function, `rand()`, to an element of the `random_array` array, where `rand()` is a library function that returns a random number.

Going backward through the listing, you can see that line 20 changes variable c from 0 to 9. This loops through the farthest right subscript of the `random_array` array. Line 18 loops through b, the middle subscript of the random array. Each time b changes, it loops through all the c elements. Line 16 increments variable a, which loops through the farthest left subscript. Each time this subscript changes, it loops through all 10 values of subscript b, which in turn loop through all 10 values of c. This loop initializes every value in the `random` array to a random number.

Lines 29 through 42 contain the second nest of `for` statements. These work like the previous `for` statements, but these loops print each of the values assigned previously. After 10 are displayed, line 38 prints a message and waits for Enter to be pressed. Line 40 takes care of the keypress using `getchar()`. If Enter hasn't been pressed, `getchar()` waits until it is. Run this program and watch the displayed values.

Summary

This lesson introduced numeric arrays, a powerful data storage method that lets you group a number of same-type data items under the same group name. Individual items, or elements, in an array are identified using a subscript after the array name. Computer programming tasks that involve repetitive data processing lend themselves to array storage.

Like nonarray variables, arrays must be declared before they can be used. Optionally, array elements can be initialized when the array is declared.

Q&A

Q **What happens if I use a subscript on an array that is larger than the number of elements in the array?**

A If you use a subscript that is out of bounds with the array declaration, the program will probably compile and even run. However, the results of such a mistake can be unpredictable. This can be a difficult error to find after it starts causing problems, so make sure you're careful when initializing and accessing array elements.

Q **What happens if I use an array without initializing it?**

A This mistake doesn't produce a compiler error. If you don't initialize an array, there can be any value in the array elements. You might get unpredictable results. You should always initialize variables and arrays so that you know exactly what's in them. Lesson 12 introduces you to one exception to the need to initialize. For now, play it safe.

Q **How many dimensions can an array have?**

A As stated in this lesson, you can have as many dimensions as you want. As you add more dimensions, you use more data storage space. You should declare an array only as large as you need to avoid wasting storage space.

Q **Is there an easy way to initialize an entire array at once?**

A Each element of an array must be initialized. The safest way for a beginning C programmer to initialize an array is either with a declaration, as shown in this lesson, or with a `for` statement. There are other ways to initialize an array, but they are beyond the scope of this book.

Q **Can I add two arrays together (or multiply, divide, or subtract them)?**

A If you declare two arrays, you can't add the two together. Each element must be added individually. Exercise 10 illustrates this point. You could, however, create a function that could add the two arrays together. Such a function will still be required to add the individual elements.

Q **Why is it better to use an array instead of individual variables?**

A With arrays, you can group like values with a single name. In Listing 8.3, 1,000 values were stored. Creating 1,000 variable names and initializing each to a random number would have taken a tremendous amount of typing. By using an array, you made the task easy.

Q What do you do if you don't know how big the array needs to be when you write the program?

A There are functions within C that enable you to allocate space for variables and arrays on-the-fly. These functions are covered in Lesson 15.

Workshop

The Workshop provides quiz questions to help you solidify your understanding of the material covered, and exercises to provide you with experience in using what you've learned.

Quiz

1. Which of C's data types can be used in an array?

2. If an array is declared with 10 elements, what is the subscript of the first element?

3. In a one-dimensional array declared with *n* elements, what is the subscript of the last element?

4. What happens if your program tries to access an array element with an out-of-range subscript?

5. How do you declare a multidimensional array?

6. An array is declared with the following statement. How many total elements does the array have?

   ```
   int array[2][3][5][8];
   ```

7. What would be the name of the tenth element in the array in question 6?

Exercises

1. Write a C program line that would declare three one-dimensional integer arrays, named `one`, `two`, and `three`, with 1,000 elements each.

2. Write the statement that would declare a 10-element integer array and initialize all its elements to 1.

3. Given the following array, write code to initialize all the array elements to 88:

   ```
   int eightyeight[88];
   ```

4. Given the following array, write code to initialize all the array elements to 0:

   ```
   int stuff[12][10];
   ```

5. **BUG BUSTER:** What is wrong with the following code fragment?

```
int x, y;
int array[10][3];
int main( void )
{
   for ( x = 0; x < 3; x++ )
      for ( y = 0; y < 10; y++ )
         array[x][y] = 0;
   return 0;
}
```

6. **BUG BUSTER:** What is wrong with the following?

```
int array[10];
int x = 1;

int main( void )
{
   for ( x = 1; x <= 10; x++ )
      array[x] = 99;

   return 0;
}
```

7. Write a program that puts random numbers into a two-dimensional array that is 5 by 4. Print the values in columns onscreen. (Hint: Use the `rand()` function from Listing 8.3.)

TIP _____

Whenever you use the `rand()` function, it is a good idea to add the following line to the beginning of your program:

```
srand ( time( NULL));
```

This function call is needed to ensure every time you run the program you get different random numbers. Believe it or not, there are times when a user would want to generate the same set of random numbers (scientific experiments, for example), so the `srand`, short for seed random, function is needed to ensure each time the program runs, it generates a new set of numbers.

8. Rewrite Listing 8.3 to use a single-dimensional array. Print the average of the 1,000 variables before printing the individual values. Note: Don't forget to pause after every 10 values are printed.

9. Write a program that initializes an array of 10 elements. Each element should be equal to its subscript. The program should then print each of the 10 elements.

10. Modify the program from exercise 9. After printing the initialized values, the program should copy the values to a new array and add 10 to each value. The new array values should be printed.

LESSON 9
Understanding Pointers

This lesson introduces you to pointers, an important part of the C language. Pointers provide a powerful and flexible method of manipulating data in your programs. In this lesson you learn

- The definition of a pointer

- The uses of pointers

- How to declare and initialize pointers

- How to use pointers with simple variables and arrays

- How to use pointers to pass arrays to functions

As you read through this lesson, the advantages of using pointers might not be immediately clear. The advantages fall into two categories: things that can be done better with pointers than without and things that can be done only with pointers. The specifics should become clear as you read this and subsequent lessons. At present, just know that you must understand pointers if you want to be a proficient C programmer.

What Is a Pointer?

To understand pointers, you need a basic knowledge of how your computer stores information in memory. The following is a somewhat simplified account of PC memory storage.

Your Computer's Memory

A PC's memory (RAM) consists of many millions of sequential storage locations, and each location is identified by a unique address. The memory addresses in a given computer range from zero to a maximum value that depends on the amount of memory installed.

When you use your computer, the operating system uses some of the system's memory. When you run a program, the program's code (the machine-language instructions for the program's various tasks) and data (the information the program uses) also use some of the system's memory. This section examines the memory storage for program data.

When you declare a variable in a C program, the compiler sets aside a memory location with a unique address to store that variable. The compiler associates that address with the variable's name. When your program uses the variable name, it automatically accesses the proper memory location. The location's address is used, but it is hidden from you, and you need not be concerned with it.

Figure 9.1 shows this schematically. A variable named `rate` has been declared and initialized to `100`. The compiler has set aside storage at address `1004` for the variable and has associated the name `rate` with the address `1004`.

FIGURE 9.1
A program variable is stored at a specific memory address.

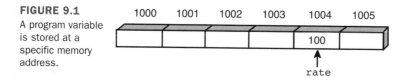

Creating a Pointer

You should note that the address of the variable `rate` (or any other variable) is a number and can be treated like any other number in C. If you know a variable's address, you can create a second variable in which to store the address of the first. The first step is to declare a variable to hold the address of `rate`. Give it the name `p_rate`, for example. At first, `p_rate` is uninitialized. Storage has been allocated for `p_rate`, but its value is undetermined, as shown in Figure 9.2.

FIGURE 9.2
Memory storage
space has been
allocated for the
variable p_rate.

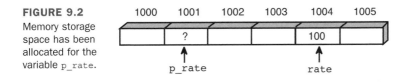

The next step is to store the address of the variable `rate` in the variable `p_rate`. Because `p_rate` now contains the address of `rate`, it indicates the location in which `rate` is stored in memory. In C parlance, `p_rate` *points* to `rate`, or is a pointer to `rate`. This is shown in Figure 9.3.

9

FIGURE 9.3
The variable
p_rate contains
the address of
the variable rate
and is therefore a
pointer to rate.

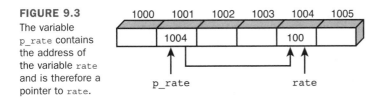

To summarize, a pointer is a variable that contains the address of another variable. Now you can get down to the details of using pointers in your C programs.

Pointers and Simple Variables

In the example just given, a pointer variable pointed to a simple (that is, nonarray) variable. This section shows you how to create and use pointers to simple variables.

Declaring Pointers

A pointer is a numeric variable and, like all variables, must be declared before it can be used. Pointer variable names follow the same rules as other variables and must be unique. This lesson uses the convention that a pointer to the variable `name` is called `p_name`. This isn't necessary, however; you can name pointers anything you want as long as they follow C's naming rules.

A pointer declaration takes the following form:

```
typename *ptrname;
```

where `typename` is any of C's variable types and indicates the type of the variable that the pointer points to. The asterisk (`*`) is the indirection operator, and it indicates that `ptrname` is a pointer to type `typename` and not a variable of type `typename`. Pointers can be declared along with nonpointer variables. Here are some more examples:

```
char *ch1, *ch2;       /* ch1 and ch2 both are pointers to type char */
float *value, percent;  /* value is a pointer to type float, and
                          /* percent is an ordinary float variable */
```

NOTE

> The * symbol is used as both the indirection operator and the multiplication operator. Don't worry about the compiler becoming confused. The context in which * is used always provides enough information for the compiler to figure out whether you mean indirection or multiplication.

Initializing Pointers

Now that you've declared a pointer, what can you do with it? You can't do anything with it until you make it point to something. Like regular variables, uninitialized pointers can be used, but the results are unpredictable and potentially disastrous. Until a pointer holds the address of a variable, it isn't useful. The address doesn't get stored in the pointer by magic; your program must put it there by using the address-of operator, the ampersand (&). When placed before the name of a variable, the address-of operator returns the address of the variable. Therefore, you initialize a pointer with a statement of the form

pointer = &variable;

Refer to the example in Figure 9.3. The program statement to initialize the variable p_rate to point at the variable rate would be

```
p_rate = &rate;     /* assign the address of rate to p_rate */
```

This statement assigns the address of rate to p_rate. Before the initialization, p_rate didn't point to anything in particular. After the initialization, p_rate is a pointer to rate.

Using Pointers

Now that you know how to declare and initialize pointers, you're probably wondering how to use them. The indirection operator (*) comes into play again. When the * precedes the name of a pointer, it refers to the variable pointed to.

Consider the previous example, in which the pointer p_rate has been initialized to point to the variable rate. If you write *p_rate, this pointer variable refers to the contents of the variable rate. If you want to print the value of rate (which is 100 in the example), you could write

```
printf("%d", rate);
```

or you could write this statement:

```
printf("%d", *p_rate);
```

In C, these two statements are equivalent. Accessing the contents of a variable by using the variable name is called *direct access*. Accessing the contents of a variable by using a pointer to the variable is called *indirect access* or *indirection*. Figure 9.4 shows that a pointer name preceded by the indirection operator refers to the value of the pointed-to variable.

FIGURE 9.4
Use of the
indirection operator
with pointers.

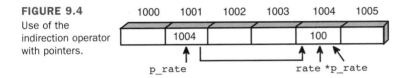

9

Pause a minute and think about this material. Pointers are an integral part of the C language, and it's essential that you understand them. Pointers have confused many people, so don't worry if you feel a bit puzzled. If you need to review, that's fine. Maybe the following summary can help.

If you have a pointer named `ptr` that has been initialized to point to the variable `var`, the following are true:

- `*ptr` and `var` both refer to the contents of `var` (that is, whatever value the program has stored there).
- `ptr` and `&var` refer to the address of `var`.

As you can see, a pointer name without the indirection operator accesses the pointer value itself, which is, of course, the address of the variable pointed to.

Listing 9.1 demonstrates basic pointer use. You should enter, compile, and run this program.

Input ▼
LISTING 9.1   pointer.c: Basic Pointer Use

```
1:  /* Demonstrates basic pointer use. */
2:
3:  #include <stdio.h>
4:
5:  /* Declare and initialize an int variable */
6:
7:  int var = 1;
```

```
8:
9:  /* Declare a pointer to int */
10:
11: int *ptr;
12:
13: int main( void )
14: {
15:     /* Initialize ptr to point to var */
16:
17:     ptr = &var;
18:
19:     /* Access var directly and indirectly */
20:
21:     printf("\nDirect access, var = %d", var);
22:     printf("\nIndirect access, var = %d", *ptr);
23:
24:     /* Display the address of var two ways */
25:
26:     printf("\n\nThe address of var = %p", &var);
27:     printf("\nThe address of var = %p\n", ptr);
28:
29:     return 0;
30: }
```

Output ▼

```
Direct access, var = 1
Indirect access, var = 1

The address of var = 4202496
The address of var = 4202496
```

NOTE | The address reported for var will probably not be 4202496 on your system.

Analysis ▼

In this listing, two variables are declared. On line 7, var is declared as an int and initialized to 1. On line 11, a pointer to a variable of type int is declared and named ptr. On line 17, the pointer ptr is assigned the address of var using the address-of operator (&). The rest of the program prints the values from these two variables to the screen. Line 21 prints the value of var, whereas line 22 prints the value stored in the location pointed to by ptr. In this program, this value is 1. Line 26 prints the address of var using the address-of operator. This is the same value printed by line 27 using the pointer variable, ptr.

This listing is good to study. It shows the relationship between a variable, its address, a pointer, and the dereferencing of a pointer.

DO	DON'T
DO understand what pointers are and how they work. The mastering of C requires mastering pointers.	**DON'T** use an uninitialized pointer until an address has been assigned. Results can be disastrous if you do.

9

Pointers and Variable Types

The previous discussion ignores the fact that different variable types occupy different amounts of memory. For the more common PC operating systems, a `short` takes 2 bytes, a `float` takes 4 bytes, and so on. Each individual byte of memory has its own address, so a multibyte variable actually occupies several addresses.

How, then, do pointers handle the addresses of multibyte variables? Here's how it works: The address of a variable is actually the address of the first (lowest) byte it occupies. This can be illustrated with an example that declares and initializes three variables:

```
short vshort = 12252;
char vchar = 90;
float vfloat = 1200.156004;
```

These variables are stored in memory, as shown in Figure 9.5. In this figure, the `short` variable occupies 2 bytes, the `char` variable occupies 1 byte, and the `float` variable occupies 4 bytes.

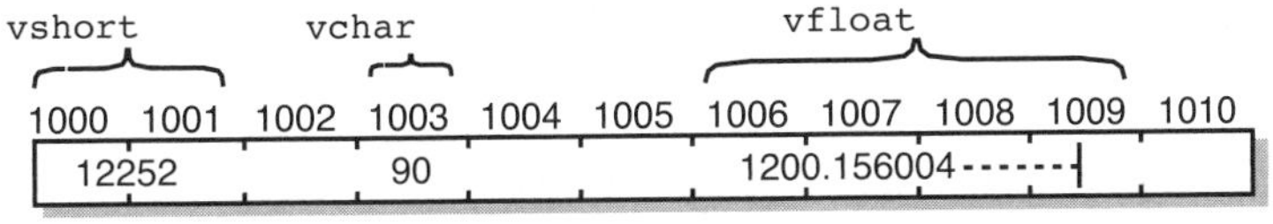

FIGURE 9.5
Different types of numeric variables occupy different amounts of storage space in memory.

Now declare and initialize pointers to these three variables:

```
int *p_vshort;
char *p_vchar;
float *p_vfloat;
/* additional code goes here */
p_vshort = &vshort;
p_vchar = &vchar;
p_vfloat = &vfloat;
```

Each pointer is equal to the address of the first byte of the pointed-to variable. Thus, p_vshort equals 1000, p_vchar equals 1003, and p_vfloat equals 1006. Remember, however, that each pointer was declared to point to a certain type of variable. The compiler knows that a pointer to type short points to the first of 2 bytes, a pointer to type float points to the first of 4 bytes, and so on. This is illustrated in Figure 9.6.

FIGURE 9.6
The compiler knows the size of the variable that a pointer points to.

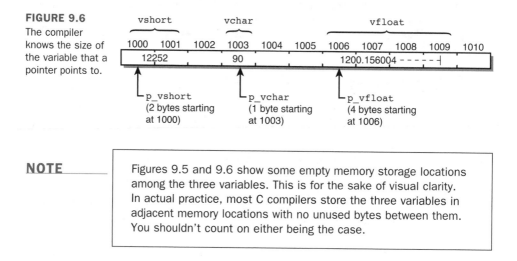

Figures 9.5 and 9.6 show some empty memory storage locations among the three variables. This is for the sake of visual clarity. In actual practice, most C compilers store the three variables in adjacent memory locations with no unused bytes between them. You shouldn't count on either being the case.

Pointers and Arrays

Pointers can be useful when you work with simple variables, but they are more helpful with arrays. There is a special relationship between pointers and arrays in C. Actually, when you use the array subscript notation that you learned in Lesson 8, "Using Numeric Arrays," you're using pointers without knowing it. The following sections explain how this works.

The Array Name as a Pointer

An array name without brackets is a pointer to the array's first element. Thus, if you declare an array data[], data is the address of the first array element.

"Wait a minute," you might be saying. "Don't you need the address-of operator to get an address?" Yes. You can also use the expression &data[0] to obtain the address of the array's first element. In C, the relationship (data == &data[0]) is true.

You've seen that the name of an array is a pointer to the array. The name of an array is a pointer constant; it can't be changed and remains fixed for the entire time the program executes. This makes sense: If you changed its value, it would point elsewhere and not to the array (which remains at a fixed location in memory).

You can, however, declare a pointer variable and initialize it to point at the array. For example, the following code initializes the pointer variable p_array with the address of the first element of array[]:

```
int array[100], *p_array;
/* additional code goes here */
p_array = array;
```

9

Because p_array is a pointer variable, it can be modified to point elsewhere. Unlike the array name (array), p_array isn't locked into pointing at the first element of array[]. For example, it could be changed to point at other elements of array[]. How would you do this? First, you need to look at how array elements are stored in memory.

Array Element Storage

As you might remember from Lesson 8, the elements of an array are stored in sequential memory locations with the first element in the lowest address. Subsequent array elements (those with an index greater than 0) are stored in higher addresses. How much higher depends on the array's data type (char, int, float, and so forth).

Take an array of type short. As you learned in Lesson 3, "Storing Data: Variables and Constants," a single short variable can occupy 2 bytes of memory. Each array element is therefore located 2 bytes above the preceding element, and the address of each array element is 2 higher than the address of the preceding element. A type float, on the other hand, can occupy 4 bytes. In an array of type float, each array element is located 4 bytes above the preceding element, and the address of each array element is 4 higher than the address of the preceding element.

Figure 9.7 illustrates the relationship between array storage and addresses for a six-element short array and a three-element float array.

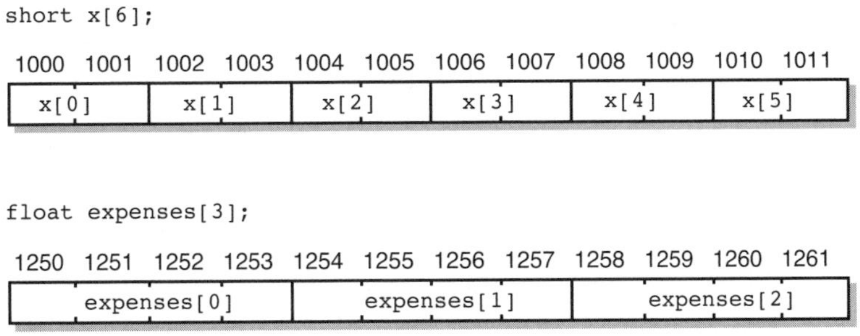

FIGURE 9.7
Array storage for different array types.

```
short x[6];
```

1000	1001	1002	1003	1004	1005	1006	1007	1008	1009	1010	1011
x[0]		x[1]		x[2]		x[3]		x[4]		x[5]	

```
float expenses[3];
```

1250	1251	1252	1253	1254	1255	1256	1257	1258	1259	1260	1261
expenses[0]				expenses[1]				expenses[2]			

By looking at Figure 9.7, you can see why the following relationships are true:

```
1: x == 1000
2: &x[0] == 1000
3: &x[1] == 1002
4: expenses == 1250
5: &expenses[0] == 1250
6: &expenses[1] == 1254
```

x without the array brackets is the address of the first element (&x[0]). You can also see that x[0] is at the address of 1000. Line 2 shows this, too. It can be read like this: "The address of the first element of the array x is equal to 1000." Line 3 shows that the address of the second element (subscripted as 1 in an array) is 1002. Again, Figure 9.7 can confirm this. Lines 4, 5, and 6 are virtually identical to 1, 2, and 3, respectively. They vary in the difference between the addresses of the two array elements. In the type short array x, the difference is 2 bytes, and in the type float array, expenses, the difference is 4 bytes.

How do you access these successive array elements using a pointer? You can see from these examples that a pointer must be increased by 2 to access successive elements of a type short array, and by 4 to access successive elements of a type float array. You can generalize and say that to access successive elements of an array of a particular data type, a pointer must be increased by sizeof(*datatype*). Remember from Lesson 3 that the sizeof() operator returns the size in bytes of a C data type.

Listing 9.2 illustrates the relationship between addresses and the elements of different type arrays by declaring arrays of type short, float, and double and by displaying the addresses of successive elements.

Input ▼
LISTING 9.2   arraysize.c: Displaying the Addresses of Successive Array Elements

```
 1:  /* Demonstrates the relationship between addresses and */
 2:  /* elements of arrays of different data types. */
 3:
 4:  #include <stdio.h>
 5:
 6:  /* Declare a counter and three arrays. */
 7:  int ctr;
 8:  short array_s[10];
 9:  float array_f[10];
10:  double array_d[10];
11:
12:  int main( void )
13:  {
```

```
14:      /* Print the table heading */
15:
16:      printf("\t\tShort\t\tFloat\t\tDouble");
17:
18:      printf("\n=================================");
19:      printf("========================");
20:
21:      /* Print the addresses of each array element. */
22:
23:      for (ctr = 0; ctr < 10; ctr++)
24:          printf("\nElement %d:\t%p\t\t%p\t\t%p", ctr,
25:              &array_s[ctr], &array_f[ctr], &array_d[ctr]);
26:
27:      printf("\n=================================");
28:      printf("=======================\n");
29:
30:      return 0;
31: }
```

9

Output ▼

	Short	Float	Double
Element 0:	4210896	4210752	4210816
Element 1:	4210898	4210756	4210824
Element 2:	4210900	4210760	4210832
Element 3:	4210902	4210764	4210840
Element 4:	4210904	4210768	4210848
Element 5:	4210906	4210772	4210856
Element 6:	4210908	4210776	4210864
Element 7:	4210910	4210780	4210872
Element 8:	4210912	4210784	4210880
Element 9:	4210914	4210788	4210888

Analysis ▼

The exact addresses that your system displays will be different from these, but the relationships are the same. In this output, there are 2 bytes between short elements, 4 bytes between float elements, and 8 bytes between double elements.

NOTE

> Some machines use different sizes for variable types. If your machine differs, the preceding output might have different-size gaps; however, they will be consistent gaps.

This listing takes advantage of the escape characters discussed in Lesson 7, "Fundamentals of Reading and Writing Information." The `printf()` calls on lines 16 and 24 use the tab escape character (`\t`) to help format the table by aligning the columns.

Looking more closely at Listing 9.2, you can see that three arrays are created on lines 8, 9, and 10. Line 8 declares array `array_s` of type `short`, line 9 declares array `array_f` of type `float`, and line 10 declares array `array_d` of type `double`. Line 16 prints the column headers for the table that will be displayed. Lines 18 and 19, along with lines 27 and 28, print dashed lines across the top and bottom of the table data. This is a nice touch for a report. Lines 23, 24, and 25 are a `for` loop that prints each of the table's rows. The number of the element `ctr` is printed first. This is followed by the address of the element in each of the three arrays.

Pointer Arithmetic

You have a pointer to the first array element; the pointer must increment by an amount equal to the size of the data type stored in the array. How do you access array elements using pointer notation? You use *pointer arithmetic.*

"Just what I don't need," you might be thinking, "another kind of arithmetic to learn!" Don't worry. Pointer arithmetic is simple, and it makes using pointers in your programs much easier. You have to be concerned with only two pointer operations: incrementing and decrementing.

Incrementing Pointers

When you *increment* a pointer, you increase its value. For example, when you increment a pointer by 1, pointer arithmetic automatically increases the pointer's value so that it points to the next array element. In other words, C knows the data type that the pointer points to (from the pointer declaration) and increases the address stored in the pointer by the size of the data type.

Suppose that `ptr_to_short` is a pointer variable to some element of a `short` array. If you execute the statement

```
ptr_to_short++;
```

the value of `ptr_to_short` is increased by the size of type `short` (usually 2 bytes), and `ptr_to_short` now points to the next array element. Likewise, if `ptr_to_float` points to an element of a type `float` array, the statement

```
ptr_to_float++;
```

increases the value of `ptr_to_float` by the size of type `float` (usually 4 bytes).

The same holds true for increments greater than 1. If you add the value *n* to a pointer, C increments the pointer by *n* array elements of the associated data type. Therefore,

```
ptr_to_short += 4;
```

increases the value stored in `ptr_to_short` by 8 (assuming that a short is 2 bytes), so it points four array elements ahead. Likewise,

```
ptr_to_float += 10;
```

increases the value stored in `ptr_to_float` by 40 (assuming that a float is 4 bytes), so it points 10 array elements ahead.

9

Decrementing Pointers

The same concepts that apply to incrementing pointers hold true for decrementing pointers. *Decrementing* a pointer is actually a special case of incrementing by adding a negative value. If you decrement a pointer with the `--` or `-=` operators, pointer arithmetic automatically adjusts for the size of the array elements.

Listing 9.3 presents an example of how pointer arithmetic can be used to access array elements. By incrementing pointers, the program can step through all the elements of the arrays efficiently.

Input ▼

LISTING 9.3   ptr_math.c: Using Pointer Arithmetic and Pointer Notation to Access Array Elements

```
1:   /* ptr_math.c--Demonstrates using pointer arithmetic to
2:       access array elements with pointer notation. */
3:
4:   #include <stdio.h>
5:   #define MAX 10
6:
7:   // Declare and initialize an integer array.
8:
9:   int i_array[MAX] = { 0,1,2,3,4,5,6,7,8,9 };
10:
11:  // Declare a pointer to int and an int variable.
12:
13:  int *i_ptr, count;
14:
15:  // Declare and initialize a float array.
16:
17:  float f_array[MAX] = { .0, .1, .2, .3, .4, .5, .6, .7, .8, .9 };
18:
19:  // Declare a pointer to float.
20:
```

```
21:   float *f_ptr;
22:
23:   int main( void )
24:   {
25:        /* Initialize the pointers. */
26:
27:        i_ptr = i_array;
28:        f_ptr = f_array;
29:
30:        /* Print the array elements. */
31:
32:        for (count = 0; count < MAX; count++)
33:             printf("%d\t%f\n", *i_ptr++, *f_ptr++);
34:
35:        return 0;
36:   }
```

Output ▼

```
0        0.000000
1        0.100000
2        0.200000
3        0.300000
4        0.400000
5        0.500000
6        0.600000
7        0.700000
8        0.800000
9        0.900000
```

Analysis ▼

In this program, a defined constant named MAX is set to 10 on line 5; it is used throughout the listing. On line 9, MAX is used to set the number of elements in an array of ints named i_array. The elements in this array are initialized at the same time that the array is declared. Line 13 declares two additional int variables. The first is a pointer named i_ptr. You know this is a pointer because the indirection operator (*) is used. The other variable is a simple type int variable named count. On line 17, a second array is defined and initialized. This array is of type float, contains MAX values, and is initialized with float values. Line 21 declares a pointer to a float named f_ptr.

The main() function is on lines 23 through 36. The program assigns the beginning address of the two arrays to the pointers of their respective types on lines 27 and 28. Remember, an array name without a subscript is the same as the address of the array's beginning. A for statement on lines 32 and 33 uses the int variable count to count from 0 to the value of MAX. For each count, line 33 dereferences the two pointers and prints their values in a `printf()` function call. The increment operator then increments each of the pointers so that each points to the next element in the array before continuing with the next iteration of the `for` loop.

You might be thinking that this program could just as well have used array subscript notation and dispensed with pointers altogether. This is true, and in simple programming tasks like this, the use of pointer notation doesn't offer any major advantages. As you start to write more complex programs, however, you will find the use of pointers advantageous.

Remember that you can't perform incrementing and decrementing operations on pointer constants. (An array name without brackets is a *pointer constant*.) Also remember that when you manipulate pointers to array elements, the C compiler doesn't keep track of the start and finish of the array. If you're not careful, you can increment or decrement the pointer so that it points somewhere in memory before or after the array. Something is stored there, but it isn't an array element. You should keep track of pointers and where they're pointing.

9

Other Pointer Manipulations

The other pointer arithmetic operation that you want to use is called *differencing,* which refers to subtracting two pointers. If you have two pointers to different elements of the same array, you can subtract them and find out how far apart they are. Again, pointer arithmetic automatically scales the answer so that it refers to the number of array elements. Thus, if `ptr1` and `ptr2` point to elements of an array (of any type), the following expression tells you how far apart the elements are:

```
ptr1 - ptr2
```

You can also compare pointers. Pointer comparisons are valid only between pointers that point to the same array. Under these circumstances, the relational operators `==`, `!=`, `>`, `<`, `>=`, and `<=` work properly. Lower array elements (that is, those having a lower subscript) always have a lower address than higher array elements. Thus, if `ptr1` and `ptr2` point to elements of the same array, the comparison

```
ptr1 < ptr2
```

is true if `ptr1` points to an earlier member of the array than `ptr2` does.

This covers all allowed pointer operations. Many arithmetic operations that can be performed with regular variables, such as multiplication and division, don't make sense with pointers. The C compiler doesn't allow them. For example, if `ptr` is a pointer, the statement

```
ptr *= 2;
```

generates an error message. Table 9.1 indicates all the operations you can do with a pointer, all of which have been covered in this lesson.

TABLE 9.1 Pointer Operations

Operation	Description
Assignment	You can assign a value to a pointer. The value should be an address, obtained with the address-of operator (&) or from a pointer constant (array name).
Indirection	The indirection operator (*) gives the value stored in the pointed-to location (often called dereferencing).
Address-of	You can use the address-of operator to find the address of a pointer, so you can have pointers to pointers. This is an advanced topic and is covered in Lesson 15, "Pointers to Pointers and Arrays of Pointers."
Incrementing	You can add an integer to a pointer to point to a different memory location.
Decrementing	You can subtract an integer from a pointer to point to a different memory location.
Differencing	You can subtract one pointer from another pointer to determine how far apart they are.
Comparison	Valid only with two pointers that point to the same array.

Pointer Cautions

When you write a program that uses pointers, you must avoid one serious error: using an uninitialized pointer on the left side of an assignment statement. For example, the following statement declares a pointer to type `int`:

```
int *ptr;
```

This pointer isn't yet initialized, so it doesn't point to anything. To be more exact, it doesn't point to anything *known*. An uninitialized pointer has some value; you just don't know what it is. In many cases, it is zero. If you use an uninitialized pointer in an assignment statement, this is what happens:

```
*ptr = 12;
```

The value `12` is assigned to whatever address `ptr` points to. That address can be almost anywhere in memory—where the operating system is stored or somewhere in the program's code. The `12` that is stored there might overwrite some important information, and the result can be anything from strange program errors to a full system crash.

The left side of an assignment statement is the most dangerous place to use an uninitialized pointer. Other errors, although less serious, can also result from using an uninitialized pointer anywhere in your program, so be sure your program's pointers are properly initialized before you use them. You must do this yourself; don't assume that the compiler will do this for you.

DO	DON'T
DO remember that subtracting from or adding to a pointer changes the pointer based on the size of the data type it points to. It doesn't change it by 1 or by the number being added (unless it's a pointer to a 1-byte character).	**DON'T** try to perform mathematical operations such as division, multiplication, and modulus on pointers. Adding (incrementing) and subtracting (differencing) pointers are acceptable.
DO understand the size of variable types on your computer. As you can begin to see, you need to know variable sizes when working with pointers and memory.	**DON'T** try to increment or decrement an array variable. Assign a pointer to the beginning address of the array and increment it (refer to Listing 9.3).

9

Array Subscript Notation and Pointers

An array name without brackets is a pointer to the array's first element. Therefore, you can access the first array element using the indirection operator. If `array[]` is a declared array, the expression `*array` is the array's first element, `*(array + 1)` is the array's second element, and so on. If you generalize for the entire array, the following relationships hold true:

```
*(array)     == array[0]
*(array + 1) == array[1]
*(array + 2) == array[2]
...
*(array + n) == array[n]
```

This illustrates the equivalence of array subscript notation and array pointer notation. You can use either in your programs; the C compiler sees them as two different ways of accessing array data using pointers.

Passing Arrays to Functions

This lesson has already discussed the special relationship that exists in C between pointers and arrays. This relationship comes into play when you need to pass an array as an argument to a function. The only way you can pass an array to a function is by using a pointer.

As you learned in Lesson 5, "Packaging Code in Functions," an argument is a value that the calling program passes to a function. It can be an `int`, a `float`, or any other simple data type, but it must be a single numerical value. It can be a single array element, but it can't be an entire array. What if you need to pass an entire array to a function? Well, you can have a pointer to an array, and that pointer is a single numeric value (the address of the array's first element). If you pass that value to a function, the function knows the address of the array and can access the array elements using pointer notation.

Consider another problem. If you write a function that takes an array as an argument, you want a function that can handle arrays of different sizes. For example, you could write a function that finds the largest element in an array of integers. The function wouldn't be much use if it were limited to dealing with arrays of one fixed size.

How does the function know the size of the array whose address it was passed? Remember, the value passed to a function is a pointer to the first array element. It could be the first of 10 elements or the first of 10,000. There are two methods of letting a function know an array's size.

You can identify the last array element by storing a special value there. As the function processes the array, it looks for that value in each element. When the value is found, the end of the array has been reached. The disadvantage of this method is that it forces you to reserve a value as the end-of-array indicator, reducing the flexibility you have for storing real data in the array.

The other method is more flexible and straightforward, and it's the one used in this book: Pass the function the array size as an argument. This can be a simple type `int` argument. Thus, the function is passed two arguments: a pointer to the first array element and an integer specifying the number of elements in the array.

Listing 9.4 accepts a list of values from the user and stores them in an array. It then calls a function named `largest()`, passing the array (both pointer and size). The function finds the largest value in the array and returns it to the calling program.

Input ▼

LISTING 9.4   arraypass.c: Passing an Array to a Function

```
1:  /* arraypass.c--Passing an array to a function. */
2:
3:  #include <stdio.h>
4:
5:  #define MAX 10
6:
7:  int array[MAX], count;
8:
9:  int largest(int num_array[], int length);
10:
11: int main( void )
12: {
13:     /* Input MAX values from the keyboard. */
14:
15:     for (count = 0; count < MAX; count++)
16:     {
17:         printf("Enter an integer value: ");
18:         scanf("%d", &array[count]);
19:     }
20:
21:     /* Call the function and display the return value. */
22:     printf("\n\nLargest value = %d\n", largest(array, MAX));
23:
24:     return 0;
25: }
26: /* Function largest() returns the largest value */
27: /* in an integer array */
28:
29: int largest(int num_array[], int length)
30: {
31:     int count, biggest;
32:
33:     for ( count = 0; count < length; count++)
34:     {
35:         if (count == 0)
36:             biggest = num_array[count];
37:         if (num_array[count] > biggest)
38:             biggest = num_array[count];
39:     }
40:
41:     return biggest;
42: }
```

9

Output ▼

```
Enter an integer value: 90
Enter an integer value: -5
Enter an integer value: 234
Enter an integer value: 0
Enter an integer value: 1
Enter an integer value: 123
Enter an integer value: -789
Enter an integer value: 18
Enter an integer value: 4
Enter an integer value: 9

Largest value = 234
```

Analysis ▼

The function used in this example to accept a pointer to an array is called `largest()`. The function prototype is on line 9 and with the exception of the semicolon, it is identical to the function header on line 29.

Most of what is presented in the function header on line 29 should make sense to you: `largest()` is a function that returns an `int` to the calling program; its second argument is an `int` represented by the parameter `length`. The only thing new is the first parameter, `int num_array[]`, which indicates that the first argument is a pointer to type `int`, represented by the parameter `num_array`. You also could write the function declaration and header as follows:

```
int largest(int *num_array, int length);
```

This is equivalent to the first form; both `int num_array[]` and `int *num_array` mean "pointer to `int`." The first form might be preferable because it reminds you that the parameter represents a pointer to an array. Of course, the pointer doesn't know that it points to an array, but the function uses it that way.

Now look at the function `largest()`. When it is called, the parameter `num_array` holds the value of the first argument and is therefore a pointer to the first element of the array. You can use x anywhere an array pointer can be used. In `largest()`, the array elements are accessed using subscript notation on lines 35 and 36. You also could use pointer notation, rewriting the `if` loop like this:

```
for (count = 0; count < length; count++)
{
    if (count == 0)
      biggest = *(num_array+count);
    if (*(num_array+count) > biggest)
      biggest = *(num_array+count);
}
```

Listing 9.5 shows the other way of passing arrays to functions.

Input ▼

LISTING 9.5   arraypass2.c: An Alternative Way of Passing an Array to a Function

```
1:  /* arraypass2.c--Passing an array to a function. Alternative way. */
2:
3:  #include <stdio.h>
4:
5:  #define MAX 10
6:
7:  int array[MAX+1], count;
8:
9:  int largest(int num_array[]);
10:
11: int main( void )
12: {
13:     /* Input MAX values from the keyboard. */
14:
15:     for (count = 0; count < MAX; count++)
16:     {
17:         printf("Enter an integer value: ");
18:         scanf("%d", &array[count]);
19:
20:         if ( array[count] == 0 )
21:             count = MAX;                    /* will exit for loop */
22:     }
23:     array[MAX] = 0;
24:
25:     /* Call the function and display the return value. */
26:     printf("\n\nLargest value = %d\n", largest(array));
27:
28:     return 0;
29: }
30: /* Function largest() returns the largest value */
31: /* in an integer array */
32:
33: int largest(int num_array[])
34: {
35:     int count, biggest;
36:
37:     for ( count = 0; num_array[count] != 0; count++)
38:     {
39:         if (count == 0)
40:             biggest = num_array[count];
41:         if (num_array[count] > biggest)
42:             biggest = num_array[count];
43:     }
44:
45:     return biggest;
46: }
```

9

Output ▼

```
Enter an integer value: 1
Enter an integer value: 2
Enter an integer value: 3
Enter an integer value: 4
Enter an integer value: 5
Enter an integer value: 10
Enter an integer value: 9
Enter an integer value: 8
Enter an integer value: 7
Enter an integer value: 6

Largest value = 10
```

Here is the output from running the program a second time:

Output ▼

```
Enter an integer value: 10
Enter an integer value: 20
Enter an integer value: 55
Enter an integer value: 3
Enter an integer value: 12
Enter an integer value: 0

Largest value = 55
```

Analysis ▼

This program uses a `largest()` function that has the same functionality as Listing 9.4. The difference is that only the array tag is needed. The `for` loop in line 37 continues looking for the largest value until it encounters a `0`, at which point it knows it is done.

Looking at the early parts of this program, you can see the differences between Listing 9.4 and Listing 9.5. First, in line 7 you need to add an extra element to the array to store the value that indicates the end. In lines 20 and 21, an `if` statement is added to see whether the user entered `0`, thus signaling that he is done entering values. If `0` is entered, `count` is set to its maximum value so that the `for` loop can be exited cleanly. Line 23 ensures that the last element is `0` in case the user entered the maximum number of values (`MAX`).

By adding the extra commands when entering the data, you can make the `largest()` function work with any size of array; however, there is one catch. What happens if you forget to put a `0` at the end of the array? `largest()` continues past the end of the array, comparing values in memory until it finds a `0`.

As you can see, passing an array to a function is not particularly difficult. You simply pass a pointer to the array's first element. In most situations, you also need to pass the number of elements in the array. In the function, the pointer value can be used to access the array elements with either subscript or pointer notation.

CAUTION

> Recall from Lesson 5 that when a simple variable is passed to a function, only a copy of the variable's value is passed. The function can use the value but can't change the original variable because it doesn't have access to the variable itself. When you pass an array to a function, things are different. A function is passed the array's address, not just a copy of the values in the array. The code in the function works with the actual array elements and can modify the values stored in the array.

9

Summary

This lesson introduced you to pointers, a central part of C programming. A pointer is a variable that holds the address of another variable; a pointer is said to "point to" the variable whose address it holds. The two operators needed with pointers are the address-of operator ($\&$) and the indirection operator ($*$). When placed before a variable name, the address-of operator returns the variable's address. When placed before a pointer name, the indirection operator returns the contents of the pointed-to variable.

Pointers and arrays have a special relationship. An array name without brackets is a pointer to the array's first element. The special features of pointer arithmetic make it easy to access array elements using pointers. Array subscript notation is in fact a special form of pointer notation.

You also learned to pass arrays as arguments to functions by passing a pointer to the array. When the function knows the array's address and length, it can access the array elements using either pointer notation or subscript notation.

Q&A

Q Why are pointers so important in C?

A Pointers give you more control over the computer and your data. When used with functions, pointers enable you to change the values of variables that were passed, regardless of where they originated. In Lesson 15 and Lesson 16, "Pointers to Functions and Linked Lists," you learn additional uses for pointers.

Q How does the compiler know the difference between * for multiplication, for dereferencing, and for declaring a pointer?

A The compiler interprets the different uses of the asterisk based on the context in which it is used. If the statement being evaluated starts with a variable type, it can be assumed that the asterisk is for declaring a pointer. If the asterisk is used with a variable that has been declared as a pointer, but not in a variable declaration, the asterisk is assumed to dereference. If it is used in a mathematical expression, but not with a pointer variable, the asterisk can be assumed to be the multiplication operator.

Q What happens if I use the address-of operator on a pointer?

A You get the address of the pointer variable. Remember, a pointer is just another variable that holds the address of the variable to which it points.

Q Are variables always stored in the same location?

A No. Each time a program runs, its variables can be stored at different addresses within the computer. You should never assign a constant address value to a pointer.

Workshop

The Workshop provides quiz questions to help you solidify your understanding of the material covered and exercises to provide you with experience in using what you've learned.

Quiz

1. What operator is used to determine the address of a variable?

2. What operator is used to determine the value at the location pointed to by a pointer?

3. What is a pointer?

4. What is indirection?

5. How are the elements of an array stored in memory?

6. Show two ways to obtain the address of the first element of the array `data[]`.

7. If an array is passed to a function, what are two ways to know where the end of that array is?

8. What are the six operations covered in this lesson that can be accomplished with a pointer?

9. Assume that you have two pointers. If the first points to the third element in an array of `ints` and the second points to the fourth element, what value is obtained if you subtract the first pointer from the second? (Assume that the size of an integer is 2 bytes.)

10. Assume that the array in question 9 is of `float` values. What value is obtained if the two pointers are subtracted? (Assume that the size of a float is 2 bytes.)

9

Exercises

1. Show a declaration for a pointer to a type `char` variable. Name the pointer `char_ptr`.

2. If you have a type `int` variable named `cost`, how would you declare and initialize a pointer named `p_cost` that points to that variable?

3. Continuing with exercise 2, how would you assign the value `100` to the variable `cost` using both direct access and indirect access?

4. Continuing with exercise 3, how would you print the value of the pointer, plus the value being pointed to?

5. Show how to assign the address of a `float` value called `radius` to a pointer.

6. Show two ways to assign the value `100` to the third element of `data[]`.

7. Write a function named `sumarrays()` that accepts two arrays as arguments, totals all values in both arrays, and returns the total to the calling program.

8. Use the function created in exercise 7 in a simple program.

9. Write a function named `addarrays()` that accepts two arrays that are the same size. The function should add each element in the arrays together and place the values in a third array.

LESSON 10
Working with Characters and Strings

A *character* is a single letter, numeral, punctuation mark, or other such symbol. A *string* is any sequence of characters. Strings are used to hold text data, which is composed of letters, numerals, punctuation marks, and other symbols. Clearly, characters and strings are extremely useful in many programming applications. In this lesson you learn:

- How to use C's `char` data type to hold single characters
- How to create arrays of type `char` to hold multiple-character strings
- How to initialize characters and strings
- How to use pointers with strings
- How to print and input characters and strings

The `char` **Data Type**

C uses the `char` data type to hold characters. You saw in Lesson 3, "Storing Information: Variables and Constants," that `char` is one of C's numeric integer data types. If `char` is a numeric type, how can it be used to hold characters?

The answer lies in how C stores characters. Your computer's memory stores all data in numeric form. There is no direct way to store characters. However, a numeric code exists for each character. This is called the *ASCII code* or the *ASCII character set.* (*ASCII* stands for American Standard Code for Information Interchange.) The code assigns values between `0` and `255` for uppercase and lowercase letters, numeric digits, punctuation marks, and other symbols. The ASCII character set is listed in Appendix A, "ASCII Chart."

NOTE

> The ASCII codes and ASCII character set is targeted toward systems using a single-byte character set. On systems using multibyte character sets, you would use a different character set. This is, however, beyond the scope of this book.

For example, 97 is the ASCII code for the letter a. When you store the character `a` in a type `char` variable, you're actually storing the value `97`. Because the allowable numeric range for type `char` matches the standard ASCII character set, `char` is ideally suited for storing characters.

At this point, you might be a bit puzzled. If C stores characters as numbers, how does your program know whether a given type `char` variable is a character or a number? As you'll learn later, declaring a variable as type `char` is not enough; you must do something else with the variable:

- If a `char` variable is used somewhere in a C program where a character is expected, it is interpreted as a character.

- If a `char` variable is used somewhere in a C program where a number is expected, it is interpreted as a number.

This gives you some understanding of how C uses a numeric data type to store character data. Now you can go on to the details.

Using Character Variables

Like other variables, you must declare chars before using them, and you can initialize them at the time of declaration. Here are some examples:

```
char a, b, c;          /* Declare three uninitialized char variables */
char code = 'x';       /* Declare the char variable named code */
                       /* and store the character x there */
code = '!';            /* Store ! in the variable named code */
```

To create literal character constants, you enclose a single character in single quotation marks. The compiler automatically translates literal character constants into the corresponding ASCII codes, and the numeric code value is assigned to the variable.

You can create symbolic character constants by using either the #define directive or the const keyword:

```
#define EX 'x'

char code = EX;        /* Sets code equal to 'x' */
const char A = 'Z';
```

10

Now that you know how to declare and initialize character variables, it's time for a demonstration. Listing 10.1 illustrates the numeric nature of character storage using the printf() function you learned in Lesson 7, "Fundamentals of Reading and Writing Information." The function printf() can be used to print both characters and numbers. The format string %c instructs printf() to print a character, whereas %d instructs it to print a decimal integer. Listing 10.1 initializes two type char variables and prints each one, first as a character and then as a number.

Input ▼

LISTING 10.1 chartest.c: The Numeric Nature of Type char Variables

```
1:  /* chartest.c--Demonstrates the numeric nature of char variables */
2:
3:  #include <stdio.h>
4:
5:  /* Declare and initialize two char variables */
6:
7:  char c1 = 'a';
8:  char c2 = 90;
9:
10: int main( void )
11: {
12:      /* Print variable c1 as a character, then as a number */
13:
```

```
14:        printf("\nAs a character, variable c1 is %c", c1);
15:        printf("\nAs a number, variable c1 is %d", c1);
16:
17:        /* Do the same for variable c2 */
18:
19:        printf("\nAs a character, variable c2 is %c", c2);
20:        printf("\nAs a number, variable c2 is %d\n", c2);
21:
22:        return 0;
23: }
```

Output ▼

```
As a character, variable c1 is a
As a number, variable c1 is 97
As a character, variable c2 is Z
As a number, variable c2 is 90
```

Analysis ▼

You learned in Lesson 3 that the allowable range for a variable of type char goes only to 127, whereas the ASCII codes go to 255. The ASCII codes are actually divided into two parts. The standard ASCII codes go only to 127; this range includes all letters, numbers, punctuation marks, and other keyboard symbols. The codes from 128 to 255 are the extended ASCII codes and represent special characters such as foreign letters and graphics symbols (see Appendix A for a full list). Thus, for standard text data, you can use type char variables; if you want to print the extended ASCII characters, you must use an unsigned char.

Listing 10.2 prints some of the extended ASCII characters.

Input ▼
LISTING 10.2 ascii.c: Printing Extended ASCII Characters

```
1:   /* Demonstrates printing extended ASCII characters */
2:
3:   #include <stdio.h>
4:
5:   unsigned char mychar;     /* Must be unsigned for extended ASCII */
6:
7:   int main( void )
8:   {
9:       /* Print extended ASCII characters 180 through 203 */
10:
11:      for (mychar = 180; mychar < 204; mychar++)
12:      {
```

```
13:          printf("ASCII code %d is character %c\n", mychar, mychar);
14:      }
15:
16:      return 0;
17: }
```

Output ▼

```
ASCII Code 180 is character ┤
ASCII Code 181 is character ╡
ASCII Code 182 is character ╢
ASCII Code 183 is character ╖
ASCII Code 184 is character ╕
ASCII Code 185 is character ╣
ASCII Code 186 is character ║
ASCII Code 187 is character ╗
ASCII Code 188 is character ╝
ASCII Code 189 is character ╜
ASCII Code 190 is character ╛
ASCII Code 191 is character ┐
ASCII Code 192 is character └
ASCII Code 193 is character ┴
ASCII Code 194 is character ┬
ASCII Code 195 is character ├
ASCII Code 196 is character ─
ASCII Code 197 is character +
ASCII Code 198 is character ╞
ASCII Code 199 is character ╟
ASCII Code 200 is character ╚
ASCII Code 201 is character ╔
ASCII Code 202 is character ╩
ASCII Code 203 is character ╦
```

10

Analysis ▼

Looking at this program, you see that line 5 declares an unsigned character variable, mychar. This gives a range of 0 to 255. As with other numeric data types, you must not initialize a char variable to a value outside the allowed range, or you might get unexpected results. On line 11, mychar is not initialized outside the range; instead, it is initialized to 180. In the for statement, mychar is incremented by 1 until it reaches 204. Each time mychar is incremented, line 13 prints the value of mychar and the character value of mychar. Remember that %c prints the character, or ASCII, value of mychar.

DO	**DON'T**
DO use %c to print the character value of a number.	**DON'T** use double quotations when initializing a character variable.
DO use single quotations when initializing a variable.	**DON'T** try to put extended ASCII character values into a signed char variable.
DO look at the ASCII chart in Appendix A to see the interesting characters that can be printed.	

CAUTION   Some computer systems might use a different character set; however, most use the same ASCII values for 0 to 127.

Using Strings

Variables of type char can hold only a single character, so they have limited usefulness. You also need a way to store *strings*. A string is simply a sequence of characters. A person's name and address are examples of strings. Although there is no special data type for strings, C handles this type of information with arrays of characters.

Arrays of Characters

To hold a string of six characters, for example, you need to declare an array of type char with seven elements. Arrays of type char are declared like arrays of other data types. For example, the statement

```
char string[10];
```

declares a 10-element array of type char. This array could be used to hold a string of nine or fewer characters.

"But wait," you might say. "It's a 10-element array, so why can it hold only nine characters?" In C, a string is defined as a sequence of characters ending with the null character. The null character is a special character represented by \0. Although it's represented by two characters (backslash and zero), the null character is interpreted as a single character and has the ASCII value of 0. It's one of C's escape sequences.

NOTE   Escape sequences were covered in Lesson 7.

When a C program stores the string `Alabama`, for example, it stores the seven characters A, l, a, b, a, m, and a, followed by the null character \0, for a total of eight characters. Thus, a character array can hold a string of characters numbering one less than the total number of elements in the array.

Initializing Character Arrays

Like other C data types, character arrays can be initialized when they are declared. Character arrays can be assigned values element by element, as shown here:

```
char string[10] = { 'A', 'l', 'a', 'b', 'a', 'm', 'a', '\0' };
```

It's more convenient, however, to use a *literal string,* which is a sequence of characters enclosed in double quotes:

```
char string[10] = "Alabama";
```

When you use a literal string in your program, the compiler automatically adds the terminating null character at the end of the string. If you don't specify the number of subscripts when you declare an array, the compiler calculates the size of the array for you. Thus, the following line creates and initializes an eight-element array:

```
char string[] = "Alabama";
```

Remember that strings require a terminating null character. The C functions that manipulate strings (covered in Lesson 18, "Manipulating Strings") determine string length by looking for the null character. These functions have no other way of recognizing the end of the string. If the null character is missing, your program thinks that the string extends until the next null character in memory. Pesky program bugs can result from this sort of error.

Strings and Pointers

You've seen that strings are stored in arrays of type `char`, with the end of the string (which might not occupy the entire array) marked by the null character. Because the end of the string is marked, all you need to define a given string is something that points to its beginning. (Is *points* the right word? Indeed it is!)

With that hint, you might be leaping ahead of the game. From Lesson 9, "Understanding Pointers," you know that the name of an array is a pointer to the first element of the array. Therefore, for a string that's stored in an array, you need only the array name to access it. In fact, using the array's name is C's standard method of accessing strings.

To be more precise, using the array's name to access strings is the method the C library functions expect. The C standard library includes a number of functions that manipulate strings. (These functions are covered in Lesson 18.) To pass a string to one of these functions, you pass the array name. The same is true of the string display functions `printf()` and `puts()`, discussed later in the chapter.

You might have noticed that "strings stored in an array" was mentioned a moment ago. Does this imply that some strings aren't stored in arrays? Indeed it does, and the next section explains why.

Strings Without Arrays

From the preceding section, you know that a string is defined by the character array's name and a null character. The array's name is a type `char` pointer to the beginning of the string. The null marks the string's end. The actual space occupied by the string in an array is incidental. In fact, the only purpose the array serves is to provide allocated space for the string.

What if you could find some memory storage space without allocating an array? You could then store a string with its terminating null character there instead. A pointer to the first character could serve to specify the string's beginning just as if the string were in an allocated array. How do you go about finding memory storage space? There are two methods: One allocates space for a literal string when the program is compiled, and the other uses the `malloc()` function to allocate space while the program is executing, a process known as *dynamic allocation*.

Allocating String Space at Compilation

The start of a string, as mentioned earlier, is indicated by a pointer to a variable of type `char`. You might recall how to declare such a pointer:

```
char *message;
```

This statement declares a pointer to a variable of type `char` named `message`. It doesn't point to anything now, but what if you changed the pointer declaration to read:

```
char *message = "Great Caesar\'s Ghost!";
```

When this statement executes, the string `Great Caesar's Ghost!` (with a terminating null character) is stored somewhere in memory, and the pointer `message` is initialized to point to the first character of the string. Don't worry where in memory the string is stored; it's handled automatically by the compiler. When defined, `message` is a pointer to the string and can be used as such.

The preceding declaration/initialization is equivalent to the following, and the two notations `*message` and `message[]` also are equivalent; they both mean "a pointer to":

```
char message[] = "Great Caesar\'s Ghost!";
```

This method of allocating space for string storage is fine when you know what string you need when writing the program. What if the program has varying string storage needs, depending on user input or other factors that are unknown when you write the program? You use the `malloc()` function, which lets you allocate storage space on-the-fly.

The `malloc()` Function

The `malloc()` function is one of C's *memory allocation* functions. When you call `malloc()`, you pass it the number of bytes of memory needed. `malloc()` finds and reserves a block of memory of the required size and returns the address of the first byte in the block. You don't need to worry about where the memory is found; it's handled automatically.

The `malloc()` function returns an address, and its return type is a pointer to type `void`. Why `void`? A pointer to type `void` is compatible with all data types. Because the memory allocated by `malloc()` can be used to store any of C's data types, the `void` return type is appropriate.

10

Syntax

The `malloc()` Function

```
#include <stdlib.h>
void *malloc(size_t size);
```

`malloc()` allocates a block of memory that is the number of bytes stated in *size*. By allocating memory as needed with `malloc()` instead of all at once when a program starts, you can use a computer's memory more efficiently. When using `malloc()`, you need to include the `stdlib.h` header file. Some compilers have other header files that can be included; for portability, however, it's best to include `stdlib.h`.

`malloc()` returns a pointer to the allocated block of memory. If `malloc()` cannot allocate the required amount of memory, it returns null. Whenever you try to allocate memory, you should always check the return value, even if the amount of memory to be allocated is small.

Example 1

```
#include <stdlib.h>
#include <stdio.h>
int main( void )
{
    /* allocate memory for a 100-character string */
    char *str;
    str = (char *) malloc(100);
```

```
    if (str == NULL)
    {
        printf( "Not enough memory to allocate buffer\n");
        exit(1);
    }
    printf( "String was allocated!\n" );
    return 0;
}
```

Example 2

```
/* allocate memory for an array of 50 integers */
int *numbers;
numbers = (int *) malloc(50 * sizeof(int));
```

Example 3

```
/* allocate memory for an array of 10 float values */
float *numbers;
numbers = (float *) malloc(10 * sizeof(float));
```

Using the `malloc()` Function

You can use `malloc()` to allocate memory to store a single type `char`. First, declare a pointer to type `char`:

```
char *ptr;
```

Next, call `malloc()` and pass the size of the wanted memory block. Because a type `char` usually occupies 1 byte, you need a block of 1 byte. The value returned by `malloc()` is assigned to the pointer:

```
ptr = malloc(1);
```

This statement allocates a memory block of 1 byte and assigns its address to `ptr`. Unlike variables that are declared in the program, this byte of memory has no name. Only the pointer can reference the variable. For example, to store the character `'x'` there, you would write

```
*ptr = 'x';
```

Allocating storage for a string with `malloc()` is almost identical to using `malloc()` to allocate space for a single variable of type `char`. The main difference is that you need to know the amount of space to allocate—the maximum number of characters in the string. This maximum depends on the needs of your program. For this example, say you want to allocate space for a string of 99 characters, plus 1 for the terminating null character, for a total of 100. First, you declare a pointer to type `char`, and then you call `malloc()`:

```
char *ptr;
ptr = malloc(100);
```

Now `ptr` points to a reserved block of 100 bytes that can be used for string storage and manipulation. You can use `ptr` just as though your program had explicitly allocated that space with the following array declaration:

```
char ptr[100];
```

Using `malloc()` lets your program allocate storage space as needed in response to demand. Of course, available space is not unlimited; it depends on the amount of memory installed in your computer and on the program's other storage requirements. If not enough memory is available, `malloc()` returns null (0). Your program should test the return value of `malloc()` so that you know the memory requested was allocated successfully. You always should test `malloc()`'s return value against the symbolic constant NULL, which is defined in `stdlib.h`. Listing 10.3 illustrates the use of `malloc()`. Any program using `malloc()` must #include the header file `stdlib.h`.

10

TIP

> Literal values were used to allocate space for characters in the above examples. You should always multiply the size of the data type you are allocating space for by the amount of space you want. The previous allocations assumed that a character was stored in just 1 byte. If a character is stored in more than 1 byte, then the previous examples overwrite other areas of memory. For example:
>
> ```
> ptr = malloc(100);
> ```
>
> should actually be declared as
>
> ```
> ptr = malloc( 100 * sizeof(char));
> ```

Input ▼
LISTING 10.3 memalloc.c: Using the `malloc()` Function to Allocate Storage Space for String Data

```
1:  /* memalloc.c--Demonstrates the use of malloc() to allocate storage */
2:  /* space for string data. */
3:
4:  #include <stdio.h>
5:  #include <stdlib.h>
6:
7:  char count, *ptr, *p;
8:
```

```
9:  int main( void )
10: {
11:    /* Allocate a block of 35 bytes. Test for success. */
12:    /* The exit() library function terminates the program. */
13:
14:    ptr = malloc(35 * sizeof(char));
15:
16:    if (ptr == NULL)
17:    {
18:        puts("Memory allocation error.");
19:        return 1;
20:    }
21:
22:    /* Fill the string with values 65 through 90, */
23:    /* which are the ASCII codes for A-Z. */
24:
25:    /* p is a pointer used to step through the string. */
26:    /* You want ptr to remain pointed at the start */
27:    /* of the string. */
28:
29:    p = ptr;
30:
31:    for (count = 65; count < 91 ; count++)
32:        *p++ = count;
33:
34:    /* Add the terminating null character. */
35:
36:    *p = '\0';
37:
38:    /* Display the string on the screen. */
39:
40:    puts(ptr);
41:
42:    free(ptr);
43:
44:    return 0;
45: }
```

Output ▼

ABCDEFGHIJKLMNOPQRSTUVWXYZ

Analysis ▼

This program uses `malloc()` in a simple way. Although the program seems long, it's filled with comments. Lines 1, 2, 11, 12, 22 through 27, 34, and 38 are all comments that detail everything the program does. Line 5 includes the `stdlib.h` header file needed for `malloc()`, and line 4 includes the `stdio.h` header file for the `puts()` functions. Line

7 declares two pointers and a character variable used later in the listing. None of these variables is initialized, so they shouldn't be used—yet!

The `malloc()` function is called in line 14 with a parameter of 35 multiplied by the *size* of a `char`. Could you have just used 35? Yes, but you're assuming that everyone running this program will be using a computer that stores `char` type variables as 1 byte in size. Remember from Lesson 3 that different compilers can use different-size variables. Using the `sizeof` operator is an easy way to create portable code.

Never assume that `malloc()` gets the memory you tell it to get. In fact, you aren't *telling* it to get memory—you're *asking* it. Line 16 shows the easiest way to check whether `malloc()` provided the memory. If the memory was allocated, `ptr` points to it; otherwise, `ptr` is null. If the program failed to get the memory, lines 18 and 19 display an error message and gracefully exit the program.

Line 29 initializes the other pointer declared on line 7, `p`. It is assigned the same address value as `ptr`. A `for` loop uses this new pointer to place values into the allocated memory. Looking at line 31, you see that `count` is initialized to `65` and incremented by `1` until it reaches `91`. For each loop of the `for` statement, the value of `count` is assigned to the address pointed to by `p`. Notice that each time `count` is incremented, the address pointed to by `p` is also incremented. This means that each value is placed one after the other in memory.

10

You should have noticed that numbers are assigned to `count`, which is a type `char` variable. Remember the discussion of ASCII characters and their numeric equivalents? The number 65 is equivalent to `A`, 66 equals `B`, 67 equals `C`, and so on. The `for` loop ends after the alphabet is assigned to the memory locations pointed to. Line 36 caps off the character values pointed to by putting a null at the final address pointed to by `p`. By appending the null, you can now use these values as a string. Remember that `ptr` still points to the first value, `A`, so if you use it as a string, it prints every character until it reaches the null. Line 40 uses `puts()` to prove this point and to show the results of what has been done.

You can notice a new function is used on line 42. This is the `free()` function. Whenever you allocate memory dynamically, you should also unallocate it—or return it—when you finish using it. The free function returns allocated memory, so on line 42, the memory allocated and assigned to `ptr` is returned to the system.

DO	DON'T
	DON'T allocate more memory than you need. Not everyone has a lot of memory, so you should try to use it sparingly. **DON'T** try to assign a new string to a character array that was previously allocated only enough memory to hold a smaller string. For example, in this declaration: `char a_string[] = "NO";` `a_string` points to `"NO"`. If you try to assign `"YES"` to this array, you could have serious problems. The array initially could hold only three characters—`'N'`, `'O'`, and a null. `"YES"` is four characters—`'Y'`, `'E'`, `'S'`, and a null. You have no idea what the fourth character, null, overwrites.

Displaying Strings and Characters

If your program uses string data, it probably needs to display the data on the screen at some time. String display is usually done with either the `puts()` function or the `printf()` function.

The `puts()` Function

You've already seen the `puts()` library function in some of the programs earlier in this book. The `puts()` function puts a string onscreen—hence its name. A pointer to the string to be displayed is the only argument `puts()` takes. Because a literal string evaluates as a pointer to a string, `puts()` can be used to display literal strings as well as string variables. The `puts()` function automatically inserts a newline character at the end of each string it displays, so each subsequent string displayed with `puts()` is on its own line.

Listing 10.4 illustrates the use of `puts()`.

Input ▼

LISTING 10.4   put.c: Using the `puts()` Function to Display Text Onscreen

```
1: /* Demonstrates displaying strings with puts(). */
2:
3: #include <stdio.h>
4:
5: char *message1 = "C";
6: char *message2 = "is the";
7: char *message3 = "best";
8: char *message4 = "programming";
9: char *message5 = "language!!";
10:
11: int main( void )
12: {
13:     puts(message1);
14:     puts(message2);
15:     puts(message3);
16:     puts(message4);
17:     puts(message5);
18:
19:     return 0;
20: }
```

Output ▼

```
C
is the
best
programming
language!!
```

Analysis ▼

This is a fairly simple listing to follow. Because `puts()` is a standard output function, the `stdio.h` header file needs to be included, as done on line 3. Lines 5 through 9 declare and initialize five different message variables. Each of these variables is a character pointer, or string variable. Lines 13 through 17 use the `puts()` function to print each string.

The `printf()` Function

You can also display strings using the `printf()` library function. Recall from Lesson 7 that `printf()` uses a format string and conversion specifiers to shape its output. To display a string, use the conversion specifier `%s`.

When `printf()` encounters a `%s` in its format string, the function matches the `%s` with the corresponding argument in its argument list. For a string, this argument must be a pointer to the string that you want displayed. The `printf()` function displays the string onscreen, stopping when it reaches the string's terminating null character, for example:

```
char *str = "A message to display";
printf("%s", str);
```

You can also display multiple strings and mix them with literal text and/or numeric variables:

```
char *bank = "First Federal";
char *name = "John Doe";
int balance = 1000;
printf("The balance at %s for %s is %d.", bank, name, balance);
```

The resulting output is

```
The balance at First Federal for John Doe is 1000.
```

For now, this information should be sufficient for you to display string data in your programs. Complete details on using `printf()` are given in Lesson 14, "Working with the Screen, Printer, and Keyboard."

Reading Strings from the Keyboard

In addition to displaying strings, programs often need to accept inputted string data from the user via the keyboard. The C library has two functions that can be used for this purpose: `gets()` and `scanf()`. Before you can read in a string from the keyboard, however, you must have somewhere to put it. You can create space for string storage using either of the methods discussed earlier—an array declaration or the `malloc()` function.

Inputting Strings Using the `gets()` Function

The `gets()` function gets a string from the keyboard. When `gets()` is called, it reads all characters typed at the keyboard up to the first newline character (which you generate by pressing Enter). This function discards the newline, adds a null character, and gives the string to the calling program. The string is stored at the location indicated by a pointer to type `char` passed to `gets()`. A program that uses `gets()` must #include the file `stdio.h`. Listing 10.5 presents an example.

Input ▼

LISTING 10.5 get.c: Using `gets()` to Input String Data from the Keyboard

```
 1:  /* Demonstrates using the gets() library function. */
 2:
 3:  #include <stdio.h>
 4:
 5:  /* Allocate a character array to hold input. */
 6:
 7:  char input[257];
 8:
 9:  int main( void )
10:  {
11:      puts("Enter some text, then press Enter: ");
12:      gets(input);
13:      printf("You entered: %s\n", input);
14:
15:      return 0;
16:  }
```

Output ▼

```
Enter some text, then press Enter:
This is a test
You entered: This is a test
```

Analysis ▼

In this example, the argument to `gets()` is the expression `input`, which is the name of a type `char` array and therefore a pointer to the first array element. The array is declared with 257 elements in line 7. Because the maximum line length possible on most computer screens is 256 characters, this array size provides space for the longest possible input line (plus the null character that `gets()` adds at the end).

The `gets()` function has a return value, which was ignored in the previous example. `gets()` returns a pointer to type `char` with the address where the input string is stored. Yes, this is the same value that is passed to `gets()`, but having the value returned to the program in this way lets your program test for a blank line. Listing 10.6 shows how to do this.

10

Input ▼

LISTING 10.6 getback.c: Using the `gets()` Return Value to Test for Input of a Blank Line

```
1:  /* getback.c--Demonstrates using the gets() return value. */
2:
3:  #include <stdio.h>
4:
5:  /* Declare a character array to hold input, and a pointer. */
6:
7:  char input[257], *ptr;
8:
9:  int main( void )
10: {
11:     /* Display instructions. */
12:
13:     puts("Enter text a line at a time, then press Enter.");
14:     puts("Enter a blank line when done.");
15:
16:     /* Loop as long as input is not a blank line. */
17:
18:     while ( *(ptr = gets(input)) != '\0')
19:         printf("You entered %s\n", input);
20:
21:     puts("Thank you and good-bye\n");
22:
23:     return 0;
24: }
```

Output ▼

```
Enter text a line at a time, then press Enter.
Enter a blank line when done.
Friend me on Facebook
You entered Friend me on Facebook
Follow me on Twitter
You entered Follow me on Twitter
You are on your way to mastering C!
You entered You are on your way to mastering C!

Thank you and good-bye
```

Analysis ▼

Now you can see how the program works. If you enter a blank line (that is, if you simply press Enter) in response to line 18, the string (which contains 0 characters) is still stored with a null character at the end. Because the string has a length of 0, the null character is stored in the first position. This is the position pointed to by the return value of `gets()`, so if you test that position and find a null character, you know that a blank line was entered.

Listing 10.6 performs this test in the `while` statement on line 18. This statement is a bit complicated, so look carefully at the details in order. Figure 10.1 illustrates the components of this statement.

CAUTION

> Because it is not always possible to know how many characters `gets()` will read, and because `gets()` will continue to store characters past the end of the buffer, it should be used with caution.

FIGURE 10.1
The components of a `while` statement that tests for input of a blank line.

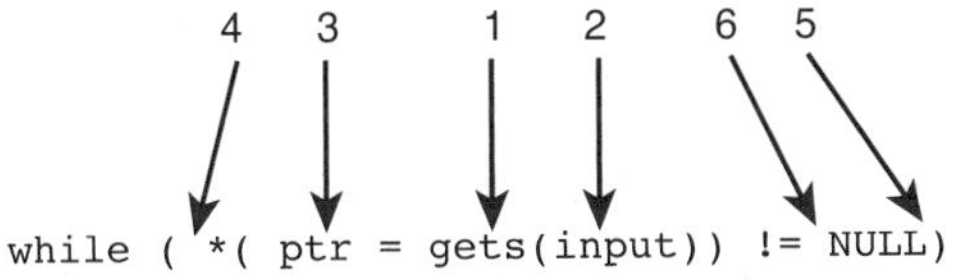

10

```
         4  3    1  2    6 5
while ( *( ptr = gets(input)) != NULL)
```

1. The `gets()` function accepts input from the keyboard until it reaches a newline character.
2. The string entered, minus the newline and with a trailing null character, is stored in the memory location pointed to by `input`.
3. The address of the string (the same value as `input`) is returned to the pointer `ptr`.
4. An *assignment statement* is an expression that evaluates to the value of the variable on the left side of the assignment operator. Therefore, the entire expression `ptr = gets(input)` evaluates to the value of `ptr`. By enclosing this expression in parentheses and preceding it with the indirection operator (`*`), you obtain the value stored at the pointed-to address. This is, of course, the first character of the input string.
5. If the first character of the input string isn't the null character (if a blank line hasn't been entered), the comparison operator returns `true`, and the `while` loop executes. If the first character is the null character (if a blank line has been entered), the comparison operator returns `false`, and the `while` loop terminates.

When you use `gets()` or any other function that stores data using a pointer, be sure that the pointer points to allocated space. It's easy to make a mistake such as this:

```
char *ptr;
gets(ptr);
```

The pointer `ptr` has been declared but not initialized. It points somewhere, but you don't know where. The `gets()` function doesn't know that `ptr` hasn't been initialized to point somewhere, so it simply goes ahead and stores the entered string at whatever address is contained in `ptr`. The string might overwrite something important, such as program code or the operating system. Most compilers won't catch this type of mistake, so you, the programmer, must be vigilant.

Syntax

The `gets()` Function

```
#include <stdio.h>
char *gets(char *str);
```

The `gets()` function gets a string, `str`, from the standard input device, usually the keyboard. The string consists of any characters entered until a newline character is read. At that point, a null is appended to the end of the string.

Then the `gets()` function returns a pointer to the string just read. If there is a problem getting the string, `gets()` returns null.

Example

```
/* gets() example */
#include <stdio.h>
char line[256];int main( void )
{
    printf( "Enter a string:\n");
    gets( line );
    printf( "\nYou entered the following string:\n" );
    printf( "%s\n", line );
}
```

Inputting Strings Using the `scanf()` Function

You saw in Lesson 7 that the `scanf()` library function accepts numeric data input from the keyboard. This function can also input strings. Remember that `scanf()` uses a *format string* that tells it how to read the information entered. To read a string, include the specifier `%s` in `scanf()`'s format string. Like `gets()`, `scanf()` is passed a pointer to the string's storage location.

How does `scanf()` decide where the string begins and ends? The beginning is the first nonwhitespace character encountered. The end can be specified in one of two ways. If you use `%s` in the format string, the string runs up to (but not including) the next whitespace character (space, tab, or newline). If you use `%ns` (where n is an integer constant that specifies field width), `scanf()` accepts the next n characters or up to the next whitespace character, whichever comes first.

You can read in multiple strings with `scanf()` by including more than one `%s` in the format string. For each `%s` in the format string, `scanf()` uses the preceding rules to find the requested number of strings in the input, for example:

```
scanf("%s%s%s", s1, s2, s3);
```

If in response to this statement you enter January February March, January is assigned to the string s1, February is assigned to s2, and March to s3.

What about using the field-width specifier? If you execute the statement

```
scanf("%3s%3s%3s", s1, s2, s3);
```

and in response you enter September, Sep is assigned to s1, tem is assigned to s2, and ber is assigned to s3.

What if you enter fewer or more strings than the `scanf()` function expects? If you enter fewer strings, `scanf()` continues to look for the missing strings, and the program doesn't continue until they're entered. For example, if in response to the statement

```
scanf("%s%s%s", s1, s2, s3);
```

you enter January February, the program sits and waits for the third string specified in the `scanf()` format string. If you enter more strings than requested, the unmatched strings remain pending (waiting in the keyboard buffer) and are read by any subsequent `scanf()` or other input statements. For example, if in response to the statements

```
scanf("%s%s", s1, s2);
scanf("%s", s3);
```

you enter January February March, the result is that January is assigned to the string s1 and February is assigned to s2 in the first `scanf()` call. March is then automatically carried over and assigned to s3 in the second `scanf()` call.

The `scanf()` function has a return value, an integer value equaling the number of items successfully inputted. The return value is often ignored. When you're reading text only, the `gets()` function is usually preferable to `scanf()`. It's best to use the `scanf()` function when you're reading in a combination of text and numeric data. This is illustrated by Listing 10.7. Remember from Lesson 7 that you must use the address-of operator (`&`) when inputting numeric variables with `scanf()`.

10

Input ▼

LISTING 10.7 input.c: Inputting Numeric and Text Data with `scanf()`

```
1:   /* Demonstrates using scanf() to input numeric and text data. */
2:
3:   #include <stdio.h>
4:
5:   char lname[257], fname[257];
6:   int count, id_num;
7:
8:   int main( void )
9:   {
10:      /* Prompt the user. */
11:
12:      puts("Enter last name, first name, ID number separated");
13:      puts("by spaces, then press Enter.");
14:
15:      /* Input the three data items. */
16:
17:      count = scanf("%s%s%d", lname, fname, &id_num);
18:
19:      /* Display the data. */
20:
21:      printf("%d items entered: %s %s %d \n", count, fname, lname, id_num);
22:
23:      return 0;
24: }
```

Output ▼

```
Enter last name, first name, ID number separated
by spaces, then press Enter.
Cunningham Norman 1023
3 items entered: Norman Cunningham 1023
```

Analysis ▼

Remember that `scanf()` requires the addresses of variables for parameters. In Listing 10.7, `lname` and `fname` are pointers (that is, addresses), so they don't need the address-of operator (`&`). In contrast, `id_num` is a regular variable name, so it requires the `&` when passed to `scanf()` on line 17.

> **TIP**
>
> This program demonstrates a limitation of the `scanf()` function. Suppose the first name you needed to enter had two names like Mary Ellen? The `scanf()` function would put only Mary into the `fname` variable due to the space, even though "Mary Ellen" is a completely acceptable string. So you would either need to create two variables for the two parts of the first name or ask the user to enter the name without a space. For this reason, `gets()` can be a more effective tool to retrieve strings from users, particularly if the strings will have spaces in them.

Some programmers feel that data entry with `scanf()` is prone to errors. They prefer to input all data, numeric and string, using `gets()`, and then have the program separate the numbers and convert them to numeric variables. Such techniques are beyond the scope of this book, but they would make a good programming exercise. For that task, you need the string manipulation functions covered in Lesson 18.

Summary

This lesson covered C's `char` data type. One use of type `char` variables is to store individual characters. You saw that characters are actually stored as numbers: The ASCII code assigns a numerical code to each character. Therefore, you can use type `char` to store small integer values as well. Both `signed` and `unsigned char` types are available.

A string is a sequence of characters terminated by the null character. Strings can be used for text data. C stores strings in arrays of type `char`. To store a string of length *n*, you need an array of type `char` with *n*+1 elements.

You can use memory allocation functions such as `malloc()` to make your programs more dynamic. By using `malloc()`, you can allocate the right amount of memory for your program. Without such functions, you would have to guess at the amount of memory storage the program needs. Your estimate would probably be high, so you would allocate more memory than needed. When you finish with the memory you have allocated, you should always take the time to return it to the system using the `free()` function.

Q&A

Q What is the difference between a string and an array of characters?

A A string is defined as a sequence of characters ending with the null character. An array is a sequence of characters. A string, therefore, is a null-terminated array of characters.

If you define an array of type `char`, the actual storage space allocated for the array is the specified size, not the size minus 1. You're limited to that size; you can't store a larger string. Here's an example:

```
char state[10]="Minneapolis";     /* Wrong! String longer than array. */
char state2[10]="MN";             /* OK, but wastes space because */
                                  /* string is shorter than array. */
```

If, on the other hand, you define a pointer to type `char`, these restrictions don't apply. The variable is a storage space only for the pointer. The actual strings are stored elsewhere in memory (but you don't need to worry about where in memory). There's no length restriction or wasted space. The actual string is stored elsewhere. A pointer can point to a string of any length.

Q   Why shouldn't I just declare big arrays to hold values instead of using a memory allocation function such as `malloc()`?

A   Although it might seem easier to declare large arrays, this isn't an effective use of memory. When you write small programs, such as those in this lesson, it might seem trivial to use a function such as `malloc()` instead of arrays, but as your programs get bigger, you want to allocate memory only as needed. When you're done with memory, you can put it back by *freeing* it. When you free memory, some other variable or array in a different part of the program can use it. (Lesson 21, "Working with Memory," covers freeing allocated memory.)

Q   Do all computers support the extended ASCII character set?

A   No. Most PCs support the extended ASCII set. Some older PCs don't, but the number of older PCs lacking this support is diminishing. Most programmers use the line and block characters of the extended set.

In addition, many international character sets contain more characters than available in ASCII. These characters are usually stored in `wchar_t` type variables instead of variables of type char. `wchar_t` is defined in the `stddef.h` header file. It can be used to hold larger characters. Check the ANSI documents for more information on using `wchar_t` and other character sets.

Q   What happens if I put a string into a character array that is bigger than the array?

A   This can cause a hard-to-find error. You can do this in C, but anything stored in the memory directly after the character array is overwritten. This could be an area of memory not used, some other data, or some vital system information. Your results depend on what you overwrite. Often, nothing happens for a while. You don't want to do this.

Workshop

The Workshop provides quiz questions to help you solidify your understanding of the material covered and exercises to provide you with experience in using what you've learned.

Quiz

1. What is the range of numeric values in the ASCII character set?

2. When the C compiler encounters a single character enclosed in single quotation marks, how is it interpreted?

3. What is C's definition of a string?

4. What is a literal string?

5. To store a string of n characters, you need a character array of $n+1$ elements. Why is the extra element needed?

6. When the C compiler encounters a literal string, how is it interpreted?

7. Using the ASCII chart in Appendix A, state the numeric value stored for each of the following:

   a. a

   b. A

   c. 9

   d. A space

   e. ╬

   f. ♠

8. Using the ASCII chart in Appendix A, translate the following numeric values to their equivalent characters:

   a. 73

   b. 32

   c. 99

   d. 97

   e. 110

   f. 0

   g. 2

10

9. How many bytes of storage are allocated for each of the following variables? (Assume that a character is 1 byte.)

   a. `char *str1 = { "String 1" };`

   b. `char str2[] = { "String 2" };`

   c. `char string3;`

   d. `char str4[20] = { "This is String 4" };`

   e. `char str5[20];`

10. Using the following declaration:

```
char *string = "A string!";
```

what are the values of the following?

   a. `string[0]`

   b. `*string`

   c. `string[9]`

   d. `string[33]`

   e. `*string+8`

   f. `string`

Exercises

1. Write a line of code that declares a type `char` variable named `letter`, and initialize it to the character $.

2. Write a line of code that declares an array of type `char`, and initialize it to the string `"Pointers are fun!"`. Make the array just large enough to hold the string.

3. Write a line of code that allocates storage for the string `"Pointers are fun!"`, as in exercise 2, but without using an array.

4. Write code that allocates space for an 80-character string and then inputs a string from the keyboard and stores it in the allocated space.

5. Write a function that copies one array of characters into another. (Hint: Do this just like the programs you wrote in Lesson 9.)

6. Write a function that accepts two strings. Count the number of characters in each, and return a pointer to the longer string.

7. **ON YOUR OWN:** Write a function that accepts two strings. Use the `malloc()` function to allocate enough memory to hold the two strings after they have been concatenated (linked). Return a pointer to this new string.

For example, if you pass `"Hello"` and `"World!"`, the function returns a pointer to `"Hello World!"`. Having the concatenated value be the third string is easiest. (You might use your answers from exercises 5 and 6.)

8. **BUG BUSTER:** Is anything wrong with the following?

```
char a_string[10] = "This is a string";
```

9. **BUG BUSTER:** Is anything wrong with the following?

```
char *quote[100] = { "Smile, Friday is almost here!" };
```

10. **BUG BUSTER:** Is anything wrong with the following?

```
char *string1;
char *string2 = "Second";
string1 = string2;
```

11. **BUG BUSTER:** Is anything wrong with the following?

```
char string1[];
char string2[] = "Second";
string1 = string2;
```

12. **ON YOUR OWN:** Using the ASCII chart, write a program that prints a box on-screen using the double-line characters.

10

LESSON 11
Implementing Structures, Unions, and TypeDefs

Many programming tasks are simplified by the C data constructs called *structures*. A structure is a data storage type designed by you, the programmer, to suit your programming needs exactly. In this lesson you learn:

- What simple and complex structures are
- How to define and declare structures
- How to access data in structures
- How to create structures that contain arrays and arrays of structures
- How to declare pointers in structures and pointers to structures
- How to pass structures as arguments to functions
- How to define, declare, and use unions
- How to use type definitions with structures

Working with Simple Structures

A *structure* is a collection of one or more variables grouped under a single name for easy manipulation. The variables in a structure, unlike those in an array, can be of different data types. A structure can contain any of C's data types, including arrays and other structures. Each variable within a structure is called a *member* of the structure. The next section shows a simple example.

You should start with simple structures. Note that the C language makes no distinction between simple and complex structures, but it's easier to explain structures in this way.

Defining and Declaring Structures

If you write a graphics program, your code needs to deal with the coordinates of points on the screen. Screen coordinates are written as an x value, giving the horizontal position, and a y value, giving the vertical position. You can define a structure named coord that contains both the x and y values of a screen location as follows:

```
struct coord
{
    int x;
    int y;
};
```

The `struct` keyword identifies the beginning of a structure definition. This `struct` keyword must be followed immediately by the name of the structure. This is the same rule that applies to the other data types you have created in C. The name of a structure is also known as the structure's *tag* or *type name*. Later you see how the tag is used.

Following the structure tag is an opening brace. Within the braces following the structure name is a list of the structure's member variables. You must give a variable type and name for each member.

The preceding code statements define a structure type named coord that contains two integer variables, x and y. This declaration of coord and its members, x and y, does not, however, actually create any instances of the structure coord or of the x and y variables. In other words, they don't *declare* (set aside storage for) any structures. There are two ways to declare structures. One is to follow the structure definition with a list of one or more variable names, as is done here:

```
struct coord {
    int x;
    int y;
} first, second;
```

These statements define the structure type `coord` and declare two structures, `first` and `second`, of type `coord`. `first` and `second` are each *instances* of type `coord`; `first` contains two integer members named `x` and `y`, and so does `second`.

This method of declaring structures combines the declaration with the definition. The second method is to declare structure variables at a different location in your source code from the definition. The following statements also declare two instances of type `coord`:

```
struct coord {
    int x;
    int y;
};
/* Additional code may go here */
struct coord first, second;
```

In this example, you can see that the definition of the `coord` structure is separate from the declaration of variables. When declaring variables separately, you use the `struct` keyword followed by the structured tag followed by the name of the variable or variables you want to create.

Accessing Members of a Structure

Individual structure members can be used like other variables of the same type. Structure members are accessed using the *structure member operator* (`.`), also called the *dot operator*, between the structure name and the member name. Thus, to have the structure named `first` refer to a screen location that has coordinates `x=50`, `y=100`, you could write

```
first.x = 50;
first.y = 100;
```

To display the screen locations stored in the structure `second`, you could write

```
printf("%d,%d", second.x, second.y);
```

At this point, you might wonder what the advantage is of using structures rather than individual variables. One major advantage is that you can copy information between structures of the same type with a simple equation statement. Continuing with the preceding example, the statement

```
first = second;
```

is equivalent to this statement:

```
first.x = second.x;
first.y = second.y;
```

11

When your program uses complex structures with many members, this notation can be a great time-saver. Other advantages of structures will become apparent as you learn some advanced techniques. In general, you'll find structures to be useful whenever information of different variable types should be treated as a group. For example, in a mailing list database, each entry could be a structure, and each piece of information (name, address, city, and so on) could be a structure member.

Listing 11.1 pulls together everything that has been covered up to this point. It is not practical; however, it illustrates the point of a simple structure.

Input ▼
LISTING 11.1   simplestruct.c: Declaring and Using a Simple Structure

```
1:  /* simplestruct.c - Demonstrates the use of a simple structures*/
2:
3:  #include <stdio.h>
4:
5:  int length, width;
6:  long area;
7:
8:  struct coord{
9:      int x;
10:     int y;
11: } myPoint;
12:
13: int main( void )
14: {
15:     /* set values into the coordinates */
16:     myPoint.x = 12;
17:     myPoint.y = 14;
18:
19:     printf("\nThe coordinates are: (%d, %d).",
20:             myPoint.x, myPoint.y);
21:
22:     return 0;
23: }
```

Output ▼

```
The coordinates are: (12, 14).
```

Analysis ▼

This listing defines a simple structure for holding the coordinates of a point. This is the same structure you've seen illustrated earlier in the lesson. On line 8, the `struct` keyword is used followed by the tag, `coord`. The body of the structure is then defined on lines 9 to 11. This structure is declared with two members, x and y, which are both variables of type int.

On line 11, a variable called myPoint is also declared as an instance of the coord structure. This declaration could also have been done on a separate line as follows:

```
struct coord myPoint;
```

On lines 16 and 17, the members of myPoint are assigned values. As stated earlier, values are assigned by using the name of the structure variable, followed by the member operator (.), and finally followed by the name of the member. On lines 19 and 20, these same variables are used in a printf statement.

Syntax

The struct Keyword

```
struct tag {
    structure_member(s);
    /* additional statements may go here */
} instance;
```

The struct keyword is used to declare structures. A structure is a collection of one or more variables (structure_members) that have been grouped under a single name for easy manipulation. The variables don't have to be of the same variable type, nor do they have to be simple variables. Structures also can hold arrays, pointers, and other structures.

The keyword struct identifies the beginning of a structure definition. It's followed by a tag that is the name given to the structure. Following the tag are the structure members, enclosed in braces. An *instance*, the actual declaration of a structure, can also be defined. If you define the structure without the instance, it's just a template, or definition, that can be used later in a program to declare structures. Here is a template's format:

```
struct tag {
    structure_member(s);
    /* additional statements may go here */
};
```

To use the template, you use the following format:

```
struct tag instance;
```

To use this format, you must have previously declared a structure with the given tag.

Example 1

```
/* Declare a structure template called SSN */
struct SSN {
```

11

```
    int first_three;
    char dash1;
    int second_two;
    char dash2;
    int last_four;
};
/* Use the structure template */
struct SSN customer_ssn;
```

Example 2

```
/* Declare a structure and instance together */
struct date {
    char month[2];
    char day[2];
    char year[4];
} current_date;
```

Example 3

```
/* Declare and initialize a structure */
struct time {
    int hours;
    int minutes;
    int seconds;
} time_of_birth = { 8, 45, 0 };
```

Using Structures That Are More Complex

Now that you have been introduced to simple structures, you can go on to the more interesting and complex types of structures. These are structures that contain other structures as members and structures that contain arrays as members.

Including Structures Within Other Structures

As mentioned earlier, a C structure can contain any of C's data types. For example, a structure can contain other structures. The preceding example can be extended to illustrate this.

Assume that your graphics program has to deal with rectangles. A rectangle can be defined by the coordinates of two diagonally opposite corners. You've already seen how to define a structure that can hold the two coordinates required for a single point. You need two such structures to define a rectangle. You can define a structure as follows (assuming, of course, that you have already defined the type coord structure):

```
struct rectangle {
    struct coord topleft;
    struct coord bottomrt;
};
```

This statement defines a structure of type `rectangle` that contains two structures of type `coord`. These two type `coord` structures are named `topleft` and `bottomrt`.

The preceding statement defines only the type `rectangle` structure. To declare a structure, you must then include a statement such as

```
struct rectangle mybox;
```

You could have combined the definition and declaration, as you did before for the type `coord`:

```
struct rectangle {
    struct coord topleft;
    struct coord bottomrt;
} mybox;
```

To access the actual data locations (the type `int` members), you must apply the member operator (.) twice. Thus, the expression

```
mybox.topleft.x
```

11

refers to the x member of the `topleft` member of the type `rectangle` structure named `mybox`. To define a rectangle with coordinates (0,10), (100,200), you would write

```
mybox.topleft.x = 0;
mybox.topleft.y = 10;
mybox.bottomrt.x = 100;
mybox.bottomrt.y = 200;
```

Maybe this is a bit confusing. You can understand better if you look at Figure 11.1, which shows the relationship between the type `rectangle` structure, the two type `coord` structures it contains, and the two type `int` variables each type `coord` structure contains. These structures are named as in the preceding example.

FIGURE 11.1

The relationship between a structure, structures within a structure, and the structure members.

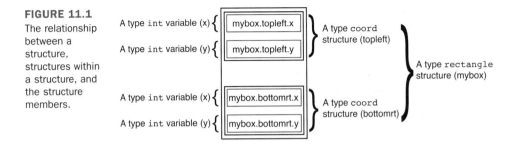

Listing 11.2 presents an example of using structures that contain other structures. This listing takes input from the user for the coordinates of a rectangle and then calculates and displays the rectangle's area. Note the program's assumptions, given in comments near the start of the program (lines 3 through 8).

Input ▼
LISTING 11.2   struct.c: A Demonstration of Structures that Contain Other Structures

```
1:  /* Demonstrates structures that contain other structures. */
2:
3:  /* Receives input for corner coordinates of a rectangle and
4:     calculates the area. Assumes that the y coordinate of the
5:     lower-right corner is greater than the y coordinate of the
6:     upper-left corner, that the x coordinate of the lower-
7:     right corner is greater than the x coordinate of the upper-
8:     left corner, and that all coordinates are positive. */
9:
10: #include <stdio.h>
11:
12: int length, width;
13: long area;
14:
15: struct coord{
16:     int x;
17:     int y;
18: };
19:
20: struct rectangle{
21:     struct coord topleft;
22:     struct coord bottomrt;
23: } mybox;
24:
25: int main( void )
26: {
27:     /* Input the coordinates */
28:
29:     printf("\nEnter the top left x coordinate: ");
```

```
30:        scanf("%d", &mybox.topleft.x);
31:
32:        printf("\nEnter the top left y coordinate: ");
33:        scanf("%d", &mybox.topleft.y);
34:
35:        printf("\nEnter the bottom right x coordinate: ");
36:        scanf("%d", &mybox.bottomrt.x);
37:
38:        printf("\nEnter the bottom right y coordinate: ");
39:        scanf("%d", &mybox.bottomrt.y);
40:
41:        /* Calculate the length and width */
42:
43:        width = mybox.bottomrt.x - mybox.topleft.x;
44:        length = mybox.topleft.y - mybox.bottomrt.y;
45:
46:        /* Calculate and display the area */
47:
48:        area = width * length;
49:        printf("\nThe area is %ld units.\n", area);
50:
51:        return 0;
52: }
```

Output ▼

```
Enter the top left x coordinate: 0

Enter the top left y coordinate: 6

Enter the bottom right x coordinate: 9

Enter the bottom right y coordinate: 1

The area is 45 units.
```

Analysis ▼

The coord structure is defined on lines 15 through 18 with its two members, x and y. Lines 20 through 23 declare and define an instance, called mybox, of the rectangle structure. The two members of the rectangle structure are topleft and bottomrt, both structures of type coord.

Lines 29 through 39 fill in the values in the mybox structure. At first, it might seem that there are only two values to fill because mybox has only two members. However, each of mybox's members has its own members. topleft and bottomrt have two members each, x and y from the coord structure. This gives a total of four members to be filled. After the members are filled with values, the area is calculated using the structure and member names. When using the x and y values, you must include the structure instance name. Because x and y are in a structure within a structure, you must use the instance names of both structures—mybox.bottomrt.x, mybox.bottomrt.y, mybox.topleft.x, and mybox. topleft.y—in the calculations.

The C programming language doesn't have to place a limit on the number of structures that can be nested; however, compliance to the ANSI standard guarantees support for only 63 levels. While memory allows, you can define structures that contain structures that contain structures that contain structures—well, you get the idea! Of course, there's a limit beyond which nesting becomes unproductive. Rarely are more than three levels of nesting used in any C program.

Structures That Contain Arrays

You can define a structure that contains one or more arrays as members. The array can be of any C data type (int, char, and so on). For example, the statements

```
struct data
{
    short x[4];
    char y[10];
};
```

define a structure of type data that contains a 4-element short array member named x and a 10-element character array member named y. You can then declare a structure named record of type data as follows:

```
struct data record;
```

The organization of this structure is shown in Figure 11.2. Note that, in this figure, the elements of array x are shown to take up twice as much space as the elements of array y. This is because a type short typically requires 2 bytes of storage, whereas a type char usually requires only 1 byte (as you learned in Lesson 3, "Storing Information: Variables and Constants").

FIGURE 11.2
The organization of a structure that contains arrays as members.

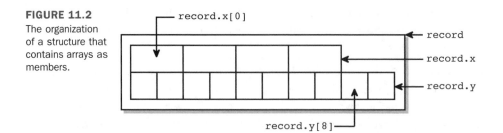

record.x[0]

record

record.x

record.y

record.y[8]

You access individual elements of arrays that are structure members using a combination of the member operator and array subscripts:

```
record.x[2] = 100;
record.y[1] = 'x';
```

You probably remember that character arrays are most frequently used to store strings. You should also remember (from Lesson 9, "Understanding Pointers") that the name of an array, without brackets, is a pointer to the array. Because this holds true for arrays that are structure members, the expression

```
record.y
```

is a pointer to the first element of array `y[]` in the structure `record`. Therefore, you could print the contents of `y[]` onscreen using the statement

```
puts(record.y);
```

Now look at another example. Listing 11.3 uses a structure that contains a type `float` variable and two type `char` arrays.

Input ▼

LISTING 11.3 arraystruct.c: A Structure that Contains Array Members

11

```
1:  /* Demonstrates a structure that has array members. */
2:
3:  #include <stdio.h>
4:  #define NAMESIZE 30
5:  /* Define and declare a structure to hold the data. */
6:  /* It contains one float variable and two char arrays. */
7:
8:  struct data{
9:      float amount;
10:     char fname[NAMESIZE];
11:     char lname[NAMESIZE];
12: } rec;
13:
14: int main( void )
15: {
16:     /* Input the data from the keyboard. */
17:
18:     printf("Enter the donor's first and last names,\n");
19:     printf("separated by a space: ");
20:     scanf("%s %s", rec.fname, rec.lname);
21:
22:     printf("\nEnter the donation amount: ");
23:     scanf("%f", &rec.amount);
24:
```

```
25:     /* Display the information. */
26:     /* Note: %.2f specifies a floating-point value */
27:     /* to be displayed with two digits to the right */
28:     /* of the decimal point. */
29:
30:     /* Display the data on the screen. */
31:
32:     printf("\nDonor %s %s gave $%.2f.\n", rec.fname, rec.lname,
33:             rec.amount);
34:
35:     return 0;
36: }
```

Output ▼

```
Enter the donor's first and last names,
separated by a space: Jayne Hatton

Enter the donation amount: 450

Donor Janye Hatton gave $450.00.
```

Analysis ▼

This program includes a structure that contains array members named `fname[NAMESIZE]` and `lname[NAMESIZE]`. Both are arrays of characters that hold a person's first name and last name, respectively. By using a constant to define the maximum length of the names, it is easier to go back and make a change if you discover the need to allow for longer names. The structure declared on lines 8 through 12 is called `data`. It contains the `fname` and `lname` character arrays with a type `float` variable called `amount`. This structure is ideal for holding a person's name (in two parts, first name and last name) and a value, such as the amount the person donated to a charitable organization.

An instance of the structure, called `rec`, has also been declared on line 12. The rest of the program uses `rec` to get values from the user (lines 18 through 23) and then print them (lines 32 and 33).

Arrays of Structures

If you can have structures that contain arrays, can you also have arrays of structures? You bet you can! In fact, arrays of structures are powerful programming tools. Here's how it's done.

You've seen how a structure definition can be tailored to fit the data your program has to work with. Usually a program has to work with more than one instance of the data. For example, in a program to maintain a list of phone numbers, you can define a structure to hold each person's name and number:

```
struct entry
{
    char fname[10];
    char lname[12];
    char phone[12];
};
```

A phone list must hold many entries, so a single instance of the `entry` structure isn't of much use. What you need is an array of structures of type `entry`. After the structure has been defined, you can declare an array as follows:

```
struct entry list[1000];
```

This statement declares an array named `list` that contains 1,000 elements. Each element is a structure of type `entry` and is identified by subscript like other array element types. Each of these structures has three elements, each of which is an array of type `char`. This entire complex creation is diagrammed in Figure 11.3.

FIGURE 11.3
The organization of the array of structures defined in the text.

11

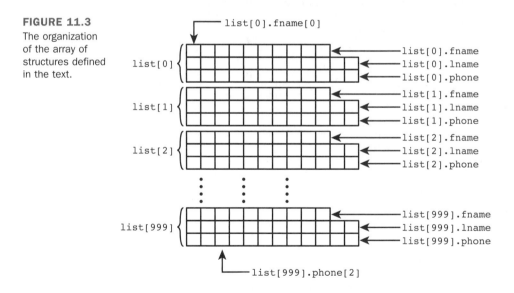

When you have declared the array of structures, you can manipulate the data in many ways. For example, to assign the data in one array element to another array element, you would write

```
list[1] = list[5];
```

This statement assigns to each member of the structure list[1] the values contained in the corresponding members of list[5]. You can also move data between individual structure members. The statement

```
strcpy(list[1].phone, list[5].phone);
```

copies the string in list[5].phone to list[1].phone. (The strcpy() library function copies one string to another string. You learn the details of this in Lesson 18, "Manipulating Strings.") If you want to, you can also move data between individual elements of the structure member arrays:

```
list[5].phone[1] = list[2].phone[3];
```

This statement moves the second character of list[5]'s phone number to the fourth position in list[2]'s phone number. (Don't forget that subscripts start at offset 0.)

Listing 11.4 demonstrates the use of arrays of structures. Moreover, it demonstrates arrays of structures that contain arrays as members.

Input ▼
LISTING 11.4   arrayrecords.c: Arrays of Structures

```
1:  /* arrayrecords.c--Demonstrates using arrays of structures. */
2:
3:  #include <stdio.h>
4:
5:  /* Define a structure to hold entries. */
6:
7:  struct entry {
8:      char fname[20];
9:      char lname[20];
10:     char phone[13];
11: };
12:
13: /* Declare an array of structures. */
14:
15: struct entry list[4];
16:
17: int i;
18:
19: int main( void )
20: {
21:
22:     /* Loop to input data for four people. */
23:
24:     for (i = 0; i < 4; i++)
25:     {
26:         printf("\nEnter first name: ");
27:         scanf("%s", list[i].fname);
```

```
28:              printf("Enter last name: ");
29:              scanf("%s", list[i].lname);
30:              printf("Enter phone in 123-456-7890 format: ");
31:              scanf("%s", list[i].phone);
32:         }
33:
34:     /* Print two blank lines. */
35:
36:     printf("\n\n");
37:
38:     /* Loop to display data. */
39:
40:     for (i = 0; i < 4; i++)
41:     {
42:              printf("Name: %s %s", list[i].fname, list[i].lname);
43:              printf("\t\tPhone: %s\n", list[i].phone);
44:     }
45:
46:     return 0;
47: }
```

Output ▼

```
Enter first name: Ellen
Enter last name: Hatton
Enter phone in 123-456-7890 format: 317-555-1267

Enter first name: Tim
Enter last name: Costello
Enter phone in 123-456-7890 format: 317-555-6723

Enter first name: Anne
Enter last name: Bono
Enter phone in 123-456-7890 format: 812-555-3400

Enter first name: Stewart
Enter last name: Costello
Enter phone in 123-456-7890 format: 317-555-9490

Name: Ellen Hatton              Phone: 317-555-1267
Name: Tim Costello             Phone: 317-555-6723
Name: Anne Bono              Phone: 812-555-3400
Name: Stewart Costello         Phone: 317-555-9490
```

Analysis ▼

This listing follows the same general format as most of the other listings. It starts with the comment on line 1 and, for the input/output functions, the #include file stdio.h on line 3. Lines 7 through 11 define a template structure called entry that contains three character arrays: `fname`, `lname`, and `phone`. Line 15 uses the template to define an array of four entry structure variables called `list`. Line 17 defines a variable of type `int` to be used as a counter throughout the program. `main()` starts on line 19. The first function of `main()` is to perform a loop four times with a `for` statement. This loop, on lines 24 through 32, is used to get information for the array of structures. Notice that `list` is being used with a subscript in the same way as the array variables in Lesson 8, "Using Numeric Arrays," were subscripted.

Line 36 prints a pair of newlines after the final input before starting with the output. Lines 40 through 44 display the data that the user entered in the preceding steps. The values in the array of structures are printed with the subscripted array name followed by the member operator (`.`) and the structure member name.

Familiarize yourself with the techniques used in Listing 11.4. Many real-world programming tasks are best accomplished by using arrays of structures containing arrays as members.

DO	DON'T
DO remember to use the `struct` keyword when declaring an instance from a previously defined structure.	**DON'T** forget the structure instance name and member operator (`.`) when using a structure's members.
DO declare structure instances with the same scope rules as other variables. (Lesson 12, "Understanding Variable Scope," covers this topic fully.)	**DON'T** confuse a structure's tag with its instances! The tag is used to define the structure's template, or format. The instance is a variable declared using the tag.

Initializing Structures

Like other C variable types, structures can be initialized when they're declared. This procedure is similar to that for initializing arrays. The structure declaration is followed by an equal sign and a list of initialization values separated by commas and enclosed in braces. For example, look at the following statements:

```
1: struct sale {
2:     char customer[20];
3:     char item[20];
4:     float amount;
5: } mysale = {
6:             "Acme Industries",
7:             "Left-handed widget",
8:               1000.00
9:           };
```

When these statements are executed, they perform the following actions:

1. Define a structure type named `sale` (lines 1 through 5).

2. Declare an instance of structure type `sale` named `mysale` (line 5).

3. Initialize the structure member `mysale.customer` to the string `"Acme Industries"` (lines 5 and 6).

4. Initialize the structure member `mysale.item` to the string `"Left-handed widget"` (line 7).

5. Initialize the structure member `mysale.amount` to the value `1000.00` (line 8).

For a structure that contains structures as members, list the initialization values in order. They are placed in the structure members in the order in which the members are listed in the structure definition. Here's an example that expands on the preceding one:

```
1:   struct customer {
2:       char firm[20];
3:       char contact[25];
4:   }
5:
6:   struct sale {
7:       struct customer buyer;
8:       char item[20];
9:       float amount;
10:  } mysale = { { "Acme Industries", "George Adams"},
11:                   "Left-handed widget",
12:                      1000.00
13:              };
```

11

These statements perform the following initializations:

1. The structure member `mysale.buyer.firm` is initialized to the string `"Acme Industries"` (line 10).

2. The structure member `mysale.buyer.contact` is initialized to the string `"George Adams"` (line 10).

3. The structure member `mysale.item` is initialized to the string `"Left-handed widget"` (line 11).

4. The structure member `mysale.amount` is initialized to the amount `1000.00` (line 12).

You can also initialize arrays of structures. The initialization data that you supply is applied, in order, to the structures in the array. For example, to declare an array of structures of type `sale` and initialize the first two array elements (that is, the first two structures), you could write

```
1:   struct customer {
2:        char firm[20];
3:        char contact[25];
4:   };
5:
6:   struct sale {
7:        struct customer buyer;
8:        char item[20];
9:        float amount;
10: };
11:
12:
13: struct sale y1990[100] = {
14:        { { "Acme Industries", "George Adams"},
15:            "Left-handed widget",
16:               1000.00
17:        }
18:        { { "Wilson & Co.", "Ed Wilson"},
19:            "Type 12 gizmo",
20:               290.00
21:        }
22: };
```

This is what occurs in this code:

1. The structure member y1990[0].buyer.firm is initialized to the string "Acme Industries" (line 14).

2. The structure member y1990[0].buyer.contact is initialized to the string "George Adams" (line 14).

3. The structure member y1990[0].item is initialized to the string "Left-handed widget" (line 15).

4. The structure member y1990[0].amount is initialized to the amount 1000.00 (line 16).

5. The structure member y1990[1].buyer.firm is initialized to the string "Wilson & Co." (line 18).

6. The structure member y1990[1].buyer.contact is initialized to the string "Ed Wilson" (line 18).

7. The structure member y1990[1].item is initialized to the string "Type 12 gizmo" (line 19).

8. The structure member y1990[1].amount is initialized to the amount 290.00 (line 20).

Structures and Pointers

Given that pointers are such an important part of C, you shouldn't be surprised to find that they can be used with structures. You can use pointers as structure members, and you can also declare pointers to structures. These topics are covered in the following sections.

Including Pointers as Structure Members

You have complete flexibility in using pointers as structure members. Pointer members are declared in the same manner as pointers that aren't members of structures—that is, by using the indirection operator (*). Here's an example:

```
struct data
{
    int *value;
    int *rate;
} first;
```

These statements define and declare a structure whose two members are both pointers to type int. As with all pointers, declaring them is not enough; you must also initialize them to point to something. Remember, this can be done by assigning them the address of a variable. If cost and interest have been declared to be type int variables, you could write

```
first.value = &cost;
first.rate = &interest;
```

11

Now that the pointers have been initialized, you can use the indirection operator (*), as explained in Lesson 9, to evaluate the values stored in each. The expression *first.value evaluates to the value of cost, and the expression *first.rate evaluates to the value of interest.

Perhaps the type of pointer most frequently used as a structure member is a pointer to type char. Recall from Lesson 10, "Working with Characters and Strings," that a *string* is a sequence of characters delineated by a pointer that points to the string's first character and a null character that indicates the end of the string. To refresh your memory, you can declare a pointer to type char and initialize it to point at a string as follows:

```
char *p_message;
p_message = "Teach Yourself C In One Hour a Day";
```

You can do the same thing with pointers to type char that are structure members:

```
struct msg {
    char *p1;
    char *p2;
} myptrs;
myptrs.p1 = "Teach Yourself C In One Hour a Day";
myptrs.p2 = "By SAMS Publishing";
```

Figure 11.4 illustrates the result of executing these statements. Each pointer member of the structure points to the first byte of a string, stored elsewhere in memory. Contrast this with Figure 11.3, which shows how data is stored in a structure that contains arrays of type char.

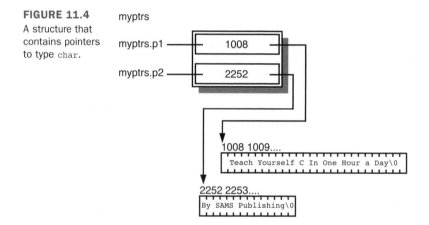

FIGURE 11.4
A structure that contains pointers to type char.

You can use pointer structure members anywhere a pointer can be used. For example, to print the pointed-to strings, you would write

```
printf("%s %s", myptrs.p1, myptrs.p2);
```

What's the difference between using an array of type char as a structure member and using a pointer to type char? These are both methods for "storing" a string in a structure, as shown here in the structure msg, which uses both methods:

```
struct msg
{
    char p1[30];
    char *p2;       /* caution: uninitialized */
} myptrs;
```

Recall that an array name without brackets is a pointer to the first array element. Therefore, you can use these two structure members in similar fashion. (Note that p2 should be initialized before you copy a value to it.)

```
strcpy(myptrs.p1, "Teach Yourself C In One Hour a Day");
strcpy(myptrs.p2, "By SAMS Publishing");
/* additional code goes here */
puts(myptrs.p1);
puts(myptrs.p2);
```

What's the difference between these methods? It is this: If you define a structure that
contains an array of type char, every instance of that structure type contains storage
space for an array of the specified size. Furthermore, you're limited to the specified size;
you can't store a larger string in the structure. Here's an example:

```
struct msg
{
    char p1[10];
    char p2[10];
} myptrs;
...
strcpy(p1, "Minneapolis");    /* Wrong! String longer than array.  */
strcpy(p2, "MN");             /* Okay, but wastes space because     */
                             /* string shorter than array.         */
```

If, on the other hand, you define a structure that contains pointers to type char, these
restrictions don't apply. Each instance of the structure contains storage space for only
the pointer. The actual strings are stored elsewhere in memory (but you don't have to
worry about *where* in memory). There's no length restriction or wasted space. The actual
strings aren't stored as part of the structure. Each pointer in the structure can point to a
string of any length. That string becomes part of the structure, even though it isn't stored
in the structure.

CAUTION

> If you do not initialize the pointer, you can inadvertently overwrite
> memory being used for something else. When using a pointer
> instead of an array, you must remember to initialize the pointer.
> You can do this by assigning it to another variable or by allocating
> memory dynamically.

Creating Pointers to Structures

In a C program, you can declare and use pointers to structures, just as you can declare
pointers to any other data storage type. As you'll see later in the lesson, pointers to
structures are often used when passing a structure as an argument to a function. Pointers
to structures are also used in a powerful data storage method known as *linked lists*.

Linked lists are explored in Lesson 16, "Pointers to Functions and Linked Lists."

For now, take a look at how your program can create and use pointers to structures. First, define a structure:

```
struct part
{
    short number;
    char name[10];
};
```

Now declare a pointer to type `part`:

```
struct part *p_part;
```

Remember, the indirection operator (*) in the declaration says that `p_part` is a pointer to type `part`, not an instance of type `part`.

Can the pointer be initialized now? No, because even though the structure `part` has been defined, no instances of it have been declared. Remember that it's a declaration, not a definition, which sets aside storage space in memory for a data object. Because a pointer needs a memory address to point to, you must declare an instance of type `part` before anything can point to it. Here's the declaration:

```
struct part gizmo;
```

Now you can perform the pointer initialization:

```
p_part = &gizmo;
```

This statement assigns the address of `gizmo` to `p_part`. (Recall the address-of operator, `&`, from Lesson 9.) Figure 11.5 shows the relationship between a structure and a pointer to the structure.

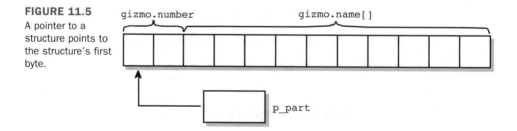

FIGURE 11.5
A pointer to a structure points to the structure's first byte.

Now that you have a pointer to the structure `gizmo`, how do you make use of it? One method uses the indirection operator (*). Recall from Lesson 9 that if `ptr` is a pointer to a data object, the expression `*ptr` refers to the object pointed to.

Applying this to the current example, you know that `p_part` is a pointer to the structure `gizmo`, so `*p_part` refers to `gizmo`. You then apply the structure member operator (`.`) to access individual members of `gizmo`. To assign the value `100` to `gizmo.number`, you could write

```
(*p_part).number = 100;
```

`*p_part` must be enclosed in parentheses because the structure member operator (`.`) has a higher precedence than the indirection operator (`*`).

A second way to access structure members using a pointer to the structure is to use the *indirect membership operator,* which consists of the characters `->` (a hyphen followed by the greater-than symbol). (Note that when they are used together in this way, C treats them as a single operator, not two.) This symbol is placed between the pointer name and the member name. For example, to access the `number` member of `gizmo` with the `p_part` pointer, you would write

```
p_part->number
```

Looking at another example, if `str` is a structure, `p_str` is a pointer to `str`, and `memb` is a member of `str`, you can access `str.memb` by writing

```
p_str->memb
```

Therefore, there are three ways to access a structure member:

- Using the structure name
- Using a pointer to the structure with the indirection operator (`*`)
- Using a pointer to the structure with the indirect membership operator (`->`)

If `p_str` is a pointer to the structure `str`, the following three expressions are all equivalent:

```
str.memb
```

```
(*p_str).memb
```

```
p_str->memb
```

NOTE Some people refer to the indirect membership operator as the *structure pointer operator.*

11

Working with Pointers and Arrays of Structures

You've seen that arrays of structures can be a powerful programming tool, as can pointers to structures. You can combine the two, using pointers to access structures that are array elements.

To illustrate, here is a structure definition from an earlier example:

```
struct part
{
    short number;
    char name[10];
};
```

After the `part` structure is defined, you can declare an array of type `part`:

```
struct part data[100];
```

Next, you can declare a pointer to type `part` and initialize it to point to the first structure in the array `data`:

```
struct part *p_part;
p_part = &data[0];
```

Recall that the name of an array without brackets is a pointer to the first array element, so the second line could also have been written as

```
p_part = data;
```

You now have an array of structures of type `part` and a pointer to the first array element (that is, the first structure in the array). For example, you could print the contents of the first element using the statement

```
printf("%d %s", p_part->number, p_part->name);
```

What if you want to print all the array elements? You would probably use a `for` loop, printing one array element with each iteration of the loop. To access the members using pointer notation, you must change the pointer `p_part` so that with each iteration of the loop it points to the next array element (that is, the next structure in the array). How do you do this?

C's pointer arithmetic comes to your aid. The unary increment operator (++) has a special meaning when applied to a pointer: It means "increment the pointer by the size of the object it points to." Put another way, if you have a pointer `ptr` that points to a data object of type `obj`, the statement

```
ptr++;
```

has the same effect as

```
ptr += sizeof(obj);
```

This aspect of pointer arithmetic is particularly relevant to arrays because array elements are stored sequentially in memory. If a pointer points to array element n, incrementing the pointer with the (++) operator causes it to point to element n + 1. This is illustrated in Figure 11.6, which shows an array named x[] that consists of 4-byte elements (for example, a structure containing two type short members, each 2 bytes long). The pointer ptr was initialized to point to x[0]; each time ptr is incremented, it points to the next array element.

FIGURE 11.6
With each increment, a pointer steps to the next array element.

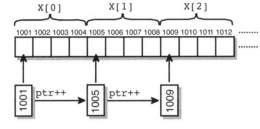

What this means is that your program can step through an array of structures (or an array of any other data type, for that matter) by incrementing a pointer. This sort of notation is usually easier to use and more concise than using array subscripts to perform the same task. Listing 11.5 shows how you do this.

11

Input ▼

LISTING 11.5   pointerstep.c: Accessing Successive Array Elements by Incrementing a Pointer

```
1:  /* pointerstep.c--Demonstrates stepping through an */
2:  /* array of structures using pointer notation. */
3:
4:  #include <stdio.h>
5:
6:  #define MAX 4
7:
8:  /* Define a structure, then declare and initialize */
9:  /* an array of 4 structures. */
10:
11: struct part {
12:     short number;
13:     char name[12];
14: } data[MAX] = { {1, "Thomas"},
15:                 {2, "Christopher"},
```

```
16:                           {3, "Andrew"},
17:                           {4, "Benjamin}"
18:                           };
19:
20: /* Declare a pointer to type part, and a counter variable. */
21:
22: struct part *p_part;
23: int count;
24:
25: int main( void )
26: {
27:      /* Initialize the pointer to the first array element. */
28:
29:      p_part = data;
30:
31:      /* Loop through the array, incrementing the pointer */
32:      /* with each iteration. */
33:
34:      for (count = 0; count < MAX; count++)
35:      {
36:          printf("At address %p: %d %s\n", p_part, p_part->number,
37:                      p_part->name);
38:          p_part++;
39:      }
40:
41:      return 0;
42: }
```

Output ▼

```
At address 4202496: 1 Thomas
At address 4202510: 2 Christopher
At address 4202524: 3 Andrew
At address 4202538: 4 Benjamin
```

Analysis ▼

First, on lines 11 through 18, this program declares and initializes an array of part structures called data. A pointer called p_part is then defined on line 22 to be used to point to the data structure. The main() function's first task on line 29 is to set the pointer, p_part, to point to the part structure that was declared. All the elements are then printed using a for loop on lines 34 through 39 that increments the pointer to the array with each iteration. The program also displays the address of each element.

Look closely at the addresses displayed. The precise values might differ on your system, but they are in equal-sized increments—just the size of the structure part. This clearly illustrates that incrementing a pointer increases it by an amount equal to the size of the data object it points to.

Passing Structures as Arguments to Functions

Like other data types, a structure can be passed as an argument to a function. Listing 11.6 shows how to do this. This program is a modification of the program shown in Listing 11.3. It uses a function to display information on the screen from a structure that is passed in, whereas Listing 11.3 uses statements that are part of main().

Input ▼
LISTING 11.6   structfunc.c: Passing a Structure as a Function Argument

```
1:  // structfunc.c--Demonstrates passing a structure to a function.
2:
3:  #include <stdio.h>
4:
5:  /* Declare and define a structure to hold the data. */
6:
7:  struct data {
8:      float amount;
9:      char fname[30];
10:     char lname[30];
11: } rec;
12:
13: /* The function prototype. The function has no return value, */
14: /* and it takes a structure of type data as its one argument. */
15:
16: void print_rec(struct data diplayRec);
17:
18: int main( void )
19: {
20:     /* Input the data from the keyboard. */
21:
22:     printf("Enter the donor's first and last names,\n");
23:     printf("separated by a space: ");
24:     scanf("%s %s", rec.fname, rec.lname);
25:
26:     printf("\nEnter the donation amount: ");
27:     scanf("%f", &rec.amount);
28:
29:     /* Call the display function. */
30:     print_rec( rec );
31:
32:     return 0;
33: }
34: void print_rec(struct data displayRec)
35: {
36:     printf("\nDonor %s %s gave $%.2f.\n", displayRec.fname,
37:             displayRec.lname, displayRec.amount);
38: }
```

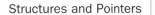

11

Output ▼

```
Enter the donor's first and last names,
separated by a space: Jayne Hatton

Enter the donation amount: 450

Donor Jayne Hatton gave $450.00.
```

Analysis ▼

Looking at line 16, you see the function prototype for the function that is to receive the structure. As you would with any other data type that was going to be passed, you must include the proper arguments. In this case, it is a structure of type `data`. This is repeated in the header for the function in line 34. When calling the function, you have to pass only the structure instance name—in this case, `rec` (line 30). That's all there is to it. Passing a structure to a function isn't very different from passing a simple variable.

You can also pass a structure to a function by passing the structure's address (that is, a pointer to the structure). In fact, in older versions of C, this was the only way to pass a structure as an argument. It's not necessary now, but you might see older programs that still use this method. If you pass a pointer to a structure as an argument, remember that you must use the indirect membership operator (`->`) to access structure members in the function. You can also use the dot operator if you format the reference as `(*ptr).<member>`.

DO	DON'T
DO take advantage of declaring a pointer to a structure—especially when using arrays of structures.	**DON'T** confuse arrays with structures.
DO use the indirect membership operator (`->`) when working with a pointer to a structure.	**DON'T** forget that when you increment a pointer, it moves a distance equivalent to the size of the data to which it points. In the case of a pointer to a structure, this is the size of the structure.

Understanding Unions

Unions are similar to structures. A union is declared and used in the same ways that a structure is. A union differs from a structure in that only one of its members can be used at a time. The reason for this is simple. All the members of a union occupy the same area of memory—they are laid on top of one another.

Defining, Declaring, and Initializing Unions

Unions are defined and declared in the same fashion as structures. The only difference in the declarations is that the keyword `union` is used instead of `struct`. To define a simple union of a `char` variable and an integer variable, you would write the following:

```
union shared
{
    char c;
    int i;
};
```

This union, `shared`, can be used to create instances of a union that can hold either a character value `c` or an integer value `i`. This is an OR condition. Unlike a structure that would hold both values, the union can hold only one value at a time. Figure 11.7 illustrates how the `shared` union would appear in memory.

FIGURE 11.7
The union can hold only one value at a time.

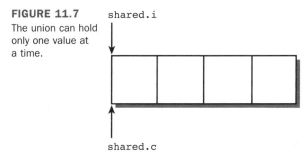

shared.i

shared.c

11

A union can be initialized on its declaration. Because only one member can be used at a time, only one member can be initialized. To avoid confusion, only the first member of the union can be initialized. The following code shows an instance of the `shared` union being declared and initialized:

```
union shared generic_variable = {'@'};
```

Notice that the `generic_variable` union was initialized just as the first member of a structure would be initialized.

Accessing Union Members

Individual union members can be used in the same way that structure members can be used—by using the member operator (`.`). However, there is an important difference in accessing union members. Only one union member should be accessed at a time. Because a union stores its members on top of each other, it's important to access only one member at a time. Listing 11.7 presents an example.

Input ▼

LISTING 11.7 union.c: An Example of the Wrong Use of Unions

```
1:   // union.c--Example of using more than one union member at a time
2:   #include <stdio.h>
3:
4:   int main( void )
5:   {
6:       union shared_tag {
7:           char    c;
8:           int     i;
9:           long    l;
10:          float   f;
11:          double  d;
12:      } shared;
13:
14:      shared.c = '$';
15:
16:      printf("\nchar c   = %c",  shared.c);
17:      printf("\nint i    = %d",  shared.i);
18:      printf("\nlong l   = %ld", shared.l);
19:      printf("\nfloat f  = %f",  shared.f);
20:      printf("\ndouble d = %f",  shared.d);
21:
22:      shared.d = 123456789.8765;
23:
24:      printf("\n\nchar c   = %c",  shared.c);
25:      printf("\nint i    = %d",  shared.i);
26:      printf("\nlong l   = %ld", shared.l);
27:      printf("\nfloat f  = %f",  shared.f);
28:      printf("\ndouble d = %f\n",  shared.d);
29:
30:      return 0;
31:  }
```

Output ▼

```
char c   = $
int i    = 65572
long l   = 65572
float f  = 0.000000
double d = 0.000000

char c   = 7
int i    = 1468107063
long l   = 1468107063
float f  = 284852666499072.000000
double d = 123456789.876500
```

Analysis ▼

In this listing, a union named `shared` is defined and declared on lines 6 through 12. `shared` contains five members, each of a different type. Lines 14 and 22 initialize individual members of `shared`. Lines 16 through 20 and 24 through 28 then output the values of each member, using `printf()` statements.

Note that, with the exceptions of `char c = $` and `double d = 123456789.876500`, the output might not be the same on your computer. Because the character variable, c, was initialized in line 14, it is the only value that should be used until a different member is initialized. The results of printing the other union member variables (`i, l, f`, and `d`) can be unpredictable (lines 16 through 20). Line 22 puts a value into the `double` variable, d. Notice that the printing of the variables again is unpredictable for all but d. The value entered into c in line 14 has been lost because it was overwritten when the value of d in line 22 was entered. This is evidence that the members all occupy the same space.

Syntax

The `union` Keyword

```
union tag {
    union_member(s);
    /* additional statements may go here */
}instance;
```

11

The `union` keyword is used for declaring unions. A union is a collection of one or more variables (`union_members`) that have been grouped under a single name. In addition, each of these union members occupies the same area of memory.

The keyword `union` identifies the beginning of a union definition. It's followed by a tag that is the name given to the union. Following the tag are the union members, enclosed in braces. An `instance`, the actual declaration of a union, also can be defined. If you define the structure without the instance, it's just a template that can be used later in a program to declare structures. The following is a template's format:

```
union tag {
    union_member(s);
    /* additional statements may go here */
};
```

To use the template, you would use the following format:

```
union tag instance;
```

To use this format, you must have previously declared a union with the given tag.

Example 1

```
/* Declare a union template called tag */
union tag {
    int nbr;
    char character;
}
/* Use the union template */
union tag mixed_variable;
```

Example 2

```
/* Declare a union and instance together */
union generic_type_tag {
    char c;
    int i;
    float f;
    double d;
} generic;
```

Example 3

```
/* Initialize a union. */
union date_tag {
    char full_date[9];
    struct part_date_tag {
        char month[2];
        char break_value1;
        char day[2];
        char break_value2;
        char year[2];
    } part_date;
}date = {"01/01/97"};
```

Listing 11.8 demonstrates a more practical use of a union. Although this use is simplistic, it's one of the more common uses of a union.

Input ▼
LISTING 11.8   union2.c: A Practical Use of a Union

```
1:   // union2.c--Example of a typical use of a union
2:
3:   #include <stdio.h>
4:
5:   #define CHARACTER   'C'
6:   #define INTEGER     'I'
7:   #define FLOAT       'F'
8:
```

```
 9:    struct generic_tag{
10:        char type;
11:        union shared_tag {
12:            char   c;
13:            int    i;
14:            float  f;
15:        } shared;
16:    };
17:
18:    void print_function( struct generic_tag generic );
19:
20:    int main( void )
21:    {
22:        struct generic_tag var;
23:
24:        var.type = CHARACTER;
25:        var.shared.c = '$';
26:        print_function( var );
27:
28:        var.type = FLOAT;
29:        var.shared.f = (float) 12345.67890;
30:        print_function( var );
31:
32:        var.type = 'x';
33:        var.shared.i = 111;
34:        print_function( var );
35:        return 0;
36:    }
37:    void print_function( struct generic_tag generic )
38:    {
39:        printf("\n\nThe generic value is...");
40:        switch( generic.type )
41:        {
42:            case CHARACTER: printf("%c",  generic.shared.c);
43:                            break;
44:            case INTEGER:   printf("%d",  generic.shared.i);
45:                            break;
46:            case FLOAT:     printf("%f",  generic.shared.f);
47:                            break;
48:            default:        printf("an unknown type: %c\n",
49:                            generic.type);
50:                            break;
51:        }
52:    }
```

11

Output ▼

```
The generic value is...$

The generic value is...12345.678711

The generic value is...an unknown type: x
```

Analysis ▼

This program is a simplistic version of what could be done with a union. This program provides a way of storing multiple data types in a single storage space. The `generic_tag` structure lets you store a character, an integer, or a floating-point number within the same area. This area is a union called `shared` that operates just like the examples in Listing 11.7. Notice that the `generic_tag` structure also adds an additional field called `type`. This field is used to store information on the type of variable contained in `shared`. `type` helps prevent `shared` from being used in the wrong way, thus helping to avoid erroneous data such as that presented in Listing 11.7.

A formal look at the program shows that lines 5, 6, and 7 define constants CHARACTER, INTEGER, and FLOAT. These are used later in the program to make the listing more readable. Lines 9 through 16 define a `generic_tag` structure that will be used later. Line 18 presents a prototype for the `void` function `print_function()`. The structure `var` is declared in line 22 and is first initialized to hold a character value in lines 24 and 25. A call to `print_function()` on line 26 lets the value be printed. Lines 28 through 30 and 32 through 34 repeat this process with other values.

The `print_function()` is the heart of this listing. Although this function is used to print the value from a `generic_tag` variable, a similar function could have been used to initialize it. `print_function()` evaluates the `type` variable in order to print a statement with the appropriate variable type. This prevents getting erroneous data such as that in Listing 11.7.

DO	DON'T
DO remember which union member is being used. If you fill in a member of one type and then try to use a different type, you can get unexpected results.	**DON'T** try to initialize more than the first union member. **DON'T** forget that the size of a union is equal to its largest member.

Creating Synonyms for Structures with typedef

You can use the `typedef` keyword to create a synonym for a structure or union type. For example, the following statements define `coord` as a synonym for the indicated structure:

```
typedef struct {
    int x;
    int y;
} coord;
```

You can then declare instances of this structure using the `coord` identifier:

```
coord topleft, bottomright;
```

Note that a `typedef` is different from a structure tag, as described earlier in this lesson. If you write

```
struct coord {
    int x;
    int y;
};
```

the identifier `coord` is a tag for the structure. You can use the tag to declare instances of the structure, but unlike using a `typedef`, you must include the `struct` keyword:

```
struct coord topleft, bottomright;
```

Whether you use `typedef` or a structure tag to declare structures makes little difference. Using `typedef` results in slightly more concise code because the `struct` keyword doesn't have to be used. On the other hand, using a tag and having the `struct` keyword explicit makes it clear that it is a structure being declared.

Summary

11

This lesson showed you how to use structures, a data type that you design to meet the needs of your program. A structure can contain any of C's data types, including other structures, pointers, and arrays. Each data item within a structure, called a *member,* is accessed using the structure member operator (.) between the structure name and the member name. Structures can be used individually and also in arrays.

Unions are similar to structures. The main difference between a union and a structure is that the union stores all its members in the same area. This means that only one member of a union can be used at a time.

Q&A

Q Is there any reason to declare a structure without an instance?

A In this lesson, you saw two ways of declaring a structure. The first is to declare a structure body, tag, and instance all at once. The second is to declare a structure body and tag without an instance. An instance can then be declared later by using the `struct` keyword, the tag, and a name for the instance. It's common programming practice to use the second method. Many programmers declare the structure body and tag without any instances. The instances are then declared later in the program. The next lesson describes variable scope. Scope applies to the instance, but not to the tag or structure body.

Q Is it more common to use a `typedef` or a structure tag?

A Many programmers use `typedef`s to make their code easier to read, but it makes little practical difference. Many add-in libraries that contain functions are available for purchase. These add-ins usually have many `typedef`s to make the product unique. This is especially true of database add-in products.

Q Can I simply assign one structure to another with the assignment operator?

A Yes and no. Newer versions of C compilers let you assign one structure to another, but older versions might not. In older versions of C, you might need to assign each member of the structure individually. This is true of unions, also.

Q How big is a union?

A Because each member in a union is stored in the same memory location, the amount of room required to store the union is equal to that of its largest member.

Workshop

The Workshop provides quiz questions to help you solidify your understanding of the material covered and exercises to provide you with experience in using what you've learned.

Quiz

1. How is a structure different from an array?
2. What is the structure member operator, and what purpose does it serve?
3. What keyword is used in C to create a structure?
4. What is the difference between a structure tag and a structure instance?
5. What does the following code fragment do?

```
struct address
{
    char name[31];
    char add1[31];
    char add2[31];
    char city[11];
    char state[3];
    char zip[11];
} myaddress = { "Bradley Jones",
                "RTSoftware",
                "P.O. Box 1213",
                "Carmel", "IN", "46082-1213"};
```

6. If you create a `typedef` called `word`, how would you declare a variable called `myWord` using it?

7. Assume you have declared an array of structures and that `ptr` is a pointer to the first array element (that is, the first structure in the array). How would you change `ptr` to point to the second array element?

Exercises

1. Write code that defines a structure named `time`, which contains three `int` members.

2. Write code that performs two tasks: defines a structure named `data` that contains one type `int` member and two type `float` members, and declares an instance of type `data` named `info`.

3. Continuing with exercise 2, how would you assign the value `100` to the integer member of the structure `info`?

4. Write code that declares and initializes a pointer to `info`.

5. Continuing with exercise 4, show two ways of using pointer notation to assign the value `5.5` to the first `float` member of `info`.

6. Write the definition for a structure type named `data` that can hold a single string of up to 20 characters.

7. Create a structure containing five strings: `address1`, `address2`, `city`, `state`, and `zip`. Create a `typedef` called `RECORD` that can be used to create instances of this structure.

8. Using the `typedef` from exercise 7, allocate and initialize an element called `myaddress`.

9. **BUG BUSTER:** What is wrong with the following code?

```
struct {
    char zodiac_sign[21];
    int month;
} sign = "Leo", 8;
```

10. **BUG BUSTER:** What is wrong with the following code?

```
/* setting up a union */
union data{
    char a_word[4];
    long a_number;
}generic_variable = { "WOW", 1000 };
```

11

LESSON 12
Understanding Variable Scope

In Lesson 5, "Packaging Code in Functions," you saw that a variable defined within a function is different from a variable defined outside a function. Without knowing it, you were introduced to the concept of *variable scope,* an important aspect of C programming. In this lesson you learn:

- About variable scope and why it's important
- What external variables are and why you should usually avoid them
- The ins and outs of local variables
- The difference between static and automatic variables
- About local variables and blocks
- How to select a storage class

What Is Scope?

The *scope* of a variable refers to the extent to which different parts of a program have access to the variable—in other words, where the variable is *visible*. When referring to C variables, the terms *accessibility* and *visibility* are used interchangeably. When speaking about scope, the term *variable* refers to all C data types: simple variables, arrays, structures, pointers, and so forth. It also refers to symbolic constants defined with the const keyword.

Scope also affects a variable's *lifetime*: how long the variable persists in memory, or in other words when the variable's storage is allocated and deallocated. After a quick demonstration of scope, this lesson examines visibility and scope in more detail.

A Demonstration of Scope

Look at the program in Listing 12.1. It defines the variable x on line 5, uses printf() to display the value of x on line 11, and then calls the function print_value() to display the value of x again. Note that the function print_value() is not passed the value of x as an argument; it simply uses x as an argument to printf() in line 19.

Input ▼

LISTING 12.1   scope.c: The Variable x Is Accessible Within the Function print_value()

```
1:   //scope.c--Illustrates variable scope.
2:
3:   #include <stdio.h>
4:
5:   int x = 999;
6:
7:   void print_value(void);
8:
9:   int main( void )
10: {
11:      printf("%d\n", x);
12:      print_value();
13:
14:      return 0;
15: }
16:
17: void print_value(void)
18: {
19:      printf("%d\n", x);
20: }
```

Output ▼

```
999
999
```

This program compiles and runs with no problems. Now make a minor modification in the program, moving the definition of the variable x to a location within the `main()` function. The new source code is shown in Listing 12.2, with the definition of x now on line 9.

Input ▼

LISTING 12.2   scope2.c: The Variable x Is not Accessible Within the Function `print_value()`

```
1:  /* Illustrates variable scope. */
2:
3:  #include <stdio.h>
4:
5:  void print_value(void);
6:
7:  int main( void )
8:  {
9:      int x = 999;
10:
11:      printf("%d\n", x);
12:      print_value();
13:
14:      return 0;
15: }
16:
17: void print_value(void)
18: {
19:      printf("%d\n", x);
20: }
```

Analysis ▼

If you try to compile Listing 12.2, the compiler generates an error message similar to the following:

```
list1202.c(19) : Error: undefined identifier 'x'.
```

Remember that in an error message, the number in parentheses refers to the program line where the error was found. Line 19 is the call to `printf()` within the `print_value()` function.

12

This error message tells you that when line 19 was compiled, within the `print_value()` function, the variable x is undefined or, in other words, not visible. Note, however, that the call to `printf()` in line 11 doesn't generate an error message; in this part of the program, outside `print_value()`, the variable x *is* visible.

The only difference between Listings 12.1 and 12.2 is where variable x is defined. By moving the definition of x, you change its scope. In Listing 12.1, x is defined outside of `main()` and is therefore an *external variable,* and its scope is the entire program. It is accessible within both the `main()` function and the `print_value()` function. In Listing 12.2, x is defined inside a function, the `main()` function, and is therefore a *local variable* with its scope limited to within the `main()` function. As far as `print_value()` is concerned, x doesn't exist, and this is why the compiler generated an error message. Later in the lesson, you learn more about local and external variables, but first you need to understand the importance of scope.

The Importance of Scope

To understand the importance of variable scope, you need to recall the discussion of structured programming in Lesson 5. The structured approach, you may remember, divides the program into independent functions that each perform a specific task. The key word here is *independent.* For true independence, it's necessary for each function's variables to be isolated from possible interference caused by code in other functions. Only by isolating each function's data can you make sure that the function goes about its job without some other part of the program throwing a monkey wrench into the works. By defining variables within functions, as you learn soon, you can "hide" those variables from other parts of the program.

If you're thinking that complete data isolation between functions isn't always desirable, you are correct. You will soon realize that by specifying the scope of variables, a programmer has a great deal of control over the degree of data isolation.

Creating External Variables

An *external variable* is a variable defined outside of any function. This means outside of `main ()` as well because `main()` is a function, too. Until now, most of the variable definitions in this book have been external, placed in the source code before the start of `main()`. External variables are sometimes referred to as *global variables.*

NOTE If you don't explicitly initialize an external variable (assign a value to it) when it's defined, the compiler initializes it to 0.

External Variable Scope

The scope of an external variable is the entire program. This means that an external variable is visible throughout `main()` and throughout every other function in the program. For example, the variable `x` in Listing 12.1 is an external variable. As you saw when you compiled and ran the program, `x` is visible within both functions, `main()` and `print_value()`, and would also be visible in any other functions you might add to the program.

Strictly speaking, it's not accurate to say that the scope of an external variable is the entire program. Instead, the scope is the entire source code file that contains the variable definition. If the entire program is contained in one source code file, the two scope definitions are equivalent. Most small-to-medium-sized C programs are contained in one file, and that's certainly true of the programs you're writing now.

It's possible, however, for a program's source code to be contained in two or more separate files. You'll learn how and why this is done in Lesson 22, "Advanced Compiler Use," and you'll see what special handling is required for external variables in these situations.

When to Use External Variables

Although the sample programs to this point have used external variables, in actual practice you should use them rarely. Why? Because when you use external variables, you are violating the principle of *modular independence* that is central to structured programming. Modular independence is the idea that each function, or module, in a program contains all the code and data it needs to do its job. With the relatively small programs you're writing now, this might not seem important, but as you progress to larger and more complex programs, over-reliance on external variables can start to cause problems.

When should you use external variables? Make a variable external only when all or most of the program's functions need access to the variable. Symbolic constants defined with the `const` keyword are often good candidates for external status. If only some of your functions need access to a variable, pass the variable to the functions as an argument rather than making it external.

The `extern` Keyword

When a function uses an external variable, it is good programming practice to declare the variable within the function using the `extern` keyword. The declaration takes the form

```
extern type name;
```

12

in which *type* is the variable type and *name* is the variable name. For example, you would add the declaration of x to the functions `main()` and `print_value()` in Listing 12.1. The resulting program is shown in Listing 12.3.

Input ▼

LISTING 12.3 extern.c: The External Variable x Is Declared as `extern` Within the Functions `main()` and `print_value()`

```
1:   /* Illustrates declaring external variables. */
2:
3:   #include <stdio.h>
4:
5:   int x = 999;
6:
7:   void print_value(void);
8:
9:   int main( void )
10:  {
11:      extern int x;
12:
13:      printf("%d\n", x);
14:      print_value();
15:
16:      return 0;
17:  }
18:
19:  void print_value(void)
20:  {
21:      extern int x;
22:      printf("%d\n", x);
23:  }
```

Output ▼

```
999
999
```

Analysis ▼

This program prints the value of x twice, first on line 13 as a part of `main()`, and then on line 22 as a part of `print_value()`. Line 5 defines x as a type `int` variable equal to 999. Lines 11 and 21 declare x as an `extern int`. Note the distinction between a variable definition, which sets aside storage for the variable, and an `extern` declaration. The latter says: "This function uses an external variable with such-and-such a name and type that is defined elsewhere." In this case, the `extern` declaration isn't needed, strictly speaking—the program will work the same without lines 11 and 21. However, if the function `print_value()` were in a different code module than the global declaration of the variable x (on line 5), the `extern` declaration would be required.

If you remove the definition of x on line 5, the listing will still compile on some platforms and produce an error in others. What you'll find, however, is that even if it does compile, an error will be given when you run the program. This is because the functions expect x to be defined elsewhere.

Creating Local Variables

A *local variable* is one that is defined within a function. The scope of a local variable is limited to the function in which it is defined. Lesson 5 describes local variables within functions, how to define them, and what their advantages are. Local variables aren't automatically initialized to 0 by the compiler. If you don't initialize a local variable when it's defined, it has an undefined or *garbage* value. You must explicitly assign a value to local variables before they're used for the first time.

A variable can be local to the `main ()` function as well. This is the case for x in Listing 12.2. It is defined within `main()`, and as compiling and executing that program illustrates, it's also only visible within `main()`.

DO	DON'T
DO use local variables for items such as loop counters. **DO** use local variables to isolate the values the variables contain from the rest of the program.	**DON'T** use external variables if they aren't needed by a majority of the program's functions.

12

Static Versus Automatic Variables

Local variables are *automatic* by default. This means that local variables are created anew each time the function is called, and they are destroyed when execution leaves the function. What this means, in practical terms, is that an automatic variable doesn't retain its value between calls to the function in which it is defined.

Suppose your program has a function that uses a local variable x. Also suppose that the first time it is called, the function assigns the value 100 to x. Execution returns to the calling program, and the function is called again later. Does the variable x still hold the value 100? No, it does not. The first instance of variable x was destroyed when execution left the function after the first call. When the function was called again, a new instance of x was created. The old x is gone.

What if the function needs to retain the value of a local variable between calls? For example, a printing function might need to remember the number of lines already sent to the printer to determine when it is necessary to start a new page. For a local variable to retain its value between calls, it must be defined as *static* with the `static` keyword, for example:

```
void print(int x)
{
    static int lineCount;
    /* Additional code goes here */
}
```

Listing 12.4 illustrates the difference between automatic and static local variables.

Input ▼
LISTING 12.4   static.c: The Difference Between Automatic and Static Local Variables

```
1:   // static.c--Demonstrates automatic and static local variables.
2:   #include <stdio.h>
3:   void func1(void);
4:   int main( void )
5:   {
6:       int count;
7:
8:       for (count = 0; count < 20; count++)
9:       {
10:          printf("At iteration %d: ", count);
11:          func1();
12:      }
13:
14:      return 0;
15: }
16:
17: void func1(void)
18: {
19:      static int x = 0;
20:      int y = 0;
21:
22:      printf("x = %d, y = %d\n", x++, y++);
23: }
```

Output ▼

```
At iteration 0: x = 0, y = 0
At iteration 1: x = 1, y = 0
At iteration 2: x = 2, y = 0
At iteration 3: x = 3, y = 0
At iteration 4: x = 4, y = 0
At iteration 5: x = 5, y = 0
At iteration 6: x = 6, y = 0
At iteration 7: x = 7, y = 0
At iteration 8: x = 8, y = 0
At iteration 9: x = 9, y = 0
At iteration 10: x = 10, y = 0
At iteration 11: x = 11, y = 0
At iteration 12: x = 12, y = 0
At iteration 13: x = 13, y = 0
At iteration 14: x = 14, y = 0
At iteration 15: x = 15, y = 0
At iteration 16: x = 16, y = 0
At iteration 17: x = 17, y = 0
At iteration 18: x = 18, y = 0
At iteration 19: x = 19, y = 0
```

Analysis ▼

This program has a function, `func1()`, on lines 17 through 23, that defines and initializes one static local variable and one automatic local variable. Each time the function is called, both variables are displayed onscreen and incremented (line 22). The `main()` function on lines 4 through 15 contains a `for` loop (lines 8 through 12) that prints a message (line 10) and then calls `func1()` (line 11). The `for` loop iterates 20 times.

In the output, note that x, the static variable, increases with each iteration because it retains its value between calls. The automatic variable y, on the other hand, is reinitialized to 0 with each call and therefore does not increment.

This program also illustrates a difference in the way explicit variable initialization is handled (that is, when a variable is initialized at the time of definition). A static variable is initialized only the first time the function is called. At later calls, the program remembers that the variable has already been initialized and therefore doesn't reinitialize. Instead, the variable retains the value it had when execution last exited the function. In contrast, an automatic variable is initialized to the specified value every time the function is called.

If you experiment with automatic variables, you might get results that disagree with what you've read here. For example, if you modify Listing 12.4 so that the two local variables aren't initialized when they're defined, the function `func1()` in lines 17 through 23 reads

12

```
17: void func1(void)
18: {
19:     static int x;
20:     int y;
21:
22:     printf("x = %d, y = %d\n", x++, y++);
23: }
```

When you run the modified program, you might find that the value of y increases by 1 with each iteration. This means that y keeps its value between calls to the function even though it is an automatic local variable. Is what you've read here about automatic variables losing their value a bunch of malarkey?

No, what you read is true. (Have faith!) If you find that an automatic variable keeps its value during repeated calls to the function, it's only by chance. Here's what happens: Each time the function is called, a new y is created. The compiler might use the same memory location for the new y that was used for y the preceding time the function was called. If y isn't explicitly initialized by the function, the storage location might contain the value that y had during the preceding call. The variable seems to have kept its old value, but it's just a chance occurrence; you definitely can't count on it happening every time. Because you can't always count on it, you should never count on it!

Because automatic is the default for local variables, it doesn't need to be specified in the variable definition. If you want to, you can include the auto keyword in the definition before the type keyword, as shown here:

```
void func1(int y)
{
    auto int count;
    /* Additional code goes here */
}
```

The Scope of Function Parameters

A variable that is contained in a function heading's parameter list has *local scope*. For example, look at the following function:

```
void func1(int x)
{
    int y;
    /* Additional code goes here */
}
```

Both x and y are local variables with a scope that is the entire function func1(). Of course, x initially contains whatever value was passed to the function by the calling program. After you make use of that value, you can use x like any other local variable.

Because parameter variables always start with the value passed as the corresponding argument, it's meaningless to think of them as either static or automatic.

External Static Variables

You can make an external variable static by including the `static` keyword in its definition:

```
static float rate;

int main( void )
{
    /* Additional code goes here */
}
```

The difference between an ordinary external variable and a static external variable is one of scope. An ordinary external variable is visible to all functions in the file and can be used by functions in other files, as well as any point below its definition. A static external variable is visible only to functions in its own file and below the point of definition.

These distinctions obviously apply mostly to programs with source code that is contained in two or more files. This topic is covered in Lesson 22.

Register Variables

The `register` keyword is used to suggest to the compiler that an automatic local variable be stored in a *processor register* rather than in regular memory. What is a processor register, and what are the advantages of using it?

The central processing unit (CPU) of your computer contains a few data storage locations called *registers*. It is in the CPU registers that actual data operations, such as addition and division, take place. To manipulate data, the CPU must move the data from memory to its registers, perform the manipulations, and then move the data back to memory. Moving data to and from memory takes a finite amount of time. If a particular variable could be kept in a register to begin with, manipulations of the variable would proceed much faster.

By using the `register` keyword in the definition of an automatic variable, you ask the compiler to store that variable in a register. Look at the following example:

```
void func1(void)
{
    register int x;
    /* Additional code goes here */
}
```

12

Note that you *ask*, not *tell*. Depending on the program's needs, a register might not be available for the variable. If no register is available, the compiler treats the variable as an ordinary automatic variable. In other words, the `register` keyword is a suggestion, not an order. The benefits of the `register` storage class are greatest for variables that the function uses frequently, such as the counter variable for a loop.

The `register` keyword can be used only with simple numeric variables, not arrays or structures. Also, it can't be used with either static or external storage classes. You can't define a pointer to a register variable.

Compilers from the last decade tend to optimize your code for you in a way that makes the `register` keyword largely unnecessary. I would not recommend using the `register` keyword, but it is worth understanding in case you run across it in older code.

DO	DON'T
DO initialize local variables, or you won't know what values they contain. **DO** initialize global variables even though they're initialized to `0` by default. If you always initialize your variables, you can avoid problems such as forgetting to initialize local variables.	**DON'T** declare all your variables as global if they are needed only in a few functions. It is often better to pass them as function parameters. **DON'T** use register variables for nonnumeric values, structures, or arrays.

Local Variables and the `main()` Function

Everything said so far about local variables applies to `main()` as well as to all other functions. Strictly speaking, `main()` is a function like any other. The `main()` function is called when the program is started from your operating system, and control is returned to the operating system from `main()` when the program terminates.

This means that local variables defined in `main()` are created when the program begins, and their lifetime is over when the program ends. The notion of a static local variable retaining its value between calls to `main()` actually does not make sense: A variable can't remain in existence between program executions. Within `main()`, therefore, there is no difference between automatic and static local variables. You can define a local variable in `main()` as being static, but it has no real effect.

DO	DON'T
DO remember that `main()` is a function similar in most respects to any other function.	**DON'T** declare static variables in `main()` because doing so gains nothing.

Which Storage Class Should You Use?

When you're deciding which storage class to use for particular variables in your programs, it might be helpful to refer to Table 12.1, which summarizes the five storage classes available in C.

TABLE 12.1 C's Five Variable Storage Classes

Storage Class	Keyword	Lifetime	Where It's Defined	Scope
Automatic	None[1]	Temporary	In a function	Local
Static	`static`	Temporary	In a function	Local
Register	`register`	Temporary	In a function	Local
External	None[2]	Permanent	Outside a function	Global (all files)
External	`static`	Permanent	Outside a function	Global (one file)

[1] The `auto` keyword is optional.

[2] The `extern` keyword is used in functions to declare a static external variable that is defined elsewhere.

When you're deciding on a storage class, you should use an automatic storage class whenever possible and use other classes only when needed. Here are some guidelines to follow:

- Give each variable an automatic local storage class to begin with.
- In functions other than `main()`, make a variable static if its value must be retained between calls to the function.
- If a variable is used by most or all the program's functions, define it with the external storage class.

Local Variables and Blocks

So far, this lesson has discussed only variables that are local to a function. This is the primary way local variables are used, but you can define variables that are local to any program block (any section enclosed in braces). When declaring variables within the

12

block, you must remember that the declarations must be first. Listing 12.5 shows an example.

Input ▼

LISTING 12.5   block.c: Defining Local Variables Within a Program Block

```
1:   /* Demonstrates local variables within blocks. */
2:
3:   #include <stdio.h>
4:
5:   int main( void )
6:   {
7:       /* Define a variable local to main(). */
8:
9:       int count = 0;
10:
11:      printf("\nOutside the block, count = %d", count);
12:
13:      /* Start a block. */
14:      {
15:        /* Define a variable local to the block. */
16:
17:        int count = 999;
18:        printf("\nWithin the block, count = %d", count);
19:      }
20:
21:      printf("\nOutside the block again, count = %d\n", count);
22:      return 0;
23: }
```

Output ▼

```
Outside the block, count = 0
Within the block, count = 999
Outside the block again, count = 0
```

Analysis ▼

In this program, the count defined within the block is independent of the count defined outside the block. Line 9 defines count as a type int variable equal to 0. Because it is declared at the beginning of main(), it can be used throughout the entire main() function. On line 11, the variable count is printed and its value is 0. A block is declared on lines 14 through 19, and within the block, another count variable is defined, also as a type int variable. This count variable is initialized to 999 on line 17. Line 18 prints the block's count variable value of 999. Because the block ends on line 19, the print statement in line 21 uses the original count initially declared in line 9 of main().

The use of this type of local variable isn't common in C programming, and you may never find a need for it. Its most common use is probably when a programmer tries to isolate a problem within a program. You can temporarily isolate sections of code in braces and establish local variables to assist in tracking down the problem. Another advantage is that the variable declaration/initialization can be placed closer to the point where it's used, which can help in understanding the program.

DO	DON'T
DO use variables at the beginning of a block (temporarily) to help track down problems.	**DON'T** try to put variable definitions anywhere other than at the beginning of a function or at the beginning of a block.
	DON'T define variables at the beginning of a block unless it makes the program clearer.

Summary

This lesson covered the concept of scope and lifetime as related to C's variable storage classes. Every C variable, whether a simple variable, an array, a structure, or whatever, has a specific storage class that determines two things: its scope, or where in the program it's visible; and its lifetime, or how long the variable persists in memory.

Proper use of storage classes is an important aspect of structured programming. By keeping most variables local to the functions that use them, you enhance the functions' independence from each other. A variable should be given automatic storage class unless there is a specific reason to make it external or static.

12

Q&A

Q If global variables can be used anywhere in the program, why not make all variables global?

A As your programs get bigger, they will contain more and more variables. Global variables take up memory as long as the program is running, whereas automatic local variables take up memory only while the function they are defined in is executing. Hence, use of local variables reduces memory usage. More important, however, is that the use of local variables greatly decreases the chance of unwanted interactions between different parts of the program, hence lessening program bugs and following the principles of structured programming.

Q **Lesson 11, "Implementing Structures, Unions, and TypeDefs" stated that scope affects a structure instance but not a structure tag or body. Why doesn't scope affect the structure tag or body?**

A When you declare a structure without instances, you are creating a template, or definition, but not actually declaring any variables. It isn't until you create an instance of the structure that you declare a variable that occupies memory and has scope. For this reason, you can leave a structure body external to any functions with no real effect on memory. Many programmers put commonly used structure bodies with tags into header files and then include these header files when they need to create an instance of the structure. (Header files are covered in Lesson 22.)

Q **How does the computer know the difference between a global variable and a local variable that have the same name?**

A The answer to this question is beyond the scope of this book. The important thing to know is that when a local variable is declared with the same name as a global variable, the program temporarily ignores the global variable when the local variable is in scope (inside the function where it is defined). It continues to ignore the global variable until the local variable goes out of scope.

Q **Can I declare a local variable and a global variable that have the same name, as long as they have different variable types?**

A Yes. When you declare a local variable with the same name as a global variable, it is a completely different variable. This means that you can make it whatever type you want. You should be careful, however, when declaring global and local variables that have the same name. Some programmers prefix all global variable names with "g" (for example, gCount instead of Count). This makes it clear in the source code which variables are global and which are local.

Workshop

The Workshop provides quiz questions to help you solidify your understanding of the material covered, and exercises to provide you with experience in using what you've learned.

Quiz

1. What does scope refer to?
2. What is the most important difference between local storage class and external storage class?
3. How does the location of a variable definition affect its storage class?

4. When defining a local variable, what are the two options for the variable's lifetime?

5. Your program can initialize both automatic and static local variables when they are defined. When do the initializations take place?

6. True or False: A register variable will always be placed in a register.

7. What value does an uninitialized global variable contain?

8. What value does an uninitialized local variable contain?

9. What will line 21 of Listing 12.5 print if lines 9 and 11 are removed? Think about this, and then try the program to see what happens.

10. If a function needs to remember the value of a local type `int` variable between calls, how should the variable be declared?

11. What does the `extern` keyword do?

12. What does the `static` keyword do?

Exercises

1. Write a declaration for a variable to be placed in a CPU register.

2. Change Listing 12.2 to prevent the error. Do this without using any external variables.

3. Write a program that declares a global variable of type `int` called `var`. Initialize `var` to any value. The program should print the value of `var` in a function (not `main()`). Do you need to pass `var` as a parameter to the function?

4. Change the program in exercise 3. Instead of declaring `var` as a global variable, change it to a local variable in `main()`. The program should still print `var` in a separate function. Do you need to pass `var` as a parameter to the function?

5. Can a program have a global and a local variable with the same name? Write a program that uses a global and a local variable with the same name to prove your answer.

6. **BUG BUSTER:** Can you spot the problem in this code? Hint: It has to do with where a variable is declared.

```
void a_sample_function( void )
{
    int ctr1;

    for ( ctr1 = 0; ctr1 < 25; ctr1++ )
        printf( "*" );

    puts( "\nThis is a sample function" );
```

12

```
    {
        char star = '*';
        puts( "\nIt has a problem\n" );
        for ( int ctr2 = 0; ctr2 < 25; ctr2++ )
        {
            printf( "%c", star);
        }
    }
}
```

7. **BUG BUSTER:** What is wrong with the following code?

```
/*Count the number of even numbers between 0 and 100. */

#include <stdio.h>

int main( void )
{
    int x = 1;
    static int tally = 0;

    for (x = 0; x < 101; x++)
    {
        if (x % 2 == 0)   /*if x is even...*/
        tally++;          /*add 1 to tally.*/

    }

    printf("There are %d even numbers.\n", tally);
    return 0;
}
```

8. **BUG BUSTER:** Is anything wrong with the following program?

```
#include <stdio.h>

void print_function( char star );

int ctr;

int main( void )
{
    char star;

    print_function( star );
    return 0;
}

void print_function( char star )
```

```
{
    char dash;

    for ( ctr = 0; ctr < 25; ctr++ )
    {
        printf( "%c%c", star, dash );
    }
}
```

9. What does the following program print? Don't run the program—try to figure it out by reading the code.

```
#include <stdio.h>
void print_letter2(void);              /* function prototype */

int ctr;
char letter1 = 'X';
char letter2 = '=';

int main( void )
{
    for( ctr = 0; ctr < 10; ctr++ )
    {
        printf( "%c", letter1 );
        print_letter2();
    }
    return 0;
}

void print_letter2(void)
{
    for( ctr = 0; ctr < 2; ctr++ )
        printf( "%c", letter2 );
}
```

10. **BUG BUSTER:** Will the preceding program run? If not, what's the problem? Rewrite it so that it is correct.

12

LESSON 13
Advanced Program Control

Lesson 6, "Basic Program Control," introduced several C program control statements that govern the execution of other statements in your program. This lesson covers more advanced aspects of program control, including the `goto` statement and some of the more interesting things you can do with loops. In this lesson you learn

- How to use the `break` and `continue` statements

- What infinite loops are and why you might use them

- What the `goto` statement is and why you should avoid it

- How to use the `switch` statement

- How to control exiting the program

- How to execute functions automatically upon program completion

- How to execute system commands in your program

Ending Loops Early

In Lesson 6, you learned how the `for` loop, the `while` loop, and the `do...while` loop can control program execution. These loop constructions execute a block of C statements never, once, or more than once, depending on conditions in the program. In all three cases, the termination or exit of the loop occurs only when a certain condition occurs.

At times, however, you might want to exert more control over loop execution. The `break` and `continue` statements provide this control.

The `break` Statement

The `break` statement can be placed only in the body of a `for` loop, `while` loop, or `do...while` loop. (It's valid in a `switch` statement, too, but that topic isn't covered until later in the lesson.) When a `break` statement is encountered, execution immediately exits the loop. The following is an example:

```
for ( count = 0; count < 10; count++ )
{
   if ( count == 5 )
      break;
}
```

Left to itself, the `for` loop would execute `10` times. On the sixth iteration, however, `count` is equal to `5`, and the `break` statement executes, causing the `for` loop to terminate. Execution then passes to the statement immediately following the `for` loop's closing brace. When a `break` statement is encountered inside a nested loop, it causes the program to exit the innermost loop only.

Listing 13.1 demonstrates the use of `break`.

Input ▼
LISTING 13.1   breaking.c: Using the `break` Statement

```
1:   /* Demonstrates the break statement. */
2:
3:   #include <stdio.h>
4:
5:   char s[] = "This is a test string. It contains two sentences.";
6:
7:   int main( void )
8:   {
9:      int count;
10:
11:      printf("\nOriginal string: %s", s);
12:
```

```
13:     for (count = 0; s[count]!='\0'; count++)
14:     {
15:         if (s[count] == '.')
16:         {
17:             s[count+1] = '\0';
18:             break;
19:         }
20:     }
21:     printf("\nModified string: %s\n", s);
22:
23:     return 0;
24: }
```

Output ▼

```
Original string: This is a test string. It contains two sentences.
Modified string: This is a test string.
```

Analysis ▼

This program extracts the first sentence from a string. It searches the string, character by character, for the first period (which should mark the end of a sentence). This is done in the `for` loop on lines 13 through 20. Line 13 starts the `for` loop, incrementing `count` to go from character to character in the string, `s`. Line 15 checks whether the current character in the string is a period. If it is, a null character is inserted immediately after the period (line 17). This, in effect, trims the string. After you trim the string, you no longer need to continue the loop, so a `break` statement in line 18 quickly terminates the loop and sends control to the first line after the loop (line 21). If no period is found, the string isn't altered.

A loop can contain multiple `break` statements, but only the first `break` executed (if any) has any effect. If no `break` is executed, the loop terminates normally (according to its test condition). Figure 13.1 shows the operation of the `break` statement.

13

FIGURE 13.1
The operation
of the break
and continue
statements.

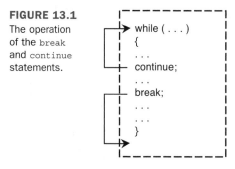

Syntax

The break **Statement**

```
break;
```

break is used inside a loop or switch statement. It causes the control of a program to immediately exit the current loop (for, while, or do...while) or switch statement. No further iterations of the loop execute; the first statement following the loop or switch statement executes.

Example

```
int x;
printf ( "Counting from 1 to 10\n" );
/* having no condition in the for loop will cause it to loop forever */

for( x = 1; ; x++ )
{
    if( x == 10 )    /* This checks for the value of 10 */
        break;       /* This ends the loop */
    printf( "\n%d", x );
}
```

The continue **Statement**

Like the break statement, the continue statement can be placed only in the body of a for loop, a while loop, or a do...while loop. When a continue statement executes, the next iteration of the enclosing loop begins immediately. The statements between the continue statement and the end of the loop aren't executed. The operation of continue is also shown in Figure 13.1. Notice how this differs from the operation of a break statement.

Listing 13.2 uses the continue statement. This program accepts a line of input from the keyboard and then displays it with all lowercase vowels removed.

Input ▼

LISTING 13.2 contin.c: Using the `continue` Statement

```
1:   // contin.c--Demonstrates the continue statement.
2:
3:   #include <stdio.h>
4:
5:   int main( void )
6:   {
7:       // Declare a buffer for input and a counter variable.
8:
9:       char buffer[81];
10:      int ctr;
11:
12:      // Input a line of text.
13:
14:      puts("Enter a line of text:");
15:      gets(buffer);
16:
17:      // Go through the string, displaying only those
18:      // characters that are not lowercase vowels.
19:
20:      for (ctr = 0; buffer[ctr] !='\0'; ctr++)
21:      {
22:
23:          // If the character is a lowercase vowel, loop back
24:          // without displaying it.
25:
26:          if (buffer[ctr] == 'a' || buffer[ctr] == 'e'
27:             || buffer[ctr] == 'i' || buffer[ctr] == 'o'
28:             || buffer[ctr] == 'u')
29:                 continue;
30:
31:          // If not a vowel, display it.
32:
33:          putchar(buffer[ctr]);
34:      }
35:      return 0;
36: }
```

13

Output ▼

```
Enter a line of text:
This is a line of text
Ths s  ln f txt
```

Analysis ▼

Although this isn't the most practical program, it does use a `continue` statement effectively. Lines 9 and 10 declare the program's variables. `buffer[]` holds the string that the user enters in line 15. The other variable, `ctr`, increments through the elements of the array `buffer[]`, while the `for` loop on lines 20 through 34 searches for vowels. For each letter in the loop, an `if` statement on lines 26 through 28 checks the letter against lowercase vowels. If there is a match, a `continue` statement executes, sending control back to line 20, the `for` statement. If the letter isn't a vowel, control passes to the next part of the loop, line 33. Line 33 contains a new library function, `putchar()`, which displays a single character onscreen.

Syntax

The `continue` **Statement**

```
continue;
```

`continue` is used inside a loop. It causes the control of a program to skip the rest of the current iteration of a loop and start the next iteration.

Example

```
int x;
printf("Printing only the even numbers from 1 to 10\n");
for( x = 1; x <= 10; x++ )
{
    if( x % 2 != 0 )      /* See if the number is NOT even */
        continue;        /* Get next instance x */
    printf( "\n%d", x );
}
```

The `goto` **Statement**

The `goto` statement is one of C's *unconditional jump,* or *branching,* statements. When program execution reaches a `goto` statement, execution immediately jumps, or branches, to the location specified by the `goto` statement. This statement is unconditional because execution always branches when a `goto` statement is encountered; the branch doesn't depend on any program conditions (unlike `if` statements, for example).

The target of a `goto` statement is identified by a text label followed by a colon at the start of a line. A target label can be on a line by itself or at the beginning of a line that contains a C statement. In a program, each target must be unique.

A `goto` statement and its target must be in the same function, but they can be in different blocks. Take a look at Listing 13.3, a simple program that uses a `goto` statement.

Input ▼
LISTING 13.3 gotoIt.c: Using the goto Statement

```c
1:  // gotoIt.c--Demonstrates the goto statement
2:
3:  #include <stdio.h>
4:
5:  int main( void )
6:  {
7:      int n;
8:
9:  start:
10:
11:     puts("Enter a number between 0 and 10: ");
12:     scanf("%d", &n);
13:
14:     if (n < 0 ||n > 10 )
15:         goto start;
16:     else if (n == 0)
17:         goto location0;
18:     else if (n == 1)
19:         goto location1;
20:     else
21:         goto location2;
22:
23: location0:
24:     puts("You entered 0.\n");
25:     goto end;
26:
27: location1:
28:     puts("You entered 1.\n");
29:     goto end;
30:
31: location2:
32:     puts("You entered something between 2 and 10.\n");
33:
34: end:
35:     return 0;
36: }
```

Output ▼

```
Enter a number between 0 and 10:
1
You entered 1.
```

Output ▼

```
Enter a number between 0 and 10:
9
You entered something between 2 and 10.
```

13

Analysis ▼

This is a simple program that accepts a number between 0 and 10. If the number isn't between 0 and 10, the program uses a `goto` statement on line 15 to go to `start`, which is on line 9. Otherwise, the program checks on line 16 to see whether the number equals 0. If it does, a `goto` statement on line 17 sends control to `location0` (line 23), which prints a statement on line 24 and executes another `goto`. The `goto` on line 25 sends control to `end` at the end of the program. The program executes the same logic for the value of 1 and all values between 2 and 10 as a whole.

The target of a `goto` statement can come either before or after that statement in the code. The only restriction, as mentioned earlier, is that both the `goto` and the target must be in the same function. They can be in different blocks, however. You can use `goto` to transfer execution both into and out of loops, such as a `for` statement, but you should never do this. In fact, we strongly recommend that you never use the `goto` statement anywhere in your programs. There are two reasons:

- You don't need it. No programming task requires the `goto` statement. You can always write the necessary code using C's other branching statements.

- It's dangerous. The `goto` statement might seem like an ideal solution for certain programming problems, but it's easy to abuse. When program execution branches with a `goto` statement, no record is kept of where the execution came from, so execution can weave through the program willy-nilly. This type of programming is known as *spaghetti code*.

Some careful programmers can write perfectly fine programs that use `goto`. There might be situations in which a judicious use of `goto` is the simplest solution to a programming problem. It's never the only solution, however. If you ignore this warning, at least be careful!

DO	DON'T
DO avoid using the `goto` statement if possible. (And it's always possible!)	**DON'T** confuse `break` and `continue`. `break` ends a loop, whereas `continue` starts the next iteration of the loop.

Syntax

The `goto` Statement

```
goto location;
```

`location` is a label statement that identifies the program location where execution is to branch. A *label statement* consists of an identifier followed by a colon and, optionally, a C statement:

```
location: a C statement;
```

You can also put a label by itself on a line. When this is done, some programmers like to follow it with the null statement (a semicolon by itself) ; although, this is not required:

```
location: ;
```

Infinite Loops

What is an infinite loop, and why would you want one in your program? An infinite loop is one that, if left to its own devices, would run forever. It can be a `for` loop, a `while` loop, or a `do...while` loop. For example, if you write

```
while (1)
{
    /* additional code goes here */
}
```

you create an infinite loop. The condition that the `while` tests is the constant `1`, which is always true and can't be changed by the program. Because `1` can never be changed on its own, the loop never terminates.

In the preceding section, you saw that the `break` statement can be used to exit a loop. Without the `break` statement, an infinite loop would be useless. With `break`, you can take advantage of infinite loops.

You can also create an infinite `for` loop, as follows:

```
for (;;)
{
    /* additional code goes here */
}
```

or an infinite `do...while` loop, as follows:

```
do
{
    /* additional code goes here */
} while (1);
```

13

The principle remains the same for all three loop types. In the following examples, the `while` loop is used.

An infinite loop can be used when there are many conditions that need to be tested to determine whether the loop should terminate. It might be difficult to include all the test conditions in parentheses after the `while` statement. It might be easier to test the conditions individually in the body of the loop and then exit by executing a break as needed. In general, you should try to avoid infinite loops if there are other alternatives.

An infinite loop can also create a menu system that directs your program's operation. You might remember from Lesson 5, "Packaging Code in Functions," that a program's main() function often serves as a sort of "traffic cop," directing execution among the various functions that do the real work of the program. This is often accomplished by a menu of some kind: The user is presented with a list of choices and makes an entry by selecting one of them. One of the available choices should be to terminate the program. When a choice is made, one of C's decision statements is used to direct program execution accordingly.

Listing 13.4 demonstrates a menu system.

Input ▼
LISTING 13.4   menu.c: Using an Infinite Loop to Implement a Menu System

```
1:   /* menu.c--Demonstrates using an infinite loop to implement */
2:   /* a menu system. */
3:   #include <stdio.h>
4:   #define DELAY   150000000       /* Used in delay loop. */
5:
6:   int menu(void);
7:   void delay(void);
8:
9:   int main( void )
10:  {
11:     int choice;
12:
13:     while (1)
14:     {
15:
16:      /* Get the user's selection. */
17:
18:      choice = menu();
19:
20:      /* Branch based on the input. */
21:
22:      if (choice == 1)
23:      {
24:          puts("\nExecuting task A.");
25:          delay();
26:      }
27:      else if (choice == 2)
28:          {
29:              puts("\nExecuting task B.");
30:              delay();
```

```
31:            }
32:     else if (choice == 3)
33:            {
34:                   puts("\nExecuting task C.");
35:                   delay();
36:            }
37:     else if (choice == 4)
38:            {
39:                   puts("\nExecuting task D.");
40:                   delay();
41:            }
42:     else if (choice == 5)          /* Exit program. */
43:            {
44:                   puts("\nExiting program now...\n");
45:                   delay();
46:                   break;
47:            }
48:            else
49:            {
50:                   puts("\nInvalid choice, try again.");
51:                   delay();
52:            }
53:      }
54:     return 0;
55: }
56:
57: /* Displays a menu and inputs user's selection. */
58: int menu(void)
59: {
60:     int reply;
61:
62:     puts("\nEnter 1 for task A.");
63:     puts("Enter 2 for task B.");
64:     puts("Enter 3 for task C.");
65:     puts("Enter 4 for task D.");
66:     puts("Enter 5 to exit program.");
67:
68:     scanf("%d", &reply);
69:
70:     return reply;
71: }
72:
73: void delay( void )
74: {
75:     long x;
76:     for ( x = 0; x < DELAY; x++ )
77:            ;
78: }
```

13

Output ▼

```
Enter 1 for task A.
Enter 2 for task B.
Enter 3 for task C.
Enter 4 for task D.
Enter 5 to exit program.
1

Executing task A.

Enter 1 for task A.
Enter 2 for task B.
Enter 3 for task C.
Enter 4 for task D.
Enter 5 to exit program.
6

Invalid choice, try again.

Enter 1 for task A.
Enter 2 for task B.
Enter 3 for task C.
Enter 4 for task D.
Enter 5 to exit program.
5

Exiting program now...
```

Analysis ▼

CAUTION
Listing 13.4 does not contain any error checking. If you enter a value other than a number, the results could be unpredictable.

In Listing 13.4, a function named menu() is called on line 18 and defined on lines 58 through 71. menu() displays a menu onscreen, accepts user input, and returns the input to the main program. In main(), a series of nested if statements test the returned value and direct execution accordingly. The only thing this program does is display messages on the screen. In a real program, the code would call various functions to perform the selected task.

This program also uses a second function, named delay(). delay() is defined on lines 73 through 78 and actually doesn't do much. Simply stated, the for statement on line 76 loops, doing nothing (line 77). The statement loops DELAY times. This is an effective method of pausing the program momentarily. If the delay is too short or too long, the defined value of DELAY can be adjusted accordingly.

CAUTION

> There are better ways to pause the computer than what is shown in Listing 13.4. If you choose to use a compiler-specific function such as usleep(), sleep(), or delay(), be cautious. These functions are not ANSI-compatible. This means that it might not work with other compilers or on all platforms.

The switch **Statement**

C's most flexible program control statement is the switch statement, which lets your program execute different statements based on an expression that can have more than two values. Earlier control statements, such as if, were limited to evaluating an expression that could have only two values: true or false. To control program flow based on more than two values, you had to use multiple nested if statements, as shown in Listing 13.4. The switch statement makes such nesting unnecessary.

The general form of the switch statement is as follows:

```
switch (expression)
{
    case   template_1: statement(s);
    case   template_2: statement(s);
    ...
    case   template_n: statement(s);
    default: statement(s);
}
```

In this statement, *expression* is any expression that evaluates to an integer value: type long, int, or char. The switch statement evaluates *expression* and compares the value against the templates following each case label. Then one of the following happens:

■ If a match is found between *expression* and one of the templates, execution is transferred to the statement that follows the case label.

■ If no match is found, execution is transferred to the statement following the optional default label.

■ If no match is found and no default label exists, execution passes to the first statement following the switch statement's closing brace.

13

The `switch` statement is demonstrated in Listing 13.5, which displays a message based on the user's input.

Input ▼
LISTING 13.5   switch1.c: Using the `switch` Statement

```
1:   /* switch1.c--Demonstrates the switch statement. */
2:
3:   #include <stdio.h>
4:
5:   int main( void )
6:   {
7:       int reply;
8:
9:       puts("Enter a number between 1 and 5:");
10:      scanf("%d", &reply);
11:
12:      switch (reply)
13:      {
14:         case 1:
15:             puts("You entered 1.");
16:         case 2:
17:             puts("You entered 2.");
18:         case 3:
19:             puts("You entered 3.");
20:         case 4:
21:             puts("You entered 4.");
22:         case 5:
23:             puts("You entered 5.");
24:         default:
25:             puts("Out of range, try again.");
26:      }
27:
28:      return 0;
29: }
```

Output ▼

```
Enter a number between 1 and 5:
2
You entered 2.
You entered 3.
You entered 4.
You entered 5.
Out of range, try again.
```

Analysis ▼

Well, that's certainly not right, is it? It looks as though the `switch` statement finds the first matching template and then executes everything that follows (not just the statements associated with the template). That's exactly what does happen; however, that's how `switch` is supposed to work. In effect, it performs a `goto` to the matching template. To ensure that only the statements associated with the matching template are executed, include a `break` statement where needed. Listing 13.6 shows the program rewritten with `break` statements. Now it functions properly.

Input ▼

LISTING 13.6   switch2.c: Correct Use of `switch`, Including `break` Statements as Needed

```
1:  /* switch2.c--Demonstrates the switch statement correctly. */
2:
3:  #include <stdio.h>
4:
5:  int main( void )
6:  {
7:      int reply;
8:
9:      puts("\nEnter a number between 1 and 5:");
10:     scanf("%d", &reply);
11:
12:     switch (reply)
13:     {
14:       case 0:
15:           break;
16:       case 1:
17:           {
18:               puts("You entered 1.\n");
19:               break;
20:           }
21:       case 2:
22:           {
23:               puts("You entered 2.\n");
24:               break;
25:           }
26:       case 3:
27:           {
28:               puts("You entered 3.\n");
29:               break;
30:           }
31:       case 4:
32:           {
33:               puts("You entered 4.\n");
34:               break;
35:           }
```

13

```
36:     case 5:
37:       {
38:          puts("You entered 5.\n");
39:          break;
40:       }
41:     default:
42:       {
43:          puts("Out of range, try again.\n");
44:       }
45:   }                   /* End of switch */
46:   return 0;
47: }
```

Output ▼

```
Enter a number between 1 and 5:
1
You entered 1.
```

Output ▼

```
Enter a number between 1 and 5:
6
Out of range, try again.
```

When you compile and run this version; you can see that it runs correctly.

One common use of the switch statement is to implement the sort of menu shown in Listing 13.4. Listing 13.7 uses switch instead of if to implement a menu. Using switch is much better than using nested if statements, which were used in the earlier version of the menu program (refer to Listing 13.4).

Input ▼
LISTING 13.7 menu2.c: Using the switch Statement to Execute a Menu System

```
1:  /* menu2.c--Demonstrates using an infinite loop and the switch */
2:  /* statement to implement a menu system. */
3:  #include <stdio.h>
4:  #include <stdlib.h>
5:
6:  #define DELAY 150000000
7:
8:  int menu(void);
9:  void delay(void);
10:
11: int main( void )
```

```
12: {
13:    int command = 0;
14:    command = menu();
15:
16:    while (command != 5 )
17:    {
18:        /* Get user's selection and branch based on the input. */
19:
20:        switch(command)
21:        {
22:            case 1:
23:                {
24:                    puts("\nExecuting task A.");
25:                    delay();
26:                    break;
27:                }
28:            case 2:
29:                {
30:                    puts("\nExecuting task B.");
31:                    delay();
32:                    break;
33:            .   }
34:            case 3:
35:                {
36:                    puts("\nExecuting task C.");
37:                    delay();
38:                    break;
39:                }
40:            case 4:
41:                {
42:                    puts("\nExecuting task D.");
43:                    delay();
44:                    break;
45:                }
46:            case 5:      /* Exit program. */
47:                {
48:                    puts("\nExiting program now...\n");
49:                    break;
50:                }
51:            default:
52:                {
53:                    puts("\nInvalid choice, try again.");
54:                }
55:        }  /* End of switch */
56:        command = menu();
57:    }         /* End of while  */
58:    return 0;
59: }
60:
61: /* Displays a menu and inputs user's selection. */
62: int menu(void)
```

13

```
63: {
64:     int reply;
65:
66:     puts("\nEnter 1 for task A.");
67:     puts("Enter 2 for task B.");
68:     puts("Enter 3 for task C.");
69:     puts("Enter 4 for task D.");
70:     puts("Enter 5 to exit program.");
71:
72:     scanf("%d", &reply);
73:
74:     return reply;
75: }
76:
77: void delay( void )
78: {
79:     long x;
80:     for( x = 0; x < DELAY; x++ )
81:         ;
82: }
```

Output ▼

```
Enter 1 for task A.
Enter 2 for task B.
Enter 3 for task C.
Enter 4 for task D.
Enter 5 to exit program.
1

Executing task A.

Enter 1 for task A.
Enter 2 for task B.
Enter 3 for task C.
Enter 4 for task D.
Enter 5 to exit program.
6

Invalid choice, try again.

Enter 1 for task A.
Enter 2 for task B.
Enter 3 for task C.
Enter 4 for task D.
Enter 5 to exit program.
5

Exiting program now...
```

Analysis ▼

This program uses a `switch` statement with cases based on the choices of an onscreen menu. Line 14 calls the menu the first time and sets a value in the `command` variable from it. If the value is anything other than 5, a `while` loop is executed. This `while` loop is primarily a `switch` statement that executes different code based on the command selected from the menu. When the appropriate case is executed, the menu is redisplayed and a new command is obtained on line 56.

Having execution "fall through" parts of a `switch` construction can be useful at times. Say, for example, that you want the same block of statements executed if one of several values is encountered. Simply omit the `break` statements and list all the `case` templates before the statements. If the test expression matches any of the `case` conditions, execution "falls through" the following `case` statements until it reaches the block of code you want to execute, as shown in Listing 13.8.

Input ▼

LISTING 13.8 fallthru.c: Another Way to Use the `switch` Statement

```
1:   /* Another use of the switch statement. */
2:
3:   #include <stdio.h>
4:   #include <stdlib.h>
5:
6:   int main( void )
7:   {
8:       int reply;
9:
10:      while (1)
11:      {
12:          puts("\nEnter a value between 1 and 10, 0 to exit: ");
13:          scanf("%d", &reply);
14:
15:          switch (reply)
16:          {
17:              case 0:
18:                  exit(0);
19:              case 1:
20:              case 2:
21:              case 3:
22:              case 4:
23:              case 5:
24:                  {
25:                      puts("You entered 5 or below.\n");
26:                      break;
27:                  }
28:              case 6:
```

13

```
29:            case 7:
30:            case 8:
31:            case 9:
32:            case 10:
33:                {
34:                    puts("You entered 6 or higher.\n");
35:                    break;
36:                }
37:            default:
38:                    puts("Between 1 and 10, please!\n");
39:          } /* end of switch */
40:       }     /*end of while */
41:     return 0;
43: }
```

Output ▼

```
Enter a value between 1 and 10, 0 to exit:
11
Between 1 and 10, please!

Enter a value between 1 and 10, 0 to exit:
1
You entered 5 or less.

Enter a value between 1 and 10, 0 to exit:
6
You entered 6 or more.

Enter a value between 1 and 10, 0 to exit:
0
```

Analysis ▼

This program accepts a value from the keyboard and then states whether the value is 5 or less, 6 or more, or not between 1 and 10. If the value is 0, line 18 executes a call to the exit() function, thus ending the program.

You can't use break n line 18, as you did in Listing 13.4 earlier. Executing a break would merely break out of the switch statement; it wouldn't break out of the infinite while loop. The exit() function terminates the program. You learn more about the exit() function in the next section.

Syntax

The `switch` **Statement**

```
switch  (expression)
{
    case   template_1: statement(s);
    case   template_2: statement(s);
    ...
    case   template_n: statement(s);
    default: statement(s);
}
```

The `switch` statement allows for multiple branches from a single expression. It's more efficient and easier to follow than a multileveled `if` statement. A `switch` statement evaluates an expression and then branches to the `case` statement that contains the template matching the expression's result. If no value matches the expression's result, control goes to the `default` statement. If there is no `default` statement, control goes to the end of the `switch` statement.

Program flow continues from the `case` statement down unless a `break` statement is encountered. If that occurs, control goes to the end of the `switch` statement.

Example 1

```
switch( letter )
{
   case 'A':
   case 'a':
       printf( "You entered A" );
       break;
   case 'B':
   case 'b':
       printf( "You entered B");
       break;
   ...
   ...
   default:
       printf( "I don't have a case for %c", letter );
}
```

13

Example 2

```
switch( number )
{
   case 0:    puts( "Your number is 0 or less.");
   case 1:    puts( "Your number is 1 or less.");
   case 2:    puts( "Your number is 2 or less.");
   case 3:    puts( "Your number is 3 or less.");
   ...
   ...
```

```
    case 99:    puts( "Your number is 99 or less.");
                break;
    default:    puts( "Your number is greater than 99.");
}
```

Because there are no `break` statements for the first `case` statements, this example finds the `case` that matches the number and prints every `case` from that point down to the `break` in `case 99`. If the number were 3, you would be told that your number is equal to 3 or less, 4 or less, 5 or less, up to 99 or less. The program continues printing until it reaches the `break` statement in `case 99`.

DO	DON'T
DO use a `default` case in a `switch` statement, even if you think you've covered all possible cases.	**DON'T** forget to use `break` statements if your `switch` statements need them.
DO use a `switch` statement instead of an `if` statement if more than two conditions are being evaluated for the same variable.	
DO line up your `case` statements so that they're easy to read.	

Exiting the Program

A C program normally terminates when execution reaches the closing brace of the `main()` function. However, you can terminate a program at any time by calling the library function `exit()`. You can also specify one or more functions to be automatically executed at termination.

The `exit()` Function

The `exit()` function terminates program execution and returns control to the operating system. This function takes a single type `int` argument that is passed back to the operating system to indicate the program's success or failure. The syntax of the `exit()` function is

```
exit(status);
```

If *status* has a value of 0, it indicates that the program terminated normally. A value of 1 indicates that the program terminated with some sort of error. The return value is usually ignored. To use the `exit()` function, a program must include the header file `stdlib.h`.

This header file also defines two symbolic constants for use as arguments to the `exit()` function:

```
#define EXIT_SUCCESS    0
#define EXIT_FAILURE    1
```

Thus, to exit with a return value of `0`, call `exit(EXIT_SUCCESS)`; for a return value of `1`, call `exit(EXIT_FAILURE)`.

DO	DON'T
DO use the `exit()` command to get out of the program if there's a problem.	
DO pass meaningful values to the `exit()` function.	

Summary

This lesson covers a variety of topics related to program control. You learned about the `goto` statement and why you should avoid using it in your programs. You saw that the `break` and `continue` statements give additional control over the execution of loops and that you can use these statements with infinite loops to perform useful programming tasks. You also learned how to use the `exit()` function to control program termination.

Q&A

Q Is it better to use a `switch` statement or a nested loop?

A If you're checking a variable that can take on more than two values, the `switch` statement is almost always better. The resulting code is easier to read, too. If you're checking a true/false condition, go with an `if` statement.

Q Why should I avoid a `goto` statement?

A When you first see a `goto` statement, it's easy to believe that it could be useful. However, `goto` can cause you more problems than it fixes. A `goto` statement is an unstructured command that takes you to another point in a program. Many *debuggers* (software that helps you trace program problems) can't interrogate a `goto` properly. `goto` statements also lead to *spaghetti* code—code that goes all over the place.

13

Q Why don't all compilers have the same functions?

A In this lesson, you saw that certain C functions aren't available with all compilers or all computer systems. For example, `sleep()` is available with Borland C compilers but not with Microsoft compilers.

Although there are standards that all ANSI compilers follow, these standards don't prohibit compiler manufacturers from adding additional functionality. They do this by creating and including new functions. Each compiler manufacturer usually adds a number of functions that it believes will be helpful to its users.

Q Isn't C supposed to be a standardized language?

A C is, in fact, highly standardized. The American National Standards Institute (ANSI) has developed the ANSI C Standard, which specifies almost all details of the C language, including the functions that are provided. Some compiler vendors have added more functions—ones that aren't part of the ANSI Standard—to their C compilers in an effort to one-up the competition. In addition, you sometimes come across a compiler that doesn't claim to meet the ANSI standard. If you limit yourself to ANSI-standard compilers, however, you'll find that 99 percent of program syntax and functions are common among them.

Workshop

The Workshop provides quiz questions to help you solidify your understanding of the material covered and exercises to provide you with experience in using what you've learned.

Quiz

1. When is it advisable to use the `goto` statement in your programs?
2. What's the difference between the `break` statement and the `continue` statement?
3. What is an infinite loop, and how do you create one?
4. What two events cause program execution to terminate?
5. To what variable types can a `switch` evaluate?
6. What does the `default` statement do?
7. What does the `exit()` function do?

Exercises

1. Write a statement that causes control of the program to go to the next iteration in a loop.

2. Write the statement(s) that send control of a program to the end of a loop.

3. **BUG BUSTER:** Is anything wrong with the following code?

```c
switch( answer )
{
    case 'Y': printf("You answered yes");
            break;
    case 'N': printf("You answered no");
}
```

4. **BUG BUSTER:** Is anything wrong with the following code?

```c
switch( choice )
{
    default:
        printf("You did not choose 1 or 2");
    case 1:
        printf("You answered 1");
        break;
    case 2:
        printf("You answered 2");
        break;
}
```

5. Rewrite exercise 5 using `if` statements.

6. Write an infinite `do...while` loop.

Because of the multitude of possible answers for the following exercises, answers are not provided. These are exercises for you to try "on your own."

7. **ON YOUR OWN:** Write a program that works like a calculator. The program should allow for addition, subtraction, multiplication, and division.

13

LESSON 14

Working with the Screen, Printer, and Keyboard

Almost every program must perform input and output. How well a program handles input and output is often the best judge of the program's usefulness. You've already learned how to perform some basic input and output. In this lesson you learn

- How C uses streams for input and output

- Various ways of accepting input from the keyboard

- Methods of displaying text and numeric data onscreen

- How to send output to the printer

- How to redirect program input and output

Streams and C

Before you get to the details of program input/output, you need to learn about streams. All C input/output is done with streams, no matter where input is coming from or where output is going to. As you see later, this standard way of handling all input and output has definite advantages for the programmer. Of course, this makes it essential that you understand what streams are and how they work. First, however, you need to know exactly what the terms *input* and *output* mean.

What Exactly Is Program Input/Output?

As you learned earlier in this book, a C program keeps data in random access memory (RAM) while executing. This data is in the form of variables, structures, and arrays that have been declared by the program. Where did this data come from, and what can the program do with it?

- Data can come from some location external to the program. Data moved from an external location into RAM, where the program can access it, is called *input*. The keyboard and disk files are the most common sources of program input.

- Data can also be sent to a location external to the program; this is called *output*. The most common destinations for output are the screen, a printer, and disk files.

Input sources and output destinations are collectively referred to as *devices*. The keyboard is a device, the screen is a device, and so on. Some devices (the keyboard) are for input only, others (the screen) are for output only, and still others (jump drives) are for both input and output.

Whatever the device, and whether it performs input or output, C carries out all input and output operations by means of streams.

What Is a Stream?

A *stream* is a sequence of characters. More exactly, it is a sequence of bytes of data. A sequence of bytes flowing into a program is an input stream; a sequence of bytes flowing out of a program is an output stream. By focusing on streams, you don't have to worry as much about where they're going or where they originated. The major advantage of streams, therefore, is that input/output programming is *device-independent*. Programmers don't need to write special input/output functions for each device (keyboard, disk, and so on). The program sees input/output as a continuous stream of bytes no matter where the input comes from or goes to.

Every C stream is connected to a file. In this context, the term *file* doesn't refer to a disk file. Rather, it is an intermediate step between the stream that your program deals with and the actual physical device used for input or output. For the most part, the beginning

C programmer doesn't need to be concerned with these files because the details of interactions among streams, files, and devices are taken care of automatically by the C library functions and the operating system.

Text Versus Binary Streams

C streams fall into two modes: text and binary. A text stream consists only of characters, such as text data sent to the screen. Text streams are organized into lines, which can be up to 255 characters long and are terminated by an end-of-line, or newline, character. Certain characters in a text stream are recognized as having special meaning, such as the newline character. This lesson deals with text streams.

A *binary* stream can handle any sort of data, including, but not limited to, text data. Bytes of data in a binary stream aren't translated or interpreted in any special way; they are read and written exactly as-is. Binary streams are used primarily with disk files, which are covered in Lesson 17, "Using Disk Files."

Predefined Streams

The ANSI standard for C has three predefined streams, also referred to as the *standard input/output files*. These streams are automatically opened when a C program starts executing and are closed when the program terminates. The programmer doesn't need to take any special action to make these streams available. Table 14.1 lists the standard streams and the devices they normally are connected with. All the standard streams are text-mode streams.

TABLE 14.1 The Three Standard Streams

Name	Streams	Device
stdin	Standard input	Keyboard
stdout	Standard output	Screen
stderr	Standard error	Screen

NOTE

In the days of DOS, there were two additional streams, stdprn (for the printer port) and stdaux (for the serial port). However, these were never ANSI Standard and were supported only by DOS and Windows. Seeing that a significant advantage of C programming is its portability, you should stick with the three streams listed in Table 14.1, and you won't have any issues. However, in case you are reading an older book or run across some older code, it's good to know these additional streams.

14

You have actually been using two of these streams already. Whenever you have used the `printf()` or `puts()` functions to display text onscreen, you have used the `stdout` stream. Likewise, when you use `gets()` or `scanf()` to read keyboard input, you use the `stdin` stream. The standard streams are opened automatically, but other streams, such as those used to manipulate information stored on disk, must be opened explicitly. You learn how to do this in Lesson 17. The remainder of this lesson deals with the standard streams.

Using C's Stream Functions

The C standard library has a variety of functions that deal with stream input and output. Most of these functions come in two varieties: one that always uses one of the standard streams, and one that requires the programmer to specify the stream. These functions are listed in Table 14.2. This table doesn't list all of C's input/output functions, nor are all the functions in the table covered in this lesson.

TABLE 14.2 The Standard Library's Stream Input/Output Functions

Uses One of the Standard Streams	Requires a Stream Name	Description
`printf()`	`fprintf()`	Formatted output
`vprintf()`	`vfprintf()`	Formatted output with a variable argument list
`puts()`	`fputs()`	String output
`putchar()`	`putc()`, `fputc()`	Character output
`scanf()`	`fscanf()`	Formatted input
`vscanf()`	`vfscanf()`	Formatted input with a variable argument list
`gets()`	`fgets()`	String input
`getchar()`	`getc()`, `fgetc()`	Character input
`perror()`		String output to `stderr` only

All these functions require that you include `stdio.h`. The function `perror()` may also require `stdlib.h`. The functions `vprintf()` and `vfprintf()` also require `stdargs.h`. On UNIX systems, `vprintf()` and `vfprintf()` may also require `varargs.h`. Your compiler's Library Reference states whether any additional or alternative header files are needed.

An Example

The short program in Listing 14.1 demonstrates the equivalence of streams.

LISTING 14.1 stream.c: The Equivalence of Streams

```
1:   // stream.c--Demonstrates the equivalence of stream input and output. */
2:   #include <stdio.h>
3:
4:   int main( void )
5:   {
6:       char buffer[256];
7:
8:       /* Input a line, then immediately output it. */
9:
10:      puts(gets(buffer));
11:
12:      return 0;
13: }
```

On line 10, the `gets()` function is used to input a line of text from the keyboard (`stdin`). Because `gets()` returns a pointer to the string, it can be used as the argument to `puts()`, which displays the string onscreen (`stdout`). When run, this program inputs a line of text from the user and then immediately displays the string onscreen.

DO	DON'T
DO take advantage of the standard input/output streams that C provides.	**DON'T** rename or change the standard streams unnecessarily.
	DON'T try to use an input stream such as `stdin` for an output function such as `fprintf()`.

For a beginner learning to program C, using `gets()` is fine. For a real-world program, however, you should use `fgets()` (explained later in this lesson) as `gets()` poses some risks to program security.

Accepting Keyboard Input

14

Most C programs require some form of input from the keyboard (that is, from the `stdin` stream). Input functions are divided into a hierarchy of three levels: character input, line input, and formatted input.

Character Input

The character input functions read input from a stream one character at a time. When called, each of these functions returns the next character in the stream, or EOF if the end of the file has been reached or an error has occurred. EOF is a symbolic constant defined in stdio.h as -1. Character input functions differ in terms of buffering and echoing:

- Some character input functions are *buffered*. This means that the operating system holds all characters in a temporary storage space until you press Enter, and then the system sends the characters to the stdin stream. Others are *unbuffered,* meaning that each character is sent to stdin as soon as the key is pressed.

- Some input functions automatically *echo* each character to stdout as it is received. Others don't echo; the character is sent to stdin and not stdout. Because stdout is assigned to the screen, that's where input is echoed.

The uses of buffered, unbuffered, echoing, and nonechoing character input are explained in the following sections.

The getchar() Function

The function getchar() obtains the next character from the stream stdin. It provides buffered character input with echo, and its prototype is

```
int getchar(void);
```

The use of getchar() is demonstrated in Listing 14.2. Notice that the putchar() function, explained in detail later in the lesson, simply displays a single character onscreen.

Input ▼
LISTING 14.2   getchar.c: The getchar() Function

```
 1: // getchar.c--Demonstrates the getchar() function.
 2:
 3: #include <stdio.h>
 4:
 5: int main( void )
 6: {
 7:     int ch;
 8:
 9:     while ((ch = getchar()) != '\n')
10:         putchar(ch);
11:
12:     return 0;
13: }
```

Output ▼

This is what's typed in.
This is what's typed in.

Analysis ▼

On line 9, the `getchar()` function is called and waits to receive a character from `stdin`. Because `getchar()` is a buffered input function, no characters are received until you press Enter. However, each key you press is echoed immediately on the screen.

When you press Enter, all the characters you entered, including the newline, are sent to `stdin` by the operating system. The `getchar()` function returns the characters one at a time, assigning each in turn to `ch`.

Each character is compared to the newline character `'\n'` and, if not equal, displayed onscreen with `putchar()`. When a newline is returned by `getchar()`, the `while` loop terminates.

You can use the `getchar()` function to input entire lines of text, as shown in Listing 14.3. However, other input functions are better-suited for this task, as you learn later in this lesson.

Input ▼
LISTING 14.3   getchar2.c: Using the `getchar()` Function to Input an Entire Line of Text

```
1:   // getchar2.c--Using getchar() to input strings.
2:
3:   #include <stdio.h>
4:
5:   #define MAX 80
6:
7:   int main( void )
8:   {
9:       char ch, buffer[MAX+1];
10:      int x = 0;
11:
12:      while ((ch = getchar()) != '\n' && x < MAX)
13:          buffer[x++] = ch;
14:
15:      buffer[x] = '\0';
16:
17:      printf("%s\n", buffer);
18:
19:      return 0;
20: }
```

14

Output ▼

```
This is a string
This is a string
```

Analysis ▼

This program is similar to Listing 14.2 in the way that it uses `getchar()`. An extra condition has been added to the loop. This time the `while` loop accepts characters from `getchar()` until either a newline character is reached or 80 characters are read. Each character is assigned to an array called `buffer`. When the characters have been input, line 15 puts a null on the end of the array so that the `printf()` function on line 17 can print the entered string.

On line 9, why was `buffer` declared with a size of MAX + 1 instead of just MAX? If you declare `buffer` with a size of MAX + 1, the string can be 80 characters plus a null terminator. Don't forget to include a place for the null terminator at the end of your strings.

The `getch()` Function

The `getch()` function obtains the next character from the stream `stdin`. It provides unbuffered character input without echo. The `getch()` function isn't part of the ANSI Standard. This means that it might not be available on every system. In addition, it might require that different header files be included. Generally, the prototype for `getch()` is in the header file `conio.h`, as follows:

```
int getch(void);
```

Because it is unbuffered, `getch()` returns each character as soon as the key is pressed, without waiting for the user to press Enter. Because `getch()` doesn't echo its input, the characters aren't displayed onscreen. Listing 14.4 illustrates the use of `getch()`.

CAUTION

Listing 14.4 uses `getch()`, which is not ANSI-compliant. You should be careful when using non-ANSI functions because there is no guarantee that all compilers support them. If you get errors from Listing 14.4, it might be because your compiler doesn't support `getch()`.

Input ▼

LISTING 14.4   getch.c: Using the `getch()` Function

```
1:   /* Demonstrates the getch() function. */
2:   /* Non-ANSI code */
3:   #include <stdio.h>
4:   #include <conio.h>
5:
6:   int main( void )
7:   {
8:       int ch;
9:
10:      while ((ch = getch()) != '\r')
11:          putchar(ch);
12:
13:      return 0;
14: }
```

Output ▼

```
Testing the getch() function
```

Analysis ▼

When this program runs, `getch()` returns each character as soon as you press a key—
it doesn't wait for you to press Enter. There's no echo, so the only reason that each
character displays onscreen is the call to `putchar()`. To get a better understanding
of how `getch()` works, add a semicolon to the end of line 10 and remove line 11
(`putchar(ch)`). When you rerun the program, you see that nothing you type is echoed to
the screen. The `getch()` function gets the characters without echoing them to the screen.
You know the characters are received because the original listing used `putchar()` to
display them.

Why does this program compare each character to \r instead of to \n? The code
\r is the escape sequence for the carriage return character. When you press Enter,
the keyboard device sends a carriage return to `stdin`. The buffered character input
functions automatically translate the carriage return to a newline, so the program must
test for \n to determine whether Enter has been pressed. The unbuffered character input
functions don't translate, so a carriage return is input as \r, and that's what the program
must test for.

Listing 14.5 uses `getch()` to input an entire line of text. Running this program clearly
illustrates that `getch()` doesn't echo its input. With the exception of substituting `getch()`
for `getchar()`, this program is virtually identical to Listing 14.3.

14

Input ▼

LISTING 14.5   getch2.c: Using the `getch()` Function to Input an Entire Line

```c
1:  // getch2.c--Using getch() to input strings.
2:  // Non-ANSI code
3:  #include <stdio.h>
4:  #include <conio.h>
5:
6:  #define MAX 80
7:
8:  int main( void )
9:  {
10:      char ch, buffer[MAX+1];
11:      int x = 0;
12:
13:      while ((ch = getch()) != '\r' && x < MAX)
14:          buffer[x++] = ch;
15:
16:      buffer[x] = '\0';
17:
18:      printf("%s", buffer);
19:
20:      return 0;
21: }
```

Output ▼

```
Here's a string
```

> **CAUTION**
>
> Remember that `getch()` isn't an ANSI-Standard command. This means that your compiler (and other compilers) might not support it. If you have problems using this command, you should check your compiler and see whether it supports `getch()`. If you're concerned about portability, you should avoid non-ANSI functions.

The `getche()` Function

This is a short section because `getche()` is exactly like `getch()`, except that it echoes each character to `stdout`. Modify the program in Listing 14.4 to use `getche()` instead of `getch()`. When the program runs, each key you press displays onscreen twice—once as echoed by `getche()` and once as echoed by `putchar()`.

CAUTION	`getch()` is not an ANSI-Standard command, but many C compilers support it.

The `getc()` and `fgetc()` Functions

The `getc()` and `fgetc()` character input functions don't automatically work with `stdin`. Instead, they let the program specify the input stream. They are used primarily to read characters from disk files. See Lesson 17 for more details.

DO	DON'T
DO understand the difference between echoed and nonechoed input.	**DON'T** use non-ANSI Standard functions if portability is a concern.
DO understand the difference between buffered and unbuffered input.	**DON'T** expect non-ANSI Standard functions to work the same if you switch compilers.

"Ungetting" a Character with `ungetc()`

What does *ungetting* a character mean? An example should help you understand. Suppose that your program reads characters from an input stream and can detect the end of input only by reading one character too many. For example, you might input digits only, so you know that input has ended when the first nondigit character is encountered. That first nondigit character might be an important part of subsequent data, but it has been removed from the input stream. Is it lost? No, it can be "ungotten" or returned to the input stream, where it is then the first character read by the next input operation on that stream.

To "unget" a character, you use the `ungetc()` library function. Its prototype is

```
int ungetc(int ch, FILE *fp);
```

The argument `ch` is the character to be returned. The argument `*fp` specifies the stream that the character is to be returned to, which can be any input stream. For now, simply specify `stdin` as the second argument: `ungetc(ch, stdin);`. The notation `FILE *fp` is used with streams associated with disk files; you learn about this in Lesson 17.

You can unget only a single character to a stream between reads, and you can't unget `EOF` at any time. The function `ungetc()` returns `ch` on success and `EOF` if the character can't be returned to the stream.

14

Line Input

The line-input functions read a line from an input stream—they read all characters up to the next newline character. The standard library has two line input functions, `gets()` and `fgets()`.

The `gets()` Function

You were introduced to the `gets()` function in Lesson 10, "Working with Characters and Strings." This is a straightforward function, reading a line from `stdin` and storing it in a string. The function prototype is

```
char *gets(char *str);
```

You probably can interpret this prototype by yourself. `gets()` takes a pointer to type `char` as its argument and returns a pointer to type `char`. The `gets()` function reads characters from `stdin` until a newline (`\n`) or end-of-file is encountered; the newline is replaced with a null character, and the string is stored at the location indicated by `str`.

The return value is a pointer to the string (the same as `str`). If `gets()` encounters an error or reads an end-of-file before any characters are input, a null pointer is returned.

Before calling `gets()`, you must allocate sufficient memory space to store the string, using the methods covered in Lesson 10. This function has no way of knowing whether space pointed to by `str` is allocated; the string is input and stored starting at `str` in either case. If the space hasn't been allocated, the string might overwrite other data and cause program errors.

Listings 10.5 and 10.6 use `gets()`.

The `fgets()` Function

The `fgets()` library function is similar to `gets()` in that it reads a line of text from an input stream. It's more flexible because it lets the programmer specify the specific input stream to use and the maximum number of characters to be input. The `fgets()` function is often used to input text from disk files, covered in Lesson 17. To use it for input from `stdin`, you specify `stdin` as the input stream. The prototype of `fgets()` is

```
char *fgets(char *str, int n, FILE *fp);
```

The last parameter, `FILE *fp`, is used to specify the input stream. For now, simply specify the standard input stream, `stdin`, as the stream argument.

The pointer `str` indicates where the input string is stored. The argument `n` specifies the maximum number of characters to be input. The `fgets()` function reads characters from the input stream until a newline or end-of-line is encountered or `n - 1` characters have been read. The newline is included in the string and terminated with a `\0` before it is stored. The return values of `fgets()` are the same as described earlier for `gets()`.

Strictly speaking, `fgets()` doesn't input a single line of text (if you define a line as a sequence of characters ending with a newline). It can read less than a full line if the line contains more than n - 1 characters. When used with `stdin`, execution doesn't return from `fgets()` until you press Enter, but only the first n - 1 characters are stored in the string. The newline is included in the string only if it falls within the first n - 1 characters. Listing 14.6 demonstrates the `fgets()` function.

Input ▼
LISTING 14.6 fgets.c: Using the `fgets()` Function for Keyboard Input

```
1:  /* Demonstrates the fgets() function. */
2:
3:  #include <stdio.h>
4:
5:  #define MAXLEN 10
6:
7:  int main( void )
8:  {
9:      char buffer[MAXLEN];
10:
11:     puts("Enter text a line at a time; enter a blank to exit.");
12:
13:     while (1)
14:     {
15:         fgets(buffer, MAXLEN, stdin);
16:
17:         if (buffer[0] == '\n')
18:             break;
19:
20:         puts(buffer);
21:     }
22:     return 0;
23: }
```

Output ▼

```
Enter text a line at a time; enter a blank to exit.
Roses are red
Roses are
 red
Violets are blue
Violets a
re blue

Programming in C
Programmi
ng in C
```

14

```
Is for people like you!
Is for pe
ople like
 you!
```

Line 15 contains the `fgets()` function. When running the program, enter lines of length less than and greater than MAXLEN to see what happens. If a line greater than MAXLEN is entered, the first MAXLEN - 1 characters are read by the first call to `fgets()`; the remaining characters remain in the keyboard buffer and are read by the next call to `fgets()` or any other function that reads from `stdin`. The program exits when a blank line is entered (lines 17 and 18).

Working with Formatted Input

The input functions covered up to this point have simply taken one or more characters from an input stream and put them somewhere in memory. No interpretation or formatting of the input has been done, and you still have no way to input numeric variables. For example, how would you input the value `12.86` from the keyboard and assign it to a type `float` variable? Enter the `scanf()` and `fscanf()` functions. You were introduced to `scanf()` in Lesson 7, "Fundamentals of Reading and Writing Information." This section explains its use in more detail.

These two functions are identical, except that `scanf()` always uses `stdin`, whereas the user can specify the input stream in `fscanf()`. This section covers `scanf()`; `fscanf()` generally is used with disk file input and is covered in Lesson 17.

The `scanf()` Function's Arguments

The `scanf()` function takes a variable number of arguments; it requires a minimum of two. The first argument is a format string that uses special characters to tell `scanf()` how to interpret the input. The second and additional arguments are the addresses of the variable(s) to which the input data is assigned. Here's an example:

```
scanf("%d", &x);
```

The first argument, `"%d"`, is the format string. In this case, `%d` tells `scanf()` to look for one signed integer value. The second argument uses the address-of operator (`&`) to tell `scanf()` to assign the input value to the variable `x`. Now you can look at the format string details.

The `scanf()` format string can contain the following:

- Spaces and tabs, which are ignored. (They can be used to make the format string more readable.)

- Characters (but not %), which are matched against nonwhite-space characters in the input.

- One or more *conversion specifications,* which consist of the % character followed by special characters. Generally, the format string contains one conversion specification for each variable.

The only required part of the format string is the conversion specifications. Each conversion specification begins with the % character and contains optional and required components in a certain order. The scanf() function applies the conversion specifications in the format string, in order, to the input fields. An *input field* is a sequence of nonwhite-space characters that ends when the next white space is encountered or when the field width, if specified, is reached. The conversion specification components include the following:

- The optional assignment suppression flag (*) immediately follows the %. If present, this character tells scanf() to perform the conversion corresponding to the current conversion specifier but to ignore the result (not assign it to any variable).

- The next component, the field width, is also optional. The field width is a decimal number specifying the width, in characters, of the input field. In other words, the field width specifies how many characters from stdin that scanf() should examine for the current conversion. If a field width isn't specified, the input field extends to the next white space.

- The next component is the optional precision modifier, a single character that can be h, l, or L. If present, the precision modifier changes the meaning of the type specifier that follows it. Details are given later in this lesson.

- The only required component of the conversion specifier (besides the %) is the type specifier. The type specifier is one or more characters that tell scanf() how to interpret the input. These characters are listed and described in Table 14.3. The Argument column lists the required type of the corresponding variable. For example, the type specifier d requires int * (a pointer to type int).

14

TABLE 14.3 The Type Specifier Characters Used in `scanf()` Conversion Specifiers

Type	Argument	Meaning of Type
d	`int *`	A decimal integer.
i	`int *`	An integer in decimal, octal (with leading `0`), or hexadecimal (with leading `0X` or `0x`) notation.
o	`int *`	An integer in octal notation with or without the leading `0`.
u	`unsigned int *`	An unsigned decimal integer.
x	`int *`	A hexadecimal integer with or without the leading `0x` or `0x`.
c	`char *`	One or more characters are read and assigned sequentially to the memory location indicated by the argument. No terminating `\0` is added. If a field width argument isn't given, one character is read. If a field width argument is given, that number of characters, including white space (if any), is read.
s	`char *`	A string of nonwhite-space characters is read into the specified memory location, and a terminating `\0` is added.
a,e,f,g	`float *`	A floating-point number. Numbers can be input in decimal or scientific notation.
[...]	`char *`	A string. Only the characters listed between the brackets are accepted. Input ends as soon as a nonmatching character is encountered, the specified field width is reached, or Enter is pressed. To accept the `]` character, list it first: `[] ...]`. A `\0` is added at the end of the string.
[^...]	`char *`	The same as `[...]`, except that only characters not listed between the brackets are accepted.
%	None	Literal `%`: Reads the `%` character. No assignment is made.

Before seeing some examples of `scanf()`, you need to understand the precision modifiers, which are listed in Table 14.4.

TABLE 14.4 The Precision Modifiers

Precision Modifier	Meaning
hh	When placed before the type specifier d, i, o, u, x, X, or n, the modifier hh specifies that the argument is a pointer to a `signed char` or `unsigned char`.
h	When placed before the type specifier d, i, o, u, x, X, or n, the modifier h specifies that the argument is a pointer to type `short int` or `unsigned short int`.

Precision Modifier	Meaning
l	When placed before the type specifier d, i, o, u, x, X, or n, the modifier l specifies that the argument is a pointer to type long or unsigned long. When placed before the type specifier a, A, e, E, f, F, g, or G, the modifier l specifies that the argument is a pointer to type double.
ll	When placed before type specifier d, i, o, u, x, X, or n, the modifier ll specifies that the argument is a pointer to a long long or unsigned long long.
L	When placed before the type specifier a, A, e, E, f, F, g, or G, the modifier L specifies that the argument is a pointer to type long double.

Handling Extra Characters

Input from scanf() is buffered; no characters are actually received from stdin until the user presses Enter. The entire line of characters then "arrives" from stdin, and is processed, in order, by scanf(). Execution returns from scanf() only when enough input has been received to match the specifications in the format string. Also, scanf() processes only enough characters from stdin to satisfy its format string. Extra, unneeded characters, if any, remain waiting in stdin. These characters can cause problems. Take a closer look at the operation of scanf() to see how.

When a call to scanf() is executed and the user has entered a single line, you can have three situations. For these examples, assume that scanf("%d %d", &x, &y); is being executed; in other words, scanf() is expecting two decimal integers. Here are the possibilities:

- The line the user inputs matches the format string. For example, suppose the user enters 12 14 followed by Enter. In this case, there are no problems. scanf() is satisfied, and no characters are left over in stdin.

- The line that the user inputs has too few elements to match the format string. For example, suppose the user enters 12 followed by Enter. In this case, scanf() continues to wait for the missing input. After the input is received, execution continues, and no characters are left over in stdin.

- The line that the user enters has more elements than required by the format string. For example, suppose the user enters 12 14 16 followed by Enter. In this case, scanf() reads the 12 and the 14 and then returns. The extra characters, the 1 and the 6, are left waiting in stdin.

It is this third situation (specifically, those leftover characters) that can cause problems. They remain waiting for as long as your program is running, until the next time the program reads input from stdin. Then the leftover characters are the first ones read,

14

ahead of any input the user makes at the time. It's clear how this could cause errors. For example, the following code asks the user to input an integer and then a string:

```
puts("Enter your age.");
scanf("%d", &age);
puts("Enter your first name.");
scanf("%s", name);
```

Say, for example, that in response to the first prompt, the user decides to be precise and enters 29.00 and then presses Enter. The first call to scanf() is looking for an integer, so it reads the characters 29 from stdin and assigns the value 29 to the variable age. The characters .00 are left waiting in stdin. The next call to scanf() is looking for a string. It goes to stdin for input and finds .00 waiting there. The result is that the string .00 is assigned to name.

How can you avoid this problem? If the people who use your programs never make mistakes when entering information, that's one solution—but it's rather impractical.

A better solution is to make sure there are no extra characters waiting in stdin before prompting the user for input. You can do this by calling gets(), which reads any remaining characters from stdin, up to and including the end of the line. Rather than calling gets() directly from the program, you can put it in a separate function with the descriptive name of clear_kb(). This function is shown in Listing 14.7.

Input ▼

LISTING 14.7   clearing.c: Clearing stdin of Extra Characters to Avoid Errors

```
1:    // clearing.c--Clearing stdin of extra characters.
2:
3:    #include <stdio.h>
4:
5:    void clear_kb(void);
6:
7:    int main( void )
8:    {
9:        int age;
10:       char name[20];
11:
12:       // Prompt for user's age.
13:
14:       puts("Enter your age:");
15:       scanf("%d", &age);
16:
17:       // Clear stdin of any extra characters.
18:
```

```
19:        clear_kb();
20:
21:        // Now prompt for user's name:
22:
23:        puts("Enter your first name:");
24:        scanf("%s", name);
25:        // Display the data.
26:
27:        printf("Your age is %d.\n", age);
28:        printf("Your name is %s.\n", name);
29:
30:        return 0;
31: }
32:
33: void clear_kb(void)
34:
35: // Clears stdin of any waiting characters.
36: {
37:        char junk[80];
38:        gets(junk);
39: }
```

Output ▼

```
Enter your age:
15 or so
Enter your first name:
Gordon
Your age is 15.
Your name is Gordon.
```

Analysis ▼

When you run Listing 14.7, enter some extra characters after your age, before pressing Enter. Make sure the program ignores them and correctly prompts you for your name. Then modify the program by removing the call to clear_kb(), and run it again. Any extra characters entered on the same line as your age are assigned to name.

Handling Extra Characters with fflush()

There is a second way in which you can clear the extra characters that were typed in. The fflush() function flushes the information in a stream—including the standard input stream. fflush() is generally used with disk files (which are covered in Lesson 17); however, it can also be used to make Listing 14.7 even simpler. Listing 14.8 uses the fflush() function instead of the clear_kb() function that was created in Listing 14.7.

14

Input ▼

LISTING 14.8 clearing2.c: Clearing `stdin` of Extra Characters Using `fflush()`

```
1:  // clearing2.c--Clearing stdin of extra characters.
2:  // Using the fflush() function
3:  #include <stdio.h>
4:
5:  int main( void )
6:  {
7:      int age;
8:      char name[20];
9:
10:     // Prompt for user's age.
11:     puts("Enter your age:");
12:     scanf("%d", &age);
13:
14:     // Clear stdin of any extra characters.
15:     fflush(stdin);
16:
17:     // Now prompt for user's name.
18:     puts("Enter your first name.");
19:     scanf("%s", name);
20:
21:     // Display the data.
22:     printf("Your age is %d.\n", age);
23:     printf("Your name is %s.\n", name);
24:
25:     return 0;
26: }
```

Output ▼

```
Enter your age.
18 until next month
Enter your first name.
Alice
Your age is 18.
Your name is Alice.
```

Analysis ▼

The `fflush()` function is used on line 15. The prototype for the `fflush()` function is as follows:

```
int fflush( FILE *stream);
```

The *stream* is the stream to be flushed. In Listing 14.8, the standard input stream, `stdin`, is passed for *stream*.

scanf() **Examples**

The best way to become familiar with the operation of the scanf() function is to use it. It's a powerful function, but it can be a bit confusing at times. Try it and see what happens. Listing 14.9 demonstrates some of the unusual ways to use scanf(). You should compile and run this program and then experiment by making changes to the scanf() format strings.

Input ▼
LISTING 14.9   scanfdemos.c: Some Ways to Use scanf() for Keyboard Input

```
1:   // scanfdemos.c--Demonstrates some uses of scanf().
2:
3:   #include <stdio.h>
4:
5:   int main( void )
6:   {
7:        int i1;
8:        int i2;
9:        long l1;
10:
11:       double d1;
12:       char buf1[80]
13:       char buf2[80];
14:
15:       // Using the l modifier to enter long integers and doubles.
16:
17:       puts("Enter an integer and a floating point number.");
18:       scanf("%ld %lf", &l1, &d1);
19:       printf("\nYou entered %ld and %lf.\n",l1, d1);
20:       puts("The scanf() format string used the l modifier to store");
21:       puts("your input in a type long and a type double.\n");
22:
23:       fflush(stdin);
24:
25:       // Use field width to split input.
26:
27:       puts("Enter a 5 digit integer (for example, 54321).");
28:       scanf("%2d%3d", &i1, &i2);
29:
30:       printf("\nYou entered %d and %d.\n", i1, i2);
31:       puts("Note how the field width specifier in the scanf() format");
32:       puts("string split your input into two values.\n");
33:
34:       fflush(stdin);
35:
36:       // Using an excluded space to split a line of input into
37:       // two strings at the space.
38:
```

14

```
39:        puts("Enter your first and last names separated by a space.");
40:        scanf("%[^ ]%s", buf1, buf2);
41:        printf("\nYour first name is %s\n", buf1);
42:        printf("Your last name is %s\n", buf2);
43:        puts("Note how [^ ] in the scanf() format string, by excluding");
44:        puts ("the space character, caused the input to be split.");
45:
46:        return 0;
47: }
```

Output ▼

```
Enter an integer and a floating point number.
123 45.6789

You entered 123 and 45.678900.
The scanf() format string used the l modifier to store
your input in a type long and a type double.

Enter a 5 digit integer (for example, 54321).
54321

You entered 54 and 321.
Note how the field width specifier in the scanf() format
string split your input into two values.

Enter your first and last names separated by a space.
Ruth Alber

Your first name is Ruth
Your last name is Alber
Note how [^ ] in the scanf() format string, by excluding
the space character, caused the input to be split.
```

Analysis ▼

This listing starts by defining several variables on lines 7 through 13 for data input. The program then walks you through the steps of entering various types of data. Lines 17 through 21 have you enter and print long integers and a `double`. Line 23 calls the `fflush()` function to clear any unwanted characters from the standard input stream. Lines 27 and 28 get the next value, a five-character integer. Because there are width specifiers, the five-digit integer is split into two integers—one that is two characters and one that is three characters. Line 34 calls `fflush()` to clear the keyboard again. The final example, in lines 36 through 44, uses the exclude character. Line 40 uses `"%[^ ]"`, which tells `scanf()` to get a string but to stop at any spaces. This effectively splits the input.

Take the time to modify this listing and enter additional values to see what the results are.

The `scanf()` function can be used for most of your input needs, particularly those involving numbers. (Strings can be input more easily with `gets()`.) It is often worthwhile, however, to write your own specialized input functions. You can see some examples of user-defined functions in Lesson 19, "Getting More from Functions."

DO	DON'T
DO use the `gets()` and `scanf()` functions instead of the `fgets()` and `fscanf()` functions if you use the standard input file (`stdin`) only.	**DON'T** forget to check the input stream for extra characters.

Controlling Output to the Screen

Screen output functions are divided into three general categories along the same lines as the input functions: character output, line output, and formatted output. You were introduced to some of these functions in earlier lessons. This section covers them in detail.

Character Output with `putchar()`, `putc()`, and `fputc()`

The C library's character output functions send a single character to a stream. The function `putchar()` sends its output to `stdout` (normally the screen). The functions `fputc()` and `putc()` send their output to a stream specified in the argument list.

Using the `putchar()` Function

The prototype for `putchar`, which is located in `stdio.h`, is as follows:

```
int putchar(int c);
```

This function writes the character stored in `c` to `stdout`. Although the prototype specifies a type `int` argument, you pass `putchar()` a type `char`. You can also pass it a type `int` as long as its value is appropriate for a character (that is, in the range 0 to 255). The function returns the character that was just written, or `EOF` if an error has occurred. Remember that `EOF` is equivalent to `-1`, so it also works as a return value for `int` type functions.

You saw `putchar()` demonstrated in Listing 14.2. Listing 14.10 displays the characters with ASCII values between 14 and 127.

14

Input ▼
LISTING 14.10   putchar.c: The `putchar()` Function

```
1:  // putchar.c--Demonstrates putchar().
2:
3:  #include <stdio.h>
4:  int main( void )
5:  {
6:    int count;
7:
8:    for (count = 14; count < 128; )
9:          putchar(count++);
10:
11:   return 0;
12: }
```

Output ▼

```
?¤????¶§?????????? !"#$%&'()*+,-./0123456789:;<=>?@ABCDEF
GHIJKLMNOPQRSTUVWXYZ[\]^_'abcdefghijklmnopqrstuvwxyz{|}~▨
```

You can also display strings with the `putchar()` function (as shown in Listing 14.11), although other functions are better-suited for this purpose.

Input ▼
LISTING 14.11   putchar2.c: Displaying a String with `putchar()`

```
1:  /* Using putchar() to display strings. */
2:
3:  #include <stdio.h>
4:
5:  #define MAXSTRING 80
6:
7:  char message[] = "Displayed with putchar().";
8:  int main( void )
9:  {
10:     int count;
11:
12:     for (count = 0; count < MAXSTRING; count++)
13:     {
14:
15:         /* Look for the end of the string. When it's found, */
16:         /* write a newline character and exit the loop. */
17:
18:         if (message[count] == '\0')
19:         {
20:             putchar('\n');
```

```
21:            break;
22:        }
23:        else
24:
25:        /* If end of string not found, write the next character. */
26:
27:            putchar(message[count]);
28:    }
29:    return 0;
30: }
```

Output ▼

```
Displayed with putchar().
```

Using the `putc()` and `fputc()` Functions

The `putc()` and `fputc()` functions perform the same action—sending a single character to a specified stream. `putc()` is a macro implementation of `fputc()`. You learn about macros in Lesson 22, "Advanced Compiler Use." For now, just stick to `fputc()`. Its prototype is

```
int fputc(int c, FILE *fp);
```

The `FILE *fp` part might puzzle you. You pass `fputc()` the output stream in this argument. (You learn more about this in Lesson 17.) If you specify `stdout` as the stream, `fputc()` behaves exactly the same as `putchar()`. Thus, the following two statements are equivalent:

```
putchar('x');
fputc('x', stdout);
```

Using `puts()` and `fputs()` for String Output

Your programs display strings onscreen more often than they display single characters. The library function `puts()` displays strings. The function `fputs()` sends a string to a specified stream; otherwise, it is identical to `puts()`. The prototype for `puts()` is

```
int puts(char *cp);
```

`*cp` is a pointer to the first character of the string that you want displayed. The `puts()` function displays the entire string up to but not including the terminating null character, adding a newline at the end. Then `puts()` returns a positive value if successful or `EOF` on error. (Remember, `EOF` is a symbolic constant with the value -1; it is defined in `stdio.h`.)

You can use the `puts()` function to display any type of string, as demonstrated in Listing 14.12.

14

Input ▼

LISTING 14.12 puts.c: Using the `puts()` Function to Display Strings

```
1:  // puts.c--Demonstrates puts().
2:
3:  #include <stdio.h>
4:  #define SIZE 5
5:  // Declare and initialize an array of pointers.
6:
7:  char *messages[SIZE] = { "This", "is", "a", "short", "message." };
8:
9:  int main( void )
10: {
11:     int x;
12:
13:     for (x=0; x<SIZE; x++)
14:         puts(messages[x]);
15:
16:     puts("And this is the end!");
17:
18:     return 0;
19: }
```

Output ▼

```
This
is
a
short
message.
And this is the end!
```

Analysis ▼

This listing declares an array of pointers, a subject not covered yet. (It will be covered in the next lesson.) Lines 13 and 14 print each of the strings stored in the message array.

Using `printf()` and `fprintf()` for Formatted Output

So far, the output functions have displayed characters and strings only. What about numbers? To display numbers, you must use the C library's formatted output functions, `printf()` and `fprintf()`. These functions can also display strings and characters. You were officially introduced to `printf()` in Lesson 7, and you've used it in almost every lesson since. This section provides the remainder of the details.

The two functions `printf()` and `fprintf()` are identical, except that `printf()` always sends output to `stdout`, whereas `fprintf()` specifies the output stream. `fprintf()` is generally used for output to disk files. It's covered in Lesson 17.

The `printf()` function takes a variable number of arguments, with a minimum of one. The first and only required argument is the format string, which tells `printf()` how to format the output. The optional arguments are variables and expressions whose values you want to display. Take a look at these few simple examples, which give you a feel for `printf()`, before you get into the nitty-gritty:

- The statement `printf("Hello, world.");` displays the message `Hello, world.` onscreen. This is an example of using `printf()` with only one argument, the format string. In this case, the format string contains only a literal string to display onscreen.

- The statement `printf("%d", i);` displays the value of the integer variable `i` onscreen. The format string contains only the format specifier `%d`, which tells `printf()` to display a single decimal integer. The second argument `i` is the name of the variable whose value displays.

- The statement `printf("%d plus %d equals %d.", a, b, a+b);` displays `2 plus 3 equals 5` onscreen (assuming that `a` and `b` are integer variables with the values of `2` and `3`, respectively). This use of `printf()` has four arguments: a format string that contains literal text as well as format specifiers, and two variables and an expression whose values display.

Now look at the `printf()` format string in more detail. It can contain the following:

- Zero, one, or more conversion commands that tell `printf()` how to display a value in its argument list. A conversion command consists of `%` followed by one or more characters.

- Characters that are not part of a conversion command and display as-is.

The third example's format string is `%d plus %d equals %d`. In this case, the three `%d`s are conversion commands, and the remainder of the string, including the spaces, is literal characters that display directly.

Now you can dissect the conversion command. The components of the command are given here and explained next. Components in brackets are optional.

`%[flag] [field_width] [.[precision]] [l] conversion_char`

The `conversion_char` is the only required part of a conversion command (other than the `%`). Table 14.5 lists the conversion characters and their meanings.

14

TABLE 14.5 The `printf()` and `fprintf()` Conversion Characters

Conversion Character	Meaning
d, i	Display a signed integer in decimal notation.
u	Display an unsigned integer in decimal notation.
o	Display an integer in unsigned octal notation.
x, X	Display an integer in unsigned hexadecimal notation. Use `x` for lowercase output and `x` for uppercase output.
c	Display a single character. (The argument gives the character's ASCII code.)
e, E	Display a `float` or `double` in scientific notation. (For example, `123.45` displays as `1.234500e+002.`). Six digits display to the right of the decimal point unless another precision is specified with the `f` specifier. Use `e` or `E` to control the case of output.
f	Display a `float` or `double` in decimal notation. (For example, `123.45` displays as `123.450000`.) Six digits display to the right of the decimal point unless another precision is specified.
g, G	Use `e`, `E`, or `f` format. The `e` or `E` format is used if the exponent is less than `-3` or greater than the precision (which defaults to `6`). `f` format is used otherwise. Trailing zeros are truncated.
n	Nothing is displayed. The argument corresponding to an `n` conversion command is a pointer to type `int`. The `printf()` function assigns to this variable the number of characters output so far.
s	Display a string. The argument is a pointer to `char`. Characters display until a null character is encountered or the number of characters specified by precision display. The terminating null character is not output.
%	Display the `%` character.

You can place the `l` modifier just before the conversion character. This modifier applies only to the conversion characters o, u, x, X, i, d, and b. When applied, this modifier specifies that the argument is a type `long` rather than a type `int`. If the `l` modifier is applied to the conversion characters e, E, f, g, or G, it specifies that the argument is a type `double`. If a `l` is placed before any other conversion character, it is ignored.

In addition to the `l` specifier, there is an `ll` specifier. The `ll` specifier works just like the `l` specifier except that the argument is type `long long` instead of type `long`.

The precision specifier consists of a decimal point (`.`) by itself or followed by a number. A precision specifier applies only to the conversion characters e, E, f, g, G, and s. It specifies the number of digits to display to the right of the decimal point or, when used with s, the number of characters to output. If the decimal point is used alone, it specifies a precision of `0`.

The field-width specifier determines the minimum number of characters output. The field-width specifier can be the following:

- A decimal integer not starting with `0`. The output is padded on the left with spaces to fill the designated field width.
- A decimal integer starting with `0`. The output is padded on the left with zeros to fill the designated field width.
- The `*` character. The value of the next argument (which must be an `int`) is used as the field width. For example, if `w` is a type `int` with a value of `10`, the statement `printf("%*d", w, a);` prints the value of `a` with a field width of `10`.

If no field width is specified, or if the specified field width is narrower than the output, the output field is just as wide as needed.

The last optional part of the `printf()` format string is the flag, which immediately follows the `%` character. There are four available flags:

-	This means that the output is left-justified in its field rather than right-justified, which is the default.
+	This means that signed numbers always display with a leading + or -.
' '	A space means that positive numbers are preceded by a space.
#	This applies only to `x`, `X`, and `o` conversion characters. It specifies that nonzero numbers display with a leading `0X` or `0x` (for `x` and `X`) or a leading `0` (for `o`).

When you use `printf()`, the format string can be a string literal enclosed in double quotes in the `printf()` argument list. It can also be a null-terminated string stored in memory, in which case you pass a pointer to the string to `printf()`. For example, this statement

```
char *fmt = "The answer is %f.";
printf(fmt, x);
```

is equivalent to this statement

```
printf("The answer is %f.", x);
```

As explained in Lesson 7, the `printf()` format string can contain escape sequences that provide special control over the output. Table 14.6 lists the most frequently used escape sequences. For example, including the newline sequence (`\n`) in a format string causes subsequent output to appear starting on the next screen line.

14

TABLE 14.6 The Most Frequently Used Escape Sequences

Sequence	Meaning
\a	Bell (alert)
\b	Backspace
\n	Newline
\t	Horizontal tab
\\	Backslash
\?	Question mark
\'	Single quote
\"	Double quote

`printf()` is somewhat complicated. The best way to learn how to use it is to look at examples and then experiment on your own. Listing 14.13 demonstrates many of the ways you can use `printf()`.

Input ▼

LISTING 14.13   printfdemo.c: Some Ways to Use the `printf()` Function

```
1:  /* printfdemo.c--Demonstration of printf(). */
2:
3:  #include <stdio.h>
4:
5:  char *m1 = "Binary";
6:  char *m2 = "Decimal";
7:  char *m3 = "Octal";
8:  char *m4 = "Hexadecimal";
9:
10: int main( void )
11: {
12:     float d1 = 10000.123;
13:     int n;
14:
15:
16:     puts("Outputting a number with different field widths.\n");
17:
18:     printf("%5f\n", d1);
19:     printf("%10f\n", d1);
20:     printf("%15f\n", d1);
21:     printf("%20f\n", d1);
22:     printf("%25f\n", d1);
23:
24:     puts("\n Press Enter to continue...");
25:     fflush(stdin);
26:     getchar();
27:
```

```
28:        puts("\nUse the * field width specifier to obtain field width");
29:        puts("from a variable in the argument list.\n");
30:
31:        for (n=5;n<=25; n+=5)
32:            printf("%*f\n", n, d1);
33:
34:        puts("\n Press Enter to continue...");
35:        fflush(stdin);
36:        getchar();
37:
38:        puts("\nInclude leading zeros.\n");
39:
40:        printf("%05f\n", d1);
41:        printf("%010f\n", d1);
42:        printf("%015f\n", d1);
43:        printf("%020f\n", d1);
44:        printf("%025f\n", d1);
45:
46:        puts("\n Press Enter to continue...");
47:        fflush(stdin);
48:        getchar();
49:
50:        puts("\nDisplay in octal, decimal, and hexadecimal.");
51:        puts("Use # to precede octal and hex output with 0 and 0X.");
52:        puts("Use - to left-justify each value in its field.");
53:        puts("First display column labels.\n");
54:
55:        printf("%-15s%-15s%-15s", m2, m3, m4);
56:
57:        for (n = 1;n< 20; n++)
58:            printf("\n%-15d%-#15o%-#15X", n, n, n);
59:
60:        puts("\n Press Enter to continue...");
61:        fflush(stdin);
62:        getchar();
63:
64:        puts("\n\nUse the %n conversion command to count characters.\n");
65:
66:        printf("%s%s%s%s%n", m1, m2, m3, m4, &n);
67:
68:        printf("\n\nThe last printf() output %d characters.\n", n);
69:
70:        return 0;
71: }
```

14

Output ▼

Outputting a number with different field widths.

10000.123047

```
10000.123047
   10000.123047
        10000.123047
              10000.123047


  Press Enter to continue...
```

Use the * field width specifier to obtain field width
from a variable in the argument list.

```
10000.123047
10000.123047
   10000.123047
        10000.123047
              10000.123047


  Press Enter to continue...
```

Include leading zeros.

```
10000.123047
10000.123047
00010000.123047
0000000010000.123047
000000000000010000.123047


  Press Enter to continue...
```

Display in octal, decimal, and hexadecimal.
Use # to precede octal and hex output with 0 and 0X.
Use - to left-justify each value in its field.
First display column labels.

```
Decimal         Octal           Hexadecimal
1               01              0X1
2               02              0X2
3               03              0X3
4               04              0X4
5               05              0X5
6               06              0X6
7               07              0X7
8               010             0X8
9               011             0X9
10              012             0XA
11              013             0XB
12              014             0XC
13              015             0XD
14              016             0XE
```

```
15              017             0XF
16              020             0X10
17              021             0X11
18              022             0X12
19              023             0X13

  Press Enter to continue...

Use the %n conversion command to count characters.

BinaryDecimalOctalHexadecimal

The last printf() output 20 characters.
```

When to Use `fprintf()`

As mentioned earlier, the library function `fprintf()` is identical to `printf()`, except that you can specify the stream to which output is sent. The main use of `fprintf()` involves disk files, as explained in Lesson 16, "Pointers to Functions and Linked Lists." There are two other uses, as explained here.

Using `stderr`

One of C's predefined streams is `stderr` (standard error). A program's error messages traditionally are sent to the stream `stderr` and not to `stdout`. Why is this?

As you just learned, output to `stdout` can be redirected to a destination other than the display screen. If `stdout` is redirected, the user might not be aware of any error messages the program sends to `stdout`. By directing error messages to `stderr`, you can be sure the user always sees them. You do this with `fprintf()`:

```
fprintf(stderr, "An error has occurred.");
```

You can write a function to handle error messages and then call the function when an error occurs rather than calling `fprintf()`:

```
error_message("An error has occurred.");

void error_message(char *msg)
{
    fprintf(stderr, msg);
}
```

14

By using your own function instead of directly calling `fprintf()`, you provide additional flexibility (one of the advantages of structured programming). For example, in special circumstances you might want a program's error messages to go to the printer or a disk file. All you need to do is modify the `error_message()` function so that the output is sent to the wanted destination.

DO	DON'T
DO use `fprintf()` to create programs that can send output to `stdout`, `stderr`, `stdprn`, or any other stream.	**DON'T** ever try to redirect `stderr`.
DO use `fprintf()` with `stderr` to print error messages to the screen.	**DON'T** use `stderr` for purposes other than printing error messages or warnings.
DO create functions such as `error_message` to make your code more structured and maintainable.	

Summary

This was a long lesson full of important information on program input and output. You learned how C uses streams, treating all input and output as a sequence of bytes. You also learned that ANSI C has three predefined streams:

`stdin`	The keyboard
`stdout`	The screen
`stderr`	The screen

Input from the keyboard arrives from the stream `stdin`. Using C's standard library functions, you can accept keyboard input character by character, a line at a time, or as formatted numbers and strings. Character input can be buffered or unbuffered, echoed or unechoed.

Output to the display screen is normally done with the `stdout` stream. Like input, program output can be by character, by line, or as formatted numbers and strings. For output to the printer, you use `fprintf()` to send data to the stream `stdprn`.

When you use `stdin` and `stdout`, you can redirect program input and output. Input can come from a disk file rather than the keyboard, and output can go to a disk file rather than to the display screen.

You learned why error messages should be sent to the stream `stderr` instead of `stdout`. Because `stderr` is usually connected to the display screen, you are assured of seeing error messages even when the program output is redirected.

Q&A

Q Is there any danger in using non-ANSI functions in a program?

A Most compilers come with many useful functions that aren't ANSI-Standard. If you plan on always using that compiler and not porting your code to other compilers or platforms, there won't be a problem. If you use other compilers and platforms, you should be concerned with ANSI compatibility.

Q Why shouldn't I always use `fprintf()` instead of `printf()`? Or `fscanf()` instead of `scanf()`?

A If you use the standard output or input streams, you should use `printf()` and `scanf()`. By using these simpler functions, you don't have to bother with any other streams.

Workshop

The Workshop provides quiz questions to help you solidify your understanding of the material covered and exercises to provide you with experience in using what you've learned.

Quiz

1. What is a stream, and what does a C program use streams for?

2. Are the following input devices or output devices?

    a. Printer

    b. Keyboard

    c. Modem

    d. Monitor

    e. Flash Drive

3. List the three preferred streams that all compilers support and the devices with which they are associated.

4. What stream do the following functions use?

    a. `printf()`

    b. `puts()`

    c. `scanf()`

    d. `gets()`

    e. `fprintf()`

14

5. What is the difference between buffered and unbuffered character input from `stdin`?

6. What is the difference between echoed and unechoed character input from `stdin`?

7. Can you "unget" more than one character at a time with `ungetc()`? Can you "unget" the `EOF` character?

8. When you use C's line input functions, how is the end of a line determined?

9. Which of the following are valid type specifiers?

    a. `"%d"`

    b. `"%4d"`

    c. `"%3i%c"`

    d. `"%q%d"`

    e. `"%%%i"`

    f. `"%9ld"`

10. What is the difference between `stderr` and `stdout`?

Exercises

1. Write a statement to print `"Hello World"` to the screen.

2. Use two different C functions to do the same thing the function in exercise 1 did.

3. Write a statement that gets a string 30 characters or shorter. If an asterisk is encountered, truncate the string.

4. Write a single statement that prints the following:

```
Jack asked, "What is a backslash?"
Jill said, "It is '\'"
```

LESSON 15
Pointers to Pointers and Arrays of Pointers

In Lesson 9, "Understanding Pointers," you were introduced to the basics of pointers, which are an important part of the C programming language. In the next two lessons, you go further, exploring some advanced pointer topics that can add flexibility to your programming. In this lesson you learn

- How to declare a pointer to a pointer

- How to use pointers with multidimensional arrays

- How to declare arrays of pointers

Declaring Pointers to Pointers

As you learned in Lesson 9, a *pointer* is a numeric variable with a value that is the address of another variable. You declare a pointer using the indirection operator (*). For example, the declaration

```
int *ptr;
```

declares a pointer named `ptr` that can point to a type `int` variable. You then use the address-of operator (`&`) to make the pointer point to a specific variable of the corresponding type. Assuming that `myVar` has been declared as a type `int` variable, the statement

```
ptr = &myVar;
```

assigns the address of `myVar` to `ptr` and makes `ptr` point to `myVar`. Again, using the indirection operator, you can access the pointed-to variable by using its pointer. Both of the following statements assign the value 12 to `myVar`:

```
myVar = 12;
*ptr = 12;
```

Because a pointer is itself a numeric variable, it is stored in your computer's memory at a particular address. Therefore, you can create a pointer to a pointer, a variable whose value is the address of a pointer. Here's how:

```
int myVar = 12;              /* myVar is a type int variable. */
int *ptr = &myVar;           /* ptr is a pointer to myVar. */
int **ptr_to_ptr = &ptr;     /* ptr_to_ptr is a pointer to a */
                             /* pointer to type int. */
```

Note the use of a double indirection operator (`**`) when declaring a pointer to a pointer. You also use the double indirection operator when accessing the pointed-to variable with a pointer to a pointer. Thus, the statement

```
**ptr_to_ptr = 12;
```

assigns the value 12 to the variable `myVar`, and the statement

```
printf("%d", **ptr_to_ptr);
```

displays the value of `myVar` onscreen. If you mistakenly use a single indirection operator, you get errors. The statement

```
*ptr_to_ptr = 12;
```

assigns the value 12 to `ptr`, which results in `ptr`'s pointing to whatever happens to be stored at address 12. This clearly is a mistake.

Declaring and using a pointer to a pointer is called *multiple indirection*. Figure 15.1 shows the relationship between a variable, a pointer, and a pointer to a pointer. There's no limit to the level of multiple indirection possible—you can have a pointer to a pointer to a pointer *ad infinitum,* but there's rarely any advantage to going beyond two levels; the complexities involved are an invitation to mistakes.

15

FIGURE 15.1
A pointer to a pointer.

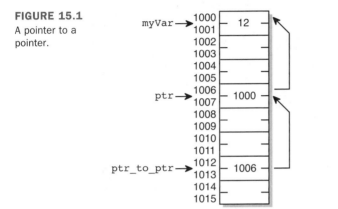

How can you use pointers to pointers? The most common use involves arrays of pointers, which are covered later in the lesson. Listing 20.5 in Lesson 20, "Exploring the C Function Library," presents an example of using multiple indirection.

Pointers and Multidimensional Arrays

Lesson 8, "Using Numeric Arrays," covered the special relationship between pointers and arrays. Specifically, the name of an array without its following brackets is a pointer to the first element of the array. As a result, it's easier to use pointer notation when you access certain types of arrays. These earlier examples, however, were limited to single-dimensional arrays. What about multidimensional arrays?

Remember that a multidimensional array is declared with one set of brackets for each dimension. For example, the following statement declares a two-dimensional array that contains eight type `int` variables:

```
int multi[2][4];
```

You can visualize an array as having a row and column structure—in this case, two rows and four columns. There's another way to visualize a multidimensional array, however, and this way is closer to the manner in which C actually handles arrays. You can consider `multi` to be a two-element array, with each of these two elements being an array of four integers.

In case this isn't clear to you, Figure 15.2 dissects the array declaration statement into its component parts.

FIGURE 15.2
The components of a multidimensional array declaration.

```
      4   1   2 3
      ↓   ↓   ↓ ↓
int multi[2][4];
```

Here's how to interpret the components of the declaration:

1. Declare an array named `multi`.
2. The array `multi` contains two elements.
3. Each of these two elements contains four elements.
4. Each of the four elements is of type `int`.

You read a multidimensional array declaration starting with the array name and moving to the right, one set of brackets at a time. When the last set of brackets (the last dimension) has been read, you jump to the beginning of the declaration to determine the array's basic data type.

Under the array-of-arrays scheme, you can visualize a multidimensional array, as shown in Figure 15.3.

FIGURE 15.3
A two-dimensional array can be visualized as an array of arrays.

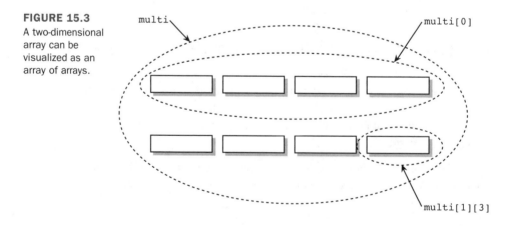

Now, let's get back to the topic of array names as pointers. (This lesson is about pointers, after all!) As with a one-dimensional array, the name of a multidimensional array is a pointer to the first array element. Continuing with our example, `multi` is a pointer to the first element of the two-dimensional array that was declared as `int multi[2][4]`. What exactly is the first element of `multi`? It isn't the type `int` variable `multi[0][0]`, as you might think. Remember that `multi` is an array of arrays, so its first element is `multi[0]`, which is an array of four type `int` variables (one of the two such arrays contained in `multi`).

Now, if `multi[0]` is also an array, does it point to anything? Yes, indeed! `multi[0]` points to its first element, `multi[0][0]`. You might wonder why `multi[0]` is a pointer. Remember that the name of an array without brackets is a pointer to the first array element. The term `multi[0]` is the name of the array `multi[0][0]` with the last pair of brackets missing, so it qualifies as a pointer.

If you're a bit confused at this point, don't worry. This material is difficult to grasp. It might help if you remember the following rules for any array of *n* dimensions used in code:

- The array name followed by *n* pairs of brackets (each pair containing an appropriate index, of course) evaluates as array data (that is, the data stored in the specified array element).
- The array name followed by fewer than *n* pairs of brackets evaluates as a pointer to an array element.

In the example, therefore, `multi` evaluates as a pointer, `multi[0]` evaluates as a pointer, and `multi[0][0]` evaluates as array data.

Now look at what all these pointers actually point to. Listing 15.1 declares a two-dimensional array—similar to those you've been using in the examples—and then prints the values of the associated pointers. It also prints the address of the first array element.

Input ▼

LISTING 15.1   multiarray.c: The Relationship Between a Multidimensional Array and Pointers

```
1:     /* Demonstrates pointers and multidimensional arrays. */
2:
3:     #include <stdio.h>
4:
5:     int multi[2][4];
6:
7:     int main( void )
8:     {
9:         printf("\nmulti = %p", multi);
10:        printf("\nmulti[0] = %p", multi[0]);
11:        printf("\n&multi[0][0] = %p\n", &multi[0][0]);
12:
13:        return 0;
14:    }
```

Output ▼

```
multi = 4210752
multi[0]  = 4210752
&multi[0][0]  = 4210752
```

Analysis ▼

The actual value might not be `4210752` on your system, but all three values will be the same. The address of the array `multi` is the same as the address of the array `multi[0]`, and both are equal to the address of the first integer in the array, `multi[0][0]`.

If all three of these pointers have the same value, what is the practical difference between them in terms of your program? Remember from Lesson 9 that the C compiler knows what a pointer points to. To be more exact, the compiler knows the size of the item a pointer is pointing to.

What are the sizes of the elements you've been using? Listing 15.2 uses the operator `sizeof()` to display the sizes, in bytes, of these elements.

Input ▼

LISTING 15.2   multiarraysize.c: Determining the Sizes of Elements

```
1:   /* Demonstrates the sizes of multidimensional array elements. */
2:
3:   #include <stdio.h>
4:
5:   int multi[2][4];
6:
7:   int main( void )
8:   {
9:       printf("\nThe size of multi = %p", sizeof(multi));
10:      printf("\nThe size of multi[0] = %p", sizeof(multi[0]));
11:      printf("\nThe size of multi[0][0] = %p\n", sizeof(multi[0][0]));
12:
13:      return 0;
14: }
```

The output of this program (assuming that your compiler uses 4-byte integers) is as follows:

Output ▼

```
The size of multi = 32
The size of multi[0] = 16
The size of multi[0][0] = 4
```

Analysis ▼

Think about these size values. The array `multi` contains two arrays, each of which contains four integers. Each integer requires 4 bytes of storage. With a total of eight integers, the size of 32 bytes makes sense.

Next, `multi[0]` is an array containing four integers. Each integer takes 4 bytes, so the size of 16 bytes for `multi[0]` also makes sense.

Finally, `multi[0][0]` is an integer, so its size is, of course, 4 bytes.

Now, keeping these sizes in mind, recall the discussion in Lesson 9 about pointer arithmetic. The C compiler knows the size of the object being pointed to, and pointer arithmetic takes this size into account. When you increment a pointer, its value is increased by the amount needed to make it point to the "next" of whatever it's pointing to. In other words, it's incremented by the size of the object to which it points.

When you apply this to the example, `multi` is a pointer to a four-element integer array with a size of 16. If you increment `multi`, its value should increase by 16 (the size of a four-element integer array). If `multi` points to `multi[0]`, therefore, `(multi + 1)` should point to `multi[1]`. Listing 15.3 tests this theory.

Input ▼
LISTING 15.3   multiarraymath.c: Pointer Arithmetic with Multidimensional Arrays

```
1:    /*  Demonstrates pointer arithmetic with pointers */
2:    /*  to multidimensional arrays. */
3:
4:    #include <stdio.h>
5:
6:    int multi[2][4];
7:
8:    int main( void )
9:    {
10:       printf("\nThe value of (multi) = %u", multi);
11:       printf("\nThe value of (multi + 1) = %u", (multi+1));
12:       printf("\nThe address of multi[1] = %u\n", &multi[1]);
13:
14:       return 0;
15:    }
```

Output ▼

```
The value of (multi) = 4210752
The value of (multi + 1) = 4210768
The address of multi[1] = 4210768
```

Analysis ▼

The precise values might be different on your system, but the relationships are the same. Incrementing `multi` by one increases its value by 16 and makes it point to the next element of the array, `multi[1]`.

In this example, you've seen that `multi` is a pointer to `multi[0]`. You've also seen that `multi[0]` is itself a pointer (to `multi[0][0]`). Therefore, `multi` is a pointer to a pointer. To use the expression `multi` to access array data, you must use double indirection. To print the value stored in `multi[0][0]`, you could use any of the following three statements:

```
printf("%d", multi[0][0]);
printf("%d", *multi[0]);
printf("%d", **multi);
```

These concepts apply equally to arrays with three or more dimensions. Thus, a three-dimensional array is an array with elements that are each two-dimensional arrays; each of these elements is itself an array of one-dimensional arrays.

This material on multidimensional arrays and pointers might seem a bit confusing. When you work with multidimensional arrays, keep this point in mind: An array with n dimensions has elements that are arrays with $n-1$ dimensions. When n becomes 1, that array's elements are variables of the data type specified at the beginning of the array declaration line.

So far, you've been using array names that are pointer constants and that can't be changed. How would you declare a pointer variable that points to an element of a multidimensional array? Look at the previous example, which declared a two-dimensional array as follows:

```
int multi[2][4];
```

To declare a pointer variable `ptr` that can point to an element of `multi` (that is, can point to a four-element integer array), you write

```
int (*ptr)[4];
```

You then make `ptr` point to the first element of `multi` by writing

```
ptr = multi;
```

You might wonder why the parentheses are necessary in the pointer declaration. Brackets (`[ ]`) have a higher precedence than `*`. If you wrote

```
int *ptr[4];
```

you would be declaring an array of four pointers to type int. Indeed, you can declare and use arrays of pointers. This isn't what you want to do now, however.

How can you use pointers to elements of multidimensional arrays? As with single-dimensional arrays, pointers must be used to pass an array to a function. This is illustrated for a multidimensional array in Listing 15.4, which uses two methods of passing a multidimensional array to a function.

15

Input ▼
LISTING 15.4 ptrmulti.c: Passing a Multidimensional Array to a Function Using a Pointer

```
1:   /* Demonstrates passing a pointer to a multidimensional */
2:   /* array to a function. */
3:
4:   #include <stdio.h>
5:
6:   void printarray_1(int (*ptr)[4]);
7:   void printarray_2(int (*ptr)[4], int n);
8:
9:   int main( void )
10: {
11:     int  multi[3][4] = { { 1, 2, 3, 4 },
12:                          { 5, 6, 7, 8 },
13:                          { 9, 10, 11, 12 } };
14:
15:     /* ptr is a pointer to an array of 4 ints. */
16:
17:     int (*ptr)[4], count;
18:
19:     /* Set ptr to point to the first element of multi. */
20:
21:     ptr = multi;
22:
23:     /* With each loop, ptr is incremented to point to the next */
24:     /* element (that is, the next 4-element integer array) of multi. */
25:
26:     for (count = 0; count < 3; count++)
27:         printarray_1(ptr++);
28:
29:     puts("\n\nPress Enter...");
30:     getchar();
31:     printarray_2(multi, 3);
32:     printf("\n");
33:     return 0;
34: }
35:
36: void printarray_1(int (*ptr)[4])
37: {
38: /* Prints the elements of a single four-element integer array. */
```

```
39: /* p is a pointer to type int. You must use a typecast */
40: /* to make p equal to the address in ptr. */
41:
42:        int *p, count;
43:        p = (int *)ptr;
44:
45:        for (count = 0; count < 4; count++)
46:             printf("\n%d", *p++);
47: }
48:
49: void printarray_2(int (*ptr)[4], int n)
50: {
51: /* Prints the elements of an n by four-element integer array. */
52:
53:        int *p, count;
54:        p = (int *)ptr;
55:
56:        for (count = 0; count < (4 * n); count++)
57:             printf("\n%d", *p++);
58: }
```

Output ▼

```
1
2
3
4
5
6
7
8
9
10
11
12

Press Enter...

1
2
3
4
5
6
7
8
9
10
11
12
```

Analysis ▼

On lines 11 through 13, the program declares and initializes an array of integers, `multi[3][4]`. Lines 6 and 7 are the prototypes for the functions `printarray_1()` and `printarray_2()`, which print the contents of the array.

The function `printarray_1()` (lines 36 through 47) is passed only one argument, a pointer to an array of four integers. This function prints all four elements of the array. The first time `main()` calls `printarray_1()` on line 27, it passes a pointer to the first element (the first four-element integer array) in `multi`. It then calls the function two more times, incrementing the pointer each time to point to the second, and then to the third element of `multi`. After all three calls are made, the 12 integers in `multi` display onscreen.

The second function, `printarray_2()`, takes a different approach. It, too, is passed a pointer to an array of four integers, but, in addition, it is passed an integer variable that specifies the number of elements (the number of arrays of four integers) that the multidimensional array contains. With a single call from line 31, `printarray_2()` displays the entire contents of `multi`.

Both functions use pointer notation to step through the individual integers in the array. The notation `(int *)ptr` in both functions (lines 43 and 54) might not be clear. The `(int *)` is a typecast, which temporarily changes the variable's data type from its declared data type to a new one. The typecast is required when assigning the value of `ptr` to `p` because they are pointers to different types. (`p` is a pointer to type `int`, whereas `ptr` is a pointer to an array of four integers.) C doesn't let you assign the value of one pointer to a pointer of a different type. The typecast tells the compiler, "For this statement only, treat `ptr` as a pointer to type `int`." Lesson 21, "Working with Memory," covers typecasts in more detail.

DO	DON'T

DO remember to use the double indirection operator (`**`) when declaring a pointer to a pointer.
 	
DO remember that a pointer increments by the size of the pointer's type (usually what is being pointed to).
	DON'T forget to use parentheses when declaring pointers to arrays.
	
	To declare a pointer to an array of characters, use this format:
	
	`char (*letters)[26];`
	
	To declare an array of pointers to characters, use this format:
	
	`char *letters[26];`

Working with Arrays of Pointers

Recall from Lesson 8 that an array is a collection of data storage locations that have the same data type and are referred to by the same name. Because pointers are one of C's data types, you can declare and use arrays of pointers. This type of program construct can be powerful in certain situations.

Perhaps the most common use of an array of pointers is with strings. A string, as you learned in Lesson 10, "Working with Characters and Strings," is a sequence of characters stored in memory. The start of the string is indicated by a pointer to the first character (a pointer to type `char`), and the end of the string is marked by a null character. By declaring and initializing an array of pointers to type `char`, you can access and manipulate a large number of strings using the pointer array. Each element in the array points to a different string, and by looping through the array, you can access each of them in turn.

Strings and Pointers: A Review

This is a good time to review some material from Lesson 10 regarding string allocation and initialization. One way to allocate and initialize a string is to declare an array of type `char` as follows:

```
char message[] = "This is the message.";
```

You could accomplish the same thing by declaring a pointer to type `char`:

```
char *message = "This is the message.";
```

Both declarations are equivalent. In each case, the compiler allocates enough space to hold the string along with its terminating null character, and the expression `message` is a pointer to the start of the string. But what about the following two declarations?

```
char message1[20];
char *message2;
```

The first line declares an array of type `char` that is 20 characters long, with `message1` being a pointer to the first array position. Although the array space is allocated, it isn't initialized, and the array contents are undetermined. The second line declares `message2`, a pointer to type `char`. No storage space for a string is allocated by this statement—only space to hold the pointer. If you want to create a string and then have `message2` point to it, you must allocate space for the string first. In Lesson 10, you learned how to use the `malloc()` memory allocation function for this purpose. Remember that any string must have space allocated for it, whether at compilation in a declaration or at runtime with `malloc()` or a related memory allocation function.

Declaring an Array of Pointers to Type `char`

Now that you're done with the review, how would you declare an array of pointers? The following statement declares an array of 10 pointers to type `char`:

```
char *message[10];
```

Each element of the array `message[]` is an individual pointer to type `char`. As you might have guessed, you can combine the declaration with initialization and allocation of storage space for the strings:

```
char *message[10] = { "one", "two", "three" };
```

This declaration does the following:

- It allocates a 10-element array named `message`; each element of `message` is a pointer to type `char`.

- It allocates space somewhere in memory (exactly where doesn't concern you) and stores the three initialization strings, each with a terminating null character.

- It initializes `message[0]` to point to the first character of the string `"one"`, `message[1]` to point to the first character of the string `"two"`, and `message[2]` to point to the first character of the string `"three"`.

This is illustrated in Figure 15.4, which shows the relationship between the array of pointers and the strings. Note that in this example, the array elements `message[3]` through `message[9]` aren't initialized to point to anything.

FIGURE 15.4
An array of pointers to type `char`.

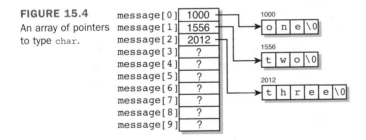

Now look at Listing 15.5, which is an example of using an array of pointers.

Input ▼

LISTING 15.5   message.c: Initializing and Using an Array of Pointers to Type `char`

```
1:  // message.c--Initializing an array of pointers to type char.
2:
3:  #include <stdio.h>
4:
5:  int main( void )
6:  {
7:      char *message[8] = { "Four", "score", "and", "seven",
8:                           "years", "ago,", "our", "forefathers" };
9:      int count;
10:
11:     for (count = 0; count < 8; count++)
12:         printf("%s ", message[count]);
13:     printf("\n");
14:
15:     return 0;
16: }
```

Output ▼

```
Four score and seven years ago, our forefathers
```

Analysis ▼

This program declares an array of eight pointers to type `char` and initializes them to point to eight strings (lines 7 and 8). It then uses a `for` loop on lines 11 and 12 to display each element of the array onscreen.

You probably can see how manipulating the array of pointers is easier than manipulating the strings themselves. This advantage is obvious in more complicated programs, such as the one presented in the next lesson. The advantage is greatest when you use functions. It's much easier to pass an array of pointers to a function than to pass several strings. This can be illustrated by rewriting the program in Listing 15.5 so that it uses a function to display the strings. The modified program is shown in Listing 15.6.

Input ▼

LISTING 15.6   message2.c: Passing an Array of Pointers to a Function

```
1:  /* Passing an array of pointers to a function. */
2:
3:  #include <stdio.h>
4:
5:  void print_strings(char *p[], int n);
6:
```

```
7:    int main( void )
8:    {
9:        char *message[8] = { "Four", "score", "and", "seven",
10:                            "years", "ago,", "our", "forefathers" };
11:
12:        print_strings(message, 8);
13:        return 0;
14:   }
15:
16:   void print_strings(char *p[], int n)
17:   {
18:       int count;
19:
20:       for (count = 0; count < n; count++)
21:           printf("%s ", p[count]);
22:       printf("\n");
23:   }
```

Output ▼

```
Four score and seven years ago, our forefathers
```

Analysis ▼

Looking at line 16, you see that the function `print_strings()` takes two arguments. One is an array of pointers to type `char`, and the other is the number of elements in the array. Thus, `print_strings()` could be used to print the strings pointed to by any array of pointers.

You might remember that in the section on pointers to pointers you were told that you would see a demonstration later. Well, you've just seen it. Listing 15.6 declared an array of pointers, and the name of the array is a pointer to its first element. When you pass that array to a function, you're passing a pointer (the array name) to a pointer (the first array element).

Pulling Things Together with an Example

Now it's time for a more robust example. Listing 15.7 uses many of the programming skills you've learned, including arrays of pointers. This program accepts lines of input from the keyboard, allocating space for each line as it is entered and keeping track of the lines by means of an array of pointers to type `char`. When you signal the end of an entry by entering a blank line, the program sorts the strings alphabetically and displays them onscreen.

If you were writing this program from scratch, you would approach the design of this program from a structured programming perspective. First, make a list of the things the program must do:

1. Accept lines of input from the keyboard one at a time until a blank line is entered.

2. Sort the lines of text into alphabetical order.

3. Display the sorted lines onscreen.

This list suggests that the program should have at least three functions: one to accept input, one to sort the lines, and one to display the lines. Now you can design each function independently. What do you need the input function—called `get_lines()`—to do? Again, make a list:

1. Keep track of the number of lines entered, and return that value to the calling program after all lines have been entered.

2. Don't allow input of more than a preset maximum number of lines.

3. Allocate storage space for each line.

4. Keep track of all lines by storing pointers to strings in an array.

5. Return to the calling program when a blank line is entered.

Now think about the second function, the one that sorts the lines. It could be called `sort()`. (Really original, right?) The sort technique used is a simple, brute-force method that compares adjacent strings and swaps them if the second string is less than the first string. More exactly, the function compares the two strings whose pointers are adjacent in the array of pointers and swaps the two pointers if necessary.

To be sure that the sorting is complete, you must go through the array from start to finish, comparing each pair of strings and swapping if necessary. For an array of n elements, you must go through the array $n-1$ times. Why is this necessary?

Each time you go through the array, a given element can be shifted by, at most, one position. For example, if the string that should be first is actually in the last position, the first pass through the array moves it to the next-to-last position, the second pass through the array moves it up one more position, and so on. It requires $n-1$ passes to move it to the first position, where it belongs.

Note that this is an inefficient and inelegant sorting method. However, it's easy to implement and understand, and it's more than adequate for the short lists that the sample program sorts.

The final function displays the sorted lines onscreen. It is, in effect, already written in Listing 15.6; and it requires only minor modification for use in Listing 15.7.

Input ▼

LISTING 15.7   sort.c: A Program that Reads Lines of Text from the Keyboard, Sorts Them Alphabetically, and Displays the Sorted List

```
1:   // sort.c--Inputs a list of strings from the keyboard,
2:   // sorts them, and then displays them on the screen.
3:   #include <stdlib.h>
4:   #include <stdio.h>
5:   #include <string.h>
6:
7:   #define MAXLINES 25
8:
9:   int get_lines(char *lines[]);
10:  void sort(char *p[], int n);
11:  void print_strings(char *p[], int n);
12:
13:  char *lines[MAXLINES];
14:
15:  int main( void )
16:  {
17:     int number_of_lines;
18:
19:     // Read in the lines from the keyboard.
20:
21:     number_of_lines = get_lines(lines);
22:
23:     if ( number_of_lines < 0 )
24:     {
25:         puts(" Memory allocation error");
26:         exit(-1);
27:     }
28:
29:     sort(lines, number_of_lines);
30:     print_strings(lines, number_of_lines);
31:     return 0;
32:  }
33:
34:  int get_lines(char *lines[])
35:  {
36:     int n = 0;
37:     char buffer[80];   // Temporary storage for each line.
38:
39:     puts("Enter one line at time; enter a blank when done.");
40:
41:     while ((n < MAXLINES) && (gets(buffer) != 0) &&
42:            (buffer[0] != '\0'))
43:     {
44:         if ((lines[n] = (char *)malloc(strlen(buffer)+1)) == NULL)
45:             return -1;
46:         strcpy( lines[n++], buffer );
```

```
47:      }
48:      return n;
49:
50:  } // End of get_lines()
51:
52:  void sort(char *p[], int n)
53:  {
54:      int a, b;
55:      char *tmp;
56:
57:      for (a = 1; a < n; a++)
58:      {
59:          for (b = 0; b < n-1; b++)
60:          {
61:              if (strcmp(p[b], p[b+1]) > 0)
62:              {
63:                  tmp = p[b];
64:                  p[b] = p[b+1];
65:                  p[b+1] = tmp;
66:              }
67:          }
68:      }
69:  }
70:
71:  void print_strings(char *p[], int n)
72:  {
73:      int count;
74:
75:      for (count = 0; count < n; count++)
76:          printf("%s\n", p[count]);
77:  }
```

Output ▼

```
Enter one line at time; enter a blank when done.
Katie
Maddie
Christopher
Benjamin
Andrew
Thomas
Margaret
John
Alice

Alice
Andrew
Benjamin
Christopher
John
```

```
Katie
Maddie
Margaret
Thomas
```

15

Analysis ▼

It will be worthwhile for you to examine some of the details of this program. Several new library functions are used for various types of string manipulation. They are explained briefly here and in more detail in Lesson 18, "Manipulating Strings." The header file string.h must be included in a program that uses these functions.

In the get_lines() function, input is controlled by the while statement on lines 41 and 42, which read as follows (condensed here onto one line):

```
while ((n < MAXLINES) && (gets(buffer) != 0) && (buffer[0] != '\0'))
```

The condition tested by the while has three parts. The first part, n < MAXLINES, ensures that the maximum number of lines has not been input yet. The second part, gets(buffer) != 0, calls the gets() library function to read a line from the keyboard into buffer and verifies that end-of-file or some other error has not occurred. The third part, buffer[0] != '\0', verifies that the first character of the line just inputted is not the null character, which would signal that a blank line had been entered.

If any of these three conditions isn't satisfied, the while loop terminates, and execution returns to the calling program, with the number of lines entered as the return value. If all three conditions are satisfied, the following if statement on line 44 is executed:

```
if ((lines[n] = (char *)malloc(strlen(buffer)+1)) == NULL)
```

This statement calls malloc() to allocate space for the string that was just input. The strlen() function returns the length of the string passed as an argument; the value is incremented by 1 so that malloc() allocates space for the string plus its terminating null character. The (char *), just before malloc() on line 44, is a *typecast* that specifies the type of pointer to be returned by malloc(), in this case a pointer to type char. You learn more about typecasts in Lesson 21.

The library function malloc(), you might remember, returns a pointer. The statement assigns the value of the pointer returned by malloc() to the corresponding element of the array of pointers. If malloc() returns NULL, the if loop returns execution to the calling program with a return value of -1. The code in main() tests the return value of get_lines() and checks whether a value less than zero is returned; lines 23 through 27 report a memory allocation error and terminate the program.

If the memory allocation were successful, the program uses the strcpy () function on line 46 to copy the string from the temporary storage location buffer to the storage space just allocated by malloc(). The while loop then repeats, getting another line of input.

After execution returns from get_lines() to main(), the following has been accomplished (assuming that a memory allocation error didn't occur):

- A number of lines of text have been read from the keyboard and stored in memory as null-terminated strings.

- The array lines[] contains pointers to all the strings. The order of pointers in the array is the order in which the strings were input.

- The variable number_of_lines holds the number of lines that were input.

Now it's time to sort. Remember, you're not actually going to move the strings around, only the order of the pointers in the array lines[]. Look at the code in the function sort(). It contains one for loop nested inside another (lines 57 through 68). The outer loop executes number_of_lines - 1 times. Each time the outer loop executes, the inner loop steps through the array of pointers, comparing (string n) with (string n+1) for n = 0 to n = number_of_lines - 1. The comparison is performed by the library function strcmp() on line 61, which is passed pointers to two strings. The function strcmp() returns one of the following:

- A value greater than zero if the first string is greater than the second string.

- Zero if the two strings are identical.

- A value less than zero if the second string is greater than the first string.

In the program, a return value from strcmp() that is greater than zero means that the first string is "greater than" the second string, and they must be swapped. (That is, their pointers in lines[] must be swapped.) This is done using a temporary variable tmp. Lines 63 through 65 perform the swap.

When program execution returns from sort(), the pointers in lines[] are ordered properly: A pointer to the "lowest" string is in lines[0], a pointer to the "next-lowest" is in lines[1], and so on. Suppose, for example, that you entered the following five lines, in this order:

```
dog
apple
zoo
program
merry
```

The situation before calling sort() is illustrated in Figure 15.5, and the situation after the return from sort() is illustrated in Figure 15.6.

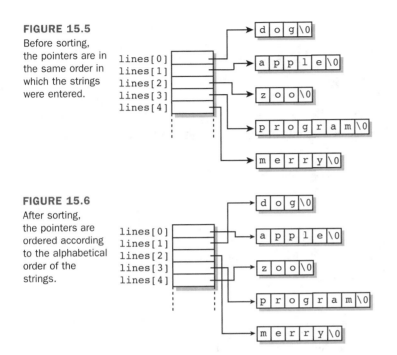

FIGURE 15.5
Before sorting, the pointers are in the same order in which the strings were entered.

FIGURE 15.6
After sorting, the pointers are ordered according to the alphabetical order of the strings.

Finally, the program calls the function `print_strings()` to display the sorted list of strings onscreen. This function should be familiar to you from previous examples in this lesson.

The program in Listing 15.7 is the most complex you have yet encountered in this book. It uses many of the C programming techniques that were covered in previous lessons. With the aid of the preceding explanation, you can follow the program's operation and understand each step. If you find areas that are unclear to you, review the related sections of this book until you understand.

Summary

This lesson covered some of the advanced uses of pointers. As you probably realize by now, pointers are a central part of the C language. C programs that don't use pointers are rare. You saw how to use pointers to pointers and how arrays of pointers can be useful when dealing with strings. You also learned how C treats multidimensional arrays as arrays of arrays, and you saw how to use pointers with such arrays.

Q&A

Q **How many levels deep can I go with pointers to pointers?**

A You need to check your compiler manuals to determine whether there are any limitations. There is rarely any reason to go more than three levels deep with pointers (pointers to pointers to pointers). Most programs rarely go over two levels.

Q **Is there a difference between a pointer to a string and a pointer to an array of characters?**

A No. A string can be considered an array of characters.

Workshop

The Workshop provides quiz questions to help you solidify your understanding of the material covered and exercises to provide you with experience in using what you've learned.

Quiz

1. Write code that declares a type `float` variable, declares and initializes a pointer to the variable, and declares and initializes a pointer to the pointer.

2. Continuing with the example in question 1, say that you want to use the pointer to a pointer to assign the value `100` to the variable `x`. What, if anything, is wrong with the following assignment statement?

   ```
   *ppx = 100;
   ```

   If it isn't correct, how should it be written?

3. Assume that you have declared an array as follows:

   ```
   int array[2][3][4];
   ```

   What is the structure of this array, as seen by the C compiler?

4. Continuing with the array declared in question 3, what does the expression `array[0][0]` mean?

5. Again using the array from question 3, which of the following comparisons is true?

   ```
   array[0][0] == &array[0][0][0];
   
   array[0][1] == array[0][0][1];
   
   array[0][1] == &array[0][1][0];
   ```

6. Write the prototype for a function that takes an array of pointers to type `char` as its one argument and returns `void`.

7. How would the function that you wrote a prototype for in question 6 know how many elements are in the array of pointers passed to it?

8. What do the following declare?

   a. `int *var1;`

   b. `int var2;`

   c. `int **var3;`

9. What do the following declare?

   a. `int a[3][12];`

   b. `int (*b)[12];`

   c. `int *c[12];`

Exercises

1. Write a statement to declare an array of 10 pointers to type `char`.

2. **BUG BUSTER:** Is anything wrong with the following code?

```
int x[3][12];
int *ptr[12];
ptr = x;
```

Because of the many possible solutions, an answer is not provided for the following exercise.

3. **ON YOUR OWN:** Write a program that declares a 12×12 array of characters. Place X's in every other element. Use a pointer to the array to print the values to the screen in a grid format.

LESSON 16
Pointers to Functions and Linked Lists

In the last lesson, you learned some new methods to take advantage of a pointer, particularly with arrays. In this lesson, you push your knowledge of a pointer even further, learning some techniques that will add significant programming power to your creations. In this lesson you learn

- How to declare pointers to functions
- How to use pointers to create linked lists for data storage

Working with Pointers to Functions

Pointers to functions provide another way of calling functions. "Hold on," you might be thinking. "How can you have a pointer to a function? Doesn't a pointer hold the address where a variable is stored?"

Well, yes and no. It's true that a pointer holds an address, but it doesn't have to be the address where a variable is stored. When your program runs, the code for each function is loaded into memory starting at a specific address. A pointer to a function holds the starting address of a function—its entry point.

Why use a pointer to a function? It provides a more flexible way of calling a function. It lets the program choose from among several functions, selecting the one that is appropriate for the current circumstances.

Declaring a Pointer to a Function

As with all C variables, you must declare a pointer to a function before using it. The general form of the declaration is as follows:

```
type (*ptr_to_func)(parameter_list);
```

This statement declares `ptr_to_func` as a pointer to a function that returns `type` and is passed the parameters in `parameter_list`. Here are some more concrete examples:

```
int (*func1)(int x);

void (*func2)(double y, double z);

char (*func3)(char *p[]);

void (*func4)();
```

The first line declares `func1` as a pointer to a function that takes one type `int` argument and returns a type `int`. The second line declares `func2` as a pointer to a function that takes two type `double` arguments and has a `void` return type (no return value). The third line declares `func3` as a pointer to a function that takes an array of pointers to type `char` as its argument and returns a type `char`. The final line declares `func4` as a pointer to a function that doesn't take any arguments and has a `void` return type.

Why do you need parentheses around the pointer name? Why can't you write, for the first example:

```
int *func1(int x);
```

The reason has to do with the precedence of the indirection operator, `*`. It has a relatively low precedence, lower than the parentheses surrounding the parameter list. The declaration just given, without the first set of parentheses, declares `func1` as a function that returns a pointer to type `int`. (Functions that return pointers are covered in Lesson 19, "Getting More from Functions.") When you declare a pointer to a function, always remember to include a set of parentheses around the pointer name and indirection operator, or you can get into trouble.

Initializing and Using a Pointer to a Function

A pointer to a function must not only be declared, but also initialized to point to something. That "something" is, of course, a function. There's nothing special about a function that gets pointed to. The only requirement is that its return type and parameter list match the return type and parameter list of the pointer declaration. For example, the following code declares and defines a function and a pointer to that function:

16

```
float square(float x);     // The function prototype.
float (*ptr)(float x);     // The pointer declaration.
float square(float x)      // The function definition.
{
  return x * x;
}
```

Because the function `square()` and the pointer `ptr` have the same parameter and return types, you can initialize `ptr` to point to `square` as follows:

```
ptr = square;
```

You can then call the function using the pointer as follows:

```
answer = ptr(x);
```

It's that simple. For a real example, compile and run Listing 16.1, which declares and initializes a pointer to a function and then calls the function twice, using the function name the first time and the pointer the second time. Both calls produce the same result.

Input ▼
LISTING 16.1   ptrfunc.c: Using a Pointer to a Function to Call the Function

```
1:  // ptrfunc.c--Demonstration of declaring and using a pointer to a function.
2:
3:  #include <stdio.h>
4:
5:  // The function prototype.
6:
7:  double square(double x);
8:
9:  // The pointer declaration.
10:
11: double (*ptr)(double x);
```

```
12:
13: int main( void )
14: {
15:     // Initialize p to point to square().
16:
17:       ptr = square;
18:
19:     // Call square() two ways.
20:     printf("%f  %f\n", square(6.6), ptr(6.6));
21:     return 0;
22: }
23:
24: double square(double x)
25: {
26:     return x * x;
27: }
```

Output ▼

```
43.560000  43.560000
```

NOTE

Precision of the values might cause some numbers to not display as the exact values entered. For example, the correct answer, 43.56, might appear as 43.559999.

Line 7 declares the function `square()`, and line 11 declares the pointer `ptr` to a function containing a `double` argument and returning a `double` value, matching the declaration of `square()`. Line 17 sets the pointer `ptr` equal to `square`. Notice that parentheses aren't used with `square` or `ptr`. Line 20 prints the return values from calls to `square()` and `ptr()`.

A function name without parentheses is a pointer to the function. (Sounds similar to the situation with arrays, doesn't it?) What's the point of declaring and using a separate pointer to the function? Well, the function name itself is a pointer constant and can't be changed (again, a parallel to arrays). A pointer variable, in contrast, can be changed. Specifically, it can be made to point to different functions as the need arises.

Listing 16.2 calls a function, passing it an integer argument. Depending on the value of the argument, the function initializes a pointer to point to one of three other functions and then uses the pointer to call the corresponding function. Each of these three functions displays a specific message onscreen.

Input ▼

LISTING 16.2   ptrfunc2.c: Using a Pointer to a Function to Call Different Functions Depending on Program Circumstances

```c
1:  /* ptrfunc2.c--Using a pointer to call different functions. */
2:
3:  #include <stdio.h>
4:
5:  /* The function prototypes. */
6:
7:  void func1(int x);
8:  void one(void);
9:  void two(void);
10: void other(void);
11:
12:  int main( void )
13: {
14:     int nbr;
15:
16:     for (;;)
17:     {
18:         puts("\nEnter an integer between 1 and 10, 0 to exit: ");
19:         scanf("%d", &nbr);
20:
21:         if (nbr == 0)
22:             break;
23:         func1(nbr);
24:     }
25:     return 0;
26: }
27:
28: void func1(int val)
29: {
30:     /* The pointer to function. */
31:
32:     void (*ptr)(void);
33:
34:     if (val == 1)
35:         ptr = one;
36:     else if (val == 2)
37:         ptr = two;
38:     else
39:         ptr = other;
40:
41:     ptr();
42: }
43:
44: void one(void)
45: {
46:     puts("You entered 1.");
```

```
47: }
48:
49: void two(void)
50: {
51:     puts("You entered 2.");
52: }
53:
54: void other(void)
55: {
56:     puts("You entered something other than 1 or 2.");
57: }
```

Output ▼

```
Enter an integer between 1 and 10, 0 to exit:
2
You entered 2.

Enter an integer between 1 and 10, 0 to exit:
9
You entered something other than 1 or 2.

Enter an integer between 1 and 10, 0 to exit:
0
```

Analysis ▼

This program employs an infinite loop starting on line 16 to continue execution until a value of 0 is entered. When a nonzero value is entered, it's passed to `func1()`. Note that line 32, in `func1()`, contains a declaration for a pointer `ptr` to a function. Being declared within a function makes `ptr` local to `func1()`, which is appropriate because no other part of the program needs access to it. `func1()` then uses this value to set `ptr` equal to the appropriate function (lines 34 through 39). Line 41 then makes a single call to `ptr()`, which calls the appropriate function.

Of course, this program is for illustration purposes only. You could have easily accomplished the same result without using a pointer to a function.

Now you can learn another way to use pointers to call different functions: passing the pointer as an argument to a function. Listing 16.3 is a revision of Listing 16.2.

Input ▼

LISTING 16.3 passptr.c: Passing a Pointer to a Function as an Argument

```
1:  // passptr.c--Passing a pointer to a function as an argument.
2:
3:  #include <stdio.h>
4:
5:  // The function prototypes. The function func1() takes as
6:  // its one argument a pointer to a function that takes no
7:  // arguments and has no return value.
8:
9:  void func1(void (*p)(void));
10: void one(void);
11: void two(void);
12: void other(void);
13:
14: int main( void )
15: {
16:     // The pointer to a function.
17:     void (*ptr)(void);
18:     int nbr;
19:
20:     for (;;)
21:     {
22:         puts("\nEnter an integer between 1 and 10, 0 to exit: ");
23:         scanf("%d", &nbr);
24:
25:         if (nbr == 0)
26:             break;
27:         else if (nbr == 1)
28:             ptr = one;
29:         else if (nbr == 2)
30:             ptr = two;
31:         else
32:             ptr = other;
33:         func1(ptr);
34:     }
35:     return 0;
36: }
37:
38: void func1(void (*p)(void))
39: {
40:     p();
41: }
42:
43: void one(void)
44: {
45:     puts("You entered 1.");
46: }
47:
```

```
48: void two(void)
49: {
50:     puts("You entered 2.");
51: }
52:
53: void other(void)
54: {
55:     puts("You entered something other than 1 or 2.");
56: }
```

Output ▼

```
Enter an integer between 1 and 10, 0 to exit:
2
You entered 2.

Enter an integer between 1 and 10, 0 to exit:
11
You entered something other than 1 or 2.

Enter an integer between 1 and 10, 0 to exit:
0
```

Analysis ▼

Notice the differences between Listing 16.2 and Listing 16.3. The declaration of the pointer to a function has been moved to line 17 in `main()`, where it is needed. Code in `main()` now initializes the pointer to point to the correct function, depending on the value the user entered (lines 25 through 32), and then passes the initialized pointer to `func1()`. `func1()` actually serves no purpose in Listing 16.3; all it does is call the function pointed to by `ptr`. Again, this program is for illustration purposes. The same principles can be used in real-world programs, such as the example in the next section.

One programming situation in which you might use pointers to functions is one in which sorting is required. Sometimes you might want different sorting rules used. For example, you might want to sort in alphabetical order one time and in reverse alphabetical order another time. By using pointers to functions, your program can call the correct sorting function. More precisely, it's usually a different comparison function that's called.

Look back at Listing 15.7 in the last lesson. In the `sort()` function, the actual sort order is determined by the value returned by the `strcmp()` library function, which tells the program whether a given string is "less than" or "greater than" another string. What if you wrote two comparison functions—one that sorts alphabetically (where A is less than Z), and another that sorts in reverse alphabetical order (where Z is less than A)?

The program can ask the user what order he wants and, by using pointers, the sorting function can call the proper comparison function. Listing 16.4 modifies Listing 15.7 to incorporate this feature.

Input ▼
LISTING 16.4   ptrsort.c: Using Pointers to Functions to Control Sort Order

```
1:   // ptrsort.c--Inputs a list of strings from the keyboard,
2:   // sorts them in ascending or descending order, and then
3:   // displays them on the screen.
4:   #include <stdlib.h>
5:   #include <stdio.h>
6:   #include <string.h>
7:
8:   #define MAXLINES 25
9:
10:  int get_lines(char *lines[]);
11:  void sort(char *p[], int n, int sort_type);
12:  void print_strings(char *p[], int n);
13:  int alpha(char *p1, char *p2);
14:  int reverse(char *p1, char *p2);
15:
16:  char *lines[MAXLINES];
17:
18:  int main( void )
19:  {
20:     int number_of_lines, sort_type;
21:
22:     // Read in the lines from the keyboard.
23:
24:     number_of_lines = get_lines(lines);
25:
26:     if ( number_of_lines < 0 )
27:     {
28:        puts("Memory allocation error");
29:        exit(-1);
30:     }
31:
32:     puts("Enter 0 for reverse order sort, 1 for alphabetical:" );
33:     scanf("%d", &sort_type);
34:
35:     sort(lines, number_of_lines, sort_type);
36:     print_strings(lines, number_of_lines);
37:     return 0;
38:  }
39:
40:  int get_lines(char *lines[])
41:  {
42:      int n = 0;
```

16

```
43:        char buffer[80];   // Temporary storage for each line.
44:
45:        puts("Enter one line at time; enter a blank when done.");
46:
47:        while (n < MAXLINES && gets(buffer) != 0 && buffer[0] != '\0')
48:        {
49:            if ((lines[n] = (char *)malloc(strlen(buffer)+1)) == NULL)
50:            return -1;
51:            strcpy( lines[n++], buffer );
52:        }
53:        return n;
54:
55:    } // End of get_lines()
56:
57:    void sort(char *p[], int n, int sort_type)
58:    {
59:        int a, b;
60:         char *x;
61:
62:        // The pointer to function.
63:
64:        int (*compare)(char *s1, char *s2);
65:
66:        // Initialize the pointer to point to the proper comparison
67:        // function depending on the argument sort_type.
68:
69:        compare = (sort_type) ? reverse : alpha;
70:
71:        for (a = 1; a < n; a++)
72:        {
73:            for (b = 0; b < n-1; b++)
74:            {
75:                if (compare(p[b], p[b+1]) > 0)
76:                {
77:                    x = p[b];
78:                    p[b] = p[b+1];
79:                    p[b+1] = x;
80:                }
81:            }
82:        }
83:    }  // end of sort()
84:
85:    void print_strings(char *p[], int n)
86:    {
87:        int count;
88:
89:        for (count = 0; count < n; count++)
90:            printf("%s\n", p[count]);
91:    }
92:
93:    int alpha(char *p1, char *p2)
```

```
94:  // Alphabetical comparison.
95:  {
96:       return(strcmp(p2, p1));
97:  }
98:
99:  int reverse(char *p1, char *p2)
100: // Reverse alphabetical comparison.
101: {
102:      return(strcmp(p1, p2));
103: }
```

Output ▼

```
Enter one line at time; enter a blank when done.
Barb
Kate
Mary
Tracy
Fran
Mike
Joe

Enter 0 for reverse order sort, 1 for alphabetical:
0

Tracy
Mike
Mary
Kate
Joe
Fran
Barb
```

Analysis ▼

Lines 32 and 33 in `main()` prompt the user for the wanted sort order. The value entered is placed in `sort_type`. This value is passed to the `sort()` function along with the other information described for Listing 15.7. The `sort()` function contains a couple of changes. Line 64 declares a pointer to a function called `compare()` that takes two character pointers (strings) as arguments. Line 69 sets `compare()` equal to one of the two new functions added to the listing based on the value of `sort_type`. The two new functions are `alpha()` and `reverse()`. `alpha()` uses the `strcmp()` library function just as it was used in Listing 15.7; `reverse()` does not. `reverse()` switches the parameters passed so that a reverse-order sort is done.

16

DO	DON'T
DO remember to use parentheses when declaring pointers to functions.	**DON'T** use a pointer without first initializing it.
Here's how you declare a pointer to a function that takes no arguments and returns a character:	**DON'T** use a function pointer that has been declared with a different return type or different arguments than you need.
`char (*func)();`	
Here's how you declare a function that returns a pointer to a character:	
`char *func();`	

Understanding Linked Lists

A *linked list* is a useful method of data storage that can easily be implemented in C. Why are we covering linked lists in a lesson on pointers? Because, as you will soon see, pointers are central to linked lists.

There are several kinds of linked lists, including single-linked lists, double-linked lists, and binary trees. Each type is suited for certain types of data storage. The one thing that these lists have in common is that the links between data items are defined by information that is contained in the items themselves, in the form of pointers. This is distinctly different from arrays, in which the links between data items result from the layout and storage of the array. This section explains the most fundamental kind of linked list: the single-linked list (referred to as simply a linked list).

Basics of Linked Lists

Each data item in a linked list is contained in a structure. (You learned about structures in Lesson 11, "Implementing Structures, Unions, and TypeDefs.") The structure contains the data elements needed to hold the data being stored; these depend on the needs of the specific program. In addition, there is one more data element: a pointer. This pointer provides the links in a linked list. Here's a simple example:

```
struct person {
char name[20];
struct person *next;
};
```

This code defines a structure named person. For the data, person contains only a 20-element array of characters. You generally wouldn't use a linked list for such simple data, but this will serve for an example. The person structure also contains a pointer to type `person`—in other words, a pointer to another structure of the same type. This means that each structure of type `person` can not only contain a chunk of data, but also can point to another `person` structure. Figure 16.1 shows how this lets the structures be linked together in a list.

FIGURE 16.1
Links in a linked list.

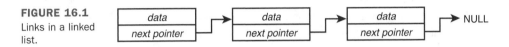

Notice that in Figure 16.1, each `person` structure points to the next `person` structure. The last `person` structure doesn't point to anything. The last element in a linked list is identified by the pointer element being assigned the value of `NULL`.

16

NOTE

The structures that make up a link in a linked list can be referred to as *links, nodes,* or *elements* of a linked list.

You have seen how the last link in a linked list is identified. What about the first link? This is identified by a special pointer (not a structure) called the *head pointer*. The head pointer always points to the first element in the linked list. The first element contains a pointer to the second element; the second element contains a pointer to the third, and so on, until you encounter an element whose pointer is `NULL`. If the entire list is empty (contains no links), the head pointer is set to `NULL`. Figure 16.2 illustrates the head pointer before the list is started and after the first list element is added.

FIGURE 16.2
A linked list's head pointer.

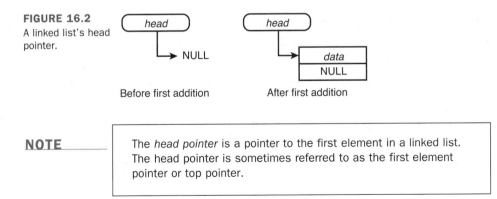

NOTE

The *head pointer* is a pointer to the first element in a linked list. The head pointer is sometimes referred to as the first element pointer or top pointer.

Working with Linked Lists

When you work with a linked list, you can add, delete, or modify elements or links. Modifying an element presents no real challenge; however, adding and deleting elements can. As stated earlier, elements in a list are connected with pointers. Much of the work of adding and deleting elements consists of manipulating these pointers. You can add elements to the beginning, middle, or end of a linked list; this determines how the pointers must be changed.

Later in this lesson, you can find a simple linked list demonstration, as well as a more complex working program. Before getting into the nitty-gritty of code, however, it's a good idea to examine some of the actions you need to perform with linked lists. For these sections, continue using the person structure that was introduced earlier.

Preliminaries

Before you start a linked list, you must define the data structure that will be used for the list, and you also need to declare the head pointer. Because the list starts out empty, the head pointer should be initialized to NULL. You also need an additional pointer to your list structure type for use in adding records. (You might need more than one pointer, as you'll soon see.) Here's how you do it:

```
struct person {
  char name[20];
  struct person *next;
};
struct person *new;
struct person *head;
head = NULL;
```

Adding an Element to the Beginning of a List

If the head pointer is NULL, the list is empty, and the new element will be its only member. If the head pointer is not NULL, the list already contains one or more elements. In either case, however, the procedure for adding a new element to the start of the list is the same:

1. Create an instance of your structure, allocating memory space using malloc().

2. Set the next pointer of the new element to the current value of the head pointer. This will be NULL if the list is empty, or the address of the current first element otherwise.

3. Make the head pointer point to the new element.

Here is the code to perform this task:

```
new = (person*)malloc(sizeof(struct person));
new->next = head;
head = new
```

Note that `malloc()` is typecast so that its return value is the proper type—a pointer to the person data structure.

CAUTION
> It's important to switch the pointers in the correct order. If you reassign the head pointer first, you will lose the list!

Figure 16.3 illustrates the procedure for adding a new element to an empty list, and Figure 16.4 illustrates adding a new first element to an existing list.

FIGURE 16.3
Adding a new element to an empty linked list.

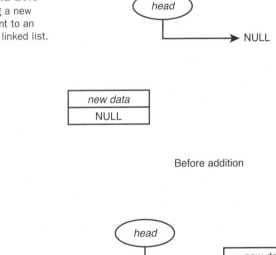

Before addition

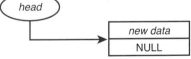

After addition

FIGURE 16.4
Adding a new first element to an existing list.

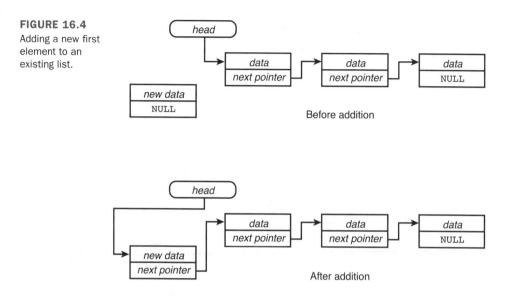

Before addition

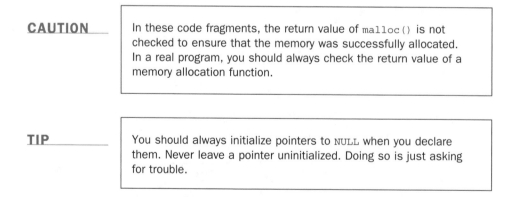

After addition

Notice that `malloc()` is used to allocate the memory for the new element. As each new element is added, only the memory needed for it is allocated. The `calloc()` function could also be used. You should be aware of the differences between these two functions. The main difference is that `calloc()` will initialize the new element; `malloc()` will not.

| CAUTION | In these code fragments, the return value of `malloc()` is not checked to ensure that the memory was successfully allocated. In a real program, you should always check the return value of a memory allocation function. |

| TIP | You should always initialize pointers to `NULL` when you declare them. Never leave a pointer uninitialized. Doing so is just asking for trouble. |

Adding an Element to the End of the List

To add an element to the end of a linked list, you start at the head pointer and go through the list until you find the last element. After you've found it, follow these steps:

1. Create an instance of your structure, allocating memory space using `malloc()`.

2. Set the next pointer in the last element to point to the new element (whose address is returned by `malloc()`).

3. Set the next pointer in the new element to NULL to signal that it is the last item in the list.

Here is the code:

```
person *current;
...
current = head;
while (current->next != NULL)
    current = current->next;
new = (person*)malloc(sizeof(struct person));
current->next = new;
new->next = NULL;
```

Figure 16.5 illustrates the procedure for adding a new element to the end of a linked list.

FIGURE 16.5
Adding a new element to the end of a linked list.

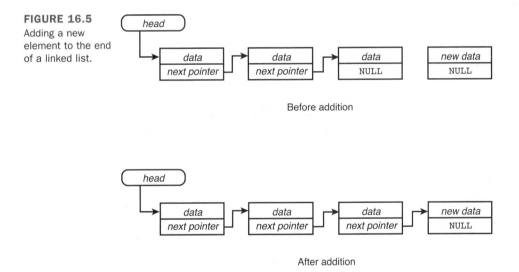

Before addition

After addition

Adding an Element to the Middle of the List

When you work with a linked list, most of the time you add elements somewhere in the middle of the list. Exactly where you place the new element depends on how you keep the list—for example, if it is sorted on one or more data elements. This process, then, requires that you first locate the position in the list where the new element should go, and then add it. Here are the steps to follow:

1. In the list, locate the existing element that the new element will be placed after. Call this the marker element.

2. Create an instance of your structure, allocating memory space using `malloc()`.

3. Set the next pointer of the marker element to point to the new element (whose address is returned by `malloc()`).

4. Set the next pointer of the new element to point to the element that the marker element used to point to.

Here's how the code might look:

```
person *marker;
/* Code here to set marker to point to the desired list location. */
...
new = (LINK)malloc(sizeof(PERSON));
new->next = marker->next;
marker->next = new;
```

Figure 16.6 illustrates this process.

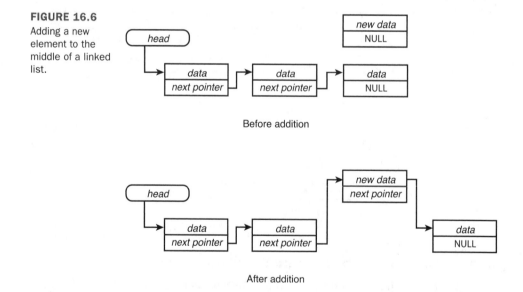

FIGURE 16.6
Adding a new element to the middle of a linked list.

Before addition

After addition

Deleting an Element from the List

Deleting an element from a linked list is a simple matter of manipulating pointers. The exact process depends on where in the list the element is located:

- To delete the first element, set the head pointer to point to the second element in the list.
- To delete the last element, set the next pointer of the next-to-last element to NULL.
- To delete any other element, set the next pointer of the element before the one being deleted to point to the element after the one being deleted.

In addition, the memory of the element that is removed from the list should be freed so that the program does not claim more memory than it needs. (This is called a *memory leak*.) Freeing memory is done with the `free()` function, which is explained in detail in Lesson 21, "Working with Memory." Here's the code to delete the first element in a linked list:

16

```
temp = head;
head = head->next;
free(temp);
```

This code deletes the last element in the list:

```
person *current1, *current2;
current1 = head;
current2= current1->next;
while (current2->next != NULL)
{
    current1 = current2;
    current2= current1->next;
}
free(current1->next);
current1->next = null;
if (head == current1)
    head = null;
```

Finally, the following code deletes an element from within the list:

```
person *current1, *current2;
/* Code goes here to have current1 point to the */
/* element just before the one to be deleted. */
current2 = current1->next;
free(current1->next);
current1->next = current2->next;
```

After any of these procedures, the deleted element is removed from the list because there is no pointer in the list pointing to it.

A Simple Linked List Demonstration

Listing 16.5 demonstrates the basics of using a linked list. This program is clearly for demonstration purposes only because it doesn't accept user input and doesn't do anything useful other than show the code required for the most basic linked list tasks. The program does the following:

1. It defines a structure and the required pointers for the list.

2. It adds the first element to the list.

3. It adds an element to the end of the list.

4. It adds an element to the middle of the list.

5. It displays the list contents onscreen.

Input ▼

LISTING 16.5　linkdemo.c: The Basics of a Linked List

```
1:   /* linkdemo.c--Demonstrates the fundamentals of using */
2:   /* a linked list. */
3:
4:   #include <stdlib.h>
5:   #include <stdio.h>
6:   #include <string.h>
7:
8:   /* The list data structure. */
9:   struct data {
10:      char name[20];
11:      struct data *next;
12:  };
13:
14:  /* Define typedefs for the structure */
15:  /* and a pointer to it. */
16:  typedef struct data PERSON;
17:  typedef PERSON *LINK;
18:
19:  int main( void )
20:  {
21:     /* Head, new, and current element pointers. */
22:     LINK head = NULL;
23:     LINK new = NULL;
24:     LINK current = NULL;
25:
26:     /* Add the first list element. We do not */
27:     /* assume the list is empty, although in */
28:     /* this demo program it always will be. */
29:
30:     new = (LINK)malloc(sizeof(PERSON));
31:     new->next = head;
32:     head = new;
33:     strcpy(new->name, "Abigail");
34:
35:     /* Add an element to the end of the list. */
```

```
36:    /* We assume the list contains at least one element. */
37:
38:    current = head;
39:    while (current->next != NULL)
40:    {
41:      current = current->next;
42:    }
43:
44:    new = (LINK)malloc(sizeof(PERSON));
45:    current->next = new;
46:    new->next = NULL;
47:    strcpy(new->name, "Carolyn");
48:
49:    /* Add a new element at the second position in the list. */
50:    new = (LINK)malloc(sizeof(PERSON));
51:    new->next = head->next;
52:    head->next = new;
53:    strcpy(new->name, "Beatrice");
54:
55:    /* Print all data items in order. */
56:    current = head;
57:    while (current != NULL)
58:    {
59:      printf("\n%s", current->name);
60:      current = current->next;
61:    }
62:
63:    printf("\n");
64:
65:    return 0;
66: }
```

Output ▼

```
Abigail
Beatrice
Carolyn
```

Analysis ▼

Lines 9 through 12 declare the data structure for the list. Lines 16 and 17 define typedefs for both the data structure and for a pointer to the data structure. Strictly speaking, this isn't necessary, but it simplifies coding by enabling you to write PERSON in place of struct data and LINK in place of struct data *.

Lines 22 through 24 declare a head pointer and a couple other pointers that will be used when manipulating the list. All these pointers are initialized to NULL.

16

Lines 30 through 33 add a new link to the start of the list. Line 30 allocates a new data structure. Note that the successful operation of `malloc()` is assumed—something you would never do in a real program!

Line 31 sets the `next` pointer in this new structure to point to whatever the head pointer contains. Why not simply assign `NULL` to this pointer? That works only if you know that the list is empty. As it is written, the code works even if the list already contains some elements. The new first element ends up pointing to the element that used to be first, which is just what you want.

Line 32 makes the head pointer point to the new record, and line 33 stores some data in the record.

Adding an element to the end of the list is a bit more complicated. Although in this case you know that the list contains only one element, you can't assume this in a real program. Therefore, it's necessary to loop through the list, starting with the first element, until you find the last element (as indicated by the `next` pointer's being `NULL`). Then you know you have found the end of the list. This task is accomplished on lines 38 through 42. After you have found the last element, it is a simple matter to allocate a new data structure, have the old last element point to it, and set the new element's `next` pointer to `NULL` because it is now the last element in the list. This is done on lines 44 through 47. Note that the return type from `malloc()` is typecast to be type `LINK`. (You learn more about typecasts in Lesson 20, "Exploring the C Function Library.")

The next task is to add an element to the middle of the list—in this case, at the second position. After a new data structure is allocated (line 50), the new element's `next` pointer is set to point to the element that used to be second and is now third in the list (line 51). The first element's `next` pointer is made to point to the new element (line 52).

Finally, the program prints all the records in the linked list. This is a simple matter of starting with the element that the head pointer points to and then progressing through the list until the last list element is found, as indicated by a `NULL` pointer. Lines 56 through 61 perform this task.

Implementing a Linked List

Now that you have seen the ways to add links to a list, it's time to see them in action. Listing 16.6 is a rather long program that uses a linked list to hold a list of five characters. The characters are stored in memory using a linked list. These characters just as easily could have been names, addresses, or any other data. To keep the example as simple as possible, only a single character is stored in each link.

What makes this linked list program complicated is the fact that it sorts the links as they are added. Of course, this also is what makes this program so valuable. Each link is added to the beginning, middle, or end, depending on its value. The link is always sorted. If you were to write a program that simply added the links to the end, the logic would be much simpler. However, the program also would be less useful.

Input ▼
LISTING 16.6 linklist.c: Implementing a Linked List of Characters

```
1:  /*=========================================================*
2:   * Program:   linklist.c                                   *
3:   * Book:      Sams Teach Yourself C in One Hour a Day      *
4:   * Purpose:   Implementing a linked list                   *
5:   *=======================================================*/
6:  #include <stdio.h>
7:  #include <stdlib.h> g
8:
9:  #ifndef NULL
10:    #define NULL 0
11: #endif
12:
13: /* List data structure */
14: struct list
15: {
16:    int    ch;      /* using an int to hold a char */
17:    struct list *next_rec;
18: };
19:
20: /* Typedefs for the structure and pointer. */
21: typedef struct list LIST;
22: typedef LIST *LISTPTR;
23:
24: /* Function prototypes. */
25: LISTPTR add_to_list( int, LISTPTR );
26: void show_list(LISTPTR);
27: void free_memory_list(LISTPTR);
28:
29: int main( void )
30: {
31:    LISTPTR first = NULL;  /* head pointer */
32:    int i = 0;
33:    int ch;
34:    char trash[256];       /* to clear stdin buffer. */
35:
36:    while ( i++ < 5 )      /* build a list based on 5 items given */
37:    {
38:       ch = 0;
39:       printf("\nEnter character %d, ", i);
40:
41:       do
42:       {
```

```
43:                    printf("\nMust be a to z: ");
44:                    ch = getc(stdin);  /* get next char in buffer  */
45:                    gets(trash);       /* remove trash from buffer */
46:            } while( (ch < 'a' || ch > 'z') && (ch < 'A' || ch > 'Z'));
47:
48:            first = add_to_list( ch, first );
49:        }
50:
51:        show_list( first );              /* Dumps the entire list */
52:        free_memory_list( first );      /* Release all memory */
53:        return 0;
54: }
55:
56: /*========================================================*
57:  * Function: add_to_list()
58:  * Purpose : Inserts new link in the list
59:  * Entry   : int ch = character to store
60:  *               LISTPTR first = address of original head pointer
61:  * Returns : Address of head pointer (first)
62:  *========================================================*/
63:
64: LISTPTR add_to_list( int ch, LISTPTR first )
65: {
66:     LISTPTR new_rec = NULL;          /* Holds address of new rec */
67:     LISTPTR tmp_rec = NULL;          /* Holds tmp pointer         */
68:     LISTPTR prev_rec = NULL;
69:
70:     /* Allocate memory. */
71:     new_rec = (LISTPTR)malloc(sizeof(LIST));
72:     if (!new_rec)        /* Unable to allocate memory */
73:     {
74:         printf("\nUnable to allocate memory!\n");
75:         exit(1);
76:     }
77:
78:     /* set new link's data */
79:     new_rec->ch = ch;
80:     new_rec->next_rec = NULL;
81:
82:     if (first == NULL)    /* adding first link to list */
83:     {
84:         first = new_rec;
85:         new_rec->next_rec = NULL;   /* redundant but safe */
86:     }
87:     else    /* not first record */
88:     {
89:         /* see if it goes before the first link */
90:         if ( new_rec->ch < first->ch)
91:         {
92:             new_rec->next_rec = first;
93:             first = new_rec;
```

```
 94:        }
 95:        else   /* it is being added to the middle or end */
 96:        {
 97:            tmp_rec = first->next_rec;
 98:            prev_rec = first;
 99:
100:            /* Check to see where link is added. */
101:
102:            if ( tmp_rec == NULL )
103:            {
104:                /* we are adding second record to end */
105:                prev_rec->next_rec = new_rec;
106:            }
107:            else
108:            {
109:                /* check to see if adding in middle */
110:                while (( tmp_rec->next_rec != NULL))
111:                {
112:                    if( new_rec->ch < tmp_rec->ch )
113:                    {
114:                        new_rec->next_rec = tmp_rec;
115:                        if (new_rec->next_rec != prev_rec->next_rec)
116:                        {
117:                            printf("ERROR");
118:                            getc(stdin);
119:                            exit(0);
120:                        }
121:                        prev_rec->next_rec = new_rec;
122:                        break;   /* link is added; exit while */
123:                    }
124:                    else
125:                    {
126:                        tmp_rec = tmp_rec->next_rec;
127:                        prev_rec = prev_rec->next_rec;
128:                    }
129:                }
130:
131:                /* check to see if adding to the end */
132:                if (tmp_rec->next_rec == NULL)
133:                {
134:                    if (new_rec->ch < tmp_rec->ch ) /* 1 b4 end */
135:                    {
136:                        new_rec->next_rec = tmp_rec;
137:                        prev_rec->next_rec = new_rec;
138:                    }
139:                    else  /* at the end */
140:                    {
141:                        tmp_rec->next_rec = new_rec;
142:                        new_rec->next_rec = NULL;  /* redundant */
143:                    }
144:                }
```

16

```
145:              }
146:          }
147:      }
148:      return(first);
149: }
150:
151: /*=======================================================*
152:  * Function: show_list
153:  * Purpose : Displays the information current in the list
154:  *=======================================================*/
155:
156: void show_list( LISTPTR first )
157: {
158:      LISTPTR cur_ptr;
159:      int counter = 1;
160:
161:      printf("\n\nRec addr  Position  Data  Next Rec addr\n");
162:      printf("========  ========  ====  =============\n");
163:
164:      cur_ptr = first;
165:      while (cur_ptr != NULL )
166:      {
167:          printf("  %p   ", cur_ptr );
168:          printf("      %2i        %c", counter++, cur_ptr->ch);
169:          printf("       %p   \n",cur_ptr->next_rec);
170:          cur_ptr = cur_ptr->next_rec;
171:      }
172: }
173:
174: /*=======================================================*
175:  * Function: free_memory_list
176:  * Purpose : Frees up all the memory collected for list
177:  *=======================================================*/
178:
179: void free_memory_list(LISTPTR first)
180: {
181:      LISTPTR cur_ptr, next_rec;
182:      cur_ptr = first;                  /* Start at beginning */
183:
184:      while (cur_ptr != NULL)           /* Go while not end of list */
185:      {
186:          next_rec = cur_ptr->next_rec;  /* Get address of next record */
187:          free(cur_ptr);                 /* Free current record */
188:          cur_ptr = next_rec;            /* Adjust current record*/
189:      }
190: }
```

Output ▼

```
Enter character 1,
Must be a to z: q

Enter character 2,
Must be a to z: b

Enter character 3,
Must be a to z: z

Enter character 4,
Must be a to z: c

Enter character 5,
Must be a to z: a


Rec addr   Position   Data   Next Rec addr
========   ========   ====   =============
 2224A0         1       a       222470
 222470         2       b       222490
 222490         3       c       222450
 222450         4       q       222480
 222480         5       z         0
```

16

NOTE	Your output will probably show different address values.

Analysis ▼

This program demonstrates adding a link to a linked list. It isn't the easiest listing to understand; however, if you walk through it, you can see that it's a combination of the three methods of adding links that were discussed earlier in the lesson. You can use this listing to add links to the beginning, middle, or end of a linked list. In addition, this listing takes into consideration the special cases of adding the first link (the one that gets added to the beginning) and the second link (the one that gets added to the middle).

TIP	The easiest way to fully understand this listing is to step through it line-by-line in your compiler's debugger and to read the following analysis. By seeing the logic executed, you can better understand the listing.

Several items at the beginning of Listing 16.6 should be familiar or easy to understand. Lines 9 through 11 check to see whether the value of NULL is already defined. If it isn't, line 10 defines it to be 0. Lines 14 through 22 define the structure for the linked list and also declare the type definitions to make working with the structure and pointers easier.

The main() function should be easy to follow. A head pointer called first is declared on line 31. Notice that this is initialized to NULL. Remember that you should never let a pointer go uninitialized. Lines 36 through 49 contain a while loop that is used to get five characters from the user. Within this outer while loop, which repeats five times, a do... while is used to ensure that each character entered is a letter. The isalpha() function could have been used just as easily.

After a piece of data is obtained, add_to_list() is called. The pointer to the beginning of the list and the data being added to the list are passed to the function.

The main() function ends by calling show_list() to display the list's data and then free_memory_list() to release all the memory that was allocated to hold the links in the list. Both these functions operate in a similar manner. Each starts at the beginning of the linked list using the head pointer first. A while loop is used to go from one link to the next using the next_ptr value. When next_ptr is equal to NULL, the end of the linked list has been reached, and the functions return.

The most important (and most complicated!) function in this listing is add_to_list() on lines 56 through 149. Lines 66 through 68 declare three pointers that can be used to point to three different links. The new_rec pointer points to the new link that is to be added. The tmp_rec pointer points to the current link in the list being evaluated. If there is more than one link in the list, the prev_rec pointer points to the previous link that was evaluated.

Line 71 allocates memory for the new link that is being added. The new_rec pointer is set to the value returned by malloc(). If the memory can't be allocated, lines 74 and 75 print an error message and exit the program. If the memory is allocated successfully, the program continues.

Line 79 sets the data in the structure to the data passed to this function. This simply consists of assigning the character passed to the function ch to the new record's character field (new_rec->ch). In a more complex program, this could entail the assigning of several fields. Line 80 sets the next_rec in the new record to NULL so that it doesn't point to some random location.

Line 82 starts the "add a link" logic by checking to see whether there are any links in the list. If the link being added is the first link in the list, as indicated by the head pointer first being NULL, the head pointer is simply set equal to the new pointer, and you're done.

If this link isn't the first, the function continues within the `else` at line 87. Line 90 checks to see whether the new link goes at the beginning of the list. As you should remember, this is one of the three cases for adding a link. If the link does go first, line 92 sets the `next_rec` pointer in the new link to point to the previous "first" link. Line 93 then sets the head pointer, `first`, to point to the new link. This results in the new link being added to the beginning of the list.

If the new link isn't the first link to be added to an empty list, and if it's being added at the first position in an existing list, you know it must be in the middle or at the end of the list. Lines 97 and 98 set up the `tmp_rec` and `prev_rec` pointers that were declared earlier. The pointer `tmp_rec` is set to the address of the second link in the list, and `prev_rec` is set to the first link in the list.

16

You should note that if there is only one link in the list, `tmp_rec` will be equal to `NULL`. This is because `tmp_rec` is set to the `next_ptr` in the first link, which will be equal to `NULL`. Line 102 checks for this special case. If `tmp_rec` is `NULL`, you know that this is the second link being added to the list. Because you know the new link doesn't come before the first link, it can go only at the end. To accomplish this, you simply set `prev_rec->next_ptr` to the new link, and then you're done.

If the `tmp_rec` pointer isn't `NULL`, you know that you already have more than two links in your list. The `while` statement on lines 110 through 129 loops through the rest of the links to determine where the new link should be placed. Line 112 checks to see whether the new link's data value is less than the link currently being pointed to. If it is, you know this is where you want to add the link. If the new data is greater than the current link's data, you need to look at the next link in the list. Lines 126 and 127 set the pointers `tmp_rec` and `next_rec` to the next links.

If the character is "less than" the current link's character, you would follow the logic presented earlier in this lesson for adding to the middle of a linked list. This process can be seen in lines 114 through 122. In line 114, the new link's next pointer is set to equal the current link's address (`tmp_rec`). Line 121 sets the previous link's next pointer to point to the new link. After this, you're done. The code uses a `break` statement to get out of the `while` loop.

NOTE

Lines 115 through 120 contain debugging code that was left in the listing for you to see. These lines could be removed; however, as long as the program is running correctly, they will never be called. After the new link's next pointer is set to the current pointer, it should be equal to the previous link's next pointer, which also points to the current record. If they aren't equal, something went wrong!

The previously covered logic takes care of links being added to the middle of the list. If the end of the list is reached, the `while` loop on lines 110 through 129 ends without adding the link. Lines 132 through 144 take care of adding the link to the end.

If the last link in the list was reached, `tmp_rec->next_rec` equals NULL. Line 132 checks for this condition. Line 134 checks to see whether the link goes before or after the last link. If it goes after the last link, the last link's `next_rec` is set to the new link (line 132), and the new link's next pointer is set to NULL (line 142).

Improving Listing 16.6

Linked lists are not the easiest thing to learn. As you can see from Listing 16.6, however, they are an excellent way of storing data in a sorted order. Because it's easy to add new data items anywhere in a linked list, the code for keeping a list of data items in sorted order with a linked list is a lot simpler that it would be if you used, say, an array. This listing could easily be converted to sort names, phone numbers, or any other data. In addition, although this listing sorted in ascending order (A to Z), it just as easily could have sorted in descending order (Z to A).

Deleting from a Linked List

The capability to add information to a linked list is essential, but there will be times when you will want to remove information, too. Deleting links, or elements, is similar to adding them. You can delete links from the beginning, middle, or end of linked lists. In each case, the appropriate pointers need to be adjusted. Also, the memory used by the deleted link needs to be freed.

NOTE | Don't forget to free memory when deleting links!

DO	**DON'T**
DO understand the difference between `calloc()` and `malloc()`. Most important, remember that `malloc()` doesn't initialize allocated memory—`calloc()` does.	**DON'T** forget to free any memory allocated for links when deleting them.

Summary

This lesson furthered your knowledge and experience with pointers. You learned how to declare and use pointers to functions, an important and flexible programming tool. Finally, you learned how to implement linked lists, a powerful and flexible data storage method.

Although the last two lessons have covered complicated topics, they're exciting as well. With your new knowledge of pointers, you're really getting into some of the sophisticated capabilities of the C language. Power and flexibility are among the main reasons C is such a popular language.

16

Q&A

Q Is it necessary to use the concepts presented in this lesson to take advantage of C?

A You can use C without ever using any advanced pointer concepts; however, you won't take advantage of the power that C offers. Pointer manipulations such as those shown in this lesson can make many programming tasks easier and more efficient.

Q Are there other times when function pointers are useful?

A Yes. Pointers to functions also are used with menus. Based on a value returned from a menu, a pointer is set to the function that should be called based on the menu choice.

Q Name two major advantages of linked lists.

A One: The size of a linked list can be increased or decreased while the program is running; it doesn't have to be predefined when you write the code. Two: It's easy to keep a linked list in sorted order because elements can easily be added or deleted anywhere in the list.

Workshop

The Workshop provides quiz questions to help you solidify your understanding of the material covered and exercises to provide you with experience in using what you've learned.

Quiz

1. What is a pointer to a function?

2. Write a declaration of a pointer to a function that returns a type `char` and takes an array of pointers to type `char` as an argument.

3. You might have answered question 2 with

   ```
   char *ptr(char *x[]);
   ```

   What is wrong with this declaration?

4. When defining a data structure to be used in a linked list, what is the one element that must be included?

5. What does it mean if the head pointer is equal to NULL?

6. How are single-linked lists connected?

7. What do the following declare?

   a. `char *z[10];`

   b. `char *y(int field);`

   c. `char (*x)(int field);`

Exercises

1. Write a declaration for a pointer to a function that takes an integer as an argument and returns a type `float` variable.

2. Write a declaration for an array of pointers to functions. The functions should all take a character string as a parameter and return an integer. What could such an array be used for?

3. Write a structure that is to be used in a single-linked list. This structure should hold your friends' names and addresses.

   Because of the many possible solutions, answers are not provided for the following exercises.

4. **ON YOUR OWN:** Write a program that uses pointers to type `double` variables to accept 10 numbers from the user, sort them, and print them to the screen. (Hint: See Listing 16.3.)

5. **ON YOUR OWN:** Modify the program in the previous exercise to allow the user to specify whether the sort order is ascending or descending.

LESSON 17
Using Disk Files

Most of the programs you write use files written to a hard drive. These files contain information that serves one purpose or another: data storage, configuration information, and so on. In this lesson you learn

- How to relate streams to disk files
- About C's two disk file types
- The commands for opening a file
- How to write data to a file
- Reading data from a file
- When to close a file
- Disk file management
- Using temporary files

Relating Streams to Disk Files

As you learned in Lesson 14, "Working with the Screen, Printer, and Keyboard," C performs all input and output, including disk files, by means of streams. You saw how to use C's predefined streams that are connected to specific devices such as the keyboard and screen. Disk file streams work essentially the same way. This is one of the advantages of stream input/output (I/O)—techniques for using one stream can be used with little or no change for other streams. The major difference with disk file streams is that your program must explicitly create a stream associated with a specific disk file.

Understanding the Types of Disk Files

In Lesson 14, you saw that C streams come in two flavors: text and binary. You can associate either type of stream with a file, and you must understand the distinction so that you use the proper mode for your files.

Text streams are associated with text-mode files. Text-mode files consist of a sequence of lines. Each line contains zero or more characters and ends with one or more characters that mark the end of the line. It's important to remember that a "line" in a text-mode file is not the same as a C string; there is no terminating NULL character (\0). When you use a text-mode stream, translation occurs between C's newline character (\n) and whatever character or characters the operating system uses to mark end-of-line in disk files. In Microsoft Windows, it's a carriage-return linefeed (CR-LF) combination. When data is written to a text-mode file, each \n is translated to a CR-LF; when data is read from a disk file, each CR-LF is translated to a \n. On UNIX systems, no translation is done—newline characters remain unchanged.

Binary streams are associated with binary-mode files. Any and all data is written and read unchanged, with no separation into lines and no use of end-of-line characters. The NULL and end-of-line characters have no special significance and are treated like any other byte of data.

Some file I/O functions are restricted to one-file mode, whereas other functions can use either mode. This lesson teaches you which mode to use with which functions.

Using Filenames

Every disk file has a name, and you must use filenames when dealing with disk files. Filenames are stored as strings, just like other text data. The rules that establish what is acceptable for filenames (and what is not) differ from one operating system to another.

A filename in a C program also can contain path information. The *path* specifies the drive and/or directory (or folder) where the file is located. If you specify a filename without a path, it will be assumed that the file is located at whatever location the operating system currently designates as the default. It's good programming practice to always specify path information as part of your filenames.

> **TIP**
>
> If the path isn't specified for a file, it is recommended that you assume the file is in the same directory as the program being executed. You might want to include programming logic to include the path of the current program.

On PCs, the backslash character is used to separate directory names in a path. For example, in Windows, the name

```
c:\data\list.txt
```

refers to a file named list.txt in the directory \data on drive C. Remember that the backslash character has a special meaning to C when it's in a string. To represent the backslash character itself, you must precede it with another backslash. Thus, in a C program, you would represent the filename as follows:

```
char *filename = "c:\\data\\list.txt";
```

However, if when running a program, you enter a filename using the keyboard, enter only a single backslash.

Not all systems use the backslash as the directory separator. For example, UNIX uses the forward slash (/).

Opening a File

The process of creating a stream linked to a disk file is called *opening* the file. When you open a file, it becomes available for reading (meaning that data is input from the file to the program), writing (meaning that data from the program is saved in the file), or both. When you're done using the file, you must close it. Closing a file is covered later in this lesson.

To open a file, you use the `fopen()` library function. The prototype of `fopen()` is located in `stdio.h` and reads as follows:

```
FILE *fopen(const char *filename, const char *mode);
```

This prototype tells you that `fopen()` returns a pointer to type FILE, which is a structure declared in `stdio.h`. The members of the FILE structure are used by the program in the various file access operations, but you don't need to be concerned about them. However, for each file that you want to open, you must declare a pointer to type FILE. When you call `fopen()`, that function creates an instance of the FILE structure and returns a pointer to that structure. You use this pointer in all subsequent operations on the file. If `fopen()` fails, it returns NULL. Such a failure can be caused, for example, by a hardware error or by trying to open a file on a flash drive that isn't attached.

The argument *filename* is the name of the file to be opened. As noted earlier, *filename* can—and should—contain a path specification. The *filename* argument can be a literal string enclosed in double quotation marks or a pointer to a string variable.

The argument *mode* specifies the mode in which to open the file. In this context, *mode* controls whether the file is binary or text and whether it is for reading, writing, or both. The permitted values for *mode* are listed in Table 17.1.

TABLE 17.1 Values of *mode* for the `fopen()` Function

mode	Meaning
r	Opens the file for reading. If the file doesn't exist, `fopen()` returns NULL.
w	Opens the file for writing. If a file of the specified name doesn't exist, it is created. If a file of the specified name does exist, it is deleted without warning, and a new, empty file is created.
a	Opens the file for appending. If a file of the specified name doesn't exist, it is created. If the file does exist, new data is appended to the end of the file.
r+	Opens the file for reading and writing. If a file of the specified name doesn't exist, it is created. If the file does exist, new data is added to the beginning of the file, overwriting existing data.
w+	Opens the file for reading and writing. If a file of the specified name doesn't exist, it is created. If the file does exist, it is overwritten.
a+	Opens a file for reading and appending. If a file of the specified name doesn't exist, it is created. If the file does exist, new data is appended to the end of the file.

The default file mode is text. To open a file in binary mode, you append a b to the *mode* argument. Thus, a *mode* argument of a would open a text-mode file for appending, whereas ab would open a binary-mode file for appending.

Remember that `fopen()` returns NULL if an error occurs. Error conditions that can cause a return value of NULL include the following:

- Using an invalid filename.

- Trying to open a file on a disk that isn't ready. (The drive door isn't closed or the disk isn't formatted, for example.)

- Trying to open a file in a nonexistent directory or on a nonexistent disk drive.

- Trying to open a nonexistent file in mode `r`.

Whenever you use `fopen()`, you need to test for the occurrence of an error. There's no way to tell exactly which error occurred, but you can display a message to the user and try to open the file again, or you can end the program. Most C compilers include non-ANSI extensions that let you obtain information about the nature of the error; refer to your compiler documentation for information.

Listing 17.1 demonstrates `fopen()`.

Input ▼

LISTING 17.1   openfiles.c: Using `fopen()` to Open Disk Files in Various Modes

```
1:   // openfiles.c--Demonstrates the fopen() function.
2:   #include <stdlib.h>
3:   #include <stdio.h>
4:
5:   int main( void )
6:   {
7:       FILE *fp;
8:       char ch, filename[40], mode[4];
9:
10:      while (1)
11:      {
12:
13:          // Input filename and mode.
14:
15:          puts("\nEnter a filename: ");
16:          gets(filename);
17:          puts("\nEnter a mode (max 3 characters): ");
18:          gets(mode);
19:
20:          // Try to open the file.
21:
22:          if ( (fp = fopen( filename, mode )) != NULL )
23:          {
24:              printf("\nSuccessful opening %s in mode %s.\n",
25:                      filename, mode);
26:              fclose(fp);
27:              puts("Enter x to exit, any other to continue.");
28:              if ( (ch = getc(stdin)) == 'x')
29:                  break;
```

```
30:              else
31:                   continue;
32:          }
33:          else
34:          {
35:               fprintf(stderr, "\nError opening file %s in mode %s.\n",
36:                        filename, mode);
37:               puts("Enter x to exit, any other to try again.");
38:               if ( (ch = getc(stdin)) == 'x')
39:                   break;
40:               else
41:                   continue;
42:          }
43:      }
43:   return;
44: }
```

Output ▼

```
Enter a filename:  My first file.txt

Enter a mode (max 3 characters): a+

Successful opening My first file.txt in mode a+.
Enter x to exit, any other to continue.
j

Enter a filename: My second file.txt

Enter a mode (max 3 characters): w

Successful opening My second file.txt in mode w.
Enter x to exit, any other to continue.
j

Enter a filename: My third file.txt

Enter a mode (max 3 characters): r


Error opening My third file.txt in mode r.
Enter x to exit, any other to try again.
x
```

Analysis ▼

This program prompts you for both the filename and the mode specifier on lines 15 through 18. After getting the names, line 22 attempts to open the file and assign its file pointer to `fp`. As an example of good programming practice, the `if` statement on line 22 checks to see that the opened file's pointer isn't equal to `NULL`. If `fp` isn't equal to `NULL`, a message is printed stating that the open was successful and that the user can continue. If the file pointer is `NULL`, the `else` condition of the `if` loop executes. The `else` condition on lines 33 through 42 prints a message stating that there is a problem. It then prompts the user to determine whether the program should continue.

You can experiment with different names and modes to see which ones give you an error. In the output just shown, you can see that trying to open My third file.txt in mode `r` resulted in an error because the file didn't exist on the disk. If an error occurs, you're given the choice of entering the information again or quitting the program. To force an error, you could enter an invalid filename such as [] or an invalid mode such as `e`.

Writing and Reading File Data

17

A program that uses a disk file can write data to a file, read data from a file, or a combination of the two. You can write data to a disk file in three ways:

- You can use formatted output to save formatted data to a file. You should use formatted output only with text-mode files. The primary use of formatted output is to create files containing text and numeric data to be read by other programs such as spreadsheets or databases. You rarely, if ever, use formatted output to create a file to be read again by a C program.

- You can use character output to save single characters or lines of characters to a file. Although technically it's possible to use character output with binary-mode files, it can be tricky. You should restrict character-mode output to text files. The main use of character output is to save text (but not numeric) data in a form that can be read by C, as well as other programs such as word processors.

- You can use direct output to save the contents of a section of memory directly to a disk file. This method is for binary files only. Direct output is the best way to save data for later use by a C program.

When you want to read data from a file, you have the same three options: formatted input, character input, or direct input. The type of input you use in a particular case depends almost entirely on the nature of the file being read. Generally, you read data in the same mode that it was saved in, but this is not a requirement. However, reading a file in a mode different from the one it was written in requires a thorough knowledge of C and file formats.

The previous descriptions of the three types of file input and output suggest tasks best suited for each type of output. This is by no means a set of strict rules. The C language is flexible (this is one of its advantages!), so a clever programmer can make any type of file output suit almost any need. As a beginning programmer, you might find it easier if you follow these guidelines, at least initially.

Formatted File Input and Output

Formatted file I/O deals with text and numeric data that is formatted in a specific way. It is directly analogous to formatted keyboard input and screen output done with the `printf()` and `scanf()` functions, as described in Lesson 14. Formatted output is discussed first, followed by input.

Formatted File Output

Formatted file output is done with the library function `fprintf()`. The prototype of `fprintf()` is in the header file `stdio.h`, and it reads as follows:

```
int fprintf(FILE *fp, char *fmt, ...);
```

The first argument is a pointer to type `FILE`. To write data to a particular disk file, you pass the pointer that was returned when you opened the file with `fopen()`.

The second argument is the format string. You learned about format strings in the discussion of `printf()` in Lesson 14. The format string used by `fprintf()` follows exactly the same rules as `printf()`. Refer to Lesson 14 for details.

The final argument is . . . . What does that mean? In a function prototype, ellipses represent a variable number of arguments. In other words, in addition to the file pointer and the format string arguments, `fprintf()` takes zero, one, or more additional arguments. This is just like `printf()`. These arguments are the names of the variables to be output to the specified stream.

Remember, `fprintf()` works just like `printf()`, except that it sends its output to the stream specified in the argument list. In fact, if you specify a stream argument of `stdout`, `fprintf()` is identical to `printf()`.

Listing 17.2 demonstrates the use of `fprintf()`.

Input ▼

LISTING 17.2 numberfile.c: The Equivalence of `fprintf()` Formatted Output to Both a File and to `stdout`

```
1:  // numberfile.c--Demonstrates the fprintf() function.
2:  #include <stdlib.h>
3:  #include <stdio.h>
4:
5:  void clear_kb(void);
6:
7:  int main( void )
8:  {
9:      FILE *fp;
10:     float data[5];
11:     int count;
12:     char filename[20];
13:
14:     puts("Enter 5 floating-point numerical values.");
15:
16:     for (count = 0; count < 5; count++)
17:         scanf("%f", &data[count]);
18:
19:     /* Get the filename and open the file. First clear stdin
20:        of any extra characters. */
21:
22:     clear_kb();
23:
24:     puts("Enter a name for the file.");
25:     gets(filename);
26:
27:     if ( (fp = fopen(filename, "w")) == NULL)
28:     {
29:         fprintf(stderr, "Error opening file %s.", filename);
30:         exit(1);
31:     }
32:
33:     // Write the numerical data to the file and to stdout.
34:
35:     for (count = 0; count < 5; count++)
36:     {
37:         fprintf(fp, "\ndata[%d] = %f", count, data[count]);
38:         fprintf(stdout, "\ndata[%d] = %f", count, data[count]);
39:     }
40:     fclose(fp);
41:     printf("\n");
42:     return(0);
43: }
44:
45: void clear_kb(void)
46: // Clears stdin of any waiting characters.
```

17

```
47: {
48:     char junk[80];
49:     gets(junk);
50: }
```

Output ▼

```
Enter 5 floating-point numerical values.
3.14159
9.99
1.50
3.
1000.0001
Enter a name for the file.
key numbers.txt

data[0] = 3.141590
data[1] = 9.990000
data[2] = 1.500000
data[3] = 3.000000
data[4] = 1000.000122
```

Analysis ▼

You might wonder why the program displays `1000.000122` when the value entered was `1000.0001`. This isn't an error in the program. It's a normal consequence of the way C stores numbers internally. Some floating-point values can't be stored exactly, so minor inaccuracies such as this one sometimes result.

This program uses `fprintf()` on lines 37 and 38 to send some formatted text and numeric data to `stdout` and to the disk file whose name you specified. The only difference between the two lines is the first argument—that is, the stream to which the data is sent. After running the program, use your editor to look at the contents of the file key numbers.txt (or whatever name you assigned to it), which will be in the same directory as the program files. You can see that the text in the file is an exact copy of the text displayed onscreen.

Note that Listing 17.2 uses the `clear_kb()` function discussed in Lesson 14. This is necessary to remove from `stdin` any extra characters that might be left over from the call to `scanf()`. If you don't clear `stdin`, these extra characters (specifically, the newline) are read by the `gets()` that inputs the filename, and the result is a file creation error.

Formatted File Input

For formatted file input, use the `fscanf()` library function, which is used like `scanf()` (see Lesson 14), except that input comes from a specified stream instead of from `stdin`. The prototype for `fscanf()` is

```
int fscanf(FILE *fp, const char *fmt, ...);
```

The argument `fp` is the pointer to type `FILE` returned by `fopen()`, and `fmt` is a pointer to the format string that specifies how `fscanf()` is to read the input. The components of the format string are the same as for `scanf()`. Finally, the ellipsis (. . .) indicates one or more additional arguments, the addresses of the variables where `fscanf()` is to assign the input.

Before getting started with `fscanf()`, you might want to review the section on `scanf()` in Lesson 14. The function `fscanf()` works exactly the same as `scanf()`, except that characters are taken from the specified stream rather than from `stdin`.

To demonstrate `fscanf()`, you need a text file containing some numbers or strings in a format that can be read by the function. Use your editor to create a file named number `input.txt`, and enter five floating-point numbers with some space between them (spaces or newlines). For example, your file might look like this:

```
123.45      87.001
100.02
0.00456     1.0005
```

Now, compile and run Listing 17.3.

Input ▼

LISTING 17.3 fscanfnums.c: Using `fscanf()` to Read Formatted Data from a Disk File

```
1:  // fscanfnums.c--Reading formatted file data with fscanf().
2:  #include <stdlib.h>
3:  #include <stdio.h>
4:
5:  int main( void )
6:  {
7:      float f1, f2, f3, f4, f5;
8:      FILE *fp;
9:
10:     if ( (fp = fopen("numberinput.txt", "r")) == NULL)
11:     {
12:         fprintf(stderr, "Error opening file.\n");
13:         exit(1);
14:     }
15:
```

17

```
16:     fscanf(fp, "%f %f %f %f %f", &f1, &f2, &f3, &f4, &f5);
17:     printf("The values are %f, %f, %f, %f, and %f\n.",
18:             f1, f2, f3, f4, f5);
19:
20:     fclose(fp);
21:     return(0);
22: }
```

Output ▼

```
The values are 123.449997, 87.000999, 100.019997, 0.004560, and 1.000500
```

NOTE	The precision of the values might cause some numbers to not display as the exact values you entered. For example, `100.02` might appear as `100.01999`.

Analysis ▼

This program reads the five values from the file you created and then displays them onscreen. The `fopen()` call on line 10 opens the file for read mode. It also checks to see that the file opened correctly. If the file weren't opened, an error message displays on line 12, and the program exits (line 13). Line 16 demonstrates the use of the `fscanf()` function. With the exception of the first parameter, `fscanf()` is identical to `scanf()`, which you have been using throughout this book. The first parameter points to the file that you want the program to read. You can do further experiments with `fscanf()`, creating input files with your programming editor and seeing how `fscanf()` reads the data.

Character Input and Output

When used with disk files, the term *character I/O* refers to single characters as well as lines of characters. Remember, a line is a sequence of zero or more characters terminated by the newline character. Use character I/O with text-mode files. The following sections describe character I/O functions, and then you see a demonstration program.

Character Input

There are three character input functions for reading from files: `getc()` and `fgetc()` for single characters, and `fgets()` for lines.

The `getc()` and `fgetc()` Functions

The functions `getc()` and `fgetc()` are identical and can be used interchangeably. They input a single character from the specified stream. Here is the prototype of `getc()`, which is in `stdio.h`:

```
int getc(FILE *fp);
```

The argument `fp` is the pointer returned by `fopen()` when the file was opened. The function returns the character that was input or `EOF` on error.

You've seen `getc()` used in earlier programs to input a character from the keyboard. This is another example of the flexibility of C's streams—the same function can be used for keyboard or file input.

If `getc()` and `fgetc()` return a single character, why are they prototyped to return a type `int`? The reason is that, when reading files, you need to read in the end-of-file marker, which on some systems isn't a type `char` but a type `int`. You can see `getc()` in action later, in Listing 17.10.

17

NOTE

The `getchar()` function is also used to read characters. It, however, reads from the `stdin` stream rather than from a file you specify.

The `fgets()` Function

To read a line of characters from a file, use the `fgets()` library function. The prototype is

```
char *fgets(char *str, int n, FILE *fp);
```

The argument `str` is a pointer to a buffer in which the input is to be stored. `n` is the maximum number of characters to be input. `fp` is the pointer to type `FILE` that was returned by `fopen()` when the file was opened.

When called, `fgets()` reads characters from `fp` into memory, starting at the location pointed to by `str`. Characters are read until a newline is encountered or until `n-1` characters have been read, whichever occurs first. By setting `n` equal to the number of bytes allocated for the buffer `str`, you prevent input from overwriting memory beyond allocated space. (The `n-1` is to allow space for the terminating `\0` that `fgets()` adds to the end of the string.) If successful, `fgets()` returns `str`. Two types of errors can occur, as indicated by the return value of `NULL`:

- If a read error or EOF is encountered before any characters have been assigned to str, NULL is returned, and the memory pointed to by str is unchanged.

- If a read error or EOF is encountered after one or more characters have been assigned to str, NULL is returned, and the memory pointed to by str contains garbage.

You can see that fgets() doesn't necessarily input an entire line (that is, everything up to the next newline character). If n-1 characters are read before a newline is encountered, fgets() stops. The next read operation from the file starts where the last one leaves off. To be sure that fgets() reads in entire strings, stopping only at newlines, be sure that the size of your input buffer and the corresponding value of n passed to fgets() are large enough.

Character Output

You need to know about a few character output functions: putc(), fputc(), puts(), and fputs().

The `putc()` and `fputc()` Functions

The library functions fputc() and putc() write a single character to a specified stream. The prototype for putc(), in stdio.h, reads

```
int putc(int ch, FILE *fp);
```

The argument ch is the character to output. As with other character functions, it is formally called a type int, but only the lower-order byte is used. The argument fp is the pointer associated with the file (the pointer returned by fopen() when the file was opened). The function putc() returns the character just written (if successful) or EOF (if an error occurs). The symbolic constant EOF is defined in stdio.h, and it has the value -1. Because no "real" character has that numeric value, EOF can be used as an error indicator (with text-mode files only).

NOTE

> The putchar() function is also used to write characters. It, however, reads from the stdout stream rather than from a file you specify.

The `fputs()` Function

To write a line of characters to a stream, use the library function `fputs()`. This function works just like `puts()`, covered in Lesson 14. The only difference is that with `fputs()`, you can specify the output stream. Also, `fputs()` doesn't add a newline to the end of the string; if you want it, you must explicitly include it. Its prototype in `stdio.h` is

```
char fputs(char *str, FILE *fp);
```

The argument `str` is a pointer to the null-terminated string to be written, and `fp` is the pointer to type `FILE` returned by `fopen()` when the file was opened. The string pointed to by `str` is written to the file, minus its terminating `\0`. The function `fputs()` returns a nonnegative value if successful or `EOF` on error.

Direct File Input and Output

You use direct file I/O most often when you save data to be read later by the same or a different C program. Direct I/O is used only with binary-mode files. With direct output, blocks of data are written from memory to disk. Direct input reverses the process: A block of data is read from a disk file into memory. For example, a single direct-output function call can write an entire array of type `double` to disk, and a single direct-input function call can read the entire array from disk back into memory. The direct I/O functions are `fread()` and `fwrite()`.

17

The `fwrite()` Function

The `fwrite()` library function writes a block of data from memory to a binary-mode file. Its prototype, in `stdio.h`, is

```
int fwrite(void *buf, int size, int count, FILE *fp);
```

The argument `buf` is a pointer to the region of memory holding the data to be written to the file. The pointer type is `void`; it can be a pointer to anything.

The argument `size` specifies the size, in bytes, of the individual data items, and `count` specifies the number of items to be written. For example, if you want to save a 100-element integer array, `size` would be 2 (because each `int` occupies 2 bytes), and `count` would be 100 (because the array contains 100 elements). To obtain the `size` argument, you can use the `sizeof()` operator.

The argument `fp` is, of course, the pointer to type `FILE`, returned by `fopen()` when the file was opened. The `fwrite()` function returns the number of items written on success; if the value returned is less than `count`, it means that an error has occurred. To check for errors, you usually program `fwrite()` as follows:

```
if( (fwrite(buf, size, count, fp)) != count)
fprintf(stderr, "Error writing to file.");
```

Here are some examples of using `fwrite()`. To write a single type `double` variable `x` to a file, use the following:

```
fwrite(&x, sizeof(double), 1, fp);
```

To write an array `data[]` of 50 structures of type `address` to a file, you have two choices:

```
fwrite(data, sizeof(address), 50, fp);

fwrite(data, sizeof(data), 1, fp);
```

The first method writes the array as 50 elements, with each element having the size of a single type `address` structure. The second method treats the array as a single element. The two methods accomplish exactly the same thing.

The following section explains `fread()` and then presents a program demonstrating `fread()` and `fwrite()`.

The `fread()` Function

The `fread()` library function reads a block of data from a binary-mode file into memory. Its prototype in `stdio.h` is

```
int fread(void *buf, int size, int count, FILE *fp);
```

The argument `buf` is a pointer to the region of memory that receives the data read from the file. As with `fwrite()`, the pointer type is `void`.

The argument `size` specifies the size, in bytes, of the individual data items being read, and `count` specifies the number of items to read. Note how these arguments parallel the arguments used by `fwrite()`. Again, the `sizeof()` operator is typically used to provide the `size` argument. The argument `fp` is (as always) the pointer to type `FILE` that was returned by `fopen()` when the file was opened. The `fread()` function returns the number of items read; this can be less than `count` if end-of-file were reached or an error occurred.

Listing 17.4 demonstrates the use of `fwrite()` and `fread()`.

Input ▼

LISTING 17.4   direct.c: Using `fwrite()` and `fread()` for Direct File Access

```
1:    // direct.c--Direct file I/O with fwrite() and fread().
2:    #include <stdlib.h>
3:    #include <stdio.h>
4:
5:    #define SIZE 20
6:
7:    int main( void )
8:    {
9:        int count, array1[SIZE], array2[SIZE];
10:       FILE *fp;
11:
12:       /* Initialize array1[]. */
13:
14:       for (count = 0; count < SIZE; count++)
15:           array1[count] = 2 * count;
16:
17:       /* Open a binary mode file. */
18:
19:       if ( (fp = fopen("direct.txt", "wb")) == NULL)
20:       {
21:           fprintf(stderr, "Error opening file.");
22:           exit(1);
23:       }
24:       /* Save array1[] to the file. */
25:
26:       if (fwrite(array1, sizeof(int), SIZE, fp) != SIZE)
27:       {
28:           fprintf(stderr, "Error writing to file.");
29:           exit(1);
30:       }
31:
32:       fclose(fp);
33:
34:       /* Now open the same file for reading in binary mode. */
35:
36:       if ( (fp = fopen("direct.txt", "rb")) == NULL)
37:       {
38:           fprintf(stderr, "Error opening file.");
39:           exit(1);
40:       }
41:
42:       /* Read the data into array2[]. */
43:
44:       if (fread(array2, sizeof(int), SIZE, fp) != SIZE)
45:       {
46:           fprintf(stderr, "Error reading file.");
47:           exit(1);
```

17

```
48:    }
49:
50:    fclose(fp);
51:
52:    /* Now display both arrays to show they're the same. */
53:
54:    for (count = 0; count < SIZE; count++)
55:        printf("%d\t%d\n", array1[count], array2[count]);
56:    return(0);
57: }
```

Output ▼

```
0      0
2      2
4      4
6      6
8      8
10     10
12     12
14     14
16     16
18     18
20     20
22     22
24     24
26     26
28     28
30     30
32     32
34     34
36     36
38     38
```

Analysis ▼

Listing 17.4 demonstrates the use of the `fwrite()` and `fread()` functions. This program initializes an array on lines 14 and 15. It then uses `fwrite()` on line 26 to save the array to disk. The program uses `fread()` on line 44 to read the data into a different array. Finally, it displays both arrays onscreen to show that they now hold the same data (lines 54 and 55).

When you save data with `fwrite()`, not much can go wrong except some type of disk error. With `fread()`, be careful, however. As far as `fread()` is concerned, the data on the disk is just a sequence of bytes. The function has no way of knowing what it represents. For example, a block of 100 bytes could be 100 `char` variables, 25 `int` variables, or 5 20-byte structures. If you ask `fread()` to read that block into memory, it obediently does so. However, if the block is saved from an array of type int and you retrieve it into an array of type float, no error occurs, but you get strange results. When writing programs, you must be sure that fread() is used properly, reading data into the appropriate types of variables and arrays. Notice that in Listing 17.4, all calls to fopen(), fwrite(), and fread() are checked to ensure that they worked correctly.

File Buffering: Closing and Flushing Files

When you finish using a file, you should close it using the fclose() function. You saw fclose() used in programs presented earlier in the lesson. Its prototype is

```
int fclose(FILE *fp);
```

The argument fp is the FILE pointer associated with the stream; fclose() returns 0 on success or -1 on error. When you close a file, the file's buffer is flushed (written to the file). You can also close all open streams except the standard ones (stdin, stdout, and stderr), and by using the fcloseall() function. Its prototype is

```
int fcloseall(void);
```

This function also flushes any stream buffers and returns the number of streams closed.

When a program terminates (either by reaching the end of main() or by executing the exit() function), all streams are automatically flushed and closed. However, it's a good idea to close streams explicitly—particularly those linked to disk files—as soon as you finish with them. The reason has to do with stream buffers.

When you create a stream linked to a disk file, a buffer is automatically created and associated with the stream. A buffer is a block of memory used for temporary storage of data being written to and read from the file. Buffers are needed because disk drives are block-oriented devices, which means that they operate most efficiently when data is read and written in blocks of a certain size. The size of the ideal block differs, depending on the specific hardware in use. It's typically on the order of a few hundred to a thousand bytes. You don't need to be concerned about the exact block size, however.

The buffer associated with a file stream serves as an interface between the stream (which is character-oriented) and the disk hardware (which is block-oriented). As your program writes data to the stream, the data is saved in the buffer until the buffer is full, and then the entire contents of the buffer are written, as a block, to the disk. An analogous process occurs when reading data from a disk file. The creation and operation of the buffer is handled by the operating system and is entirely automatic; you don't have to be concerned with it. (C does offer some functions for buffer manipulation, but they are beyond the scope of this book.)

17

In practical terms, this buffer operation means that, during program execution, data that your program wrote to the disk might still be in the buffer, not on the disk. If your program hangs up, if there's a power failure, or if some other problem occurs, the data that's still in the buffer might be lost, and you won't know what's contained in the disk file.

You can flush a stream's buffers without closing it by using the `fflush()` or `flushall()` library functions. Use `fflush()` when you want a file's buffer to be written to disk while still using the file. Use `flushall()` to flush the buffers of all open streams. The prototypes of these two functions are as follows:

```
int fflush(FILE *fp);

int flushall(void);
```

The argument `fp` is the `FILE` pointer returned by `fopen()` when the file was opened. If a file were opened for writing, `fflush()` writes its buffer to disk. If the file were opened for reading, the buffer is cleared. The function `fflush()` returns 0 on success or `EOF` if an error occurred. The function `flushall()` returns the number of open streams.

DO	DON'T
DO open a file before trying to read or write to it.	**DON'T** assume that a file access is okay. Always check after doing a read, write, or open to ensure that the function worked.
DO use the `sizeof()` operator with the `fwrite()` and `fread()` functions.	
DO close all files that you've opened.	**DON'T** use `fcloseall()` unless you have a reason to close all the streams.

Understanding Sequential Versus Random File Access

Every open file has a file position indicator associated with it. The position indicator specifies where read and write operations take place in the file. The position is always given in terms of bytes from the beginning of the file. When a new file is opened, the position indicator is always at the beginning of the file, position 0. (Because the file is new and has a length of 0, there's no other location to indicate.) When an existing file is opened, the position indicator is at the end of the file if the file is opened in append mode, or at the beginning of the file if the file is opened in any other mode.

The file I/O functions, covered earlier in this lesson, make use of the position indicator, although the manipulations go on behind the scenes. Writing and reading operations occur at the location of the position indicator and update the position indicator as well. For example, if you open a file for reading, and 10 bytes are read, you input the first 10 bytes in the file (the bytes at positions 0 through 9). After the read operation, the position indicator is at position 10, and the next read operation begins there. Thus, if you want to read all the data in a file sequentially or write data to a file sequentially, you don't need to be concerned about the position indicator. The stream I/O functions take care of it automatically.

When you need more control, use the C library functions that enable you to determine and change the value of the file position indicator. By controlling the position indicator, you can perform random file access. Here, *random* means that you can read data from or write data to any position in a file without reading or writing all the preceding data.

The `ftell()` and `rewind()` Functions

To set the position indicator to the beginning of the file, use the library function `rewind()`. Its prototype, in `stdio.h`, is

```
void rewind(FILE *fp);
```

The argument `fp` is the `FILE` pointer associated with the stream. After `rewind()` is called, the file's position indicator is set to the beginning of the file (byte 0). Use `rewind()` if you've read some data from a file and you want to start reading from the beginning of the file again without closing and reopening the file.

To determine the value of a file's position indicator, use `ftell()`. This function's prototype, located in `stdio.h`, reads

```
long ftell(FILE *fp);
```

The argument `fp` is the `FILE` pointer returned by `fopen()` when the file was opened. The function `ftell()` returns a type `long` that gives the current file position in bytes from the start of the file. (The first byte is at position 0.) If an error occurs, `ftell()` returns `-1L` (a type `long -1`).

To get a feel for the operation of `rewind()` and `ftell()`, look at Listing 17.5.

Input ▼

LISTING 17.5   fileposition.c: Using `ftell()` and `rewind()`

```
1:  // fileposition.c--Demonstrates ftell() and rewind().
2:  #include <stdlib.h>
3:  #include <stdio.h>
4:
5:  #define BUFLEN 6
6:
7:  char msg[] = "abcdefghijklmnopqrstuvwxyz";
8:
9:  int main( void )
10: {
11:     FILE *fp;
12:     char buf[BUFLEN];
13:
14:     if ( (fp = fopen("fileposition.txt", "w")) == NULL)
15:     {
16:         fprintf(stderr, "Error opening file.");
17:         exit(1);
18:     }
19:
20:     if (fputs(msg, fp) == EOF)
21:     {
22:         fprintf(stderr, "Error writing to file.");
23:         exit(1);
24:     }
25:
26:     fclose(fp);
27:
28:     // Now open the file for reading.
29:
30:     if ( (fp = fopen("file position.txt", "r")) == NULL)
31:     {
32:         fprintf(stderr, "Error opening file.");
33:         exit(1);
34:     }
35:     printf("\nImmediately after opening, position = %ld", ftell(fp));
36:
37:     // Read in 5 characters.
38:
39:     fgets(buf, BUFLEN, fp);
40:     printf("\nAfter reading in %s, position = %ld", buf, ftell(fp));
41:
42:     // Read in the next 5 characters.
43:
44:     fgets(buf, BUFLEN, fp);
45:     printf("\n\nThe next 5 characters are %s, and position now = %ld",
46:             buf, ftell(fp));
47:
```

```
48:        // Rewind the stream.
49:
50:        rewind(fp);
51:
52:        printf("\n\nAfter rewinding, the position is back at %ld",
53:                   ftell(fp));
54:
55:        // Read in 5 characters.
56:
57:        fgets(buf, BUFLEN, fp);
58:        printf("\nand reading starts at the beginning again: %s\n", buf);
59:        fclose(fp);
60:        return(0);
61: }
```

Output ▼

```
Immediately after opening, position = 0
After reading in abcde, position = 5

The next 5 characters are fghij, and position now = 10

After rewinding, the position is back at 0
and reading starts at the beginning again: abcde
```

Analysis ▼

This program writes a string, msg, to a file called file position.txt. The message consists of the 26 letters of the alphabet, in order. Lines 14 through 18 open file position.txt for writing and test to ensure that the file was opened successfully. Lines 20 through 24 write msg to the file using fputs() and check to ensure that the write was successful. Line 26 closes the file with fclose(), completing the process of creating a file for the rest of the program to use.

Lines 30 through 34 open the file again, only this time for reading. Line 35 prints the return value of ftell(). Notice that this position is at the beginning of the file. Line 39 performs an fgets() to read five characters. The five characters and the new file position are printed on line 40. Notice that ftell() returns the correct offset. Line 50 calls rewind() to put the pointer back at the beginning of the file, before line 52 prints the file position again. This should confirm for you that rewind() resets the position. An additional read on line 57 further confirms that the program is indeed back at the beginning of the file. Line 59 closes the file before ending the program.

The `fseek()` Function

More precise control over a stream's position indicator is possible with the `fseek()` library function. By using `fseek()`, you can set the position indicator anywhere in the file. The function prototype, in `stdio.h`, is

```
int fseek(FILE *fp, long offset, int origin);
```

The argument `fp` is the `FILE` pointer associated with the file. The distance that the position indicator is to be moved is given by `offset` in bytes. The argument `origin` specifies the move's relative starting point. There can be three values for `origin`, with symbolic constants defined in `io.h`, as shown in Table 17.2.

TABLE 17.2 Possible Origin Values for `fseek()`

Constant	Value	Description
SEEK_SET	0	Moves the indicator *offset* bytes from the beginning of the file
SEEK_CUR	1	Moves the indicator *offset* bytes from its current position
SEEK_END	2	Moves the indicator *offset* bytes from the end of the file

The function `fseek()` returns 0 if the indicator were successfully moved or nonzero if an error occurred. Listing 17.6 uses `fseek()` for random file access.

Input ▼
LISTING 17.6　randomfile.c: Random File Access with `fseek()`

```
1:  /* randomfile.c--Random access with fseek(). */
2:
3:  #include <stdlib.h>
4:  #include <stdio.h>
5:
6:  #define MAX 50
7:
8:  int main( void )
9:  {
10:     FILE *fp;
11:     int data, count, array[MAX];
12:     long offset;
13:
14:     /* Initialize the array. */
15:
16:     for (count = 0; count < MAX; count++)
17:         array[count] = count * 10;
18:
19:     /* Open a binary file for writing. */
```

```
20:
21:     if ( (fp = fopen("RANDOM.DAT", "wb")) == NULL)
22:     {
23:         fprintf(stderr, "\nError opening file.");
24:         exit(1);
25:     }
26:
27:     /* Write the array to the file, then close it. */
28:
29:     if ( (fwrite(array, sizeof(int), MAX, fp)) != MAX)
30:     {
31:         fprintf(stderr, "\nError writing data to file.");
32:         exit(1);
33:     }
34:
35:     fclose(fp);
36:
37:     /* Open the file for reading. */
38:
39:     if ( (fp = fopen("RANDOM.DAT", "rb")) == NULL)
40:     {
41:         fprintf(stderr, "\nError opening file.");
42:         exit(1);
43:     }
44:
45:     /* Ask user which element to read. Input the element */
46:     /* and display it, quitting when -1 is entered. */
47:
48:     while (1)
49:     {
50:         printf("\nEnter element to read, 0-%d, -1 to quit: ",MAX-1);
51:         scanf("%ld", &offset);
52:
53:         if (offset < 0)
54:             break;
55:         else if (offset > MAX-1)
56:             continue;
57:
58:         /* Move the position indicator to the specified element. */
59:
60:         if ( (fseek(fp, (offset*sizeof(int)), SEEK_SET)) != 0)
61:         {
62:             fprintf(stderr, "\nError using fseek().");
63:             exit(1);
64:         }
65:
66:         /* Read in a single integer. */
67:
68:         fread(&data, sizeof(int), 1, fp);
69:
70:         printf("\nElement %ld has value %d.", offset, data);
```

17

```
71:     }
72:
73:     fclose(fp);
74:     return(0);
75: }
```

Output ▼

```
Enter element to read, 0-49, -1 to quit: 5

Element 5 has value 50.
Enter element to read, 0-49, -1 to quit: 6

Element 6 has value 60.
Enter element to read, 0-49, -1 to quit: 49

Element 49 has value 490.
Enter element to read, 0-49, -1 to quit: 1

Element 1 has value 10.
Enter element to read, 0-49, -1 to quit: 0

Element 0 has value 0.
Enter element to read, 0-49, -1 to quit: -1
```

Analysis ▼

Lines 14 through 35 are similar to Listing 17.5. Lines 16 and 17 initialize an array called data with 50 type int values. The value stored in each array element is equal to 10 times the index. Then the array is written to a binary file called RANDOM.DAT. You know it is binary because the file was opened with mode "wb" on line 21.

Line 39 reopens the file in binary read mode before going into an infinite while loop. The while loop prompts users to enter the number of the array element that they want to read. Notice that lines 53 through 56 check that the entered element is within the range of the file. Does C let you read an element that is beyond the end of the file? Yes. Like going beyond the end of an array with values, C also lets you read beyond the end of a file. If you do read beyond the end (or before the beginning), your results are unpredictable. It's always best to check what you're doing (as lines 53 through 56 do in this listing).

After you have input the element to find, line 60 jumps to the appropriate offset with a call to fseek(). Because SEEK_SET is being used, the seek is done from the beginning of the file. Notice that the distance into the file is not just offset, but offset multiplied by the size of the elements being read. Line 68 then reads the value, and line 70 prints it.

Detecting the End of a File

Sometimes you know exactly how long a file is, so there's no need to detect the file's end. For example, if you used `fwrite()` to save a 100-element integer array, you know the file is 400 bytes long (assuming 4-byte integers). At other times, however, you don't know how long the file is, but you still want to read data from the file, starting at the beginning and proceeding to the end. There are two ways to detect end-of-file.

When reading from a text-mode file character-by-character, you can look for the end-of-file character. The symbolic constant `EOF` is defined in `stdio.h` as `-1`, a value never used by a "real" character. When a character input function reads `EOF` from a text-mode stream, you can be sure that you've reached the end of the file. For example, you could write the following:

```
while ( (c = fgetc( fp )) != EOF )
```

With a binary-mode stream, you can't detect the end-of-file by looking for –1 because a byte of data from a binary stream could have that value, which would result in premature end of input. Instead, you can use the library function `feof()`, which can be used for both binary- and text-mode files:

```
int feof(FILE *fp);
```

The argument `fp` is the `FILE` pointer returned by `fopen()` when the file was opened. The function `feof()` returns `0` if the end of file `fp` hasn't been reached, or a nonzero value if end-of-file has been reached. If a call to `feof()` detects end-of-file, no further read operations are permitted until a `rewind()` has been done, `fseek()` is called, or the file is closed and reopened.

Listing 17.7 demonstrates the use of `feof()`. When you're prompted for a filename, enter the name of any text file—one of your C source files, for example, or a header file such as `stdio.h`. Just be sure that the file is in the current directory, or else enter a path as part of the filename. The program reads the file one line at a time, displaying each line on `stdout`, until `feof()` detects end-of-file.

Input ▼

LISTING 17.7 endOfFile.c: Using `feof()` to Detect the End of a File

```
1:   // endOfFile.c--Detecting end-of-file.
2:   #include <stdlib.h>
3:   #include <stdio.h>
4:
5:   #define BUFSIZE 100
6:
7:   int main( void )
```

```
 8:   {
 9:       char buf[BUFSIZE];
10:       char filename[60];
11:       FILE *fp;
12:
13:       puts("Enter name of text file to display: ");
14:       gets(filename);
15:
16:       /* Open the file for reading. */
17:       if ( (fp = fopen(filename, "r")) == NULL)
18:       {
19:           fprintf(stderr, "Error opening file.");
20:           exit(1);
21:       }
22:
23:       /* If end of file not reached, read a line and display it. */
24:
25:       while ( !feof(fp) )
26:       {
27:           fgets(buf, BUFSIZE, fp);
28:           printf("%s",buf);
29:       }
30:
31:       fclose(fp);
32:       return(0);
33:   }
```

Output ▼

```
Enter name of text file to display:
hello.c
#include <stdio.h>
int main( void )
{
    printf("Hello, world.");
    return(0);
}
```

Analysis ▼

The while loop in this program (lines 25 through 29) is typical of a while loop used in more complex programs that do sequential processing. As long as the end of the file hasn't been reached, the code within the while statement (lines 27 and 28) continues to execute repeatedly. When the call to feof() returns a nonzero value, the loop ends, the file is closed, and the program ends.

DO	DON'T
DO use either `rewind()` or `fseek( fp, SEEK_SET, 0 )` to reset the file position to the beginning of the file.	**DON'T** read beyond the end of a file or before the beginning of a file. Avoid this by checking your position.
DO use `feof()` to check for the end of the file when working with binary files.	**DON'T** use `EOF` with binary files.

File Management Functions

The term *file management* refers to dealing with existing files—not reading from or writing to them—but deleting, renaming, and copying them. The C standard library contains functions for deleting and renaming files, and you can also write your own file-copying program.

Deleting a File

To delete a file, you use the library function `remove()`. Its prototype is in `stdio.h`, as follows:

```
int remove( const char *filename );
```

The variable `*filename` is a pointer to the name of the file to be deleted. (See the section on filenames, "Using Filenames," earlier in this lesson.) The specified file must not be open. If the file exists, it is deleted, and `remove()` returns `0`. If the file doesn't exist, if it's read-only, if you don't have sufficient access rights, or if some other error occurs, `remove()` returns `-1`.

Listing 17.8 demonstrates the use of `remove()`. Be careful: If you `remove()` a file, it's gone forever.

Input ▼
LISTING 17.8   filedeleter.c: Using the `remove()` Function to Delete a Disk File

```
1:  // filedeleter.c--Demonstrates the remove() function.
2:
3:  #include <stdio.h>
4:
5:  int main( void )
6:  {
7:      char filename[80];
8:
9:      printf("Enter the filename to delete: ");
10:     gets(filename);
11:
```

17

```
12:      if ( remove(filename) == 0)
13:          printf("The file %s has been deleted.\n", filename);
14:      else
15:          fprintf(stderr, "Error deleting the file %s.\n", filename);
16:      return(0);
17: }
```

Output ▼

```
Enter the filename to delete: *.bak
Error deleting the file *.bak.
Enter the filename to delete: list1414.bak
The file list1414.bak has been deleted.
```

Analysis ▼

This program prompts the user on line 9 for the name of the file to be deleted. Line 12 then calls `remove()` to delete the entered file. If the return value is `0`, the file was removed, and a message displays stating this fact. If the return value is not zero, an error occurred, and the file was not removed.

TIP	It is always a good idea to verify the user actually wants to delete a file.

Renaming a File

The `rename()` function changes the name of an existing disk file. The function prototype, in `stdio.h`, is as follows:

```
int rename( const char *oldname, const char *newname );
```

The filenames pointed to by `oldname` and `newname` follow the rules given earlier in this lesson. The only restriction is that both names must refer to the same disk drive; you can't rename a file to a different disk drive. The function `rename()` returns `0` on success, or `-1` if an error occurs. Errors can be caused by the following conditions (among others):

- The file `oldname` does not exist.
- A file with the name `newname` already exists.
- You try to rename to another disk.

Listing 17.9 demonstrates the use of `rename()`.

Input ▼

```
1:   /* Using rename() to change a filename. */
2:
3:   #include <stdio.h>
4:
5:   int main( void )
6:   {
7:       char oldname[80], newname[80];
8:
9:       printf("Enter current filename: ");
10:      gets(oldname);
11:      printf("Enter new name for file: ");
12:      gets(newname);
13:
14:      if ( rename( oldname, newname ) == 0 )
15:          printf("%s has been renamed %s.\n", oldname, newname);
16:      else
17:          fprintf(stderr, "An error has occurred renaming %s.\n", oldname);
18:      return(0);
19:  }
```

17

Output ▼

```
Enter current filename: My first file
Enter new name for file: SuperNewFile.txt
My first file has been renamed SuperNewFile.txt.
```

Analysis ▼

Listing 17.9 shows how powerful C can be. With only 18 lines of code, this program replaces an operating system command, and it's a friendly function. Line 9 prompts for the name of the file to be renamed. Line 11 prompts for the new filename. The call to the `rename()` function is wrapped in an `if` statement on line 14. The `if` statement checks to ensure that the renaming of the file was carried out correctly. If so, line 15 prints an affirmative message; otherwise, line 17 prints a message stating that there was an error.

Copying a File

It's frequently necessary to make a copy of a file—an exact duplicate with a different name (or with the same name but in a different drive or directory). In Windows, you do this by copying the file and pasting it in the new directory, and other operating systems have equivalents. How do you copy a file in C? There's no library function, so you need to write your own.

This might sound a bit complicated, but it's quite simple because of C's use of streams for input and output. Here are the steps you follow:

1. Open the source file for reading in binary mode. (Using binary mode ensures that the function can copy all sorts of files, not just text files.)

2. Open the destination file for writing in binary mode.

3. Read a character from the source file. Remember, when a file is first opened, the pointer is at the start of the file, so there's no need to position the file pointer explicitly.

4. If the function `feof()` indicates that you've reached the end of the source file, you're finished and can close both files and return to the calling program.

5. If you haven't reached end-of-file, write the character to the destination file, and then loop back to step 3.

Listing 17.10 contains a function, `copy_file()`, that is passed the names of the source and destination files and then performs the copy operation just as the preceding steps outlined. If there's an error opening either file, the function doesn't attempt the copy operation and returns `-1` to the calling program. When the copy operation is complete, the program closes both files and returns `0`.

Input ▼
LISTING 17.10 filecopier.c: A Function that Copies a File

```
1:  // filecopier.c--Copying a file.
2:
3:  #include <stdio.h>
4:
5:  int file_copy( char *oldname, char *newname );
6:
7:  int main( void )
8:  {
9:      char source[80], destination[80];
10:
11:     /* Get the source and destination names. */
12:
13:     printf("\nEnter source file: ");
14:     gets(source);
15:     printf("\nEnter destination file: ");
16:     gets(destination);
17:
18:     if ( file_copy( source, destination ) == 0 )
19:         puts("Copy operation successful");
20:     else
21:         fprintf(stderr, "Error during copy operation");
```

```
22:     return(0);
23: }
24: int file_copy( char *oldname, char *newname )
25: {
26:     FILE *fold, *fnew;
27:     int c;
28:
29:     /* Open the source file for reading in binary mode. */
30:
31:     if ( ( fold = fopen( oldname, "rb" ) ) == NULL )
32:         return -1;
33:
34:     /* Open the destination file for writing in binary mode. */
35:
36:     if ( ( fnew = fopen( newname, "wb" ) ) == NULL )
37:     {
38:         fclose ( fold );
39:         return -1;
40:     }
41:
42:     /* Read one byte at a time from the source; if end of file */
43:     /* has not been reached, write the byte to the */
44:     /* destination. */
45:
46:     while (1)
47:     {
48:         c = fgetc( fold );
49:
50:         if ( !feof( fold ) )
51:             fputc( c, fnew );
52:         else
53:             break;
54:     }
55:
56:     fclose ( fnew );
57:     fclose ( fold );
58:
59:     return 0;
60: }
```

17

Output ▼

```
Enter source file: list1710.c

Enter destination file: tmpfile.c
Copy operation successful
```

Analysis ▼

The function `copy_file()` works perfectly well, letting you copy anything from a small text file to a huge program file. It does have limitations, however. If the destination file already exists, the function deletes it without asking. A good programming exercise for you is to modify `copy_file()` to check whether the destination file already exists, and then query the user as to whether the old file should be overwritten.

`main()` in Listing 17.10 should look familiar. It's nearly identical to the `main()` in Listing 17.9, with the exception of line 14. Instead of `rename()`, this function uses `copy()`. Because C doesn't have a copy function, lines 24 through 60 create a copy function. Lines 31 and 32 open the source file, `fold`, in binary read mode. Lines 36 through 40 open the destination file, `fnew`, in binary write mode. Notice that line 38 closes the source file if there is an error opening the destination file. The `while` loop on lines 46 through 54 does the actual copying of the file. Line 48 gets a character from the source file, `fold`. Line 50 checks to see whether the end-of-file marker was read. If the end of the file has been reached, a `break` statement is executed in order to get out of the `while` loop. If the end of the file has not been reached, the character is written to the destination file, `fnew`. Lines 56 and 57 close the two files before returning to `main()`.

Using Temporary Files

Some programs make use of one or more temporary files during execution. A temporary file is a file that is created by the program, used for some purpose during program execution, and then deleted before the program terminates. When you create a temporary file, you don't care what its name is because it gets deleted. All that is necessary is that you use a name that isn't already in use for another file. The C standard library includes a function `tmpnam()` that creates a valid filename that doesn't conflict with any existing file. Its prototype in `stdio.h` is as follows:

```
char *tmpnam(char *s);
```

The argument `s` must be a pointer to a buffer large enough to hold the filename. You can also pass a null pointer (`NULL`), in which case the temporary name is stored in a buffer internal to `tmpnam()`, and the function returns a pointer to that buffer. Listing 17.11 demonstrates both methods of using `tmpnam()` to create temporary filenames.

Input ▼

LISTING 17.11 tempfilemaker.c: Using `tmpnam()` to Create Temporary Filenames

```
 1:  // tempfilemaker.c--Demonstration of temporary filenames.
 2:
 3:  #include <stdio.h>
 4:
 5:  int main( void )
 6:  {
 7:      char buffer[10], *c;
 8:
 9:      // Get a temporary name in the defined buffer.
10:
11:      tmpnam(buffer);
12:
13:      /* Get another name, this time in the function's
14:         internal buffer. */
15:
16:      c = tmpnam(NULL);
17:
18:      // Display the names.
19:
20:      printf("Temporary name 1: %s", buffer);
21:      printf("\nTemporary name 2: %s\n", c);
22:
23:      return 0;
24:
25:  }
```

Output ▼

```
Temporary name 1: \s3us.
Temporary name 2: \s3us.1
```

> **NOTE** The temporary names created in your system will probably be different from these.

Analysis ▼

This program generates and prints only the temporary names; it doesn't actually create any files. Line 11 stores a temporary name in the character array, `buffer`. Line 16 assigns the character pointer to the name returned by `tmpnam()` to `c`. Your program must use the generated name to open the temporary file and then delete the file before program execution terminates. The following code fragment illustrates this:

17

```
char tempname[80];
FILE *tmpfile;
tmpnam(tempname);
tmpfile = fopen(tempname, "w");   /* Use appropriate mode */
fclose(tmpfile);
remove(tempname);
```

DO	**DON'T**
DO remember to remove temporary files that you create. They aren't deleted automatically.	**DON'T** remove a file that you might need again.

Summary

In this lesson, you learned how C programs can use disk files. C treats a disk file like a stream (a sequence of characters), just like the predefined streams you learned about in Lesson 14. A stream associated with a disk file must be opened before it can be used, and it must be closed after use. A disk file stream can be opened in either text or binary mode.

After a disk file has been opened, you can read data from the file into your program, write data from the program to the file, or both. There are three general types of file I/O: formatted, character, and direct. Each type of I/O is best used for certain types of data storage and retrieval tasks.

Each open disk file has a file position indicator associated with it. This indicator specifies the position in the file, measured as the number of bytes from the start of the file, where subsequent read and write operations occur. With some types of file access, the position indicator is updated automatically, and you don't have to be concerned with it. For random file access, the C standard library provides functions for manipulating the position indicator.

Finally, C provides some rudimentary file management functions, enabling you to delete and rename disk files. In this lesson, you developed your own function for copying a file.

Q&A

Q Can I use drives and paths with filenames when using `remove()`, `rename()`, `fopen()`, **and the other file functions?**

A Yes. You can use a full filename with a path and a drive or just the filename by itself. If you use the filename by itself, the function looks for the file in the current directory. Remember, when using a backslash (\), you need to use the escape sequence. Also remember that UNIX uses the forward slash (/) as a directory separator.

Q Can I read beyond the end of a file?

A Yes. You can also read before the beginning of a file. Results from such reads can be disastrous. Reading files is just like working with arrays. You're looking at offsets within memory. If you're using `fseek()`, you should check to make sure that you don't go beyond the end of the file.

Q What happens if I don't close a file?

A It's good programming practice to close any files you open. By default, the file should be closed when the program exits; however, you should never count on this. If the file isn't closed, you might not be able to access it later because the operating system will think that the file is already in use.

Q How many files can I open at once?

A This question can't be answered with a simple number. The limitation on the number of files that can be opened is based on variables set within your operating system. Consult your operating system manuals for more information.

Q Can I read a file sequentially with random-access functions?

A When reading a file sequentially, there is no need to use such functions as `fseek()`. Because the file pointer is left at the last position it occupied, it is always where you want it for sequential reads. You can use `fseek()` to read a file sequentially; however, you gain nothing.

17

Workshop

The Workshop provides quiz questions to help you solidify your understanding of the material covered and exercises to provide you with experience in using what you've learned.

Quiz

1. What's the difference between a text-mode stream and a binary-mode stream?
2. What must your program do before it can access a disk file?
3. When you open a file with `fopen()`, what information must you specify, and what does this function return?
4. What are the three general methods of file access?
5. What are the two general methods of reading a file's information?

6. What is the value of EOF?

7. When is EOF used?

8. How do you detect the end of a file in text and binary modes?

9. What is the file position indicator, and how can you modify it?

10. When a file is first opened, where does the file position indicator point to? (If you're unsure, refer to Listing 16.5 in the previous lesson.)

Exercises

1. Write code to close all file streams.

2. Show two different ways to reset the file position pointer to the beginning of the file.

3. **BUG BUSTER:** Is anything wrong with the following code?

```
FILE *fp;
int c;

if ( ( fp = fopen( oldname, "rb" ) ) == NULL )
    return -1;

while (( c = fgetc( fp)) != EOF )
    fprintf( stdout, "%c", c );

fclose ( fp );
```

Because of the many possible solutions, answers are not provided for the following exercises.

4. Write a program that displays a file to the screen.

5. Write a program that opens a file and counts the number of characters. The program should print the number of characters when finished.

6. Write a program that opens an existing text file and copies it to a new text file with all lowercase letters changed to uppercase and all other characters unchanged.

7. Write a program that opens any disk file, reads it in 128-byte blocks, and displays the contents of each block onscreen in both hexadecimal and ASCII formats.

8. Write a function that opens a new temporary file with a specified mode. All temporary files created by this function should automatically be closed and deleted when the program terminates. (Hint: Use the atexit() library function.)

LESSON 18
Manipulating Strings

Text data, which C stores in strings, is an important part of many programs. So far, you have learned how a C program stores strings and how you can input and output strings. C offers a variety of functions for other types of string manipulations as well. In this lesson you learn

- How to determine the length of a string

- How to copy and join strings

- Functions that compare strings

- How to search strings

- How to convert strings

- How to test characters

Determining String Length

You should remember from earlier chapters that in C programs, a string is a sequence of characters, with its beginning indicated by a pointer and its end marked by the null character \0. At times, you need to know the length of a string—the number of characters it contains. This length is obtained with the library function `strlen()`. Its prototype, in `string.h`, is

```
size_t strlen(char *str);
```

You might be puzzling over the `size_t` return type. This type is defined in `string.h` as `unsigned`, so the function `strlen()` returns an unsigned integer. The `size_t` type is used with many of the string functions. Just remember that it means `unsigned`.

The argument passed to `strlen` is a pointer to the string whose length you want to know. The function `strlen()` returns the number of characters between `str` and the next null character, not counting the null character. Listing 18.1 demonstrates `strlen()`.

Input ▼

LISTING 18.1   stringlen.c: Using the `strlen()` Function to Determine the Length of a String

```c
1:  // stringlen.c--Using the strlen() function.
2:
3:  #include <stdio.h>
4:  #include <string.h>
5:
6:  int main( void )
7:  {
8:      size_t length;
9:      char buf[80];
10:
11:     while (1)
12:     {
13:         puts("\nEnter a line of text, a blank line to exit.");
14:         gets(buf);
15:
16:         length = strlen(buf);
17:
18:         if (length != 0)
19:             printf("\nThat line is %u characters long.", length);
20:         else
21:             break;
22:     }
23:     return(0);
24: }
```

Output ▼

```
Enter a line of text, a blank line to exit.
I am Iron Man!

That line is 14 characters long.
Enter a line of text, a blank line to exit.
```

Analysis ▼

This program does little more than demonstrate the use of `strlen()`. Lines 13 and 14 display a message and get a string called `buf`. Line 16 uses `strlen()` to assign the length of `buf` to the variable `length`. Line 18 checks whether the string was blank by checking for a length of `0`. If the string is not blank, line 19 prints the string's size.

Copying Strings

The C library has two functions for copying strings. Because of the way C handles strings, you can't simply assign one string to another, as you can in some other computer languages. You must copy the source string from its location in memory to the memory location of the destination string. The string-copying functions are `strcpy()` and `strncpy()`. These functions require the header file `string.h`.

The `strcpy()` Function

The library function `strcpy()` copies an entire string to another memory location. Its prototype is as follows:

```
char *strcpy( char *destination, const char *source );
```

The function `strcpy()` copies the string (including the terminating null character `\0`) pointed to by `source` to the location pointed to by `destination`. The return value is a pointer to the new string, `destination`.

When using `strcpy()`, you must first allocate storage space for the destination string. The function has no way of knowing whether `destination` points to allocated space. If space hasn't been allocated, the function overwrites `strlen(source)` bytes of memory, starting at `destination`. This can cause unpredictable problems. The use of `strcpy()` is illustrated in Listing 18.2.

NOTE

When a program uses `malloc()` to allocate memory, as Listing 18.2 does, good programming practice requires the use of the `free()` function to free up the memory when the program finishes with it. You learn about `free()` in Lesson 21, "Working with Memory."

Input ▼
LISTING 18.2   stringcopy.c: Before Using `strcpy()`, You Must Allocate Storage Space for the Destination String

```
1:  // stringcopy.c--Demonstrates strcpy().
2:  #include <stdlib.h>
3:  #include <stdio.h>
4:  #include <string.h>
5:
6:  char source[] = "The source string.";
7:
8:  int main( void )
9:  {
10:     char dest1[80];
11:     char *dest2, *dest3;
12:
13:     printf("\nsource: %s", source );
14:
15:     // Copy to dest1 is okay because dest1 points to
16:     // 80 bytes of allocated space.
17:
18:     strcpy(dest1, source);
19:     printf("\ndest1: %s", dest1);
20:
21:     // To copy to dest2 you must allocate space.
22:
23:     dest2 = (char *)malloc(strlen(source) +1);
24:     strcpy(dest2, source);
25:     printf("\ndest2: %s\n", dest2);
26:
27:     // Copying without allocating destination space is a no-no.
28:     // The following could cause serious problems.
29:
30:     // strcpy(dest3, source);
31:     return(0);
32: }
```

Output ▼

```
source:  The source string.
dest1:   The source string.
dest2:   The source string.
```

Analysis ▼

This program demonstrates copying strings both to character arrays such as dest1 (declared on line 10) and to character pointers such as dest2 (declared along with dest3 on line 11). Line 13 prints the original source string. This string is then copied to dest1 with strcpy() on line 18. Line 24 copies source to dest2. Both dest1 and dest2 are printed to show that the function was successful. Notice that line 23 allocates the appropriate amount of space for dest2 with the malloc() function. If you copy a string to a character pointer that hasn't been allocated memory, you get unpredictable results.

The strncpy() Function

The strncpy() function is similar to strcpy(), except that strncpy() enables you to specify how many characters to copy. Its prototype is

```
char *strncpy(char *destination, const char *source, size_t n);
```

The arguments destination and source are pointers to the destination and source strings. The function copies, at most, the first n characters of source to destination. If source is shorter than n characters, enough null characters are added at the end of source to make a total of n characters copied to destination. If source is longer than n characters, no terminating \0 is added to destination. The function's return value is destination.

Listing 18.3 demonstrates the use of strncpy().

Input ▼
LISTING 18.3 stringcopy2.c: The strncpy() Function

```
1:  /* stringcopy2.c--Using the strncpy() function. */
2:
3:  #include <stdio.h>
4:  #include <string.h>
5:
6:  char dest[]  = "........................";
7:  char source[] = "abcdefghijklmnopqrstuvwxyz";
8:
9:  int main( void )
10: {
```

18

```
11:     size_t n;
12:
13:     while (1)
14:     {
15:         puts("Enter the number of characters to copy (1-26)");
16:         scanf("%d", &n);
17:
18:         if (n > 0 && n< 27)
19:             break;
20:     }
21:
22:     printf("\nBefore strncpy destination = %s", dest);
23:
24:     strncpy(dest, source, n);
25:
26:     printf("\nAfter strncpy destination = %s\n", dest);
27:     return(0);
28: }
```

Output ▼

```
Enter the number of characters to copy (1-26)
15

Before strncpy destination = ........................
After strncpy destination = abcdefghijklmno..........
```

Analysis ▼

In addition to demonstrating the `strncpy()` function, this program also illustrates an effective way to ensure that only correct information is entered by the user. Lines 13–20 contain a `while` loop that prompts the user for a number from 1–26. The loop continues until a valid value is entered, so the program can't continue until the user enters a valid value. When a number between 1 and 26 is entered, line 22 prints the original value of `dest`, line 24 copies the number of characters specified by the user from `source` to `dest`, and line 26 prints the final value of `dest`.

CAUTION Be sure that the number of characters copied doesn't exceed the allocated size of the destination. Also, be aware that `strncpy()` does not add a null terminator.

Concatenating Strings

If you're not familiar with the term *concatenation,* you might be asking, "What is it?" and "Is it legal?" Well, it means to join two strings—to tack one string onto the end of another—and, in most states, it is legal. The C standard library contains two string concatenation functions—`strcat()` and `strncat()`—both of which require the header file `string.h`.

Using the `strcat()` Function

The prototype of `strcat()` is

```
char *strcat(char *str1, const char *str2);
```

The function appends a copy of `str2` onto the end of `str1`, moving the terminating null character to the end of the new string. You must allocate enough space for `str1` to hold the resulting string. The return value of `strcat()` is a pointer to `str1`. Listing 18.4 demonstrates `strcat()`.

Input ▼
LISTING 18.4   stringcat.c: Using `strcat()` to Concatenate Strings

```
1:  // stringcat.c--The strcat() function.
2:
3:  #include <stdio.h>
4:  #include <string.h>
5:
6:  char str1[27] = "a";
7:  char str2[2];
8:
9:  int main( void )
10: {
11:     int n;
12:
13:     // Put a null character at the end of str2[].
14:
15:     str2[1] = '\0';
16:
17:     for (n = 98; n< 123; n++)
18:     {
19:         str2[0] = n;
20:         strcat(str1, str2);
21:         puts(str1);
22:     }
23:      return(0);
24: }
```

18

Output ▼

```
ab
abc
abcd
abcde
abcdef
abcdefg
abcdefgh
abcdefghi
abcdefghij
abcdefghijk
abcdefghijkl
abcdefghijklm
abcdefghijklmn
abcdefghijklmno
abcdefghijklmnop
abcdefghijklmnopq
abcdefghijklmnopqr
abcdefghijklmnopqrs
abcdefghijklmnopqrst
abcdefghijklmnopqrstu
abcdefghijklmnopqrstuv
abcdefghijklmnopqrstuvw
abcdefghijklmnopqrstuvwx
abcdefghijklmnopqrstuvwxy
abcdefghijklmnopqrstuvwxyz
```

Analysis ▼

The ASCII codes for the letters b–z are 98–122. This program uses these ASCII codes in its demonstration of `strcat()`. The `for` loop on lines 17–22 assigns these values in turn to `str2[0]`. Because `str2[1]` is already the null character (line 15), the effect is to assign the strings `"b"`, `"c"`, and so on to `str2`. Each of these strings is concatenated with `str1` (line 20), and then `str1` displays onscreen (line 21).

Using the `strncat()` Function

The library function `strncat()` also performs string concatenation, but it enables you to specify how many characters of the source string are appended to the end of the destination string. The prototype is

```
char *strncat(char *str1, const char *str2, size_t n);
```

If `str2` contains more than `n` characters, the first `n` characters are appended to the end of `str1`. If `str2` contains fewer than `n` characters, all of `str2` is appended to the end of `str1`. In either case, a terminating null character is added at the end of the resulting string. You must allocate enough space for str1 to hold the resulting string. The function returns a pointer to str1. Listing 18.5 uses strncat() to produce the same output as Listing 18.4.

Input ▼

LISTING 18.5   stringcat2.c: Using the strncat() Function to Concatenate Strings

```
1:   // stringcat2.c--The strncat() function.
2:
3:   #include <stdio.h>
4:   #include <string.h>
5:
6:   char str2[] = "abcdefghijklmnopqrstuvwxyz";
7:
8:   int main( void )
9:   {
10:      char str1[27];
11:      int n;
12:
13:      for (n=1; n< 27; n++)
14:      {
15:          strcpy(str1, "");
16:          strncat(str1, str2, n);
17:          puts(str1);
18:      }
19:      return 0;
20: }
```

Output ▼

```
a
ab
abc
abcd
abcde
abcdef
abcdefg
abcdefgh
abcdefghi
abcdefghij
abcdefghijk
abcdefghijkl
abcdefghijklm
abcdefghijklmn
abcdefghijklmno
abcdefghijklmnop
abcdefghijklmnopq
abcdefghijklmnopqr
```

```
abcdefghijklmnopqrs
abcdefghijklmnopqrst
abcdefghijklmnopqrstu
abcdefghijklmnopqrstuv
abcdefghijklmnopqrstuvw
abcdefghijklmnopqrstuvwx
abcdefghijklmnopqrstuvwxy
abcdefghijklmnopqrstuvwxyz
```

Analysis ▼

You might wonder about the purpose of line 15, `strcpy(str1, "");`. This line copies to `str1` an empty string consisting of only a single null character. The result is that the first character in `str1`—`str1[0]`—is set equal to 0 (the null character). The same thing could have been accomplished with the statements `str1[0] = 0;` or `str1[0] = '\0';`.

Comparing Strings

Strings are compared to determine whether they are equal or unequal. If they are unequal, one string is "greater than" or "less than" the other. Determinations of "greater" and "less" are made with the ASCII codes of the characters. For letters, this is equivalent to alphabetical order, with the one seemingly strange exception that all uppercase letters are "less than" the lowercase letters. This is true because the uppercase letters have ASCII codes 65–90 for A–Z, whereas lowercase a–z are represented by 97–122. Thus, `"ZEBRA"` would be considered to be less than `"apple"` evaluating by these C functions.

The ANSI C library contains functions for two types of string comparisons: comparing two entire strings and comparing a certain number of characters in two strings.

Comparing Two Entire Strings

The function `strcmp()` compares two strings, character by character. Its prototype is

```
int strcmp(const char *str1, const char *str2);
```

The arguments `str1` and `str2` are pointers to the strings being compared. The function's return values are given in Table 18.1. You should notice that both strings are passed as constants because neither will be changed. Listing 18.6 demonstrates `strcmp()`.

TABLE 18.1 The Values Returned by `strcmp()`

Return Value	Meaning
< 0	`str1` is less than `str2`.
0	`str1` is equal to `str2`.
> 0	`str1` is greater than `str2`.

Input ▼

LISTING 18.6 stringcompare.c: Using `strcmp()` to Compare Strings

```
1:  // stringcompare.c--The strcmp() function.
2:
3:  #include <stdio.h>
4:  #include <string.h>
5:
6:  int main( void )
7:  {
8:      char str1[80], str2[80];
9:      int x;
10:
11:     while (1)
12:     {
13:
14:         /* Input two strings. */
15:
16:         printf("\n\nInput the first string, a blank to exit: ");
17:         gets(str1);
18:
19:         if ( strlen(str1) == 0 )
20:             break;
21:
22:         printf("\nInput the second string: ");
23:         gets(str2);
24:
25:         /* Compare them and display the result. */
26:
27:         x = strcmp(str1, str2);
28:
29:         printf("\nstrcmp(%s,%s) returns %d", str1, str2, x);
30:     }
31:     return(0);
32: }
```

Output ▼

```
Input the first string, a blank to exit: First string

Input the second string: Second string

strcmp(First string,Second string) returns -1

Input the first string, a blank to exit: test string

Input the second string: test string

strcmp(test string,test string) returns 0
```

```
Input the first string, a blank to exit: zebra

Input the second string: aardvark

strcmp(zebra,aardvark) returns 1

Input the first string, a blank to exit:
```

NOTE — On some UNIX systems, string comparison functions don't necessarily return -1 when the strings aren't the same. They do, however, always return a nonzero value for unequal strings.

The ANSI Standard states that only the return value is less than, equal to, or greater than zero.

Analysis ▼

This program demonstrates `strcmp()`, prompting the user for two strings (lines 16, 17, 22, and 23) and displays the result returned by `strcmp()` on line 29. Experiment with this program to get a feel for how `strcmp()` compares strings. Try entering two strings that are identical except for case, such as `Smith` and `SMITH`. You learn that `strcmp()` is case-sensitive, meaning that the program considers uppercase and lowercase letters to be different.

Comparing Partial Strings

The library function `strncmp()` compares a specified number of characters of one string to another string. Its prototype is

```
int strncmp(const char *str1, const char *str2, size_t n);
```

The function `strncmp()` compares n characters of `str2` to `str1`. The comparison proceeds until n characters have been compared or the end of `str1` has been reached. The method of comparison and return values are the same as for `strcmp()`. The comparison is case-sensitive. Listing 18.7 demonstrates `strncmp()`.

Input ▼
LISTING 18.7   stringcompare2.c: Comparing Parts of Strings with `strncmp()`

```
1:  // stringcompare2.c--The strncmp() function.
2:
3:  #include <stdio.h>
4:  #include <string.h>
5:
```

```
6:   char str1[] = "The first string.";
7:   char str2[] = "The second string.";
8:
9:   int main( void )
10:  {
11:      size_t n, x;
12:
13:      puts(str1);
14:      puts(str2);
15:
16:      while (1)
17:      {
18:          puts("\n\nEnter number of characters to compare, 0 to exit.");
19:          scanf("%d", &n);
20:
21:          if (n <= 0)
22:              break;
23:
24:          x = strncmp(str1, str2, n);
25:
26:          printf("\nComparing %d characters, strncmp() returns %d.", n, x);
27:      }
28:      return(0);
29:  }
```

Output ▼

```
The first string.
The second string.


Enter number of characters to compare, 0 to exit.
3

Comparing 3 characters, strncmp() returns 0.

Enter number of characters to compare, 0 to exit.
6

Comparing 6 characters, strncmp() returns -13.

Enter number of characters to compare, 0 to exit.
0
```

18

Analysis ▼

This program compares two strings defined on lines 6 and 7. Lines 13 and 14 print the strings to the screen so that the user can see what they are. The program executes a while loop on lines 16–27 so that multiple compares can be done. If the user asks to compare zero characters on lines 18 and 19, the program breaks on line 22; otherwise, a strncmp() executes on line 24, and the result is printed on line 26.

Searching Strings

The C library contains a number of functions that search strings. To put it another way, these functions determine whether one string occurs within another string and, if so, where. You can choose from six string searching functions, all of which require the header file string.h:

- strchr()
- strrchr()
- strcspn()
- strspn()
- strpbrk()
- strstr()

The strchr() Function

The strchr() function finds the first occurrence of a specified character in a string. The prototype is

```
char *strchr(const char *str, int ch);
```

The function strchr() searches str from left to right until the character ch is found or the terminating null character is found. If ch is found, a pointer to it is returned. If not, NULL is returned.

When strchr() finds the character, it returns a pointer to that character. Knowing that str is a pointer to the first character in the string, you can obtain the position of the found character by subtracting str from the pointer value returned by strchr(). Listing 18.8 illustrates this. Remember that the first character in a string is at position 0. Like many of C's string functions, strchr() is case-sensitive and, therefore, reports that the character "F" isn't found in the string "raffle".

Input ▼

LISTING 18.8 stringsearch1.c: Using `strchr()` to Search a String for a Single Character

```
1:  // stringsearch1.c--Searching for a single character with strchr().
2:
3:  #include <stdio.h>
4:  #include <string.h>
5:
6:  int main( void )
7:  {
8:      char *loc, buf[80];
9:      int ch;
10:
11:     // Input the string and the character.
12:
13:     printf("Enter the string to be searched: ");
14:     gets(buf);
15:     printf("Enter the character to search for: ");
16:     ch = getchar();
17:
18:     // Perform the search.
19:
20:     loc = strchr(buf, ch);
21:
22:     if ( loc == NULL )
23:         printf("The character %c was not found.", ch);
24:     else
25:         printf("The character %c was found at position %d.\n",
26:                 ch, loc-buf);
27:     return(0);
28: }
```

Output ▼

```
Enter the string to be searched: How now Brown Cow?
Enter the character to search for: C
The character C was found at position 14.
```

Analysis ▼

This program uses `strchr()` on line 20 to search for a character within a string. `strchr()` returns a pointer to the location where the character is first found or NULL if the character isn't found. Line 22 checks whether the value of `loc` is NULL and prints an appropriate message. As described in the section "The `strchr()` Function," the position of the character within the string is determined by subtracting the string pointer from the value returned by the function.

18

The `strrchr()` **Function**

The library function `strrchr()` is identical to `strchr()`, except that it searches a string for the last occurrence of a specified character in a string. Its prototype is

```
char *strrchr(const char *str, int ch);
```

The function `strrchr()` returns a pointer to the last occurrence of `ch` in `str` and NULL if it finds no match. To see how this function works, modify line 20 in Listing 18.8 to use `strrchr()` instead of `strchr()`.

The `strcspn()` **Function**

The library function `strcspn()` searches one string for the first occurrence of any of the characters in a second string. Its prototype is

```
size_t strcspn(const char *str1, const char *str2);
```

The function `strcspn()` starts searching at the first character of `str1`, looking for any of the individual characters contained in `str2`. This is important to remember. The function doesn't look for the string `str2`, but only the characters it contains. If the function finds a match, it returns the offset from the beginning of `str1` where the matching character is located. If it finds no match, `strcspn()` returns the value of `strlen(str1)`. This indicates that the first match was the null character terminating the string. Listing 18.9 shows you how to use `strcspn()`.

Input ▼

LISTING 18.9   stringsearch2.c: Searching for a Set of Characters with `strcspn()`

```
 1:  // stringsearch2.c--Searching with strcspn().
 2:
 3:  #include <stdio.h>
 4:  #include <string.h>
 5:
 6:  int main( void )
 7:  {
 8:      char  buf1[80], buf2[80];
 9:      size_t loc;
10:
11:      // Input the strings.
12:
13:      printf("Enter the string to be searched: ");
14:      gets(buf1);
15:      printf("Enter the string containing target characters: ");
16:      gets(buf2);
17:
18:      // Perform the search.
19:
```

```
20:     loc = strcspn(buf1, buf2);
21:
22:     if ( loc ==  strlen(buf1) )
23:         printf("No match was found.");
24:     else
25:         printf("The first match was found at position %lu.\n", loc);
26:     return(0);
27: }
```

Output ▼

```
Enter the string to be searched: How now Brown Cow?
Enter the string containing target characters: Cat
The first match was found at position 14.
```

Analysis ▼

This listing is similar to Listing 18.8. Instead of searching for the first occurrence of a single character, it searches for the first occurrence of any of the characters entered in the second string. The program calls `strcspn()` on line 20 with `buf1` and `buf2`. If any of the characters in `buf2` are in `buf1`, `strcspn()` returns the offset from the beginning of `buf1` to the location of the first occurrence. Line 22 checks the return value to determine whether it is NULL. If the value is NULL, no characters were found, and an appropriate message displays on line 23. If a value is found, a message displays stating the character's position in the string.

The `strspn()` Function

This function is related to the previous one, `strcspn()`, as the following paragraph explains. Its prototype is

```
size_t strspn(const char *str1, const char *str2);
```

The function `strspn()` searches `str1`, comparing it character by character with the characters contained in `str2`. It returns the position of the first character in `str1` that doesn't match a character in `str2`. In other words, `strspn()` returns the length of the initial segment of `str1` that consists entirely of characters found in `str2`. The return is `0` if no characters match. Listing 18.10 demonstrates `strspn()`.

18

Input ▼

LISTING 18.10 stringsearch3.c: Searching for the First Nonmatching Character with
strspn()

```
1:   /* Searching with strspn(). */
2:
3:   #include <stdio.h>
4:   #include <string.h>
5:
6:   int main( void )
7:   {
8:       char  buf1[80], buf2[80];
9:       size_t loc;
10:
11:      /* Input the strings. */
12:
13:      printf("Enter the string to be searched: ");
14:      gets(buf1);
15:      printf("Enter the string containing target characters: ");
16:      gets(buf2);
17:
18:      /* Perform the search. */
19:
20:      loc = strspn(buf1, buf2);
21:
22:      if ( loc ==  0 )
23:          printf("No match was found.\n");
24:      else
25:          printf("Characters match up to position %d.\n", loc-1);
26:
27:  }
```

Output ▼

```
Enter the string to be searched: How now Brown Cow?
Enter the string containing target characters: How now what?
Characters match up to position 7.
```

Analysis ▼

This program is similar to the previous example, except that it calls strspn() instead
of strcspn() on line 20. The function returns the offset into buf1 where the first
character that is not in buf2 is found. Lines 22–25 evaluate the return value and print an
appropriate message.

The `strpbrk()` Function

The library function `strpbrk()` is similar to `strcspn()`, searching one string for the first occurrence of any character contained in another string. It differs in that it doesn't include the terminating null characters in the search. The function prototype is

```c
char *strpbrk( const char *str1, const char *str2);
```

The function `strpbrk()` returns a pointer to the first character in `str1` that matches any of the characters in `str2`. If it doesn't find a match, the function returns NULL. As previously explained for the function `strchr()`, you can obtain the offset of the first match in `str1` by subtracting the pointer `str1` from the pointer returned by `strpbrk()` (if it isn't NULL, of course). For example, replace `strcspn()` on line 20 of Listing 18.9 with `strpbrk()`.

The `strstr()` Function

The final and, perhaps, most useful C string searching function is `strstr()`. This function searches for the first occurrence of one string within another, and it searches for the entire string, not just for individual characters within the string. Its prototype is

```c
char *strstr(const char *str1, const char *str2);
```

The function `strstr()` returns a pointer to the first occurrence of `str2` within `str1`. If it finds no match, the function returns NULL. If the length of `str2` is 0, the function returns `str1`. When `strstr()` finds a match, you can obtain the offset of `str2` within `str1` by pointer subtraction, as explained earlier for `strchr()`. The matching procedure that `strstr()` uses is case-sensitive. Listing 18.11 demonstrates how to use `strstr()`.

Input ▼
LISTING 18.11 stringsearch4.c: Using `strstr()` to Search for One String Within Another

```c
1:   // stringsearch4.c--Searching with strstr().
2:
3:   #include <stdio.h>
4:   #include <string.h>
5:
6:   int main( void )
7:   {
8:        char *loc, buf1[80], buf2[80];
9:
10:       // Input the strings.
11:
12:       printf("Enter the string to be searched: ");
13:       gets(buf1);
14:       printf("Enter the target string: ");
```

18

```
15:      gets(buf2);
16:
17:      // Perform the search.
18:
19:      loc = strstr(buf1, buf2);
20:
21:      if ( loc ==  NULL )
22:          printf("No match was found.\n");
23:      else
24:          printf("%s was found at position %d.\n", buf2, loc-buf1);
25:      return(0);
26: }
```

Output ▼

```
Enter the string to be searched: How now brown cow?
Enter the target string: cow
Cow was found at position 14.
```

Analysis ▼

This function provides an alternative way to search a string. This time you can search for an entire string within another string. Lines 12–15 prompt for two strings. Line 19 uses strstr() to search for the second string, buf2, within the first string, buf1. A pointer to the first occurrence is returned, or NULL is returned if the string isn't found. Lines 21–24 evaluate the returned value, loc, and print an appropriate message.

DO	DON'T
DO remember that for many of the string functions, equivalent functions enable you to specify a number of characters to manipulate. The functions that enable specification of the number of characters are usually named strnxxx(), where xxx is specific to the function.	**DON'T** forget that C is case-sensitive. A and a are different.

String-to-Number Conversions

Sometimes, you need to convert the string representation of a number to an actual numeric variable. For example, the string "123" can be converted to a type int variable with the value 123. You can use four functions to convert a string to a number. They are explained in the following paragraphs, and their prototypes are in stdlib.h.

Converting Strings to Integers

The library function `atoi()` converts a string to an integer. The prototype is

```
int atoi(const char *ptr);
```

The function `atoi()` converts the string pointed to by `ptr` to an integer. Besides digits, the string can contain leading whitespace and a + or – sign. Conversion starts at the beginning of the string and proceeds until an unconvertible character (for example, a letter or punctuation mark) is encountered. The resulting integer is returned to the calling program. If it finds no convertible characters, `atoi()` returns 0. Table 18.2 lists some examples.

TABLE 18.2   String-to-Number Conversions with `atoi()`

String	Value Returned by `atoi()`
"157"	157
"-1.6"	-1
"+50x"	50
"twelve"	0
"x506"	0

The first example is straightforward. In the second example, you might be confused about why the `".6"` didn't translate. Remember that this is a string-to-integer conversion. The floating-point portion of a number is dropped.

The third example is also straightforward; the function understands the plus sign and considers it a part of the number. The fourth example uses `"twelve"`. The `atoi()` function can't translate words; it sees only characters. Because the string didn't start with a number, `atoi()` returns 0. This is true of the last example also.

Converting Strings to Longs

The library function `atol()` works exactly like `atoi()`, except that it returns a type `long`. The function prototype is

```
long atol(const char *ptr);
```

The values returned by `atol()` would be the same as shown for `atoi()` in Table 18.2, except that each return value would be a type `long` instead of a type `int`.

18

Converting Strings to Long Longs

Just like the `atoi()` and `atol()` functions, the `atoll()` function converts a string value to a `long long` value. The prototype for the `atoll()` function is

```
long long atoll(const char *ptr);
```

Converting Strings to Floating-Point Numeric Values

The function `atof()` converts a string to a type `double`. The prototype is

```
double atof(const char *str);
```

The argument `str` points to the string to be converted. This string can contain leading whitespace and a + or – character. The number can contain the digits 0–9, the decimal point, and the exponent indicator `E` or `e`. If there are no convertible characters, `atof()` returns 0. Table 18.3 lists some examples of using `atof()`.

TABLE 18.3 String-to-Number Conversions with `atof()`

String	Value Returned by `atof()`
`"12"`	12.000000
`"-0.123"`	-0.123000
`"123E+3"`	123000.000000
`"123.1e-5"`	0.001231

Listing 18.12 illustrates the use of `atof()`. It lets you enter your own strings for conversion.

Input ▼

LISTING 18.12 stringtodouble.c: Using `atof()` to Convert Strings to Type `double` Numeric Variables

```
1:  // stringtodouble.c--Demonstration of atof().
2:
3:  #include <string.h>
4:  #include <stdio.h>
5:  #include <stdlib.h>
6:
7:  int main( void )
8:  {
9:      char buf[80];
10:     double d;
11:
12:     while (1)
13:     {
```

```
14:            printf("\nEnter the string to convert (blank to exit):     ");
15:            gets(buf);
16:
17:            if ( strlen(buf) == 0 )
18:                break;
19:
20:            d = atof( buf );
21:
22:            printf("The converted value is %f.", d);
23:        }
24:        return(0);
25: }
```

Output ▼

```
Enter the string to convert (blank to exit):     1009.12
The converted value is 1009.120000.
Enter the string to convert (blank to exit):     abc
The converted value is 0.000000.
Enter the string to convert (blank to exit):     3
The converted value is 3.000000.
Enter the string to convert (blank to exit):
```

Analysis ▼

The while loop on lines 12–23 lets you keep running the program until you enter a blank line. Lines 14 and 15 prompt for the value. Line 17 checks whether a blank line is entered. If it is, the program breaks out of the while loop and ends. Line 20 calls atof(), converting the value entered (buf) to a type double, d. Line 22 prints the final result.

Character-Test Functions

The header file ctype.h contains the prototypes for a number of functions that test characters, returning TRUE or FALSE depending on whether the character meets a certain condition. For example, is it a letter or is it a numeral? The isxxxx() functions are actually macros, defined in ctype.h. You learn about macros in Lesson 22, "Advanced Compiler Use." At that time, you might want to look at the definitions in ctype.h to see how they work. For now, you need to only see how they're used.

The isxxxx() macros all have the same prototype:

```
int isxxxx(int ch);
```

In the preceding line, ch is the character tested. The return value is TRUE (nonzero) if the condition is met, or FALSE (zero) if it isn't. Table 18.4 lists the complete set of isxxxx() macros.

TABLE 18.4   The is*xxxx*() Macros

Macro	Action
isalnum()	Returns TRUE if ch is a letter or a digit.
isalpha()	Returns TRUE if ch is a letter.
isblank()	Returns TRUE if ch is blank.
iscntrl()	Returns TRUE if ch is a control character.
isdigit()	Returns TRUE if ch is a digit.
isgraph()	Returns TRUE if ch is a printing character (other than a space).
islower()	Returns TRUE if ch is a lowercase letter.
isprint()	Returns TRUE if ch is a printing character (including a space).
ispunct()	Returns TRUE if ch is a punctuation character.
isspace()	Returns TRUE if ch is a whitespace character (space, tab, vertical tab, line feed, form feed, or carriage return).
isupper()	Returns TRUE if ch is an uppercase letter.
isxdigit()	Returns TRUE if ch is a hexadecimal digit (0–9, a–f, A–F).

You can do many interesting things with the character-test macros. One example is the function get_int() in Listing 18.13. This function inputs an integer from stdin and returns it as a type int variable. The function skips over leading whitespace and returns 0 if the first nonspace character isn't a numeric character.

Input ▼
LISTING 18.13   getaninteger.c: Using the is*xxxx*() Macros to Implement a Function that Inputs an Integer

```
1:  // getaninteger.c--Using character-test macros to create an integer
2:  // to create an integer input function.
3:
4:  #include <stdio.h>
5:  #include <ctype.h>
6:
7:  int get_int(void);
8:
9:  int main( void )
10: {
11:     int x;
12:     x =  get_int();
13:
14:     printf("You entered %d.\n", x);
15:     return 0;
16: }
17:
```

```
18: int get_int(void)
19: {
20:     int ch, i, sign = 1;
21:
22:     // Skip over any leading whitespace.
23:
24:     while ( isspace(ch = getchar()) )
25:         ;
26:
27:     /* If the first character is nonnumeric, unget
28:        the character and return 0. */
29:
30:     if (ch != '-' && ch != '+' && !isdigit(ch) && ch != EOF)
31:     {
32:         ungetc(ch, stdin);
33:         return 0;
34:     }
35:
36:     /* If the first character is a minus sign, set
37:        sign accordingly. */
38:
39:     if (ch == '-')
40:         sign = -1;
41:
42:     /* If the first character was a plus or minus sign,
43:        get the next character. */
44:
45:     if (ch == '+' || ch == '-')
46:         ch = getchar();
47:
48:     /* Read characters until a nondigit is input. Assign
49:        values, multiplied by proper power of 10, to i. */
50:
51:     for (i = 0; isdigit(ch); ch = getchar() )
52:         i = 10 * i + (ch - '0');
53:
54:     // Make result negative if sign is negative.
55:
56:     i *= sign;
57:
58:     /* If EOF was not encountered, a nondigit character
59:        must have been read in, so unget it. */
60:
61:     if (ch != EOF)
62:         ungetc(ch, stdin);
63:
64:     // Return the input value.
65:
66:     return i;
67: }
```

18

Output ▼

```
-100
You entered -100.

abc3.145
You entered 0.

9 9 9
You entered 9.

2.5
You entered 2.
```

Analysis ▼

This program uses the library function `ungetc()` on lines 32 and 62, which you learned about in Lesson 14, "Working with the Screen, Printer, and Keyboard." Remember that this function "ungets," or returns, a character to the specified stream. This returned character is the first one input the next time the program reads a character from that stream. This is necessary because when the function `get_int()` reads a nonnumeric character from `stdin`, you want to put that character back, in case the program needs to read it later.

In this program, `main()` is simple. An integer variable, x, is declared (line 11), assigned the value of the `get_int()` function (line 12), and printed to the screen (line 14). The `get_int()` function makes up the rest of the program.

The `get_int()` function isn't so simple. To remove leading whitespace that might be entered, line 24 loops with a `while` command. The `isspace()` macro tests a character, `ch`, obtained with the `getchar()` function. If `ch` is a space, another character is retrieved, until a nonwhite-space character is received. Line 30 checks whether the character is one that can be used. Line 30 could be read, "If the character input isn't a negative sign, a plus sign, a digit, or the end of the file(s)." If this is true, `ungetc()` is used on line 32 to put the character back, and the function returns to `main()`. If the character is usable, execution continues.

Lines 39–46 handle the sign of the number. Line 39 checks whether the character entered is a negative sign. If it is, a variable (`sign`) is set to -1. `sign` is used to make the final number either positive or negative (line 56). Because positive numbers are the default, after you have taken care of the negative sign, you are almost ready to continue. If a sign is entered, the program must get another character. Lines 45 and 46 take care of this.

The heart of the function is the `for` loop on lines 51 and 52, which continues to get characters as long as the characters gotten are digits. Line 52 might be a little confusing at first. This line takes the individual character entered and turns it into a number. Subtracting the character `'0'` from your number changes a character number to a real number. (Remember the ASCII values.) When the correct numerical value is obtained, the numbers are multiplied by the proper power of 10. The `for` loop continues until a nondigit number is entered. At that point, line 56 applies the sign to the number, making it complete.

Before returning, the program needs to do a little cleanup. If the last number weren't the end of file, it needs to be put back (in case it's needed elsewhere). Line 62 does this before line 66 returns.

NOTE

Although this program is simple, it's not user-friendly. As an extra programming exercise, try altering the program to improve the user interface.

DO	DON'T
DO take advantage of the string functions that are available.	**DON'T** confuse characters with numbers. It's easy to forget that the character `"1"` isn't the same thing as the number `1`.

18

ANSI Support for Uppercase and Lowercase

Although some compilers include functions that convert a string to lowercase or uppercase (such as `strlwr()` and `strupr()`), they are not part of the ANSI Standard. The ANSI Standard does, however, define two macros for converting information to uppercase or lowercase. Along with the `isxxxx()` macros there are two ANSI-defined macros for changing a character's case: `toupper()` and `tolower()`. You can see the use of these macros in Listing 18.14.

Input ▼

LISTING 18.14   stringconversion.c: Converting the Case of Characters in a String with `tolower()` and `toupper()`

```
1:  // The character conversion functions tolower() and toupper().
2:  #include <ctype.h>
3:  #include <stdio.h>
4:  #include <string.h>
5:
6:  int main( void )
7:  {
8:      char buf[80];
9:      int  ctr;
10:
11:     while (1)
12:     {
13:         puts("\nEnter a line of text, a blank to exit.");
14:         gets(buf);
15:
16:         if ( strlen(buf) == 0 )
17:             break;
18:
19:         for ( ctr = 0; ctr< strlen(buf); ctr++)
20:         {
21:             printf("%c", tolower(buf[ctr]));
22:         }
23:
24:         printf("\n");
25:         for ( ctr = 0; ctr< strlen(buf); ctr++)
26:         {
27:             printf("%c", toupper(buf[ctr]));
28:         }
29:         printf("\n");
30:     }
31:     return(0);
32: }
```

Output ▼

```
Enter a line of text, a blank to exit.
Time to shuffle off to Buffalo, New York.
time to shuffle off to buffalo, new york.
TIME TO SHUFFLE OFF TO BUFFALO, NEW YORK.
Enter a line of text, a blank to exit.
```

Analysis ▼

This listing prompts for a string on line 13 and uses `gets()` in line 14 to obtain it. It then checks to ensure that the string isn't blank (line 16). Because the `toupper` and `tolower` macros work with individual characters, on line 19 a `for` loop is used to cycle through the characters. Each is then converted.

NOTE	Where possible, you should use the `toupper()` and `tolower()` macros rather than your compiler's included non-ANSI functions. You can create your own functions using `toupper()` and `tolower()`. Your functions would then be ANSI-compliant.

Summary

This lesson showed the various ways you can use C to manipulate strings. Using C standard library functions, you can copy, concatenate, compare, and search strings. These are all necessary tasks in most programming projects. The standard library also contains functions for converting the case of characters in strings and for converting strings to numbers. Finally, C provides a variety of character-test functions or, more accurately, macros that perform a variety of tests on individual characters. By using these macros to test characters, you can create your own custom input functions.

18

Q&A

Q How do I know whether a function is ANSI-compatible?

A Most compilers have a Library Function Reference manual or section. This manual or section of a manual lists all the compiler's library functions and how to use them. Usually, the manual includes information on the compatibility of the function. Sometimes, the descriptions state not only whether the function is ANSI-compatible, but also whether it is compatible with your operating system. (Most compilers tell you only what is relevant to their compiler.)

Q Are all the available string functions presented in this lesson?

A No. However, the string functions presented in this lesson should cover virtually all your needs. Consult your compiler's Library Reference to see what other functions are available.

Q Does `strcat()` ignore trailing spaces when doing a concatenation?

A No. `strcat()` looks at a space as just another character.

Q Can I convert numbers to strings?

A Yes. You can write a function similar to the one in Listing 17.16, or you can check your Library Reference for available functions. Some functions available include `itoa()`, `ltoa()`, and `ultoa()`. `sprint(f)` can also be used.

Workshop

The Workshop provides quiz questions to help you solidify your understanding of the material covered and exercises to provide you with experience in using what you've learned.

Quiz

1. What is the length of a string, and how can the length be determined?

2. Before copying a string, what must you be sure to do?

3. What does the term *concatenate* mean?

4. When comparing strings, what is meant by "One string is greater than another string"?

5. What is the difference between `strcmp()` and `strncmp()`?

6. What values does `isascii()` test for?

7. Using Table 18.4, which macros would return TRUE for `var`?

   ```
   int var = 1;
   ```

8. Using Table 18.4, which macros would return TRUE for `x`?
   ```
   char x = 65;
   ```

9. What are the character-test functions used for?

Exercises

1. What values do the test functions return?

2. What would the `atoi()` function return if passed the following values?

   a. `"65"`

   b. `"81.23"`

   c. `"-34.2"`

   d. `"ten"`

e. `"+12hundred"`

f. `"negative100"`

3. What would the `atof()` function return if passed the following?

a. `"65"`

b. `"81.23"`

c. `"-34.2"`

d. `"ten"`

e. `"+12hundred"`

f. `"1e+3"`

4. **BUG BUSTER:** Is anything wrong with the following?

```
char *string1, string2;
string1 = "Hello World";
strcpy( string2, string1);
printf( "%s %s", string1, string2 );
```

Because of the many possible solutions, answers aren't provided for the following exercises.

5. Write a program that prompts for the user's last name, first name, and middle name individually. Then store the name in a new string as first initial, period, space, middle initial, period, space, and last name. For example, if Ruth, Claire, and Alber are entered, store R. C. Alber. Display the new name to the screen.

6. Write a program to prove your answers to quiz questions 8 and 9.

7. The function `strstr()` finds the first occurrence of one string within another, and it is case-sensitive. Write a function that performs the same task without case-sensitivity.

8. Write a function that determines the number of times one string occurs within another.

9. Write a program that searches a text file for occurrences of a user-specified target string and then reports the line numbers where the target is found. For example, if you search one of your C source code files for the string `"printf()"`, the program should list all the lines where the `printf()` function is called by the program.

10. Listing 18.13 demonstrates a function that inputs an integer from `stdin`. Write a function `get_float()` that inputs a floating-point value from `stdin`.

18

LESSON 19
Getting More from Functions

As you know by now, functions are central to C programming. In this chapter you learn more ways to use functions in your programs, including

- Passing pointers as arguments to functions

- Passing type `void` pointers as arguments

- Using functions with a variable number of arguments

- Returning a pointer from a function

Some of these topics have been mentioned earlier in this book, but this lesson provides more detailed information.

Passing Pointers to Functions

The default method of passing an argument to a function is by value. *Passing by value* means that the function is passed a copy of the argument's value. This method has three steps:

1. The argument expression is evaluated.

2. The result is copied onto the *stack,* a temporary storage area in memory.

3. The function retrieves the argument's value from the stack.

The main point is that if a variable is passed as the argument, code in the function cannot modify the value of the variable. Figure 19.1 illustrates passing an argument by value. In this case, the argument is a simple type int variable, but the principle is the same for other variable types and more complex expressions.

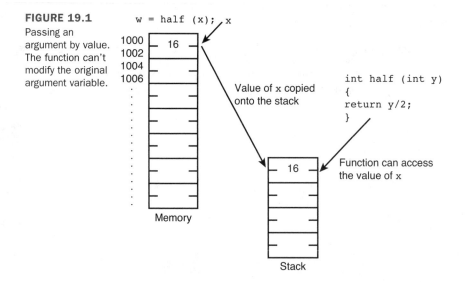

FIGURE 19.1
Passing an argument by value. The function can't modify the original argument variable.

When a variable is passed to a function by value, the function has access to the variable's value but not to the original copy of the variable. As a result, the code in the function can't modify the original variable. This is the main reason why passing by value is the default method of passing arguments: Data outside a function is protected from inadvertent modification.

There is another way to pass an argument to a function. Passing arguments by value is possible with the basic data types (char, short, int, long, long long, float, double, and long double) and structures. The alternative method is to pass a pointer to the argument variable rather than the value of the variable itself. This method of passing an argument is called *passing by reference*. Because the function has the address of the actual variable, the function can modify the variable's value.

As you learned in Lesson 9, "Understanding Pointers," passing by reference is the only way to pass an array to a function; passing an array by value is not possible. With other data types, however, you can use either method. If your program uses large structures, passing them by value might cause your program to run out of stack space. Aside from this consideration, passing an argument by reference instead of by value offers an advantage as well as a disadvantage:

- The advantage of passing by reference is that the function can modify the value of the argument variable.

- The disadvantage of passing by reference is that the function can modify the value of the argument variable.

"What?" you might be saying. "An advantage that's also a disadvantage?" Yes. It all depends on the specific situation. If your program requires that a function modify an argument variable, passing by reference is an advantage. If there is no such need, it is a disadvantage because of the possibility of inadvertent modifications.

You might be wondering why you don't use the function's return value to modify the argument variable. You can do this, of course, as shown in the following example:

```
x = half(x);

float half(float y)
{
    return y/2;
}
```

19

Remember, however, that a function can return only a single value. By passing one or more arguments by reference, you enable a function to "return" more than one value to the calling program. Figure 19.2 illustrates passing by reference for a single argument.

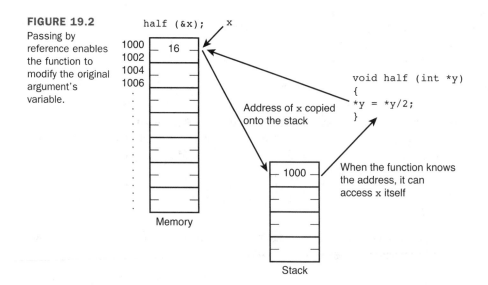

FIGURE 19.2
Passing by reference enables the function to modify the original argument's variable.

The function used in Figure 19.2 is not a good example of a real program in which you would use passing by reference, but it does illustrate the concept. When you pass by reference, you must ensure that the function definition and prototype reflect that the argument passed to the function is a pointer. Within the body of the function, you must also use the indirection operator to access the variable(s) passed by reference.

Listing 19.1 demonstrates passing by reference and the default passing by value. Its output clearly shows that a variable passed by value can't be changed by the function, whereas a variable passed by reference can be changed. Of course, a function doesn't need to modify a variable passed by reference. In such a case, there's no reason to pass by reference.

Input ▼

LISTING 19.1   differentarguments.c: Passing by Value and Passing by Reference

```
1:   // differentarguments.c--Passing arguments by value and by reference. */
2:
3:   #include <stdio.h>
4:
5:   void by_value(int a, int b, int c);
6:   void by_ref(int *a, int *b, int *c);
7:
8:   int main( void )
9:   {
10:       int x = 2, y = 4, z = 6;
11:
```

```
12:     printf("\nBefore calling by_value(), x = %d, y = %d, z = %d.",
13:          x, y, z);
14:
15:     by_value(x, y, z);
16:
17:     printf("\nAfter calling by_value(), x = %d, y = %d, z = %d.",
18:            x, y, z);
19:
20:     by_ref(&x, &y, &z);
21:     printf("\nAfter calling by_ref(), x = %d, y = %d, z = %d.\n",
22:            x, y, z);
23:     return(0);
24: }
25:
26: void by_value(int a, int b, int c)
27: {
28:     a = 0;
29:     b = 0;
30:     c = 0;
31: }
32:
33: void by_ref(int *a, int *b, int *c)
34: {
35:     *a = 0;
36:     *b = 0;
37:     *c = 0;
38: }
```

Output ▼

```
Before calling by_value(), x = 2, y = 4, z = 6.
After calling by_value(), x = 2, y = 4, z = 6.
After calling by_ref(), x = 0, y = 0, z = 0.
```

19

Analysis ▼

This program demonstrates the difference between passing variables by value and passing them by reference. Lines 5 and 6 contain prototypes for the two functions called in the program. In line 5, notice that the by_value() function takes three type int arguments. In contrast, line 6 defines _by_ref() to take three pointers to type int variables as arguments. The function headers for these two functions on lines 26 and 33 follow the same format as the prototypes. The bodies of the two functions are similar, but not identical. Both functions assign 0 to the three variables passed to them. In the by_value() function, 0 is assigned directly to the variables. In the by_ref() function, pointers are used, so the variables must be dereferenced before the assignment is made.

Each function is called once by `main()`. First, the three variables to be passed are assigned values other than 0 on line 10. Line 12 prints these values to the screen. Line 15 calls the first of the two functions, `by_value()`. Line 17 prints the three variables again. Notice that they are not changed. The `by_value()` function receives the variables by value and, therefore, can't change their original content. Line 20 calls `by_ref()`, and line 22 prints the values again. This time, the values have all changed to 0. Passing the variables by reference gives `by_ref()` access to the actual contents of the variables.

You can write a function that receives some arguments by reference and others by value. Just remember to keep them straight inside the function, using the indirection operator (`*`) to dereference arguments passed by reference.

DO	DON'T
DO pass variables by value if you don't want the original value altered.	**DON'T** pass large amounts of data by value if it isn't necessary. You can run out of stack space.
DO remember to use the indirection operator to dereference the variable passed by reference to a function.	**DON'T** forget that a variable passed by reference should be a pointer.

Type `void` Pointers

You've seen the `void` keyword used in a function declaration to specify that the function either doesn't take arguments or doesn't return a value. You can also use the `void` keyword to create a generic pointer—a pointer that can point to any type of data object. For example, the statement

```
void *ptr;
```

declares `ptr` as a generic pointer. `ptr` points to something; you just haven't yet specified what.

The most common use for type `void` pointers is in declaring function parameters. You might want to create a function that can handle different types of arguments. You can pass it a type `int` one time, a type `float` the next time, and so on. By declaring that the function takes a `void` pointer as an argument, you don't restrict it to accepting only a single data type. If you declare the function to take a `void` pointer as an argument, you can pass the function a pointer to anything.

Here's a simple example: You want to write a function that accepts a numeric variable as an argument and divides it by two, returning the answer in the argument variable. Thus, if the variable `val` holds the value 4, after a call to `half(val)`, the variable `val` is equal to 2. Because you want to modify the argument, you pass it by reference. Because you want to use the function with any of C's numeric data types, you declare the function to take a void pointer:

```
void half(void *val);
```

Now you can call the function, passing it any pointer as an argument. There's one more thing you need, however. Although you can pass a void pointer without knowing what data type it points to, you can't dereference the pointer. Before the code in the function can do anything with the pointer, it must know the data type. You do this with a *typecast,* which is nothing more than a way of telling the program to treat this void pointer as a pointer to a specific type. If pval is a void pointer, you typecast it as follows:

```
(type *)pval
```

Here, type is the appropriate data type. To tell the program that pval is a pointer to type int, write

```
(int *)pval
```

To dereference the pointer—that is, to access the int that pval points to—write

```
*(int *)pval
```

Typecasts are covered in more detail in Lesson 21, "Working with Memory." Getting back to the original topic (passing a void pointer to a function), you can see that to use the pointer, the function must know the data type to which it points. In the case of the function you are writing that will divide its argument by two, there are four possibilities for type that will be used: int, long, float, and double. In addition to passing the void pointer to the variable to be divided by two, you must also tell the function which of the four types the void pointer points. You can modify the function definition as follows:

```
void half(void *pval, char type);
```

Based on the argument type, the function casts the void pointer pval to the appropriate type. Then the pointer can be dereferenced, and the value of the pointed-to variable can be used. The final version of the half() function is shown in Listing 19.2.

Input ▼
LISTING 19.2   typecast.c: Using a void Pointer to Pass Different Data Types to a Function

```
1:  // typecast.c--Using type void pointers.
2:
3:  #include <stdio.h>
4:
5:  void half(void *pval, char type);
6:
```

19

```
 7:  int main( void )
 8:  {
 9:      // Initialize one variable of each type.
10:
11:      int i = 20;
12:      long l = 100000;
13:      float f = 12.456;
14:      double d = 123.044444;
15:
16:      // Display their initial values.
17:
18:      printf("\n%d", i);
19:      printf("\n%ld", l);
20:      printf("\n%f", f);
21:      printf("\n%lf\n\n", d);
22:
23:      // Call half() for each variable.
24:
25:      half(&i, 'i');
26:      half(&l, 'l');
27:      half(&d, 'd');
28:      half(&f, 'f');
29:
30:      // Display their new values.
31:      printf("\n%d", i);
32:      printf("\n%ld", l);
33:      printf("\n%f", f);
34:      printf("\n%lf\n", d);
35:      return(0);
36:  }
37:
38:  void half(void *pval, char type)
39:  {
40:      // Depending on the value of type, cast the
41:      // pointer val appropriately and divide by 2.
42:
43:      switch (type)
44:      {
45:          case 'i':
46:              {
47:              *((int *)pval) /= 2;
48:              break;
49:              }
50:          case 'l':
51:              {
52:              *((long *)pval) /= 2;
53:              break;
54:              }
55:          case 'f':
56:              {
57:              *((float *)pval) /= 2;
```

```
58:                break;
59:                }
60:         case 'd':
61:                {
62:                *((double *)pval) /= 2;
63:                break;
64:                }
65:      }
66: }
```

Output ▼

```
20
100000
12.456000
123.044444


10
50000
6.228000
61.522222
```

Analysis ▼

As implemented in this listing, the function `half()` on lines 38–66 includes no error checking (for example, if an invalid `type` argument is passed). This is because, in a real program, you wouldn't use a function to perform a task as simple as dividing a value by two. This is an illustrative example only.

You might think that the need to pass the type of the pointed-to variable would make the function less flexible. The function would be more general if it didn't need to know the type of the pointed-to data object, but that's not the way C works. You must always cast a `void` pointer to a specific type before you dereference it. By taking this approach, you write only one function. If you don't make use of a `void` pointer, you need to write four separate functions—one for each data type.

When you need a function that can deal with different data types, you can often write a macro to take the place of the function. The example just presented—in which the task performed by the function is relatively simple—would be a good candidate for a macro. (Lesson 22, "Advanced Compiler Use," covers macros.)

19

DO	DON'T
DO cast a `void` pointer when you use the value it points to.	**DON'T** try to increment or decrement a `void` pointer.

Using Functions That Have a Variable Number of Arguments

You have used several library functions, such as `printf()` and `scanf()`, that take a variable number of arguments. You can write your own functions that take a variable argument list. Programs that have functions with variable argument lists must include the header file `stdarg.h`.

When you declare a function that takes a variable argument list, you first list the fixed parameters—those that are always present. (There must be at least one fixed parameter.) You then include an ellipsis (. . .) at the end of the parameter list to indicate that zero or more additional arguments are passed to the function. During this discussion, please remember the distinction between a parameter and an argument, as explained in Lesson 5, "Packaging Code in Functions."

How does the function know how many arguments have been passed to it on a specific call? You tell it. One of the fixed parameters informs the function of the total number of arguments. For example, when you use the `printf()` function, the number of conversion specifiers in the format string tells the function how many additional arguments to expect. More directly, one of the function's fixed arguments can be the number of additional arguments. The example you see in a moment uses this approach, but first you need to look at the tools that C provides for dealing with a variable argument list.

The function must also know the type of each argument in the variable list. In the case of `printf()`, the conversion specifiers indicate the type of each argument. In other cases, such as the following example, all arguments in the variable list are of the same type, so there's no problem. To create a function that accepts different types in the variable argument list, you must devise a method of passing information about the argument types. For example, you could use a character code, as was done in the function `half()` in Listing 19.2.

The tools for using a variable argument list are defined in `stdarg.h`. These tools are used within the function to retrieve the arguments in the variable list. They are as follows:

`va_list`	A pointer data type.
`va_start()`	A macro used to initialize the argument list.
`va_arg()`	A macro used to retrieve each argument, in turn, from the variable list.
`va_end()`	A macro used to "clean up" when all arguments have been retrieved.

We've outlined how these macros are used in a function, and then included an example. When the function is called, the code in the function must follow these steps to access its arguments:

1. Declare a pointer variable of type `va_list`. This pointer is used to access the individual arguments. It is common practice, although certainly not required, to call this variable `arg_ptr`.

2. Call the macro `va_start()`, passing it the pointer `arg_ptr` as well as the name of the last fixed argument. The macro `va_start()` has no return value; it initializes the pointer `arg_ptr` to point at the first argument in the variable list.

3. To retrieve each argument, call `va_arg()`, passing it the pointer `arg_ptr` and the data type of the next argument. The return value of `va_arg()` is the value of the next argument. If the function has received n arguments in the variable list, call `va_arg()` n times to retrieve the arguments in the order listed in the function call.

4. When all the arguments in the variable list have been retrieved, call `va_end()`, passing it the pointer `arg_ptr`. In some implementations, this macro performs no action, but in others, it performs necessary clean-up actions. You should get in the habit of calling `va_end()` in case you use a C implementation that requires it.

Now for that example: The function `average()` in Listing 19.3 calculates the arithmetic average of a list of integers. This program passes the function a single fixed argument, indicating the number of additional arguments followed by the list of numbers.

19

Input ▼
LISTING 19.3   variableaverage.c: Using a Variable-Size Argument List

```
1:   // variableaverage.c--Functions with a variable argument list.
2:
3:   #include <stdio.h>
4:   #include <stdarg.h>
5:
6:   float average(int num, ...);
7:
8:   int main( void )
9:   {
10:      float x;
11:
```

```
12:     x = average(0, 1, 2, 3, 4, 5, 6, 7, 8, 9, 10);
13:     printf("\nThe first average is %.2f.", x);
14:     x = average(5, 121, 206, 76, 31, 5);
15:     printf("\nThe second average is %.2f.\n", x);
16:     return(0);
17: }
18:
19: float average(int num, ...)
20: {
21:     // Declare a variable of type va_list.
22:
23:     va_list arg_ptr;
24:     int count, total = 0;
25:
26:     // Initialize the argument pointer.
27:
28:     va_start(arg_ptr, num);
29:
30:     // Retrieve each argument in the variable list.
31:
32:     for (count = 0; count < num; count++)
33:         total += va_arg( arg_ptr, int );
34:
35:     // Perform clean up.
36:
37:     va_end(arg_ptr);
38:
39:     /* Divide the total by the number of values to get the
40:        average. Cast the total to type float so the value
41:        returned is type float. */
42:
43:     return ((float)total/num);
44: }
```

Output ▼

```
The first average is 5.500000.
The second average is 87.800000.
```

Analysis ▼

The function average() is first called on line 12. The first argument passed, the only fixed argument, specifies the number of values in the variable argument list. In the function, as each argument in the variable list is retrieved on lines 32–33, each argument is added to the variable total. After all arguments have been retrieved, line 43 casts total as type float and then divides total by num to obtain the average.

Two other things should be pointed out in this listing. Line 28 calls `va_start()` to initialize the argument list. This must be done before the values are retrieved. Line 37 calls `va_end()` to "clean up" because the function is done with the values. You should use both of these functions in your programs whenever you write a function with a variable number of arguments.

Strictly speaking, a function that accepts a variable number of arguments doesn't need to have a fixed parameter informing it of the number of arguments being passed. For example, you could mark the end of the argument list with a special value not used elsewhere. This method places limitations on the arguments that can be passed, however, so it's best avoided.

Functions That Return a Pointer

In previous chapters, you have seen several functions from the C standard library whose return value is a pointer. You can write your own functions that return a pointer. As you might expect, the indirection operator (`*`) is used in both the function declaration and the function definition. The general form of the declaration is

```
type *func(parameter_list);
```

This statement declares a function `func()` that returns a pointer to `type`. Here are two concrete examples:

```
double *func1(parameter_list);
struct address *func2(parameter_list);
```

The first line declares a function that returns a pointer to type `double`. The second line declares a function that returns a pointer to type `address` (which you assume is a user-defined structure).

Don't confuse a function that returns a pointer with a pointer to a function. If you include an additional pair of parentheses in the declaration, you declare a pointer to a function, as shown in these two examples:

```
double (*func)(...);    // Pointer to a function that returns a double.
double *func(...);      // Function that returns a pointer to a double.
```

Now that you have the declaration format straight, how do you use a function that returns a pointer? There's nothing special about such functions—you use them just as you do any other function, assigning their return value to a variable of the appropriate type (in this case, a pointer). Because the function call is a C expression, you can use it anywhere you would use a pointer of that type.

19

Listing 19.4 presents a simple example, a function that is passed two arguments and determines which is larger. The listing shows two ways of doing this: One function returns an `int`, and the other returns a pointer to `int`.

Input ▼

LISTING 19.4   pointerreturn.c: Returning a Pointer from a Function

```
1:    // pointerreturn.c--Function that returns a pointer.
2:
3:    #include <stdio.h>
4:
5:    int larger1(int x, int y);
6:    int *larger2(int *x, int *y);
7:
8:    int main( void )
9:    {
10:        int a, b, bigger1, *bigger2;
11:
12:        printf("Enter two integer values: ");
13:        scanf("%d %d", &a, &b);
14:
15:        bigger1 = larger1(a, b);
16:        printf("\nThe larger value is %d.", bigger1);
17:        bigger2 = larger2(&a, &b);
18:        printf("\nThe larger value is %d.\n", *bigger2);
19:        return(0);
20: }
21:
22: int larger1(int x, int y)
23: {
24:        if (y > x)
25:            return y;
26:        return x;
27: }
28:
29: int *larger2(int *x, int *y)
30: {
31:        if (*y > *x)
32:            return y;
33:
34:        return x;
35: }
```

Output ▼

```
Enter two integer values: 1111 3000

The larger value is 3000.
The larger value is 3000.
```

Analysis ▼

This is a relatively easy program to follow. Lines 5 and 6 contain the prototypes for the two functions. The first, `larger1()`, receives two `int` variables and returns an `int`. The second, `larger2()`, receives two pointers to `int` variables and returns a pointer to an `int`. The `main()` function on lines 8–20 is straightforward. Line 10 declares four variables. `a` and `b` hold the two variables to be compared. `bigger1` and `bigger2` hold the return values from the `larger1()` and `larger2()` functions, respectively. Notice that `bigger2` is a pointer to an `int`, and `bigger1` is just an `int`.

Line 15 calls `larger1()` with the two `int`s, `a` and `b`. The value returned from the function is assigned to `bigger1`, which is printed on line 16. Line 17 calls `larger2()` with the address of the two `int`s. The value returned from `larger2()`, a pointer, is assigned to `bigger2`, also a pointer. This value is dereferenced and printed on the following line.

The two comparison functions are similar. They both compare the two values and return the larger one. The difference between the functions is that `larger2()` works with pointers, whereas `larger1()` does not. In `larger2()`, notice that the dereference operator is used in the comparisons, but not in the `return` statements on lines 32 and 34.

In many cases, as in Listing 19.4, it is equally feasible to write a function to return a value or a pointer. Which one you select depends on the specifics of your program—mainly on how you intend to use the return value.

DO	DON'T
DO use all the elements described in this lesson when writing functions that have variable arguments. This is true even if your compiler doesn't require all the elements. The elements are `va_list`, `va_start()`, `va_arg()`, and `va_end()`.	**DON'T** confuse pointers to functions with functions that return pointers.

19

Summary

In this chapter, you learned some more advanced things your C programs can do with functions. You learned the difference between passing arguments by value and by reference, and how the latter technique enables a function to "return" more than one value to the calling program. You also saw how the `void` type can be used to create a generic pointer that can point to any type of C data object. Type `void` pointers are most commonly used with functions that can be passed arguments that aren't restricted to a single data type. Remember that a type `void` pointer must be cast to a specific type before you can dereference it.

This lesson also showed you how to use the macros defined in `stdarg.h` to write a function that accepts a variable number of arguments. Such functions provide considerable programming flexibility. Finally, you saw how to write a function that returns a pointer.

Q&A

Q Is passing pointers as function arguments a common practice in C programming?

A Definitely! In many instances, a function needs to change the value of multiple variables, and there are two ways this can be accomplished. The first is to declare and use global variables. The second is to pass pointers so that the function can modify the data directly. The first option is advisable only if nearly every function uses the variable; otherwise, you should avoid it. (See Lesson 12, "Understanding Variable Scope.")

Q Is it better to modify a variable by assigning a function's return value to it or by passing a pointer to the variable to the function?

A When you need to modify only one variable with a function, usually it's best to return the value from the function rather than pass a pointer to the function. The logic behind this is simple. By not passing a pointer, you don't run the risk of changing any data that you didn't intend to change, and you keep the function independent of the rest of the code.

Workshop

The Workshop provides quiz questions to help you solidify your understanding of the material covered and exercises to provide you with experience in using what you've learned.

Quiz

1. When passing arguments to a function, what's the difference between passing by value and passing by reference?

2. What is a type `void` pointer?

3. What is one reason you would use a `void` pointer?

4. When using a `void` pointer, what is meant by a typecast, and when must you use it?

5. Can you write a function that takes a variable argument list only, with no fixed arguments?

6. What macros should be used when you write functions with variable argument lists?

7. What value is added to a `void` pointer when it's incremented?

8. Can a function return a pointer?

9. What macro is used to retrieve values from a variable list of arguments passed to a function?

10. What are the elements that need to be used when using variable argument lists?

Exercises

1. Write the prototype for a function that returns an integer. It should take a pointer to a character array as its argument.

2. Write a prototype for a function called `numbers` that takes three integer arguments. The integers should be passed by reference.

3. Show how you would call the `numbers` function in exercise 2 with the three integers `int1`, `int2`, and `int3`.

4. **BUG BUSTER:** Is anything wrong with the following?

```
void squared(void *nbr)
{
   *nbr *= *nbr;
}
```

5. **BUG BUSTER:** Is anything wrong with the following?

```
float total( int num, ...)
{
   int count, total = 0;
   for ( count = 0; count < num; count++ )
     total += va_arg( arg_ptr, int );
   return ( total );
}
```

Because of the many possible solutions, answers are not provided for the following exercises.

19

6. Write a function that (a) is passed a variable number of strings as arguments, (b) concatenates the strings, in order, into one longer string, and (c) returns a pointer to the new string to the calling program.

7. Write a function that (a) is passed an array of any numeric data type as an argument, (b) finds the largest and smallest values in the array, and (c) returns pointers to these values to the calling program. (Hint: You need some way to tell the function how many elements are in the array.)

8. Write a function that accepts a string and a character. The function should look for the first occurrence of the character in the string and return a pointer to that location.

LESSON 20
Exploring the C Function Library

As you've seen throughout this book, much of C's power comes from the functions in the C standard library. In this lesson, you explore some of the functions that don't fit into the subject matter of other lessons. In this lesson you learn about

- Mathematical functions
- Functions that deal with time
- Error-handling functions
- Functions for searching and sorting data

Mathematical Functions

The C standard library contains a variety of functions that perform mathematical operations. Prototypes for the mathematical functions are in the header file `math.h`. The math functions all return a type `double`. For the trigonometric functions, angles are expressed in radians rather than degrees, which you may be more used to. One radian equals 57.296 degrees, and a full circle (360 degrees) contains 2π radians.

Trigonometric Functions

The trigonometric functions perform calculations that are used in some graphical and engineering applications:

Function	Prototype	Description
acos()	double acos(double x)	Returns the arccosine of its argument. The argument must be in the range `-1 <= x <= 1`, and the return value is in the range `0 <= acos <= [pi]`.
asin()	double asin(double x)	Returns the arcsine of its argument. The argument must be in the range `-1 <= x <= 1`, and the return value is in the range `-[pi]/2 <= asin <= [pi]/2`.
atan()	double atan(double x)	Returns the arctangent of its argument. The return value is in the range `-[pi]/2 <= atan <= [pi]/2`.
atan2()	double atan2(double x, double y)	Returns the arctangent of `x/y`. The value returned is in the range `-[pi] <= atan2 <= [pi]`.
cos()	double cos(double x)	Returns the cosine of its argument.
sin()	double sin(double x)	Returns the sine of its argument.
tan()	double tan(double x)	Returns the tangent of its argument.

Exponential and Logarithmic Functions

The exponential and logarithmic functions are needed for certain types of mathematical calculations:

Function	Prototype	Description
exp()	double exp(double x)	Returns the natural exponent of its argument, that is, e^x where e equals 2.7182818284590452354.
log()	double log(double x)	Returns the natural logarithm of its argument. The argument must be greater than 0.
log10()	double log10(double x)	Returns the base-10 logarithm of its argument. The argument must be greater than 0.
frexp()	double frexp(double x, int *y)	The function calculates the normalized fraction representing the value x. The function's return value r is a fraction in the range 0.5 <= r <= 1.0. The function assigns to y an integer exponent such that x = r * 2^y. If the value passed to the function is 0, both r and y are 0.
ldexp()	double ldexp(double x, int y)	Returns x * 2^y.

Hyperbolic Functions

The hyperbolic functions perform hyperbolic trigonometric calculations:

Function	Prototype	Description
cosh()	double cosh(double x)	Returns the hyperbolic cosine of its argument.
sinh()	double sinh(double x)	Returns the hyperbolic sine of its argument.
tanh()	double tanh(double x)	Returns the hyperbolic tangent of its argument.

Other Mathematical Functions

The standard C library contains the following miscellaneous mathematical functions:

Function	Prototype	Description
sqrt()	double sqrt(double x)	Returns the square root of its argument. The argument must be zero or greater.
ceil()	double ceil(double x)	Returns the smallest integer not less than its argument. For example, ceil(4.5) returns 5.0, and ceil(-4.5) returns -4.0. Although ceil() returns an integer value, it is returned as a type double.
abs() labs()	int abs(int x) long labs(long x)	Return the absolute value of their arguments.
floor()	double floor(double x)	Returns the largest integer not greater than its argument. For example, floor(4.5) returns 4.0, and floor(-4.5) returns -5.0.

20

Function	Prototype	Description
modf()	double modf(double x, double *y)	Splits x into integral and fractional parts, each with the same sign as x. The fractional part is returned by the function, and the integral part is assigned to *y.
pow()	double pow(double x, double y)	Returns x^y. An error occurs if x == 0 and y <= 0, or if x < 0 and y is not an integer.
fmod()	double fmod(double x, double y)	Returns the floating-point remainder of x/y, with the same sign as x. The function returns 0 if x == 0.

A Demonstration of the Math Functions

An entire book could be filled with programs demonstrating all the math functions. Listing 20.1 contains a single program that demonstrates several of these functions.

Input ▼
LISTING 20.1 math.c: Using the C Library Math Functions

```
1:  // math.c--Demonstrates some of C's math functions
2:
3:  #include <stdio.h>
4:  #include <math.h>
5:
6:  int main( void )
7:  {
8:
9:      double x;
10:     int power;
11:
12:     puts("Enter a number: ");
13:     scanf( "%lf", &x);
14:
15:     printf("\n\nOriginal value: %lf", x);
16:
17:     printf("\nCeil: %lf", ceil(x));
18:     printf("\nFloor: %lf", floor(x));
19:     if( x >= 0 )
20:         printf("\nSquare root: %lf", sqrt(x) );
21:     else
22:        puts("\nNegative number" );
23:
24:     printf("\nCosine: %lf\n", cos(x));
25:      puts("Enter a whole number between 2 and 10: ");
26:      scanf( "%d", &power);
27:      printf("\n%lf to the %d power is %lf\n", x, power, pow(x, power));
28:     return(0);
29: }
```

Output ▼

```
Enter a number: 98.6


Original value: 98.600000
Ceil: 99.000000
Floor: 98.000000
Square root: 9.929753
Cosine: -0.352432
Enter a whole number between 2 and 10: 5

98.600000 to the 5 power is 9319327515.421757
```

Analysis ▼

This listing uses just a few of the math functions that are available in the C standard library. Line 13 inputs a number from the user, which is then printed. Next this value is passed to four of the C library math functions: `ceil()`, `floor()`, `sqrt()`, and `cos()`. Notice that `sqrt()` is called only if the number isn't negative because, by definition, negative numbers don't have square roots. Line 26 then asks for a second number, an integer, to test the `pow()` function that needs two arguments. You can add any of the other math functions to a program such as this to test its functionality. You could even build some menus and make a rudimentary calculator program.

Dealing with Time

The C library contains several functions that let your program work with times. In C, the term *times* refers to dates as well as times. The function prototypes and the definition of the structure used by many of the time functions are in the header file `time.h`.

Representing Time

The C time functions represent time in two ways. The more basic method is the number of seconds elapsed since midnight on January 1, 1970. Negative values are used to represent times before that date. These time values are stored as type `long` integers. In `time.h`, the symbols `time_t` and `clock_t` are both defined with a `typedef` statement as `long`. These symbols are used in the time function prototypes rather than `long`.

The second method represents a time broken down into its components: year, month, day, and so on. For this kind of time representation, the time functions use a structure `tm`, defined in `time.h` as follows:

20

```
struct tm {
  int tm_sec;     // seconds after the minute - [0,59]
  int tm_min;     // minutes after the hour - [0,59]
  int tm_hour;    // hours since midnight - [0,23]
  int tm_mday;    // day of the month - [1,31]
  int tm_mon;     // months since January - [0,11]
  int tm_year;    // years since 1900
  int tm_wday;    // days since Sunday - [0,6]
  int tm_yday;    // days since January 1 - [0,365]
  int tm_isdst;   // daylight savings time flag
};
```

The Time Functions

This section describes the various C library functions that deal with time. Remember that the term *time* refers to the date as well as hours, minutes, and seconds. A demonstration program follows the descriptions.

Obtaining the Current Time

To obtain the current time as set on your system's internal clock, use the `time()` function. The prototype is

```
time_t time(time_t *timeptr);
```

Remember, `time_t` is defined in `time.h` as a synonym for `long`. The function `time()` returns the number of seconds elapsed since midnight, January 1, 1970. If it is passed a non-`NULL` pointer, `time()` also stores this value in the type `time_t` variable pointed to by `timeptr`. Thus, to store the current time in the type `time_t` variable `now`, you could write

```
time_t now;

now = time(0);
```

You also could write

```
time_t now;
time_t *ptr_now = &now;
time(ptr_now);
```

Converting Between Time Representations

Knowing the number of seconds since January 1, 1970, is not often useful. Therefore, C provides the capability to convert time represented as a `time_t` value to a `tm` structure, using the `localtime()` function. A `tm` structure contains day, month, year, and other time information in a format more appropriate for display and printing. The prototype of this function is

```
struct tm *localtime(time_t *ptr);
```

This function returns a pointer to a static type tm structure, so you don't need to declare a type tm structure to use—only a pointer to type tm. This static structure is reused and overwritten each time localtime() is called; if you want to save the value returned, your program must declare a separate type tm structure and copy the values from the static structure.

The reverse conversion—from a type tm structure to a type time_t value—is performed by the function mktime(). The prototype is

```
time_t mktime(struct tm *ntime);
```

This function returns the number of seconds between midnight, January 1, 1970, and the time represented by the type tm structure pointed to by ntime.

Displaying Times

To convert times into formatted strings appropriate for display, use the functions ctime() and asctime(). Both these functions return the time as a string with a specific format. They differ because ctime() is passed the time as a type time_t value, whereas asctime() is passed the time as a type tm structure. Their prototypes are

```
char *asctime(struct tm *ptr);
char *ctime(time_t *ptr);
```

Both functions return a pointer to a static, null-terminated, 26-character string that gives the time of the function's argument in the following format:

```
Thu Jun 13 10:22:23 1991
```

The time is formatted in 24-hour "military" time. Both functions use a static string, overwriting it each time they're called.

For more control over the format of the time, use the strftime() function. This function is passed a time as a type tm structure. It formats the time according to a format string. The function prototype is

```
size_t strftime(char *s, size_t max, char *fmt, struct tm *ptr);
```

This function takes the time in the type tm structure pointed to by ptr, formats it according to the format string fmt, and writes the result as a null-terminated string to the memory location pointed to by s. The argument max should specify the amount of space

20

allocated at s. If the resulting string (including the terminating null character) has more than max characters, the function returns 0, and the string s is invalid. Otherwise, the function returns the number of characters written—strlen(s).

The format string consists of one or more conversion specifiers from Table 20.1.

TABLE 20.1 Conversion Specifiers That Can Be Used with strftime()

Specifier	What It's Replaced By
%a	Abbreviated weekday name.
%A	Full weekday name.
%b	Abbreviated month name.
%B	Full month name.
%c	Date and time representation (for example, 10:41:50 30-Jun-91).
%C	The year as a decimal number from 00 to 99.
%d	Day of month as a decimal number 01 through 31.
%D	Is equivalent to "%m/%d/%y".
%e	The day of the month as a decimal number from 1 to 31.
%F	Is equivalent to "%Y-%m-%d".
%h	The same as "%b", the abbreviated month name.
%H	The hour (24-hour clock) as a decimal number 00 through 23.
%I	The hour (12-hour clock) as a decimal number 00 through 11.
%j	The day of the year as a decimal number 001 through 366.
%m	The month as a decimal number 01 through 12.
%M	The minute as a decimal number 00 through 59.
%p	AM or PM.
%r	The locale's 12 hour clock time.
%R	Is equivalent to "%H:%M".
%S	The second as a decimal number 00 through 59.
%T	Is equivalent to "%H:%M:%S".
%u	The day of week as a decimal number 1 through 7 where 1 is Monday.
%U	The week of the year as a decimal number 00 through 53. Sunday is considered the first day of the week.
%w	The weekday as a decimal number 0 through 6 (Sunday = 0).
%W	The week of the year as a decimal number 00 through 53. Monday is considered the first day of the week.
%x	The date representation (for example, 30-Jun-91).
%X	The time representation (for example, 10:41:50).

%y	The year, without century, as a decimal number 00 through 99.
%Y	The year, with century, as a decimal number.
%z	The locale's time zone or abbreviation. If the time zone isn't known, then this would be blank.
%Z	The time zone name if the information is available or blank if not.
%%	A single percent sign %.

Calculating Time Differences

You can calculate the difference, in seconds, between two times with the `difftime()` macro, which subtracts two `time_t` values and returns the difference. The prototype is

```
double difftime(time_t later, time_t earlier);
```

This function subtracts `earlier` from `later` and returns the difference, the number of seconds between the two times. A common use of `difftime()` is to calculate elapsed time, as demonstrated (along with other time operations) in Listing 20.2.

You can determine duration of a different sort using the `clock()` function, which returns the amount of time that has passed since the program started execution, in 1/100-second units. The prototype is

```
clock_t clock(void);
```

To determine the duration of some portion of a program, call `clock()` twice—before and after the process occurs—and subtract the two return values.

Using the Time Functions

Listing 20.2 demonstrates how to use the C library time functions.

Input ▼
LISTING 20.2   whattime.c: Using the C Library Time Functions

```
1:  /* Demonstrates the time functions. */
2:
3:  #include <stdio.h>
4:  #include <time.h>
5:
6:  int main( void )
7:  {
8:      time_t start, finish, now;
9:      struct tm *ptr;
10:     char *c, buf1[80];
11:     double duration;
12:
```

20

```
13:        /* Record the time the program starts execution. */
14:
15:        start = time(0);
16:
17:        /* Record the current time, using the alternate method of */
18:        /* calling time(). */
19:
20:        time(&now);
21:
22:        /* Convert the time_t value into a type tm structure. */
23:
24:        ptr = localtime(&now);
25:
26:        // Create and display a formatted string containing
27:        // the current time.
28:
29:        c = asctime(ptr);
30:        puts(c);
31:        getc(stdin);
32:
33:        // Now use the strftime() function to create several different
34:        // formatted versions of the time.
35:
36:        strftime(buf1, 80, "This is week %U of the year %Y", ptr);
37:        puts(buf1);
38:        getc(stdin);
39:
40:        strftime(buf1, 80, "Today is %A, %x", ptr);
41:        puts(buf1);
42:        getc(stdin);
43:
44:        strftime(buf1, 80, "It is %M minutes past hour %I.", ptr);
45:        puts(buf1);
46:        getc(stdin);
47:
48:        // Now get the current time and calculate program duration.
49:
50:        finish = time(0);
51:        duration = difftime(finish, start);
52:        printf("\nProgram execution time using time() = %f seconds.",
53:                    duration);
54:
55:        // Also display program duration in hundredths of seconds
56:        // using clock().
57:
58:        printf("\nProgram execution time using clock() = %ld \
59:            hundredths of sec.", clock());
60:        return(0);
61: }
```

Output ▼

```
Sat May 11 13:49:41 2013


This is week 18 of the year 2013

Today is Saturday, 05/11/13

It is 49 minutes past hour 01.


Program execution time using time() = 109.000000 seconds.
Program execution time using clock() = 109454 hundredths of sec.
```

Analysis ▼

This program has numerous comment lines, so it should be easy to follow. Because the time functions are being used, the `time.h` header file is included on line 4. Line 8 declares three variables of type `time_t`—`start`, `finish`, and `now`. These variables can hold the time as an offset from January 1, 1970, in seconds. Line 9 declares a pointer to a `tm` structure. The `tm` structure was described earlier. The rest of the variables have types that should be familiar to you.

The program records its starting time on line 15. This is done with a call to `time()`. The program then does virtually the same thing in a different way. Instead of using the value returned by the `time()` function, line 20 passes `time()` a pointer to the variable `now`. As explained in the comment on line 22, line 24 converts the `time_t` value of `now` to a type `tm` structure. The next few sections of the program print the value of the current time to the screen in various formats. Line 29 uses the `asctime()` function to assign the information to a character pointer, `c`. Line 30 prints the formatted information. The program then waits for the user to press Enter.

Lines 36 through 46 use the `strftime()` function to print the date in three different formats. Using Table 20.1, you should determine what these lines print.

The program then determines the time again on line 50. This is the program-ending time. Line 51 uses this ending time along with the starting time to calculate the program's duration by means of the `difftime()` function. This value is printed on line 52. The program concludes by printing the program execution time from the `clock()` function.

20

Error-Handling

The C standard library contains a variety of functions and macros that help you deal with program errors.

The `assert()` Macro

The macro `assert()` can diagnose program bugs. It is defined in `assert.h`, and its prototype is

```
void assert(int expression);
```

The argument `expression` can be anything you want to test—a variable or any C expression. If `expression` evaluates to TRUE, `assert()` does nothing. If `expression` evaluates to FALSE, `assert()` displays an error message on `stderr` and aborts program execution.

How do you use `assert()`? It is most frequently used to track down program bugs (which are distinct from compilation errors). A bug doesn't prevent a program from compiling, but it causes the program to give incorrect results or to run improperly (locking up, for example). For instance, a financial-analysis program you're writing might occasionally give incorrect answers. You suspect that the problem is caused by the variable `interest_rate` taking on a negative value, which should never happen. To check this, place the statement

```
assert(interest_rate >= 0);
```

at locations in the program where `interest_rate` is used. If the variable ever does become negative, the `assert()` macro alerts you. You can then examine the relevant code to locate the cause of the problem.

To see how `assert()` works, run Listing 20.3. If you enter a nonzero value, the program displays the value and terminates normally. If you enter zero, the `assert()` macro forces abnormal program termination. The exact error message you see depends on your compiler, but here's a typical example:

```
Assertion failed: x, file list1903.c, line 13
```

Note that, for `assert()` to work, your program must be compiled in debug mode. Refer to your compiler documentation for information on enabling debug mode (as explained in a moment). When you later compile the final version in release mode, the `assert()` macros are disabled.

Input ▼

LISTING 20.3   assert.c: Using the `assert()` Macro

```
1:   /* The assert() macro. */
2:
3:   #include <stdio.h>
4:   #include <assert.h>
5:
6:   int main( void )
7:   {
8:       int x;
9:
10:      printf("\nEnter an integer value: ");
11:      scanf("%d", &x);
12:
13:      assert(x != 0);
14:
15:      printf("You entered %d.\n", x);
16:      return(0);
17:  }
```

Output ▼

```
Enter an integer value: 10
You entered 10.
Enter an integer value: 0

Assertion failed: x, file list1903.c, line 13

Abnormal program termination
```

Your error message might differ, depending on your system and compiler, but the general idea is the same. For example, the Code::Blocks compiler generates the following output when 0 is entered:

Output ▼

```
Enter an integer value: 0
Assertion failed: x != 0, file C:\Users\Dean\assert.c

This application has requested the Runtime to terminate it in an unusual way.
Please contact the application's support team for more information.
```

20

Analysis ▼

Run this program to see that the error message displayed by `assert()` on line 13 includes the expression whose test failed, the name of the file, and the line number where the `assert()` is located.

The action of `assert()` depends on another macro named NDEBUG (which stands for "no debugging"). If the macro NDEBUG isn't defined (the default), `assert()` is active. If NDEBUG is defined, `assert()` is turned off and has no effect. If you place `assert()` in various program locations to help with debugging and then solve the problem, you can define NDEBUG to turn `assert()` off. This is much easier than going through the program and removing the `assert()` statements (only to discover later that you want to use them again). To define the macro NDEBUG, use the `#define` directive. You can demonstrate this by adding the line

```
#define NDEBUG
```

to Listing 20.3, on line 2. Now the program prints the value entered and then terminates normally, even if you enter 0.

Note that NDEBUG doesn't need to be defined as anything in particular, as long as it's included in a `#define` directive. You'll learn more about the `#define` directive in Lesson 22, "Advanced Compiler Use."

The `errno.h` Header File

The header file `errno.h` defines several macros used to define and document runtime errors. These macros are used with the `perror()` function, described in the next section.

The `errno.h` definitions include an external integer named `errno`. Many of the C library functions assign a value to this variable if an error occurs during function execution. The file `errno.h` also defines a group of symbolic constants for these errors, listed in Table 20.2.

TABLE 20.2 The Symbolic Error Constants Defined in `errno.h`

Name	Value	Message and Meaning
E2BIG	1000	Argument list too long. (The list length exceeds 128 bytes.)
EACCES	5	Permission denied (for example, trying to write to a file opened for read-only).
EBADF	6	Bad file descriptor.
EDOM	1002	Math argument out of domain. (An argument passed to a math function is outside the allowable range.)
EEXIST	80	File exists.

EMFILE	4	Too many open files.
ENOENT	2	No such file or directory.
ENOEXEC	1001	Exec format error.
ENOMEM	8	Not enough core (for example, not enough memory to execute the `exec()` function).
ENOPATH	3	Path not found.
ERANGE	1003	Result out of range (for example, result returned by a math function is too large or too small for the return data type).

You can use `errno` two ways. Some functions signal, by means of their return values, that an error has occurred. If this happens, you can test the value of `errno` to determine the nature of the error and take appropriate action. Otherwise, when you have no specific indication that an error occurred, you can test `errno`. If it's nonzero, an error has occurred, and the specific value of `errno` indicates the nature of the error. Be sure to reset `errno` to zero after handling the error. The next section explains `perror()`, and then Listing 20.4 illustrates the use of `errno`.

The `perror()` Function

The `perror()` function is another of C's error-handling tools. When called, `perror()` displays a message on `stderr` describing the most recent error that occurred during a library function call or system call. The prototype, in `stdio.h`, is

```
void perror(const char *msg);
```

The argument `msg` points to an optional, user-defined message. This message is printed first, followed by a colon and the implementation-defined message that describes the most recent error. If you call `perror()` when no error has occurred, the message displayed is `no error`.

A call to `perror()` does nothing to deal with the error condition. It's up to the program to take action. The action might consist of prompting the user to do something such as terminate the program. The action the program takes can be determined by testing the value of `errno` and by the nature of the error. Note that a program need not include the header file `errno.h` to use the external variable `errno`. That header file is required only if your program uses the symbolic error constants listed in Table 20.2. Listing 20.4 illustrates the use of `perror()` and `errno` for handling runtime errors.

20

Input ▼

LISTING 20.4   perror.c: Using `perror()` and `errno` to Deal with Runtime Errors

```
1:   // errorhandling.c--Demonstration of error-handling with perror() and errno.
2:
3:   #include <stdio.h>
4:   #include <stdlib.h>
5:   #include <errno.h>
6:
7:   int main( void )
8:   {
9:        FILE *fp;
10:       char filename[80];
11:
12:       printf("Enter filename: ");
13:       gets(filename);
14:
15:       if (( fp = fopen(filename, "r")) == NULL)
16:       {
17:            perror("You goofed!");
18:            printf("errno = %d.\n", errno);
19:            exit(1);
20:       }
21:       else
22:       {
23:            puts("File opened for reading.");
24:            fclose(fp);
25:       }
26:       return(0);
27:  }
```

Output ▼

```
Enter file name: math.c
File opened for reading.

Enter file name: notafile.xxx
You goofed!: No such file or directory
errno = 2.
```

Analysis ▼

This program prints one of two messages based on whether a file can be opened for reading. Line 15 tries to open a file. If the file opens, the `else` part of the `if` branch executes, printing the following message:

```
File opened for reading.
```

If there is an error when the file is opened, such as the file not existing, lines 17–19 of the `if` loop execute. Line 17 calls the `perror()` function with the string `"You goofed!"`. The error number is then printed. The result of entering a file that does not exist is

```
You goofed!: No such file or directory.
errno = 2.
```

DO	**DON'T**
DO check for possible errors in your programs. Never assume that everything is okay.	**DON'T** include the `errno.h` header file if you aren't going to use the symbolic error constants listed in Table 20.2.

Searching and Sorting

Among the most common tasks that programs perform are searching and sorting data. The C standard library contains general-purpose functions that you can use for each task.

Searching with `bsearch()`

The library function `bsearch()` performs a binary search of a data array, looking for an array element that matches a key. To use `bsearch()`, the array must be sorted into ascending order. Also, the program must provide the comparison function used by `bsearch()` to determine whether one data item is greater than, less than, or equal to another item. The prototype of `bsearch()` is in `stdlib.h`:

```
void *bsearch(const void *key, const void *base, size_t num, size_t width,
int (*cmp)(const void *element1, const void *element2));
```

This is a fairly complex prototype, so go through it carefully. The argument `key` is a pointer to the data item being searched for, and `base` is a pointer to the first element of the array being searched. Both are declared as type `void` pointers, so they can point to any of C's data objects. The `const` modifiers simply indicate that the values being passed are constants that won't be changed by the functions.

The argument `num` is the number of elements in the array, and `width` is the size (in bytes) of each element. The type specifier `size_t` refers to the data type returned by the `sizeof()` operator, which is `unsigned`. The `sizeof()` operator is usually used to obtain the values for `num` and `width`.

The final argument, `cmp`, is a pointer to the comparison function. This can be a user-written function or, when searching string data, it can be the library function `strcmp()`. The comparison function must meet the following two criteria:

20

- It is passed pointers to two data items.
- It returns a type `int` as follows:

   < 0   Element 1 is less than element 2.

     0   Element 1 is equal to element 2.

   > 0   Element 1 is greater than element 2.

The return value of `bsearch()` is a type `void` pointer. The function returns a pointer to the first array element it finds that matches the key, or `NULL` if no match is found. You must cast the returned pointer to the proper type before using it.

The `sizeof()` operator can provide the `num` and `width` arguments as follows. If `array[]` is the array to be searched, the statement

```
sizeof(array[0]);
```

returns the value of `width`—the size (in bytes) of one array element. Because the expression `sizeof(array)` returns the size, in bytes, of the entire array, the following statement obtains the value of `num`, the number of elements in the array:

```
sizeof(array)/sizeof(array[0])
```

The binary search algorithm is very efficient; it can search a large array quickly. Its operation is dependent on the array elements being arranged in ascending order. Here's how the algorithm works:

1. The key is compared to the element at the middle of the array. If there's a match, the search is done. Otherwise, the key must be either less than or greater than the array element.

2. If the key is less than the array element, the matching element, if any, must be located in the first half of the array. Likewise, if the key is greater than the array element, the matching element must be located in the second half of the array.

3. The search is restricted to the appropriate half of the array, and then the algorithm returns to step 1.

You can see that each comparison performed by a binary search eliminates half the array being searched. For example, a 1,000-element array can be searched with only 10 comparisons, and a 16,000-element array can be searched with only 14 comparisons. In general, a binary search requires n comparisons to search an array of 2^n elements.

Sorting with `qsort()`

The library function `qsort()` is an implementation of the quicksort algorithm, invented by C.A.R. Hoare. This function sorts an array into order. Usually the result is in ascending order, but `qsort()` can be used for descending order as well. The function prototype, defined in `stdlib.h`, is

```
void qsort(void *base, size_t num, size_t size,
int (*cmp)(const void *element1, const void *element2));
```

The argument `base` points at the first element in the array, `num` is the number of elements in the array, and `size` is the size (in bytes) of one array element. The argument `cmp` is a pointer to a comparison function. The rules for the comparison function are the same as for the comparison function used by `bsearch()`, described in the preceding section: You often use the same comparison function for both `bsearch()` and `qsort()`. The function `qsort()` has no return value.

Searching and Sorting: Two Demonstrations

Listing 20.5 demonstrates the use of `qsort()` and `bsearch()`. The program sorts and searches an array of values. Note that the non-ANSI function `getch()` is used. If your compiler doesn't support it, you should replace it with the ANSI Standard function `getchar()`.

Input ▼
LISTING 20.5 searchandsort.c: Using the `qsort()` and `bsearch()` Functions with Values

```
1:  // searchandsort.c--Using qsort() and bsearch() with values.
2:
3:  #include <stdio.h>
4:  #include <stdlib.h>
5:
6:  #define MAX 20
7:
8:  int intcmp(const void *v1, const void *v2);
9:
10: int main( void )
11: {
12:      int arr[MAX], count, key, *ptr;
13:
14:      // Enter some integers from the user.
15:
16:      printf("Enter %d integer values; press Enter after each.\n", MAX);
17:
18:      for (count = 0; count < MAX; count++)
```

20

```
19:                scanf("%d", &arr[count]);
20:
21:        puts("Press Enter to sort the values.");
22:        getc(stdin);
23:
24:        // Sort the array into ascending order.
25:
26:        qsort(arr, MAX, sizeof(arr[0]), intcmp);
27:
28:        // Display the sorted array.
29:
30:        for (count = 0; count < MAX; count++)
31:            printf("\narr[%d] = %d.", count, arr[count]);
32:
33:        puts("\nPress Enter to continue.");
34:        getc(stdin);
35:
36:        // Enter a search key.
37:
38:        printf("Enter a value to search for: ");
39:        scanf("%d", &key);
40:
41:        // Perform the search.
42:
43:        ptr = (int *)bsearch(&key, arr, MAX, sizeof(arr[0]),intcmp);
44:
45:        if ( ptr != NULL )
46:            printf("%d found at arr[%d].", key, (ptr - arr));
47:        else
48:            printf("%d not found.", key);
49:        return(0);
50: }
51:
52: int intcmp(const void *v1, const void *v2)
53: {
54:        return (*(int *)v1 - *(int *)v2);
55: }
```

Output ▼

```
Enter 20 integer values; press Enter after each.
45
12
999
1000
321
123
2300
954
1968
```

```
12
2
1999
1776
1812
1456
1
9999
3
76
200
Press Enter to sort the values.

arr[0]  = 1.
arr[1]  = 2.
arr[2]  = 3.
arr[3]  = 12.
arr[4]  = 12.
arr[5]  = 45.
arr[6]  = 76.
arr[7]  = 123.
arr[8]  = 200.
arr[9]  = 321.
arr[10] = 954.
arr[11] = 999.
arr[12] = 1000.
arr[13] = 1456.
arr[14] = 1776.
arr[15] = 1812.
arr[16] = 1968.
arr[17] = 1999.
arr[18] = 2300.
arr[19] = 9999.
Press Enter to continue.

Enter a value to search for:
1776
1776 found at arr[14]
```

20

Analysis ▼

Listing 20.5 incorporates everything described previously about sorting and searching. This program enables you to enter up to MAX values (20 in this case). It sorts the values and prints them in order. Then it enables you to enter a value to search for in the array. A printed message states the search's status.

Familiar code is used to obtain the values for the array on lines 18 and 19. Line 26 contains the call to qsort() to sort the array. The first argument is a pointer to the array's first element. This is followed by MAX, the number of elements in the array. The size of the first element is then provided so that qsort() knows the width of each item. The call is finished with the argument for the sort function, intcmp.

The function intcmp() is defined on lines 52–55. It returns the difference of the two values passed to it. This might seem too simple at first, but remember what values the comparison function is supposed to return. If the elements are equal, 0 should be returned. If element one is greater than element two, a positive number should be returned. If element one is less than element two, a negative number should be returned. This is exactly what intcmp() does.

The searching is done with bsearch(). Notice that its arguments are virtually the same as those of qsort(). The difference is that the first argument of bsearch() is the key to be searched for. bsearch() returns a pointer to the location of the found key or NULL if the key isn't found. On line 43, ptr is assigned the returned value of bsearch(). ptr is used in the if block of code on lines 45–48 to print the status of the search.

Listing 20.6 has the same functionality as Listing 20.5; however, Listing 20.6 sorts and searches strings.

Input ▼

LISTING 20.6   searchandsort2.c: Using qsort() and bsearch() with Strings

```
1:  // searchandsort2.c--Using qsort() and bsearch() with strings.
2:
3:  #include <stdio.h>
4:  #include <stdlib.h>
5:  #include <string.h>
6:
7:  #define MAX 20
8:
9:  int comp(const void *s1, const void *s2);
10:
11: int main( void )
12: {
13:     char *data[MAX], buf[80], *ptr, *key, **key1;
14:     int count;
15:
16:     // Input a list of words or phrases.
17:
18:     printf("Enter %d words or phrases, pressing Enter after each.\n",MAX);
19:
20:     for (count = 0; count < MAX; count++)
21:     {
22:         printf("Word %d: ", count+1);
23:         gets(buf);
```

```
24:            data[count] = malloc(strlen(buf)+1);
25:            strcpy(data[count], buf);
26:        }
27:
28:        // Sort the words (actually, sort the pointers).
29:
30:        qsort(data, MAX, sizeof(data[0]), comp);
31:
32:        // Display the sorted words.
33:
34:        for (count = 0; count < MAX; count++)
35:            printf("\n%d: %s", count+1, data[count]);
36:
37:        // Get a search key.
38:
39:        printf("\n\nEnter a search key: ");
40:        gets(buf);
41:
42:        // Perform the search. First, make key1 a pointer
43:        // to the pointer to the search key.
44:
45:        key = buf;
46:        key1 = &key;
47:        ptr = bsearch(key1, data, MAX, sizeof(data[0]), comp);
48:
49:        if (ptr != NULL)
50:            printf("%s found.\n", buf);
51:        else
52:            printf("%s not found.\n", buf);
53:        return(0);
54: }
55:
56: int comp(const void *s1, const void *s2)
57: {
58:        return (strcmp(*(char **)s1, *(char **)s2));
59: }
```

Output ▼

20

```
Enter 20 words or phrases, pressing Enter after each.
Word 1: Massachusetts
Word 2: Colorado
Word 3: New Hampshire
Word 4: Vermont
Word 5: Georgia
Word 6: Indiana
Word 7: Illinois
Word 8: Connecticut
Word 9: North Carolina
Word 10: New York
```

```
Word 11: Texas
Word 12: Florida
Word 13: Alaska
Word 14: Alabama
Word 15: Arkansas
Word 16: New Mexico
Word 17: South Carolina
Word 18: Kentucky
Word 19: Ohio
Word 20: California

1: Alabama
2: Alaska
3: Arkansas
4: California
5: Colorado
6: Connecticut
7: Florida
8: Georgia
9: Illinois
10: Indiana
11: Kentucky
12: Massachusetts
13: New Hampshire
14: New Mexico
15: New York
16: North Carolina
17: Ohio
18: South Carolina
19: Texas
20: Vermont

Enter a search key: Indiana
Indiana found.
```

Analysis ▼

A couple of points about Listing 20.6 bear mentioning. This program makes use of an array of pointers to strings, a technique introduced in Lesson 15, "Pointers to Pointers and Arrays of Pointers." As you saw in that lesson, you can "sort" the strings by sorting the array of pointers. However, this method requires a modification in the comparison function. This function is passed pointers to the two items in the array that are compared. However, you want the array of pointers sorted based not on the values of the pointers themselves but on the values of the strings they point to.

Because of this, you must use a comparison function that is passed pointers to pointers. Each argument to comp() is a pointer to an array element, and because each element is itself a pointer (to a string), the argument is, therefore, a pointer to a pointer. Within the function itself, you dereference the pointers so that the return value of `comp()` depends on the values of the strings pointed to.

The fact that the arguments passed to `comp()` are pointers to pointers creates another problem. You store the search key in `buf[]`, and you also know that the name of an array (`buf` in this case) is a pointer to the array. However, you need to pass not `buf` itself but a pointer to `buf`. The problem is that `buf` is a pointer constant, not a pointer variable. `buf` itself has no address in memory; it's a symbol that evaluates to the address of the array. Because of this, you can't create a pointer that points to `buf` by using the address-of operator in front of `buf`, as in `&buf`.

What to do? First, create a pointer variable and assign the value of `buf` to it. In the program, this pointer variable has the name `key`. Because `key` is a pointer variable, it has an address, and you can create a pointer that contains that address—in this case, `key1`. When you finally call `bsearch()`, the first argument is `key1`, a pointer to a pointer to the key string. The function `bsearch()` passes that argument on to `comp()`, and everything works properly.

DO	**DON'T**
DO check out your compiler's documentation or the ANSI documentation to see the other standard functions you can use.	**DON'T** forget to put your search array into ascending order before using `bsearch()`.

Summary

In this lesson, you explored some of the more useful functions supplied in the C function library. There are functions that perform mathematical calculations, deal with time, and assist your program with error-handling. The functions for sorting and searching data are particularly useful; they can save you considerable time when you write your programs.

20

Q&A

Q Why do nearly all the math functions return `doubles`?

A The answer to this question is to achieve precision, not consistency. A `double` is more precise than the other variable types; therefore, your answers are more accurate. In Lesson 21, "Working with Memory," you learn the specifics of casting variables and variable promotion. These topics are also applicable to precision.

Q Are `bsearch()` and `qsort()` **the only ways in C to sort and search?**

A These two functions are provided in the standard library; however, you don't have to use them. Many computer-programming textbooks teach you how to write your own searching and sorting programs. C contains all the commands you need to write your own. You can purchase especially written searching and sorting routines. The biggest benefits of `bsearch()` and `qsort()` are that they are already written, and they are provided with any ANSI-compatible compiler.

Q **Do the math functions validate bad data?**

A Never assume that data entered is correct. Always validate user-entered data. For example, if you pass a negative value to `sqrt()`, the function generates an error. If you're formatting the output, you probably don't want this error displayed as it is. Remove the `if` statement in Listing 20.1 and enter a negative number to see what I mean.

Workshop

The Workshop provides quiz questions to help you solidify your understanding of the material covered and exercises to provide you with experience in using what you've learned.

Quiz

1. What is the return data type for all of C's mathematical functions?

2. What C variable type is `time_t` equivalent to?

3. What are the differences between the `time()` function and the `clock()` function?

4. When you call the `perror()` function, what does it do to correct an existing error condition?

5. Before you search an array with `bsearch()`, what must you do?

6. Using `bsearch()`, how many comparisons would be required to find an element if the array had 16,000 items?

7. Using `bsearch()`, how many comparisons would be required to find an element if an array had only 10 items?

8. Using `bsearch()`, how many comparisons would be required to find an element if an array had 2 million items?

9. What values must a comparison function for `bsearch()` and `qsort()` return?

10. What does `bsearch()` return if it can't find an element in an array?

Exercises

1. Write a call to `bsearch()`. The array to be searched is called `names`, and the values are characters. The comparison function is called `comp_names()`. Assume that all the names are the same size.

2. **BUG BUSTER:** What is wrong with the following program?

    ```c
    #include <stdio.h>
    #include <stdlib.h>
    int main( void )
    {
        int values[10], count, key, *ptr;

        printf("Enter values");
        for( ctr = 0; ctr < 10; ctr++ )
            scanf( "%d", &values[ctr] );

        qsort(values, 10, compare_function());
    }
    ```

3. **BUG BUSTER:** Is anything wrong with the following compare function?

    ```c
    int intcmp( int element1, int element2)
    {
        if ( element 1 > element 2 )
            return -1;
        else if ( element 1 < element2 )
            return 1;
        else
            return 0;
    }
    ```

    Because of the many possible solutions, answers are not provided for the following exercises.

4. **ON YOUR OWN:** Modify Listing 20.1 so that the `sqrt()` function works with negative numbers. Do this by taking the absolute value of `x`.

5. **ON YOUR OWN:** Write a program that consists of a menu that performs various math functions. Use as many of the math functions as you can.

6. **ON YOUR OWN:** Using the time functions discussed in this lesson, write a function that causes the program to pause for approximately 5 seconds.

7. **ON YOUR OWN:** Add the `assert()` function to the program in exercise 4. The program should print a message if a negative value is entered.

8. **ON YOUR OWN:** Write a program that accepts 30 names and sorts them using `qsort()`. The program should print the sorted names.

20

9. **ON YOUR OWN:** Modify the program in exercise 8 so that if the user enters QUIT, the program stops accepting input and sorts the entered values.

10. **ON YOUR OWN:** Refer to Lesson 15 for a "brute-force" method of sorting an array of pointers to strings based on the string values. Write a program that measures the time required to sort a large array of pointers with that method and then compares that time with the time required to perform the same sort with the library function qsort().

LESSON 21
Working with Memory

This chapter covers some of the more advanced aspects of managing memory within your C programs. In this lesson you learn

- About type conversions
- How to allocate and free memory storage
- How to manipulate memory blocks
- How to manipulate individual bits

Type Conversions

All of C's data objects have a specific type. A numeric variable can be an `int` or a `float`, a pointer can be a pointer to a `double` or `char`, and so on. Programs often require that different types be combined in expressions and statements. What happens in such cases? Sometimes C automatically handles the different types, so you don't need to be concerned. Other times, you must explicitly convert one data type to another to avoid erroneous results. You've seen this in earlier chapters when you had to convert or cast a type `void` pointer to a specific type before using it. In this and other situations, you need a clear understanding of when explicit type conversions are necessary and what types of errors can result when the proper conversion isn't applied. The following sections cover C's automatic and explicit type conversions.

Automatic Type Conversions

As the name implies, automatic type conversions are performed automatically by the C compiler without any action on your part. However, you should be aware of what's going on so that you can understand how C evaluates expressions.

NOTE Automatic type conversion is often referred to as *implicit* conversion.

Type Promotion in Expressions

When a C expression is evaluated, the resulting value has a particular data type. If all the components in the expression have the same type, the resulting type is that type as well. For example, if `x` and `y` are both type `int`, the following expression is type `int` also:

```
x + y
```

What if the components of an expression have different types? In that case, the expression has the same type as its most comprehensive component. From least-comprehensive to most-comprehensive, the numerical data types are

```
char
short
int
long
long long
float
double
long double
```

Thus, an expression containing an `int` and a `char` evaluates to type `int`, an expression containing a `long` and a `float` evaluates to type `float`, and so on.

When creating expressions, the compiler uses two variables or values at a time. For example, if you have the expression:

```
Y + X * 2
```

the compiler would first use the operand x and the operand 2. When it completes, it would use the resulting value and the operand y.

Within expressions, individual operands are promoted as necessary to match the associated operands in the expression. Operands are promoted, in pairs, for each binary operator in the expression. Of course, promotion isn't needed if both operands are the same type. If they aren't, promotion follows these rules:

- If either operand is a `long double`, the other operand is promoted to type `long double`.
- If either operand is a `double`, the other operand is promoted to type `double`.
- If either operand is a `float`, the other operand is promoted to type `float`.
- If either operand is a `long`, the other operand is converted to type `long`.

For example, if x is an `int` and y is a `float`, evaluating the expression x/y causes x to be promoted to type `float` before the expression is evaluated. This doesn't mean that the type of variable x is changed. It means that a type `float` copy of x is created and used in the expression evaluation. The value of the expression is, as you just learned, type `float`. Likewise, if x is a type `double` and y is a type `float`, y will be promoted to `double`.

Conversion by Assignment

Promotions also occur with the assignment operator. The expression on the right side of an assignment statement is always promoted to the type of the data object on the left side of the assignment operator. Note that this might cause a "demotion" rather than a promotion. If f is a type `float` and i is a type `int`, i is promoted to type `float` in this assignment statement:

```
f = i;
```

In contrast, the assignment statement

```
i = f;
```

causes f to be demoted to type `int`. Its fractional part is lost on assignment to i. Remember that f itself isn't changed at all; promotion affects only a copy of the value. Thus, after the following statements are executed

```
float f = 1.23;
int i;
i = f;
```

the variable `i` has the value `1`, and `f` still has the value `1.23`. As this example illustrates, the fractional part is lost when a floating-point number is converted to an integer type.

NOTE	Most compilers give a warning if a variable is demoted without explicitly asking for it to be.

You should be aware that when an integer type is converted to a floating-point type, the resulting floating-point value might not exactly match the integer value. This is because the floating-point format used internally by the computer can't accurately represent every possible integer number. For example, the following code could result in a display of 2.999995 instead of 3:

```
float f;
int i = 3;
f = i;
printf("%f", f);
```

In most cases, any loss of accuracy caused by this would be insignificant. To be sure, however, keep integer values in type `short`, `int`, `long`, or `long long` variables.

Explicit Conversions Using Typecasts

A *typecast* uses the cast operator to explicitly control type conversions in your program. A typecast consists of a type name, in parentheses, before an expression. Casts can be performed on arithmetic expressions and pointers. The result is that the expression is converted to the type specified by the cast. In this manner, you can control the type of expressions in your program rather than relying on C's automatic conversions.

Casting Arithmetic Expressions

Casting an arithmetic expression tells the compiler to represent the value of the expression in a certain way. In effect, a cast is similar to a promotion, which was discussed earlier. However, a cast is under your control, not the compiler's. For example, if `i` is a type `int`, the expression

```
(float)i
```

casts i to type `float`. In other words, the program makes an internal copy of the value of i in floating-point format.

When would you use a typecast with an arithmetic expression? The most common use is to avoid losing the fractional part of the answer in an integer division. Listing 21.1 illustrates this. You should compile and run this program.

Input ▼
LISTING 21.1   casting.c: When One Integer Is Divided by Another, Any Fractional Part of the Answer Is Lost

```
1:   #include <stdio.h>
2:
3:   int main( void )
4:   {
5:       int i1 = 100, i2 = 40;
6:       float f1;
7:
8:       f1 = i1/i2;
9:       printf("%lf\n", f1);
10:      return(0);
11: }
```

Output ▼

```
2.000000
```

Analysis ▼

The answer displayed by the program is `2.000000`, but 100/40 evaluates to 2.5. What happened? The expression `i1/i2` on line 8 contains two type `int` variables. Following the rules explained earlier today, you should determine that the value of the expression `i1/i2` is type `int` itself. This is because the two operands are both of type `int`. As such, the result can represent only whole numbers, so the fractional part of the answer is lost.

You might think that assigning the result of `i1/i2` to a type `float` variable promotes it to type `float`. This is correct, but now it's too late; the fractional part of the answer is already gone.

To avoid this sort of inaccuracy, you must cast one of the type `int` variables to type `float`. If one of the variables is cast to type `float`, the previous rules tell you that the other variable is promoted automatically to type `float`, and the value of the expression is also type `float`. The fractional part of the answer is thus preserved. To demonstrate this, change line 8 in the source code so that the assignment statement reads as follows:

21

```
f1 = (float)i1/i2;
```

The program then displays the correct answer.

NOTE | In more complex expressions, you might want to cast more than one value.

Casting Pointers

You have already been introduced to the casting of pointers. As you saw in Lesson 19, "Getting More from Functions," a type `void` pointer is a generic pointer; it can point to anything. Before you can use a `void` pointer, you must cast it to the proper type. Note that you don't need to cast a pointer to assign a value to it or to compare it with `NULL`. However, you must cast it before dereferencing it or performing pointer arithmetic with it. For more details on casting `void` pointers, review Lesson 19.

DO	**DON'T**
DO use a cast to promote or demote variable values when necessary.	**DON'T** use a cast just to prevent a compiler warning. You might find that using a cast gets rid of a warning, but before removing the warning this way, be sure you understand why you're getting the warning.

Allocating Memory Storage Space

The C library contains functions for allocating memory storage space at runtime, a process called *dynamic memory allocation*. This technique can have significant advantages over explicitly allocating memory in the program source code by declaring variables, structures, and arrays. This latter method, called *static memory allocation*, requires you to know, when you're writing the program, exactly how much memory you need. Dynamic memory allocation enables the program to react, while it's executing, to demands for memory, such as user input. All the functions for handling dynamic memory allocation require the header file stdlib.h; with some compilers, malloc.h is required as well. Note that all allocation functions return a type `void` pointer. As you learned in Lesson 19, a type `void` pointer must be cast to the appropriate type before being used.

Before moving on to the details, a few words are in order about memory allocation. What exactly does it mean? Each computer has a certain amount of memory (random access memory, or RAM) installed. This amount varies from system to system. When you run a program, whether a word processor, a graphics program, or a C program you wrote yourself, the program is loaded from disk into the computer's memory. The memory space the program occupies includes the program code, as well as space for all the program's static data—that is, data items that are declared in the source code. The memory left over is what's available for allocation using the functions in this section.

How much memory is available for allocation? It all depends. If you run a large program on a system with only a modest amount of memory installed, the amount of free memory will be small. Conversely, when a small program runs on a multigigabyte system, plenty of memory will be available. This means that your programs can't make any assumptions about memory availability. When a memory allocation function is called, you must check its return value to ensure that the memory was allocated successfully. In addition, your programs must gracefully handle the situation when a memory allocation request fails. Later in this lesson, you learn a technique for determining exactly how much memory is available.

Also note that your operating system might have an effect on memory availability. Some operating systems make only a portion of physical RAM available. In contrast, UNIX usually makes all physical RAM available to a program. To complicate matters further, some operating systems, such as Windows, provide virtual memory that permits storage space on the hard disk to be allocated as if it were RAM. In this situation, the amount of memory available to a program includes not only the RAM installed, but also the virtual-memory space on the hard disk.

For the most part, these operating system differences in memory allocation should be transparent to you. If you use one of the C functions to allocate memory, the call either succeeds or fails, and you don't need to worry about the details of what's happening.

Allocating Memory with the `malloc()` Function

In earlier lessons, you learned how to use the `malloc()` library function to allocate storage space for strings. The `malloc()` function isn't limited to allocating memory for strings, of course; it can allocate space for any storage need. This function allocates memory by the byte. Recall that `malloc()`'s prototype is

```
void *malloc(size_t num);
```

The argument `size_t` is defined in stdlib.h as `unsigned`. The `malloc()` function allocates `num` bytes of storage space and returns a pointer to the first byte. This function returns NULL if the requested storage space couldn't be allocated or if `num == 0`. Review the

21

section "The `malloc()` Function" in Lesson 10, "Working with Characters and Strings," if you're still a bit unclear on its operation.

Allocating Memory with the `calloc()` Function

The `calloc()` function also allocates memory. Rather than allocating a group of bytes as `malloc()` does, `calloc()` allocates a group of objects. The function prototype is

```
void *calloc(size_t num, size_t size);
```

Remember that `size_t` is a synonym for `unsigned` on most compilers. The argument *num* is the number of objects to allocate, and *size* is the size (in bytes) of each object. If allocation is successful, all the allocated memory is cleared (set to 0), and the function returns a pointer to the first byte. If allocation fails or if either `num` or `size` is 0, the function returns NULL.

Listing 21.2 illustrates the use of `calloc()`.

Input ▼

LISTING 21.2 callocmem.c: Using the `calloc()` Function to Allocate Memory Storage Space Dynamically

```
1:  /* callocmem.c--Demonstrates calloc(). */
2:
3:  #include <stdlib.h>
4:  #include <stdio.h>
5:
6:  int main( void )
7:  {
8:      unsigned long num;
9:      int *ptr;
10:
11:     printf("Enter the number of type int to allocate: ");
12:     scanf("%ld", &num);
13:
14:     ptr = (int*)calloc(num, sizeof(long long));
15:
16:     if (ptr != NULL)
17:         puts("Memory allocation was successful.");
18:     else
19:         puts("Memory allocation failed.");
20:     return(0);
21: }
```

Output ▼

```
Enter the number of type int to allocate: 100
Memory allocation was successful.
Enter the number of type int to allocate: 99999999
Memory allocation was successful.
```

This program prompts for a value on lines 11 and 12. This number determines how much space the program attempts to allocate. The program attempts to allocate enough memory (line 14) to hold the specified number of `long long` variables. If the allocation fails, the return value from `calloc()` is NULL; otherwise, it's a pointer to the allocated memory. In the case of this program, the return value from `calloc()` is placed in the `int` pointer, `ptr`. An `if` statement on lines 16–19 checks the status of the allocation based on `ptr`'s value and prints an appropriate message.

Allocating More Memory with the `realloc()` Function

The `realloc()` function changes the size of a block of memory that was previously allocated with `malloc()` or `calloc()`. The function prototype is

```
void *realloc(void *ptr, size_t size);
```

The `ptr` argument is a pointer to the original block of memory. The new size, in bytes, is specified by *size*. There are several possible outcomes with `realloc()`:

- If sufficient space exists to expand the memory block pointed to by `ptr`, the additional memory is allocated and the function returns `ptr`.
- If sufficient space does not exist to expand the current block in its current location, a new block of the size for `size` is allocated, and existing data is copied from the old block to the beginning of the new block. The old block is freed, and the function returns a pointer to the new block.
- If the `ptr` argument is NULL, the function acts like `malloc()`, allocating a block of `size` bytes and returning a pointer to it.
- If the argument size is 0, the memory that `ptr` points to is freed, and the function returns NULL.
- If memory is insufficient for the reallocation (either expanding the old block or allocating a new one), the function returns NULL, and the original block is unchanged.

Listing 21.3 demonstrates the use of `realloc()`.

21

Input ▼

LISTING 21.3 reusingmem.c: Using `realloc()` to Increase the Size of a Block of Dynamically Allocated Memory

```
1:    // reusingmem.c--Using realloc() to change memory allocation.
2:
3:    #include <stdio.h>
4:    #include <stdlib.h>
5:    #include <string.h>
6:
7:    int main( void )
8:    {
9:        char buf[80], *message;
10:
11:       // Input a string.
12:
13:       puts("Enter a line of text.");
14:       gets(buf);
15:
16:       // Allocate the initial block and copy the string to it.
17:
18:       message = realloc(NULL, strlen(buf)+1);
19:       strcpy(message, buf);
20:
21:       // Display the message.
22:
23:       puts(message);
24:
25:       // Get another string from the user.
26:
27:       puts("Enter another line of text.");
28:       gets(buf);
29:
30:       // Increase the allocation, then concatenate the string to it.
31:
32:       message = realloc(message,(strlen(message) + strlen(buf)+1));
33:       strcat(message, buf);
34:
35:       // Display the new message.
36:       puts(message);
37:       return(0);
38: }
```

Output ▼

```
Enter a line of text.
This is the first line of text.
This is the first line of text.
Enter another line of text.
This is the second line of text.
This is the first line of text.This is the second line of text.
```

Analysis ▼

This program gets an input string on line 14, reading it into an array of characters called `buf`. The string is then copied into a memory location pointed to by `message` (line 19). `message` was allocated using `realloc()` on line 18. `realloc()` was called even though there was no previous allocation. By passing `NULL` as the first parameter, `realloc()` knows that this is a first allocation.

Line 28 gets a second string in the `buf` buffer. This string is concatenated to the string already held in `message`. Because `message` is just big enough to hold the first string, it needs to be reallocated to make room to hold both the first and second strings. This is exactly what line 32 does. The program concludes by printing the final concatenated string.

Releasing Memory with the `free()` Function

When you allocate memory with either `malloc()` or `calloc()`, it is taken from the dynamic memory pool that is available to your program. This pool is sometimes called the *heap*, and it is finite—it has a limit. When your program finishes using a particular block of dynamically allocated memory, you should deallocate, or free, the memory to make it available for future use. To free memory that was allocated dynamically, use `free()`. Its prototype is

```
void free(void *ptr);
```

The `free()` function releases the memory pointed to by `ptr`. This memory must have been allocated with `malloc()`, `calloc()`, or `realloc()`. If `ptr` is `NULL`, `free()` does nothing. Listing 21.4 demonstrates the `free()` function.

Input ▼

LISTING 21.4 freemem.c: Using `free()` to Release Previously Allocated Dynamic Memory

```
1:  // freemem.c--Using free() to release allocated dynamic memory.
2:
3:  #include <stdio.h>
4:  #include <stdlib.h>
5:  #include <string.h>
6:
7:  #define BLOCKSIZE 300000000
8:
9:  int main( void )
10: {
11:     void *ptr1, *ptr2;
12:
13:     // Allocate one block.
14:
```

21

```
15:     ptr1 = malloc(BLOCKSIZE);
16:
17:     if (ptr1 != NULL)
18:         printf("\nFirst allocation of %d bytes successful.",BLOCKSIZE);
19:     else
20:     {
21:         printf("\nAttempt to allocate %d bytes failed.\n",BLOCKSIZE);
22:         exit(1);
23:     }
24:
25:     // Try to allocate another block.
26:
27:     ptr2 = malloc(BLOCKSIZE);
28:
29:     if (ptr2 != NULL)
30:     {
31:         // If allocation successful, print message and exit.
32:
33:         printf("\nSecond allocation of %d bytes successful.\n",
34:                 BLOCKSIZE);
35:         exit(0);
36:     }
37:
38:     // If not successful, free the first block and try again.
39:
40:     printf("\nSecond attempt to allocate %d bytes failed.",BLOCKSIZE);
41:     free(ptr1);
42:     printf("\nFreeing first block.");
43:
44:     ptr2 = malloc(BLOCKSIZE);
45:
46:     if (ptr2 != NULL)
47:         printf("\nAfter free(), allocation of %d bytes successful.\n",
48:                 BLOCKSIZE);
49:     return(0);
50: }
```

Output ▼

```
First allocation of 300000000 bytes successful.
Second allocation of 300000000 bytes successful.
```

Analysis ▼

This program tries to dynamically allocate two blocks of memory. It uses the defined constant BLOCKSIZE to determine how much to allocate. Line 15 does the first allocation using malloc(). Lines 17 through 23 check the status of the allocation by determining whether the return value was equal to NULL. A message displays, stating the status of the allocation. If the allocation failed, the program exits. Line 27 tries to allocate a second block of memory, again checking to see whether the allocation was successful (lines 29 through 36). If the second allocation were successful, a call to `exit()` ends the program. If it were not successful, a message states that the attempt to allocate memory failed. The first block is then freed with `free()` (line 41), and a new attempt is made to allocate the second block.

DO	DON'T
DO free allocated memory when you're done with it.	**DON'T** assume that a call to `malloc()`, `calloc()`, or `realloc()` was successful. In other words, always check to see that the memory was indeed allocated.

Manipulating Memory Blocks

So far in this lesson, you've seen how to allocate and free blocks of memory. The C library also contains functions that can be used to manipulate blocks of memory—setting all bytes in a block to a specified value, copying, and moving information from one location to another.

Initializing Memory with the `memset()` Function

To set all the bytes in a block of memory to a particular value, use `memset()`. The function prototype is

```
void *memset(void *dest, int c, size_t count);
```

The argument `dest` points to the block of memory. `c` is the value to set, and `count` is the number of bytes, starting at `dest`, to be set. Note that while `c` is a type `int`, it is treated as a type `char`. In other words, only the low-order byte is used, and you can specify values of `c` only in the range `0` through `255`.

Use `memset()` to initialize a block of memory to a specified value. Because this function can use only a type `char` as the initialization value, it is not useful for working with blocks of data types other than type `char`, except when you want to initialize to `0`. In other words, it wouldn't be efficient to use `memset()` to initialize an array of type `int` to the value `99`, but you could initialize all array elements to the value `0`. `memset()` is demonstrated in Listing 21.5.

21

Copying Memory with the `memcpy()` Function

`memcpy()` copies bytes of data between memory blocks, sometimes called *buffers*. This function doesn't care about the type of data being copied—it simply makes an exact byte-for-byte copy. The function prototype is

```
void *memcpy(void *dest, void *src, size_t count);
```

The arguments `dest` and `src` point to the destination and source memory blocks, respectively. `count` specifies the number of bytes to be copied. The return value is `dest`. If the two blocks of memory overlap, the function might not operate properly—some of the data in `src` might be overwritten before being copied. Use the `memmove()` function, discussed next, to handle overlapping memory blocks. `memcpy()` will be demonstrated in Listing 21.5.

Moving Memory with the `memmove()` Function

`memmove()` is very much like `memcpy()`, copying a specified number of bytes from one memory block to another. It's more flexible, however, because it can handle overlapping memory blocks properly. Because `memmove()` can do everything `memcpy()` can do (with the added flexibility of dealing with overlapping blocks), you rarely, if ever, have a reason to use `memcpy()`. The prototype is

```
void *memmove(void *dest, void *src, size_t count);
```

`dest` and `src` point to the destination and source memory blocks, and `count` specifies the number of bytes to be copied. The return value is `dest`. If the blocks overlap, this function ensures that the source data in the overlapped region is copied before being overwritten. Listing 21.5 demonstrates `memset()`, `memcpy()`, and `memmove()`.

Input ▼

LISTING 21.5 memfunctions.c: A Demonstration of `memset()`, `memcpy()`, and `memmove()`

```
1:  // memfunctions.c--Demonstrating memset(), memcpy(), and memmove().
2:
3:  #include <stdio.h>
4:  #include <string.h>
4:
5:  char message1[60] = "Four score and seven years ago ...";
6:  char message2[60] = "abcdefghijklmnopqrstuvwxyz";
7:  char temp[60];
8:
9:  int main( void )
10: {
11:     printf("\nmessage1[] before memset():\t%s", message1);
```

```
12:     memset(message1 + 5, '@', 10);
13:     printf("\nmessage1[] after memset():\t%s", message1);
14:
15:     strcpy(temp, message2);
16:     printf("\n\nOriginal message: %s", temp);
17:     memcpy(temp + 4, temp + 16, 10);
18:     printf("\nAfter memcpy() without overlap:\t%s", temp);
19:     strcpy(temp, message2);
20:     memcpy(temp + 6, temp + 4, 10);
21:     printf("\nAfter memcpy() with overlap:\t%s", temp);
22:
23:     strcpy(temp, message2);
24:     printf("\n\nOriginal message: %s", temp);
25:     memmove(temp + 4, temp + 16, 10);
26:     printf("\nAfter memmove() without overlap:\t%s", temp);
27:     strcpy(temp, message2);
28:     memmove(temp + 6, temp + 4, 10);
29:     printf("\nAfter memmove() with overlap:\t%s\n", temp);
30:     return 0;
31: }
```

Output ▼

```
message1[] before memset():    Four score and seven years ago ...
message1[] after memset():     Four @@@@@@@@@@seven years ago ...

Original message: abcdefghijklmnopqrstuvwxyz
After memcpy() without overlap: abcdqrstuvwxyzopqrstuvwxyz
After memcpy() with overlap:    abcdefefefefefefqrstuvwxyz

Original message: abcdefghijklmnopqrstuvwxyz
After memmove() without overlap:        abcdqrstuvwxyzopqrstuvwxyz
After memmove() with overlap:   abcdefefghijklmnqrstuvwxyz
```

Analysis ▼

The operation of `memset()` is straightforward. Note how the pointer notation `message1 + 5` is used to specify that `memset()` is to start setting characters at the sixth character in `message1[]`. (Remember, arrays are zero-based.) As a result, the 6th through 15th characters in `message1[]` have been changed to `@`.

When source and destination do not overlap, `memcpy()` works fine. The 10 characters of `temp[]` starting at position 17 (the letters q through z) have been copied to positions 5 though 14, where the letters e through n were originally located. If, however, the source and destination overlap, things are different. When the function tries to copy 10 characters starting at position 4 to position 6, an overlap of 8 positions occurs. You

21

might expect the letters e through n to be copied over the letters g through p. Instead, the letters e and f are repeated five times.

If there's no overlap, `memmove()` works just like `memcpy()`. With overlap, however, `memmove()` copies the original source characters to the destination.

DO	DON'T
DO use `memmove()` instead of `memcpy()` in case you deal with overlapping memory regions.	**DON'T** try to use `memset()` to initialize type `int`, `float`, or `double` arrays to any value other than `0`.

Working with Bits

As you may know, the most basic unit of computer data storage is the bit. There are times when manipulating individual bits in your C program's data is useful. C has several tools that enable you to do this.

The C bitwise operators enable you to manipulate the individual bits of integer variables. Remember, a *bit* is the smallest possible unit of data storage, and it can have only one of two values: `0` or `1`. The bitwise operators can be used only with integer types: `char`, `int`, and `long`. Before continuing with this section, you should be familiar with binary notation—the way the computer internally stores integers.

The bitwise operators are most frequently used when your C program interacts directly with your system's hardware—a topic that is beyond the scope of this book. They do have other uses, however, which are introduced.

The Shift Operators

Two shift operators shift the bits in an integer variable by a specified number of positions. The `<<` operator shifts bits to the left, and the `>>` operator shifts bits to the right. The syntax for these binary operators is

```
x << n
```

and

```
x >> n
```

Each operator shifts the bits in `x` by `n` positions in the specified direction. For a right shift, zeros are placed in the `n` high-order bits of the variable; for a left shift, zeros are placed in the `n` low-order bits of the variable. Here are a few examples:

Binary `00001100` (decimal `12`) right-shifted by 2 evaluates to binary `00000011` (decimal `3`).

Binary `00001100` (decimal `12`) left-shifted by 3 evaluates to binary `01100000` (decimal `96`).

Binary `00001100` (decimal `12`) right-shifted by 3 evaluates to binary `00000001` (decimal `1`).

Binary `00110000` (decimal `48`) left-shifted by 3 evaluates to binary `10000000` (decimal `128`).

Under certain circumstances, you can use the shift operators to multiply and divide an integer variable by a power of 2. Left-shifting an integer by n places has the same effect as multiplying it by 2^n, and right-shifting an integer has the same effect as dividing it by 2^n. The results of a left-shift multiplication are accurate only if there is no overflow—that is, if no bits are "lost" by being shifted out of the high-order positions. A right-shift division is an integer division, in which any fractional part of the result is lost. For example, if you right-shift the value `5` (binary `00000101`) by one place, intending to divide by 2, the result is `2` (binary `00000010`) instead of the correct `2.5` because the fractional part (the `.5`) is lost. Listing 21.6 demonstrates the shift operators.

Input ▼
LISTING 21.6 shiftit.c: Using the Shift Operators

```
1:   // shiftit.c--Demonstrating the shift operators.
2:
3:   #include <stdio.h>
4:
5:   int main( void )
6:   {
7:       unsigned int y, x = 255;
8:       int count;
9:
10:      printf("Decimal\t\tshift left by\tresult\n");
11:
12:      for (count = 1; count < 8; count++)
13:      {
14:          y = x << count;
15:          printf("%d\t\t%d\t\t%d\n", x, count, y);
16:      }
17:      printf("\n\nDecimal\t\tshift right by\tresult\n");
18:
19:      for (count = 1; count < 8; count++)
20:      {
21:          y = x >> count;
22:          printf("%d\t%d\t\t%d\n", x, count, y);
23:      }
24:      return(0);
25: }
```

21

Output ▼

```
Decimal          shift left by    result
255              1                510
255              2                1020
255              3                2040
255              4                4080
255              5                8160
255              6                16320
255              7                32640
Decimal          shift right by   result
255              1                127
255              2                63
255              3                31
255              4                15
255              5                7
255              6                3
255              7                1
```

The Bitwise Logical Operators

Three bitwise logical operators are used to manipulate individual bits in an integer data type, as shown in Table 21.1. These operators have names similar to the TRUE/FALSE logical operators you learned about in earlier chapters, but their operations differ.

TABLE 21.1   The Bitwise Logical Operators

Operator	Action
&	AND
|	Inclusive OR
^	Exclusive OR

These are all binary operators, setting bits in the result to 1 or 0 depending on the bits in the operands. They operate as follows:

- Bitwise AND sets a bit in the result to 1 only if the corresponding bits in both operands are 1; otherwise, the bit is set to 0. The AND operator is used to turn off, or clear, one or more bits in a value.

- Bitwise inclusive OR sets a bit in the result to 0 only if the corresponding bits in both operands are 0; otherwise, the bit is set to 1. The OR operator is used to turn on, or set, one or more bits in a value.

- Bitwise exclusive OR sets a bit in the result to 1 if the corresponding bits in the operands are different (if one is 1 and the other is 0); otherwise, the bit is set to 0.

The following are examples of how these operators work:

Operation	Example
AND	11110000 & 01010101 01010000
Inclusive OR	11110000 | 01010101 11110101
Exclusive OR	11110000 ^ 01010101 10100101

You just read that bitwise AND and bitwise inclusive OR can be used to clear or set, respectively, specified bits in an integer value. Here's what that means. Suppose you have a type char variable, and you want to ensure that the bits in positions 0 and 4 are cleared (that is, equal to 0) and that the other bits stay at their original values. If you AND the variable with a second value that has the binary value 11101110, you'll obtain the wanted result. Here's how this works.

In each position where the second value has a 1, the result will have the same value, 0 or 1, as was present in that position in the original variable:

```
0 & 1 == 0
1 & 1 == 1
```

In each position where the second value has a 0, the result will have a 0 regardless of the value that was present in that position in the original variable:

```
0 & 0 == 0
1 & 0 == 0
```

Setting bits with OR works in a similar way. In each position where the second value has a 1, the result will have a 1, and in each position where the second value has a 0, the result will be unchanged:

```
0 | 1 == 1
1 | 1 == 1
0 | 0 == 0
1 | 0 == 1
```

21

The Complement Operator

The final bitwise operator covered is the complement operator, ~. This is a unary operator. Its action is to reverse every bit in its operand, changing all 0s to 1s, and vice versa. For example, ~254 (binary 11111110) evaluates to 1 (binary 00000001).

All the examples in this section have used type char variables containing 8 bits. For larger variables, such as type int and type long, things work exactly the same.

Bit Fields in Structures

The final bit-related topic is the use of bit fields in structures. In Lesson 11, "Implementing Structures, Unions, and TypeDefs," you learned how to define your own data structures, customizing them to fit your program's data needs. By using bit fields, you can accomplish even greater customization and save memory space as well.

A *bit field* is a structure member that contains a specified number of bits. You can declare a bit field to contain one bit, two bits, or whatever number of bits are required to hold the data stored in the field. What advantage does this provide?

Suppose that you're programming an employee database program that keeps records on your company's employees. Many of the items of information that the database stores are of the yes/no variety, such as "Is the employee enrolled in the dental plan?" or "Did the employee graduate from college?" Each piece of yes/no information can be stored in a single bit, with 1 representing yes and 0 representing no.

Using C's standard data types, the smallest type you could use in a structure is a type char. You could indeed use a type char structure member to hold yes/no data, but 7 of the char's 8 bits would be wasted space. By using bit fields, you can store 8 yes/no values in a single char.

Bit fields aren't limited to yes/no values. Continuing with this database example, imagine that your firm has three different health insurance plans. Your database needs to store data about the plan in which each employee is enrolled (if any). You could use 0 to represent no health insurance and use the values 1, 2, and 3 to represent the three plans. A bit field containing 2 bits is sufficient because 2 binary bits can represent values of 0 through 3. Likewise, a bit field containing 3 bits could hold values in the range 0 through 7, 4 bits could hold values in the range 0 through 15, and so on.

Bit fields are named and accessed in the same way as regular structure members. All bit fields have type unsigned int, and you specify the size of the field (in bits) by following the member name with a colon and the number of bits. To define a structure with a 1-bit member named dental, another 1-bit member named college, and a 2-bit member named health, you write the following:

```
struct emp_data
{
  unsigned dental      : 1;
  unsigned college     : 1;
  unsigned health      : 2;
  ...
};
```

The ellipsis (. . .) indicates space for other structure members. The members can be bit fields or fields made up of regular data types. Note that bit fields must be placed first in the structure definition before any nonbit field structure members. To access the bit fields, use the structure member operator just as you do with any structure member. For the example, you can expand the structure definition to something more useful:

```
struct emp_data
{
  unsigned dental      : 1;
  unsigned college     : 1;
  unsigned health      : 2;
  char fname[20];
  char lname[20];
  char ssnumber[10];
};
```

You can then declare an array of structures:

```
struct emp_data workers[100];
```

To assign values to the first array element, write something like this:

```
workers[0].dental = 1;
workers[0].college = 0;
workers[0].health = 2;
strcpy(workers[0].fname, "Mildred");
```

Your code would be clearer, of course, if you used symbolic constants YES and NO with values of 1 and 0 when working with 1-bit fields. In any case, you treat each bit field as a small, unsigned integer with the given number of bits. The range of values that can be assigned to a bit field with n bits is from 0 to 2^{n-1}. If you try to assign an out-of-range value to a bit field, the compiler won't report an error, but you will get unpredictable results.

21

DO	DON'T
DO use defined constants YES and NO or TRUE and FALSE when working with bits. These are much easier to read and understand than 1 and 0.	**DON'T** define a bit field that takes 8 or 16 bits. These are the same as other available variables such as type char or int.

Summary

Today's lesson covered a variety of C programming topics. You learned how to allocate, reallocate, and free memory at runtime, and you saw commands that give you flexibility in allocating storage space for program data. You also saw how and when to use typecasts with variables and pointers. Forgetting about typecasts, or using them improperly, is a common cause of hard-to-find program bugs, so this is a topic worth reviewing. You also learned how to use the memset(), memcpy(), and memmove() functions to manipulate blocks of memory. Finally, you saw the ways in which you can manipulate and use individual bits in your programs.

Q&A

Q **What's the advantage of dynamic memory allocation? Why can't I just declare the storage space I need in my source code?**

A If you declare all your data storage in your source code, the amount of memory available to your program is fixed. You have to know ahead of time, when you write the program, how much memory will be needed. Dynamic memory allocation enables your program to control the amount of memory used to suit the current conditions and user input. The program can use as much memory as it needs, up to the limit of what's available in the computer.

Q **Why would I ever need to free memory?**

A When you first learn to use C, your programs aren't big. As your programs grow, their use of memory also grows. You should try to write your programs to use memory as efficiently as possible. When you finish with memory, you should release it. If you write programs that work in a multitasking environment, other applications might need memory that you aren't using. Although some systems automatically return memory when a program ends, not all systems do.

Q **What happens if I reuse a string without calling realloc()?**

A You don't need to call realloc() if the string you use was allocated enough room. Call realloc() when your current string isn't big enough. Remember, the C compiler enables you to do almost anything, even things you shouldn't! You can overwrite one string with a bigger string as long as the new string's length is equal to or smaller than the original string's allocated space. However, if the new string is bigger, you can also overwrite whatever came after the string in memory. This could be nothing, or it could be vital data. If you need a bigger allocated section of memory, call `realloc()`.

Q **What's the advantage of the `memset()`, `memcpy()`, and `memmove()` functions? Why can't I just use a loop with an assignment statement to initialize or copy memory?**

A You can use a loop with an assignment statement to initialize memory in some cases. In fact, sometimes this is the only way to do it—for example, setting all elements of a type `float` array to the value `1.23`. In other situations, however, the memory will not have been assigned to an array or list, and the `mem...()` functions are your only choice. There are also times when a loop and assignment statement work, but the `mem...()` functions are simpler and faster.

Q **When would I use the shift operators and the bitwise logical operators?**

A The most common use for these operators is when a program is interacting directly with the computer hardware—a task that often requires specific bit patterns to be generated and interpreted. This topic is beyond the scope of this book. Even if you never need to manipulate hardware directly, you can use the shift operators, in certain circumstances, to divide or multiply integer values by powers of two.

Q **Do I really gain that much by using bit fields?**

A Yes, you can gain quite a bit with bit fields. (Pun intended!) Consider a circumstance similar to the example in this chapter in which a file contains information from a survey. People are asked to answer TRUE or FALSE to the questions asked. If you ask 100 questions of 10,000 people and store each answer as a type `char` as T or F, you will need 10,000 × 100 bytes of storage (because a character is 1 byte). This is 1 million bytes of storage. If you use bit fields instead and allocate 1 bit for each answer, you need 10,000 × 100 bits. Because 1 byte holds 8 bits, this amounts to 130,000 bytes of data, which is significantly less than 1 million bytes.

21

Workshop

The Workshop provides quiz questions to help you solidify your understanding of the material covered and exercises to provide you with experience in using what you've learned.

Quiz

1. What is the difference between the `malloc()` and `calloc()` memory-allocation functions?

2. What is the most common reason for using a typecast with a numeric variable?

3. What variable type do the following expressions evaluate to? Assume that `c` is a type `char` variable, `i` is a type `int` variable, `l` is a type `long` variable, and `f` is a type `float` variable.

   a. `( c + i + l )`

   b. `( i + 32 )`

   c. `( c + 'A')`

   d. `( i + 32.0 )`

   e. `( 100 + 1.0 )`

4. What is meant by dynamically allocating memory?

5. What is the difference between the `memcpy()` function and the `memmove()` function?

6. Imagine that your program uses a structure that must (as one of its members) store the day of the week as a value between `1` and `7`. What's the most memory-efficient way to do so?

7. What is the smallest amount of memory in which the current date can be stored? (Hint: month/day/year—think of year as an offset from 1900.)

8. What does `10010010 << 4` evaluate to?

9. What does `10010010 >> 4` evaluate to?

10. Describe the difference between the results of the following two expressions:
    ```
    (01010101 ^ 11111111 )
    ( ~01010101 )
    ```

Exercises

1. Write a `malloc()` command that allocates memory for 1,000 `long`s.

2. Write a `calloc()` command that allocates memory for 1,000 `long`s.

3. Assume that you have declared an array as follows:

```
float data[1000];
```

Show two ways to initialize all elements of the array to `0`. Use a loop and an assignment statement for one method, and the `memset()` function for the other.

4. **BUG BUSTER:** Is anything wrong with the following code?

```
void func()
{
  int number1 = 100, number2 = 3;
  float answer;
  answer = number1 / number2;
  printf("%d/%d = %lf", number1, number2, answer)
}
```

5. **BUG BUSTER:** What, if anything, is wrong with the following code?

```
void *p;
p = (float*) malloc(sizeof(float));
*p = 1.23;
```

6. **BUG BUSTER:** Is the following structure allowed?

```
struct quiz_answers
{
  char student_name[15];
  unsigned answer1   : 1;
  unsigned answer2   : 1;
  unsigned answer3   : 1;
  unsigned answer4   : 1;
  unsigned answer5   : 1;
}
```

Because of the many possible solutions, answers are not provided for the following exercises.

7. Write a program that uses each of the bitwise logical operators. The program should apply the bitwise operator to a number and then reapply it to the result. You should observe the output to be sure you understand what's going on.

8. Write a program that displays the binary value of a number. For instance, if the user enters `3`, the program should display `00000011`. (Hint: You need to use the bitwise operators.)

21

LESSON 22
Advanced Compiler Use

This is the last lesson of your C learning journey. At this time, you have actually learned nearly all the key topics you need to know about programming with the C language syntax. This lesson covers some additional features of C. You learn

- Programming with multiple source-code files

- Using the C preprocessor

- Using command-line arguments

Programming with Multiple Source-Code Files

Until now, all your C programs have consisted of a single source-code file (not counting the header files, of course). A single source-code file is often all you need, particularly for small programs, but you can also divide the source code for a single program among two or more files, a practice called *modular programming*. Why would you want to do this? The following sections explain.

Advantages of Modular Programming

The primary reason to use modular programming is closely related to structured programming and its reliance on functions. As you become a more experienced programmer, you develop more general-purpose functions that you can use, not only in the program for which they were originally written, but in other programs as well. For example, you might write a collection of general-purpose functions for displaying information onscreen. By keeping these functions in a separate file, you can use them again in different programs that also display information onscreen. When you write a program that consists of multiple source-code files, each source file is called a *module*.

Modular Programming Techniques

A C program can have only one `main()` function. The module that contains the `main()` function is called the *main module,* and other modules are called *secondary modules*. A separate header file is usually associated with each secondary module. (You learn why later in this lesson). For now, look at a few simple examples that illustrate the basics of multiple module programming. Listings 22.1, 22.2, and 22.3 show the main module, the secondary module, and the header file, respectively, for a program that inputs a number from the user and displays its square.

Input ▼
LISTING 22.1 list2101.c: The Main Module

```
1:   /* list2101.c--Inputs a number and displays its square. */
2:
3:   #include <stdio.h>
4:   #include "calc.h"
5:
6:   int main( void )
7:   {
8:       int x;
9:
10:      printf("Enter an integer value: ");
11:      scanf("%d", &x);
```

```
12:      printf("\nThe square of %d is %ld.\n", x, sqr(x));
13:      return(0);
14: }
```

Input ▼

LISTING 22.2 calc.c: The Secondary Module

```
1:  /* Module containing calculation functions. */
2:
3:  #include "calc.h"
4:
5:  long sqr(int x)
6:  {
7:      return ((long)x * x);
8:  }
```

Input ▼

LISTING 22.3 calc.h: The Header File for calc.c

```
1:  /* calc.h--header file for calc.c. */
2:
3:  long sqr(int x);
4:
5:  /* end of calc.h */
```

Output ▼

Enter an integer value: **100**

The square of 100 is 10000.

Analysis ▼

Now look at the components of these three files in greater detail. The header file, calc.h, contains the prototype for the sqr() function in calc.c. Because any module that uses sqr() needs to know sqr()'s prototype, the module must include calc.h.

The secondary module file, calc.c, contains the definition of the sqr() function. The #include directive is used to include the header file, calc.h. Note that the header filename is enclosed in quotation marks rather than angle brackets. (You learn the reason for this later in this lesson.)

The main module, list2201.c, contains the main() function. This module also includes the header file, calc.h.

After you use your editor to create these three files, how do you compile and link the final executable program? Your integrated development environment can create a project that takes care of compiling multiple source files for you. For example, if you use the Code::Blocks compiler, you can compile the previous listings using the following steps:

1. Open Code::Blocks.

2. Select File | New | Project. The New from Template dialog box displays, as shown in Figure 22.1.

FIGURE 22.1
Code::Blocks New
from Template.

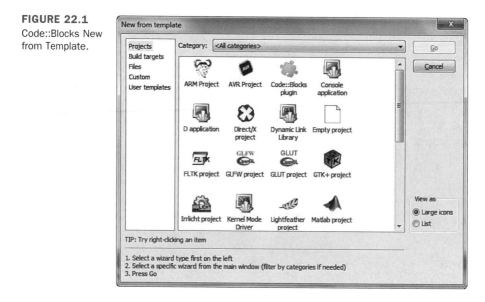

3. Select Empty project and then click Next. The Empty Project dialog displays, as shown in Figure 22.2.

FIGURE 22.2
Code::Blocks
Empty Project
dialog box.

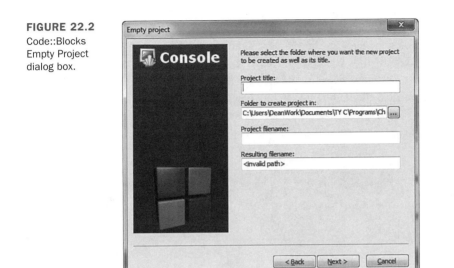

22

4. Enter the title of your project, such as **Project2201**. The default folder is wherever you last saved a file, and the Project filename defaults to your project title. You can change these if you want. Click Next.

5. An additional dialog box (shown in Figure 22.3) displays other options concerning your compiler, debug configurations, and release configurations. Use the defaults. You can later play with these options, but they are beyond the scope of this book. Click Finish.

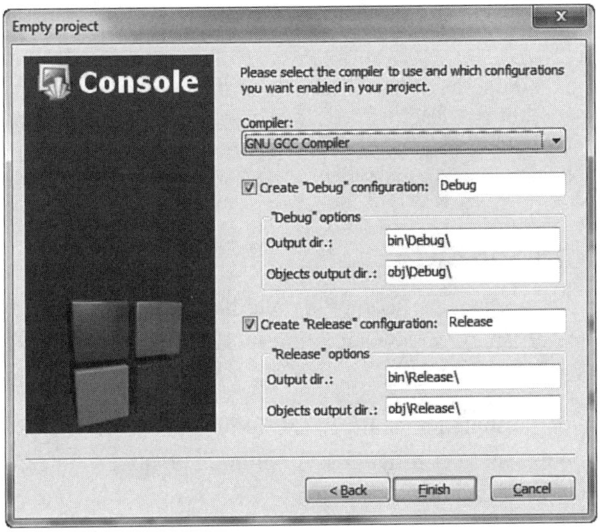

FIGURE 22.3
Additional
options for your
Code::Blocks
project.

6. The Integrated Development Environment (IDE) opens, and you can now add files to your project by clicking the Project menu, highlighting Add Files to Project, and choosing the files you entered earlier in this lesson into the project. Each time you do this, the file is listed on the left as a Source for the Project. Figure 22.4 shows the calc.h file highlighted in the dialog box and the two .c files (calc.c and list2201.c) listed on the tree on the left under a Sources folder as they were already added to the project. After you add calc.h, a new folder named Headers is added.

FIGURE 22.4
Adding files to a Code::Blocks Project.

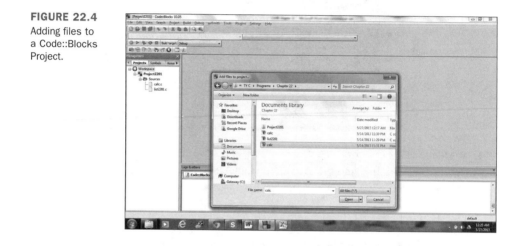

7. Click the Build button (which you've probably used to compile your source files before).

NOTE

These steps and screen shots are specific to the Code::Block IDE, but your IDE (if you use a different one) should lead to a similar set of steps.

Module Components

As you can see, the mechanics of compiling and linking a multiple-module program are quite simple. The only question is what to put in each file. This section gives you some general guidelines.

The secondary module should contain general utility functions—that is, functions that you might want to use in other programs. A common practice is to create one secondary module for each type of function—for example, keyboard.c for your keyboard functions, screen.c for your screen display functions, and so on. To compile and link more than two modules, include all source files in your project.

The main module should contain `main()`, of course, and any other functions that are program-specific (meaning that they have no general utility).

There is usually one header file for each secondary module. Each file has the same name as the associated module, with an .h extension. In the header file, put

- Prototypes for functions in the secondary module
- `#define` directives for any symbolic constants and macros used in the module
- Definitions of any structures or external variables used in the module

Because this header file might be included in more than one source file, you want to prevent portions of it from compiling more than once. You can do this by using the preprocessor directives for conditional compilation (discussed later in this lesson).

External Variables and Modular Programming

In many cases, the only data communication between the main module and the secondary module is through arguments passed to and returned from the functions. In this case, you don't need to take special steps regarding data visibility; but what about an external variable that needs to be visible in both modules?

Recall from Lesson 12, "Understanding Variable Scope," that an external variable is one declared outside of any function. An external variable is visible throughout the entire source-code file in which it is declared. However, it is not automatically visible in other modules. To make it visible, you must declare the variable in each module, using the `extern` keyword. For example, if you have an external variable declared in the main module as

```
float interest_rate;
```

you make `interest_rate` visible in a secondary module by including the following declaration in that module (outside of any function):

```
extern float interest_rate;
```

The `extern` keyword tells the compiler that the original declaration of `interest_rate` (the one that set aside storage space for it) is located elsewhere, but that the variable should be made visible in this module. All `extern` variables have static duration and are visible to all functions in the module. Figure 22.5 illustrates the use of the `extern` keyword in a multiple-module program.

CAUTION

If you use `extern` declarations and then don't actually declare the variable elsewhere, you get an error. This error can occur either when you link the final program or at runtime.

FIGURE 22.5

Using the `extern` keyword to make an external variable visible across modules.

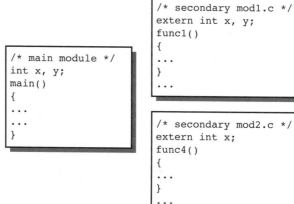

```
/* main module */
int x, y;
main()
{
...
...
}
```

```
/* secondary mod1.c */
extern int x, y;
func1()
{
...
}
...
```

```
/* secondary mod2.c */
extern int x;
func4()
{
...
}
...
```

In Figure 22.5, the variable `x` is visible throughout all three modules. In contrast, `y` is visible only in the main module and secondary module 1.

DO	DON'T
DO create generic functions in their own source files. This way, they can be linked into any other programs that need them.	**DON'T** try to compile multiple source files together if more than one module contains a `main()` function. You can have only one `main()`. (You can have only one function of any name.)
	DON'T always use the C source files when compiling multiple files together. If you compile a source file into an object file, recompile only when the file changes. This saves a great deal of time.

The C Preprocessor

The preprocessor is a part of all C compiler packages. When you compile a C program, the preprocessor is the first compiler component that processes your program. In most C compilers, the preprocessor is part of the compiler program. When you run the compiler, it automatically runs the preprocessor.

22

The preprocessor changes your source code based on instructions, or *preprocessor directives,* in the source code. The output of the preprocessor is a modified source-code file that is then used as the input for the next compilation step. Normally, you never see this file because the compiler deletes it after it's used. However, later in this lesson, you learn how to look at this intermediate file. First, you need to learn about the preprocessor directives, which all begin with the # symbol.

The `#define` Preprocessor Directive

The `#define` preprocessor directive has two uses: creating symbolic constants and creating macros.

Simple Substitution Macros Using `#define`

You learned about substitution macros in Lesson 3, "Storing Information: Variables and Constants," although the term used to describe them in that lesson was *symbolic constants.* You create a substitution macro by using `#define` to replace text with other text. For example, to replace `text1` with `text2`, you write

```
#define text1 text2
```

This directive causes the preprocessor to go through the entire source-code file, replacing every occurrence of `text1` with `text2`. The only exception occurs if `text1` is found within double quotation marks, in which case no change is made.

The most frequent use for substitution macros is to create symbolic constants, as explained in Lesson 3. For example, if your program contains the following lines:

```
#define MAX 1000
x = y * MAX;
z = MAX - 12;
```

during preprocessing, the source code is changed to read as follows:

```
x = y * 1000;
z = 1000 - 12;
```

The effect is the same as using your editor's search-and-replace feature to change every occurrence of MAX to 1000. Your original source-code file isn't changed, of course. Instead, a temporary copy is created with the changes. Note that #define isn't limited to creating symbolic numeric constants. For example, you can write

```
#define ZINGBOFFLE printf ZINGBOFFLE("Hello, world.");
```

although there is little reason to do so. You should also be aware that some authors refer to symbolic constants defined with #define as being macros themselves. (Symbolic constants are also called *manifest constants*.) However, in this book, the word *macro* is reserved for the type of construction described next.

Creating Function Macros with #define

You can use the #define directive also to create function macros. A *function macro* is a type of shorthand, using something simple to represent something more complicated. The reason for the "function" name is that this type of macro can accept arguments, just like a real C function does. One advantage of function macros is that their arguments aren't type-sensitive. Therefore, you can pass any numeric variable type to a function macro that expects a numeric argument.

Now look at an example. The preprocessor directive

```
#define HALFOF(value) ((value)/2)
```

defines a macro named HALFOF that takes a parameter named value. Whenever the preprocessor encounters the text HALFOF(value) in the source code, it replaces it with the definition text and inserts the argument as needed. Thus, the source-code line

```
result = HALFOF(10);
```

is replaced by this line:

```
result = ((10)/2);
```

Likewise, the program line

```
printf("%f", HALFOF(x[1] + y[2]));
```

is replaced by this line:

```
printf("%f", ((x[1] + y[2])/2));
```

A macro can have more than one parameter, and each parameter can be used more than once in the replacement text. For example, the following macro, which calculates the average of five values, has five parameters:

```
#define AVG5(v, w, x, y, z) (((v)+(w)+(x)+(y)+(z))/5)
```

The following macro, in which the conditional operator determines the larger of two values, also uses each of its parameters twice. (You learned about the conditional operator in Lesson 4, "The Pieces of a C Program: Statements, Expressions, and Operators.")

```
#define LARGER(x, y) ((x) > (y) ? (x) : (y))
```

A macro can have as many parameters as needed, but all the parameters in the list must be used in the substitution string. For example, the macro definition

```
#define ADD(x, y, z) ((x) + (y))
```

is invalid because the parameter z is not used in the substitution string. Also, when you invoke the macro, you must pass it the correct number of arguments.

When you write a macro definition, the opening parenthesis must immediately follow the macro name; there can be no whitespace. The opening parenthesis tells the preprocessor that a function macro is being defined and that this isn't a simple symbolic constant type substitution. Look at the following definition:

```
#define SUM (x, y, z) ((x)+(y)+(z))
```

Because of the space between SUM and (, the preprocessor treats this like a simple substitution macro. Every occurrence of SUM in the source code is replaced with (x, y, z) ((x)+(y)+(z)), clearly not what you wanted.

Also note that in the substitution string, each parameter is enclosed in parentheses. This is necessary to avoid unwanted side effects when passing expressions as arguments to the macro. Look at the following example of a macro defined without parentheses:

```
#define SQUARE(x) x*x
```

If you invoke this macro with a simple variable as an argument, there's no problem. But what if you pass an expression as an argument?

```
result = SQUARE(x + y);
```

The resulting macro expansion is as follows, which doesn't give the proper result:

```
result = x + y * x + y;
```

If you use parentheses, you can avoid the problem, as shown in this example:

```
#define SQUARE(x) (x)*(x)
```

This definition expands to the following line, which does give the proper result:

```
result = (x + y)*(x + y);
```

You can obtain additional flexibility in macro definitions by using the *stringizing operator* (#) (sometimes called the *string-literal operator*). When a macro parameter is preceded by # in the substitution string, the argument is converted into a quoted string when the macro is expanded. Thus, if you define a macro as

```
#define OUT(x) printf(#x)
```

and you invoke it with the statement

```
OUT(Hello Mom);
```

it expands to this statement:

```
printf("Hello Mom");
```

The conversion performed by the stringizing operator takes special characters into account. Thus, if a character in the argument normally requires an escape character, the # operator inserts a backslash before the character. Continuing with the example, the invocation

```
OUT("Hello Mom");
```

expands to

```
printf("\"Hello Mom\"");
```

The # operator is demonstrated in Listing 22.4. First, you need to look at one other operator used in macros, the *concatenation operator* (##).This operator concatenates, or joins, two strings in the macro expansion. It doesn't include quotation marks or special treatment of escape characters. Its main use is to create sequences of C source code. For example, if you define and invoke a macro as

```
#define CHOP(x) func ## x
salad = CHOP(3)(q, w);
```

the macro invoked in the second line is expanded to

```
salad = func3 (q, w);
```

You can see that, by using the ## operator, you determine which function is called. You have actually modified the C source code.

Listing 22.4 shows an example of one way to use the # operator.

Input ▼

LISTING 22.4   macrorepl.c: Using the # Operator in Macro Expansion

```
1:  // macrorepl.c--Demonstrates the # operator in macro expansion.
2:
3:  #include <stdio.h>
4:
5:  #define OUT(x) printf(#x " is equal to %d.\n", x)
6:
7:  int main( void )
8:  {
9:    int value = 123;
10:   OUT(value);
11:   return(0);
12: }
```

Output ▼

```
value is equal to 123.
```

Analysis ▼

By using the # operator on line 5, the call to the macro expands with the variable name value as a quoted string passed to the printf() function. After expansion on line 9, the macro OUT looks like this:

```
printf("value" " is equal to %d.",  value );
```

Macros Versus Functions

You have seen that function macros can be used in place of real functions, at least in situations where the resulting code is relatively short. Function macros can extend beyond one line, but they usually become impractical beyond a few lines. When you can use either a function or a macro, which should you use? It's a trade-off between program speed and program size.

A macro's definition is expanded into the code each time the macro is encountered in the source code. If your program invokes a macro 100 times, 100 copies of the expanded macro code are in the final program. In contrast, a function's code exists only as a single copy. Therefore, in terms of program size, the better choice is a true function.

When a program calls a function, a certain amount of processing overhead is required to pass execution to the function code and then return execution to the calling program. There is no processing overhead in "calling" a macro because the code is right there in the program. In terms of speed, a function macro has the advantage.

These size/speed considerations aren't usually of much concern to the beginning programmer. Only with large, time-critical applications do they become important.

DO	DON'T
DO use #defines, especially for symbolic constants. Symbolic constants make your code much easier to read. Examples of things to put into defined constants are colors, true/false, yes/no, the keyboard keys, and maximum values. Symbolic constants are used throughout this book.	**DON'T** overuse macro functions. Use them where needed, but be sure they are a better choice than a normal function.

Using the #include **Directive**

You have already learned how to use the #include preprocessor directive to include header files in your program. When it encounters an #include directive, the preprocessor reads the specified file and inserts it at the location of the directive. You can't use the * or ? wildcards to read in a group of files with one #include directive. You can, however, nest #include directives. In other words, an included file can contain #include directives, which can contain #include directives, and so on. Most compilers limit the number of levels deep that you can nest, but if the compiler supports the ANSI Standard, then you usually already learned how to use the #include preprocessor directive to include header files that can nest up to 15 levels.

There are two ways to specify the filename for an #include directive. If the filename is enclosed in angle brackets, such as #include <stdio.h> (as you have seen throughout this book), the preprocessor first looks for the file in the standard directory. If the file isn't found, or no standard directory is specified, the preprocessor looks for the file in the current directory.

The second method of specifying the file to be included is enclosing the filename in double quotation marks: #include "myfile.h". In this case, the preprocessor doesn't search the standard directories; instead, it looks in the directory containing the source-code file being compiled. Generally speaking, header files that you write should be kept in the same directory as the C source-code files, and they are included by using double quotation marks. The standard directory is reserved for header files supplied with your compiler.

Using `#if`, `#elif`, `#else`, **and** `#endif`

These four preprocessor directives control conditional compilation. The term *conditional compilation* means that blocks of C source code are compiled only if certain conditions are met. In many ways, the `#if` family of preprocessor directives operates like the C language's `if` statement. The difference is that `if` controls whether certain statements are executed, whereas `#if` controls whether they are compiled.

The structure of an `#if` block is as follows:

```
#if condition_1
    statement_block_1
#elif condition_2
    statement_block_2
    ...
#elif condition_n
    statement_block_n
#else
    default_statement_block
#endif
```

The test expression that `#if` uses can be almost any expression that evaluates to a constant. You can't use the `sizeof()` operator, typecasts, or the `float` type. Most often you use `#if` to test symbolic constants created with the `#define` directive.

Each `statement_block` consists of one or more C statements of any type, including preprocessor directives. They don't need to be enclosed in braces, although they can be.

The `#if` and `#endif` directives are required, but `#elif` and `#else` are optional. You can have as many `#elif` directives as you want, but only one `#else`. When the compiler reaches an `#if` directive, it tests the associated condition. If it evaluates to TRUE (nonzero), the statements following the `#if` are compiled. If it evaluates to FALSE (zero), the compiler tests, in order, the conditions associated with each `#elif` directive. The statements associated with the first TRUE `#elif` are compiled. If none of the conditions evaluates as TRUE, the statements following the `#else` directive are compiled.

Note that, at most, a single block of statements within the `#if...#endif` construction is compiled. If the compiler finds no `#else` directive, it might not compile any statements.

The possible uses of these conditional compilation directives are limited only by your imagination. Here's one example: Suppose you're writing a program that uses a great deal of country-specific information. This information is contained in a header file for each country. When you compile the program for use in different countries, you can use an `#if...#endif` construction as follows:

```
#if ENGLAND == 1
#include "england.h"
#elif FRANCE == 1
#include "france.h"
#elif ITALY == 1
#include "italy.h"
#else
#include "usa.h"
#endif
```

Then, by using `#define` to define the appropriate symbolic constant, you can control which header file is included during compilation.

Using `#if...#endif` to Help Debug

Another common use of `#if...#endif` is to include conditional debugging code in the program. You could define a DEBUG symbolic constant set to either `1` or `0`. Throughout the program, you can insert debugging code as follows:

```
#if DEBUG == 1
  debugging code here
#endif
```

During program development, if you define DEBUG as `1`, the debugging code is included to help track down any bugs. After the program works properly, you can redefine DEBUG as `0` and recompile the program without the debugging code.

The `defined()` operator is useful when you write conditional compilation directives. This operator tests to see whether a particular name is defined. Thus, the expression

```
defined( NAME )
```

evaluates to TRUE or FALSE, depending on whether NAME is defined. By using `defined()`, you can control compilation, based on previous definitions, without regard to the specific value of a name. Referring to the previous debugging code example, you could rewrite the `#if...#endif` section as follows:

```
#if defined( DEBUG )
  debugging code here
#endif
```

You can also use `defined()` to assign a definition to a name only if it hasn't been previously defined. Use the NOT operator (`!`) as follows:

```
#if !defined( TRUE )      /* if TRUE is not defined. */
#define TRUE 1
#endif
```

Notice that the defined() operator doesn't require that a name be defined as anything in particular. For example, after the following program line, the name RED is defined, but not as anything in particular:

```
#define RED
```

Even so, the expression defined(RED) still evaluates as TRUE. Of course, occurrences of RED in the source code are removed and not replaced with anything, so you must use caution.

Avoiding Multiple Inclusions of Header Files

As programs grow, or as you use header files more often, you run the risk of accidentally including a header file more than once. This can cause the compiler to balk in confusion. Using the directives that you've learned, you can easily avoid this problem. Look at the example shown in Listing 22.5.

Input ▼
LISTING 22.5   prog.h: Using Preprocessor Directives with Header Files

```
1:  // prog.h--A header file with a check to prevent multiple includes!
2:
3.  #if defined( prog_h )
4:  // the file has been included already
5:  #else
6:  #define prog_h
7:
8:  // Header file information goes here...
9:
10:
11:
12: #endif
```

Analysis ▼

Examine what this header file does. On line 3, it checks whether prog_h is defined. Notice that prog_h is similar to the name of the header file. If prog_h is defined, a comment is included on line 4, and the program looks for the #endif at the end of the header file. This means that nothing more is done.

How does prog_h get defined? It is defined on line 6. The first time this header is included, the preprocessor checks whether prog_h is defined. It won't be, so control goes to the #else statement. The first thing done after the #else is to define prog_h so that any other inclusions of this file skip the body of the file. Lines 7 through 11 can contain any number of commands or declarations.

<table>
<tr><td>TIP</td><td>You should include preprocessor directive checks, as shown in Listing 22.5, with all the header files you create. This prevents them from being included multiple times.</td></tr>
</table>

The #undef **Directive**

The #undef directive is the opposite of #define; it removes the definition from a name. Here's an example:

```
#define DEBUG 1
   /* In this section of the program, occurrences of DEBUG      */
   /* are replaced with 1, and the expression defined( DEBUG ) */
   /* evaluates to TRUE. *.
#undef DEBUG
   /* In this section of the program, occurrences of DEBUG   */
   /* are not replaced, and the expression defined( DEBUG ) */
   /* evaluates to FALSE. */
```

You can use #undef and #define to create a name that is defined only in parts of your source code. You can use this in combination with the #if directive, as explained earlier, for more control over conditional compilations.

Predefined Macros

Most compilers have a number of predefined macros. The most useful of these are __DATE__, __TIME__, __LINE__, and __FILE__. Notice that each of these are preceded and followed by double underscores. This is done to prevent you from redefining them, on the theory that programmers are unlikely to create their own definitions with leading and trailing underscores.

These macros work just like the macros described earlier in this lesson. When the precompiler encounters one of these macros, it replaces the macro with the macro's code. __DATE__ and __TIME__ are replaced with the current date and time. This is the date and time the source file is precompiled. This can be useful information as you work with different versions of a program. By having a program display its compilation date and time, you can tell whether you're running the latest version of the program or an earlier one.

The other two macros are even more valuable. __LINE__ is replaced by the current source-file line number. __FILE__ is replaced with the current source-code filename. These two macros are best used when you debug a program or deal with errors. Consider the following printf() statement:

```
31:
32: printf( "Program %s: (%d) Error opening file ", __FILE__, __LINE__ );
33:
```

If these lines were part of a program called myprog.c, they would print

```
Program myprog.c: (32) Error opening file
```

This might not seem important at this point, but as your programs grow and spread across multiple source files, finding errors becomes more difficult. Using __LINE__ and __FILE__ makes debugging much easier.

22

DO	DON'T
DO use the __LINE__ and __FILE__ macros to make your error messages more helpful.	**DON'T** forget the #endif when using the #if statement.
DO put parentheses around the value to be passed to a macro. This prevents errors. For example, use this:	
`#define CUBE(x)    (x)*(x)*(x)`	
instead of this:	
`#define CUBE(x)    x*x*x`	

Using Command-Line Arguments

Your C program can access arguments passed to the program on the command line. This refers to information entered after the program name when you start the program. If you start a program named progname from the C:\> prompt, for example, you could enter

```
C:\>progname smith jones
```

The two command-line arguments smith and jones can be retrieved by the program during execution. You can think of this information as arguments passed to the program's main() function. Such command-line arguments permit information to be passed to the program at startup rather than during execution, which can be convenient at times. You can pass as many command-line arguments as you like. Note that command-line arguments can be retrieved only within main(). To do so, declare main () as follows:

```
main(int argc, char *argv[])
{
    /* Statements go here */
}
```

The first parameter, `argc`, is an integer giving the number of command-line arguments available. This value is always at least `1` because the program name is counted as the first argument. The parameter `argv[]` is an array of pointers to strings. The valid subscripts for this array are `0` through `argc - 1`. The pointer `argv[0]` points to the program name (including path information), `argv[1]` points to the first argument that follows the program name, and so on. Note that the names `argc` and `argv[]` aren't required—you can use any valid C variable names you like to receive the command-line arguments. However, these two names are traditionally used for this purpose, so you should probably stick with them.

The command line is divided into discrete arguments by any whitespace. If you need to pass an argument that includes a space, enclose the entire argument in double quotation marks. For example, if you enter

```
C:>progname smith "and jones"
```

`smith` is the first argument (pointed to by `argv[1]`); and `jones` is the second (pointed to by `argv[2]`). Listing 22.6 demonstrates how to access command-line arguments in your programs.

Input ▼

LISTING 22.6 commandargs.c: Passing Command-Line Arguments to `main()`

```
1:  // commandargs.c--Accessing command-line arguments.
2:
3:  #include <stdio.h>
4:
5:  int main(int argc, char *argv[])
6:  {
7:      int count;
8:
9:      printf("Program name: %s\n", argv[0]);
10:
11:     if (argc > 1)
12:     {
13:         for (count = 1; count < argc; count++)
14:             printf("Argument %d: %s\n", count, argv[count]);
15:     }
16:     else
17:         puts("No command-line arguments entered.");
18:     return(0);
19: }
```

Output ▼

```
list22_6
Program name: C:\LIST2206.EXE
No command line arguments entered.

list2206 first second "3 4"
Program name: C:\LIST22_6.EXE
Argument 1: first
Argument 2: second
Argument 3: 3 4
```

Analysis ▼

This program does no more than print the command-line parameters entered by the user. Notice that line 5 uses the `argc` and `argv` parameters shown previously. Line 9 prints the one command-line parameter that you always have, the program name. Notice this is `argv[0]`. Line 11 checks to see whether there is more than one command-line parameter. Why more than one and not more than zero? Because there is always at least one—the program name. If there are additional arguments, a `for` loop prints each to the screen (lines 13 and 14). Otherwise, an appropriate message is printed (line 17).

Command-line arguments generally fall into two categories: those that are required because the program can't operate without them, and those that are optional, such as flags that instruct the program to act in a certain way. For example, imagine a program that sorts the data in a file. If you write the program to receive the input filename from the command line, the name is required information. If the user forgets to enter the input filename on the command line, the program must somehow deal with the situation. The program could also look for the argument `/r`, which signals a reverse-order sort. This argument isn't required; the program looks for it and behaves one way if it's found and another way if it isn't.

NOTE

Graphical IDEs usually enable you to enter command-line arguments into a dialog box. Each IDE handles this differently, so you just need to consult the help on your specific program.

DO	DON'T
DO use `argc` and `argv` as the variable names for the command-line arguments for `main()`. Most C programmers are familiar with these names.	**DON'T** assume that users will enter the correct number of command-line parameters. Check to be sure they did, and if not, display a message explaining the arguments they should enter.

Summary

In this lesson, you covered some of the more advanced programming tools available with C compilers. You learned how to write a program that has source code divided among multiple files or modules. This practice, called modular programming, makes it easy to reuse general-purpose functions in more than one program. You saw how you can use preprocessor directives to create function macros, for conditional compilation and other tasks. Finally, you saw that the compiler provides some function macros for you.

Q&A

Q **When compiling multiple files, how does the compiler know which filename to use for the executable file?**

A You might think the compiler uses the name of the file containing the `main()` function; however, this isn't usually the case. When compiling from the command line, the first file listed is used to determine the name.

Q **Do header files need to have an .h extension?**

A No. You can give a header file any name you want. It is standard practice to use the .h extension.

Q **When including header files, can I use an explicit path?**

A Yes. If you want to state the path where a file to be included is, you can. In such a case, you put the name of the include file between quotation marks.

Q **Are all the predefined macros and preprocessor directives presented in this lesson?**

A No. The predefined macros and directives presented in this lesson are ones common to most compilers. However, most compilers also have additional macros and constants.

Q **Is the following header also acceptable when using `main()` with command-line parameters?**

```
main( int argc, char **argv);
```

A You can probably answer this one on your own. This declaration uses a pointer to a character pointer instead of a pointer to a character array. Because an array is a pointer, this definition is virtually the same as the one presented in this lesson. This declaration is also commonly used. (See Lesson 8, "Using Numeric Arrays," and Lesson 10, "Working with Characters and Strings," for more details.)

Workshop

The Workshop provides quiz questions to help you solidify your understanding of the material covered and exercises to provide you with experience in using what you've learned.

Quiz

1. What does the term *modular programming* mean?

2. In modular programming, what is the main module?

3. When you define a macro, why should each argument be enclosed in parentheses?

4. What are the pros and cons of using a macro in place of a regular function?

5. What does the `defined()` operator do?

6. What must always be used if `#if` is used?

7. What extension do compiled C files have? (Assume that they have not been linked.)

8. What does `#include` do?

9. What is the difference between this line of code

   ```
   #include <myfile.h>
   ```

   and the following line of code?

   ```
   #include "myfile.h"
   ```

10. What is `__DATE__` used for?

11. What does `argv[0]` point to?

Exercises

Because many solutions are possible for the following exercises, answers are not provided.

1. Use your compiler to compile multiple source files into a single executable file. (You can use Listings 22.1, 22.2, and 22.3 or your own listings.)

2. Write an error routine that receives an error number, line number, and module name. The routine should print a formatted error message and then exit the program. Use the predefined macros for the line number and module name. (Pass the line number and module name from the location where the error occurs.) Here's a possible example of a formatted error:

   ```
   module.c (Line ##): Error number ##
   ```

3. Modify exercise 2 to make the error message more descriptive. Create a text file with your editor that contains an error number and message. Call this file ERRORS.TXT. It could contain information such as the following:

   ```
   1     Error number 1
   2     Error number 2
   90    Error opening file
   100   Error reading file
   ```

   Have your error routine search this file and display the appropriate error message based on a number passed to it.

4. Some header files might be included more than once when you write a modular program. Use preprocessor directives to write the skeleton of a header file that compiles only the first time it is encountered during compilation.

5. Write a program that takes two filenames as command-line parameters. The program should copy the first file into the second file. (See Lesson 17, "Using Disk Files," if you need help working with files.)

6. This is the last exercise of the book and its content is up to you. Select a programming task of interest to you that also meets a real need you have. For example, you could write programs to catalog your MP3 collection, keep track of your checkbook, or calculate financial figures related to a planned house purchase. There's no substitute for tackling a real-world programming problem to sharpen your programming skills and help you remember all the things you learned in this book.

APPENDIX A
ASCII Chart

Dec	Hex	ASCII	Dec	Hex	ASCII
0	00	null	31	1F	▼
1	01	☺	32	20	space
2	02	☻	33	21	!
3	03	♥	34	22	"
4	04	♦	35	23	#
5	05	♣	36	24	$
6	06	♠	37	25	%
7	07	•	38	26	&
8	08	◘	39	27	'
9	09	○	40	28	(
10	0A	◙	41	29	)
11	0B	♂	42	2A	*
12	0C	♀	43	2B	+
13	0D	♪	44	2C	'
14	0E	♫	45	2D	-
15	0F	☼	46	2E	.
16	10	►	47	2F	/
17	11	◄	48	30	0
18	12	↕	49	31	1
19	13	‼	50	32	2
20	14	¶	51	33	3
21	15	§	52	34	4
22	16	▬	53	35	5
23	17	↨	54	36	6
24	18	↑	55	37	7
25	19	↓	56	38	8
26	1A	→	57	39	9
27	1B	←	58	3A	:
28	1C	∟	59	3B	;
29	1D	↔	60	3C	<
30	1E	▲	61	3D	=
			62	3E	>
			63	3F	?
			64	40	@
			65	41	A

Dec	Hex	ASCII	Dec	Hex	ASCII
66	42	B	101	65	e
67	43	C	102	66	f
68	44	D	103	67	g
69	45	E	104	68	h
70	46	F	105	69	i
71	47	G	106	6A	j
72	48	H	107	6B	k
73	49	I	108	6C	l
74	4A	J	109	6D	m
75	4B	K	110	6E	n
76	4C	L	111	6F	o
77	4D	M	112	70	p
78	4E	N	113	71	q
79	4F	O	114	72	r
80	50	P	115	73	s
81	51	Q	116	74	t
82	52	R	117	75	u
83	53	S	118	76	v
84	54	T	119	77	w
85	55	U	120	78	x
86	56	V	121	79	y
87	57	W	122	7A	z
88	58	X	123	7B	{
89	59	Y	124	7C	¦
90	5A	Z	125	7D	}
91	5B	[	126	7E	~
92	5C	\	127	7F	Δ
93	5D	]	128	80	Ç
94	5E	^	129	81	ü
95	5F	–	130	82	é
96	60	`	131	83	â
97	61	a	132	84	ä
98	62	b	133	85	à
99	63	c	134	86	å
100	64	d	135	87	ç

A

Dec	Hex	ASCII	Dec	Hex	ASCII
136	88	ê	170	AA	¬
137	89	ë	171	AB	½
138	8A	è	172	AC	¼
139	8B	ï	173	AD	
140	8C	î	174	AE	«
141	8D	ì	175	AF	»
142	8E	Ä	176	B0	
143	8F	Å	177	B1	
144	90	É	178	B2	
145	91	æ	179	B3	│
146	92	Æ	180	B4	┤
147	93	ô	181	B5	╡
148	94	ö	182	B6	╢
149	95	ò	183	B7	╖
150	96	û	184	B8	╕
151	97	ù	185	B9	╣
152	98	ÿ	186	BA	║
153	99	Ö	187	BB	╗
154	9A	Ü	188	BC	╝
155	9B	¢	189	BD	╜
156	9C	£	190	BE	╛
157	9D	¥	191	BF	┐
158	9E	₧	192	C0	└
159	9F	ƒ	193	C1	┴
160	A0	á	194	C2	┬
161	A1	í	195	C3	├
162	A2	ó	196	C4	─
163	A3	ú	197	C5	┼
164	A4	ñ	198	C6	╞
165	A5	Ñ	199	C7	╟
166	A6	ª	200	C8	╚
167	A7	º			
168	A8	¿			
169	A9	⌐			

Dec	Hex	ASCII	Dec	Hex	ASCII
201	C9	╔	232	E8	Φ
202	CA	╩	233	E9	θ
203	CB	╦	234	EA	Ω
204	CC	╠	235	EB	δ
205	CD	=	236	EC	∞
206	CE	╬	237	ED	ø
207	CF	╧	238	EE	∈
208	D0	╨	239	EF	∩
209	D1	╤	240	F0	Å
210	D2	╥	241	F1	±
211	D3	╙	242	F2	≥
212	D4	╘	243	F3	≤
213	D5	╒	244	F4	⌠
214	D6	╓	245	F5	⌡
215	D7	╫	246	F6	÷
216	D8	╪	247	F7	≈
217	D9	┘	248	F8	°
218	DA	┌	249	F9	•
219	DB		250	FA	·
220	DC	▄	251	FB	√
221	DD	▌	252	FC	ⁿ
222	DE	▐	253	FD	^{2}
223	DF	▀	254	FE	■
224	E0	α	255	FF	
225	E1	β			
226	E2	Γ			
227	E3	π			
228	E4	Σ			
229	E5	σ			
230	E6	μ			
231	E7	γ			

A

APPENDIX B
C/C++ Reserved Words

The identifiers listed in Table B.1 are reserved keywords for C. You shouldn't use them for any other purpose in a C program. They are allowed, of course, within double quotation marks.

Also included is a list of words that aren't reserved in C but are C++ reserved words. These C++ reserved words aren't described here, but if there's a chance your C programs might eventually be ported to C++, you need to avoid these words as well.

TABLE B.1   Reserved C Keywords

Keyword	Description
asm	Keyword that denotes inline assembly language code.
auto	The default storage class. Means to create the variable on entry to the block and destroy it on exit from the block.
break	Command that exits `for`, `while`, `switch`, and `do...while` statements unconditionally.
case	Command used within the `switch` statement.
char	The simplest C data type.
const	Data modifier that prevents a variable from being changed. See `volatile`.
continue	Command that resets a `for`, `while`, or `do...while` statement to the next iteration.
default	Command used within the `switch` statement to catch any instances not specified with a `case` statement.
do	Looping command used with the `while` statement. The loop will always execute at least once.
double	Data type that can hold double-precision floating-point values.
else	Statement signaling alternative statements to be executed when an `if` statement evaluates to FALSE.

Keyword	Description
enum	Data type that enables variables to be declared that accept only certain values.
extern	Data modifier indicating that a variable will be declared in another area of the program.
float	Data type used for floating-point numbers.
for	Looping command that contains initialization, incrementation, and conditional sections.
goto	Command that causes a jump to a predefined label.
if	Command used to change program flow based on a TRUE/FALSE decision.
inline	Used to declare a function as inline. Inline functions can be copied into the listing rather than called like a regular function.
int	Data type used to hold integer values.
long	Data type used to hold larger integer values than int.
register	Storage modifier that specifies that a variable should be stored in a register if possible.
restrict	An access modifier used with pointers.
return	Command that causes program flow to exit from the current function and return to the calling function. It can also be used to return a single value.
short	Data type used to hold integers. It isn't commonly used, and it's the same size as an int on most computers.
signed	Modifier used to signify that a variable can have both positive and negative values. See unsigned.
sizeof	Operator that returns the size of the item in bytes.
static	Modifier used to signify that the compiler should retain the variable's value. Also can be used to limit the scope of a variable or function.
struct	Keyword used to combine C variables of any data type into a group.
switch	Command used to change program flow in a multitude of directions. Used with the case statement.
typedef	Modifier used to create new names for existing variable and function types.
union	Keyword used to allow multiple variables to share the same memory space.
unsigned	Modifier used to signify that a variable will contain only positive values. See signed.
void	Keyword used to signify either that a function doesn't return anything or that a pointer being used is considered generic or able to point to any data type.
volatile	Modifier that signifies that a variable can be changed. See const.

Keyword	Description
while	Looping statement that executes a section of code as long as a condition remains TRUE.
_Bool	A type large enough to store a value of 0 or 1.
_Complex	Support for complex types. It is not required that _Complex be supported.
_Imaginary	Support for imaginary types. It is not required that _Imaginary be supported.

In addition to the preceding keywords, the following are C++ reserved words:

catch	new	template
class	operator	this
delete	private	throw
except	protected	try
finally	public	virtual
friend		

B

APPENDIX C
Common C Functions

This appendix lists the function prototypes contained in each of the header files supplied with most C compilers. Functions that have an asterisk after them were covered in this book.

The functions are listed alphabetically. Following each name and header file is the complete prototype. Notice that the header file prototypes use a notation different from that used in this book. For each parameter a function takes, only the type is given in the prototype; no parameter name is included. Here are two examples:

```
int func1(int, int *);
int func1(int x, int *y);
```

Both declarations specify two parameters—the first a type `int`, and the second a pointer to type `int`. As far as the compiler is concerned, these two declarations are equivalent.

TABLE C.1   Common C Functions Listed in Alphabetical Order

Function	Header File	Function Prototype
abort*	stdlib.h	void abort(void);
abs	stdlib.h	int abs(int);
acos*	math.h	double acos(double);
asctime*	time.h	char *asctime(const struct tm *);
asin*	math.h	double asin(double);
assert*	assert.h	void assert(int);
atan*	math.h	double atan(double);
atan2*	math.h	double atan2(double, double);
atexit*	stdlib.h	int atexit(void (*)(void));
atof*	stdlib.h	double atof(const char *);
atof*	math.h	double atof(const char *);
atoi*	stdlib.h	int atoi(const char *);

Function	Header File	Function Prototype
atol*	stdlib.h	long atol(const char *);
bsearch*	stdlib.h	void *bsearch(const void *, const void *, size_t, size_t, int(*) (const void *, const void *));
calloc*	stdlib.h	void *calloc(size_t, size_t);
ceil*	math.h	double ceil(double);
clearerr	stdio.h	void clearerr(FILE *);
clock*	time.h	clock_t clock(void);
cos*	math.h	double cos(double);
cosh*	math.h	double cosh(double);
ctime*	time.h	char *ctime(const time_t *);
difftime	time.h	double difftime(time_t, time_t);
div	stdlib.h	div_t div(int, int);
exit*	stdlib.h	void exit(int);
exp*	math.h	double exp(double);
fabs*	math.h	double fabs(double);
fclose*	stdio.h	int fclose(FILE *);
fcloseall*	stdio.h	int fcloseall(void);
feof*	stdio.h	int feof(FILE *);
fflush*	stdio.h	int fflush(FILE *);
fgetc*	stdio.h	int fgetc(FILE *);
fgetpos	stdio.h	int fgetpos(FILE *, fpos_t *);
fgets*	stdio.h	char *fgets(char *, int, FILE *);
floor*	math.h	double floor(double);
flushall*	stdio.h	int flushall(void);
fmod*	math.h	double fmod(double, double);
fopen*	stdio.h	FILE *fopen(const char *, const char *);
fprintf*	stdio.h	int fprintf(FILE *, const char *, ...);
fputc*	stdio.h	int fputc(int, FILE *);
fputs*	stdio.h	int fputs(const char *, FILE *);
fread*	stdio.h	size_t fread(void *, size_t, size_t, FILE *);
free*	stdlib.h	void free(void *);
freopen	stdio.h	FILE *freopen(const char *, const char *, FILE *);
frexp*	math.h	double frexp(double, int *);
fscanf*	stdio.h	int fscanf(FILE *, const char *, ...);

Function	Header File	Function Prototype
fseek[*]	stdio.h	int fseek(FILE *, long, int);
fsetpos	stdio.h	int fsetpos(FILE *, const fpos_t *);
ftell[*]	stdio.h	long ftell(FILE *);
fwrite[*]	stdio.h	size_t fwrite(const void *, size_t, size_t, FILE *);
getc[*]	stdio.h	int getc(FILE *);
getch[*]	stdio.h	int getch(void);
getchar[*]	stdio.h	int getchar(void);
getche[*]	stdio.h	int getche(void);
getenv	stdlib.h	char *getenv(const char *);
gets[*]	stdio.h	char *gets(char *);
gmtime	time.h	struct tm *gmtime(const time_t *);
isalnum[*]	ctype.h	int isalnum(int);
isalpha[*]	ctype.h	int isalpha(int);
isascii[*]	ctype.h	int isascii(int);
iscntrl[*]	ctype.h	int iscntrl(int);
isdigit[*]	ctype.h	int isdigit(int);
isgraph[*]	ctype.h	int isgraph(int);
islower[*]	ctype.h	int islower(int);
isprint[*]	ctype.h	int isprint(int);
ispunct[*]	ctype.h	int ispunct(int);
isspace[*]	ctype.h	int isspace(int);
isupper[*]	ctype.h	int isupper(int);
isxdigit[*]	ctype.h	int isxdigit(int);
labs	stdlib.h	long int labs(long int);
ldexp	math.h	double ldexp(double, int);
ldiv	stdlib.h	ldiv_t div(long int, long int);
localtime[*]	time.h	struct tm *localtime(const time_t *);
log[*]	math.h	double log(double);
log10[*]	math.h	double log10(double);
malloc[*]	stdlib.h	void *malloc(size_t);
mblen	stdlib.h	int mblen(const char *, size_t);
mbstowcs	stdlib.h	size_t mbstowcs(wchar_t *, const char *, size_t);
mbtowc	stdlib.h	int mbtowc(wchar_t *, const char *, size_t);

C

Function	Header File	Function Prototype
memchr	string.h	void *memchr(const void *, int, size_t);
memcmp	string.h	int memcmp(const void *, const void *, size_t);
memcpy	string.h	void *memcpy(void *, const void *, size_t);
memmove	string.h	void *memmove(void *, const void*, size_t);
memset	string.h	void *memset(void *, int, size_t);
mktime*	time.h	time_t mktime(struct tm *);
modf	math.h	double modf(double, double *);
perror*	stdio.h	void perror(const char *);
pow*	math.h	double pow(double, double);
printf*	stdio.h	int printf(const char *, ...);
putc*	stdio.h	int putc(int, FILE *);
putchar*	stdio.h	int putchar(int);
puts*	stdio.h	int puts(const char *);
qsort*	stdlib.h	void qsort(void*, size_t, size_t, int (*) (const void*, const void *));
rand	stdlib.h	int rand(void);
realloc*	stdlib.h	void *realloc(void *, size_t);
remove*	stdio.h	int remove(const char *);
rename*	stdio.h	int rename(const char *, const char *);
rewind*	stdio.h	void rewind(FILE *);
scanf*	stdio.h	int scanf(const char *, ...);
setbuf	stdio.h	void setbuf(FILE *, char *);
setvbuf	stdio.h	int setvbuf(FILE *, char *, int, size_t);
sin*	math.h	double sin(double);
sinh*	math.h	double sinh(double);
sleep*	time.h	void sleep(time_t);
sprintf	stdio.h	int sprintf(char *, const char *, ...);
sqrt*	math.h	double sqrt(double);
srand	stdlib.h	void srand(unsigned);
sscanf	stdio.h	int sscanf(const char *, const char *, ...);
strcat*	string.h	char *strcat(char *,const char *);
strchr*	string.h	char *strchr(const char *, int);
strcmp*	string.h	int strcmp(const char *, const char *);

Function	Header File	Function Prototype
strcmpl*	string.h	int strcmpl(const char *, const char *);
strcpy*	string.h	char *strcpy(char *, const char *);
strcspn*	string.h	size_t strcspn(const char *, const char *);
strdup*	string.h	char *strdup(const char *);
strerror	string.h	char *strerror(int);
strftime*	time.h	size_t strftime(char *, size_t, const char *, const struct tm *);
strlen*	string.h	size_t strlen(const char *);
strlwr*	string.h	char *strlwr(char *);
strncat*	string.h	char *strncat(char *, const char *, size_t);
strncmp*	string.h	int strncmp(const char *, const char *, size_t);
strncpy*	string.h	char *strncpy(char *, const char *, size_t);
strnset*	string.h	char *strnset(char *, int, size_t);
strpbrk*	string.h	char *strpbrk(const char *, const char *);
strrchr*	string.h	char *strrchr(const char *, int);
strspn*	string.h	size_t strspn(const char *, const char *);
strstr*	string.h	char *strstr(const char *, const char *);
strtod	stdlib.h	double strtod(const char *, char **);
strtok	string.h	char *strtok(char *, const char*);
strtol	stdlib.h	long strtol(const char *, char **, int);
strtoul	stdlib.h	unsigned long strtoul(const char*, char **, int);
strupr*	string.h	char *strupr(char *);
system*	stdlib.h	int system(const char *);
tan*	math.h	double tan(double);
tanh*	math.h	double tanh(double);
time*	time.h	time_t time(time_t *);
tmpfile	stdio.h	FILE *tmpfile(void);
tmpnam*	stdio.h	char *tmpnam(char *);
tolower	ctype.h	int tolower(int);
toupper	ctype.h	int toupper(int);

C

Function	Header File	Function Prototype
ungetc*	stdio.h	int ungetc(int, FILE *);
va_arg*	stdarg.h	(type) va_arg(va_list, (type));
va_end*	stdarg.h	void va_end(va_list);
va_start*	stdarg.h	void va_start(va_list, lastfix);
vfprintf	stdio.h	int vfprintf(FILE *, constchar *, ...);
vprintf	stdio.h	int vprintf(FILE*, constchar *, ...);
vsprintf	stdio.h	int vsprintf(char *, constchar *, ...);
wcstombs	stdlib.h	size_t wcstombs(char *, const wchar_t *, size_t);
wctomb	stdlib.h	int wctomb(char *, wchar_t);

APPENDIX D
Answers

Answers for Lesson 1

Quiz

1. C is powerful, popular, and portable.

2. The compiler translates C source code into machine-language instructions that your computer can understand.

3. Editing, compiling, linking, and testing.

4. The answer to this question depends on your compiler. Consult your compiler's manuals.

5. The answer to this question depends on your compiler. Consult your compiler's manuals.

6. The appropriate extension for C source files is .C (or .c).

   Note: C++ uses the extension .CPP. You can write and compile your C programs with a .CPP extension, but it's more appropriate to use a .C extension.

7. FILENAME.TXT would compile. However, it's more appropriate to use a .C extension rather than .TXT.

8. You should make changes to the source code to correct the problems. You should then recompile and relink. After relinking, you should run the program again to see whether your corrections fixed the program.

9. Machine language is made up of digital or binary instructions that the computer can understand. Because the computer can't understand C source code, a compiler translates source code to machine code, also called object code.

10. The linker combines the object code from your program with the object code from the function library and creates an executable file.

Exercises

1. When you look at the object file, you see many unusual characters and other gibberish. Mixed in with the gibberish, you also see pieces of the source file.

2. This program calculates the area of a circle. It prompts the user for the radius and then displays the area.

3. This program prints a 10×10 block made of the character x. A similar program is covered in Lesson 6, "Basic Program Control."

4. This program generates a compiler error. You should get a message similar to the following:

```
Error: ch1ex4.c: Declaration terminated incorrectly
```

This error is caused by the semicolon at the end of line 3. If you remove the semicolon, this program should compile and link correctly.

5. This program compiles okay, but it generates a linker error. You should get a message similar to the following:

```
Error: Undefined symbol _do_it in module...
```

This error occurs because the linker can't find a function called `do_it`. To fix this program, change `do_it` to `printf`.

6. Rather than printing a 10×10 block filled with the character x, the program now prints a 10×10 block of smiley faces.

Answers for Lesson 2

Quiz

1. A block.

2. The `main()` function.

3. You use program comments to make notations about the program's structure and operation. Any text between `/*` and `*/` is a program comment and is ignored by the compiler. In addition, you can use single-line comments. Any text on the same line following two forward slashes (`//`) is considered a comment.

4. A function is an independent section of program code that performs a certain task and has been assigned a name. By using a function's name, a program can execute the code in the function.

5. A user-defined function is created by the programmer. A library function is supplied with the C compiler.

6. An `#include` directive instructs the compiler to add the code from another file into your source code during the compilation process.

7. Comments shouldn't be nested. Although some compilers enable you to do this, others don't. To keep your code portable, you shouldn't nest comments.

8. Yes. Comments can be as long as needed. A comment can start with `/*` and won't end until a `*/` is encountered.

9. An include file is also known as a header file.

10. An include file is a separate disk file that contains information needed by the compiler to use various functions, variables, constants, and macros.

Exercises

1. Remember, only the `main()` function is required in C programs. The following is the smallest possible program, but it doesn't do anything:

```
void main(void)
{
}
```

This also could be written

```
void main(void){}
```

2. a. Statements are on lines 8, 9, 10, 12, 18, 20, and 21.

b. The only variable definition is on line 18.

c. The only function prototype (for `display_line()`) is on line 4.

d. The function definition for `display_line()` is on lines 16 through 22.

e. Comments are on lines 1, 15, and 23.

3. A comment is any text included between `/*` and `*/` or after `//`. Examples include the following:

```
/* This is a comment */
/*???*/

// Here is a comment in a different style

/ * This is a
   multiline
   comment */
```

4. This program prints the alphabet in all capital letters. You should understand this program better after you finish Chapter 10, "Working with Characters and Strings."

D

The output is

```
ABCDEFGHIJKLMNOPQRSTUVWXYZ
```

5. This program counts and prints the number of characters and spaces you enter. This program also will be clearer after you finish Chapter 10.

Answers for Lesson 3

Quiz

1. An integer variable can hold a whole number (a number without a fractional part), and a floating-point variable can hold a real number (a number with a fractional part).

2. A type `double` variable has a greater range than type `float`. (It can hold larger and smaller values.) A type `double` variable also is more precise than type `float`.

3. a. The size of a `char` is 1 byte.

    b. The size of a `short` is less than or equal to the size of an `int`.

    c. The size of an `int` is less than or equal to the size of a `long`.

    d. The size of an `unsigned` is equal to the size of an `int`.

    e. The size of a `float` is less than or equal to the size of a `double`.

4. The names of symbolic constants make your source code easier to read. They also make it much easier to change the constant's value.

5. a. `#define MAXIMUM 100`

    b. `const int MAXIMUM = 100;`

6. Letters, numerals, and underscores.

7. Names of variables and constants should describe the data being stored. Variable names should be in lowercase, and constant names should be in uppercase.

8. Symbolic constants are symbols that represent literal constants.

9. If it's an `unsigned int` that is 2 bytes long, the minimum value it can hold is 0. If it is signed, –32,768 is the minimum.

Exercises

1. a. Because a person's age can be considered a whole number, and a person can't be a negative age, an `unsigned int` is suggested.

    b. `unsigned int`

c. `float`

d. If your expectations for a yearly salary aren't high, a simple `unsigned int` variable would work. If you feel you have the potential to go above $65,535, you probably should use a `long`. (Have faith in yourself; use a `long`.)

e. `float`. (Don't forget the decimal places for the cents.)

f. Because the highest grade will always be 100, it is a constant. Use either `const short` or a `#define` statement.

g. `char`

h. `float`. (If you're going to use only whole numbers, use either `int` or `long`.)

i. Definitely a signed field. Either `int`, `long`, or `float`. See answer 1.d.

j. `long double`

2. Answers for exercises 2 and 3 are combined here.

   Remember, a variable name should be representative of the value it holds. A variable declaration is the statement that initially creates the variable. The declaration might or might not initialize the variable to a value. You can use any name for a variable, except the C keywords.

   a. `unsigned int age;`

   b. `unsigned int friends;`

   c. `float radius = 3;`

   d. `long annual_salary;`

   e. `float cost = 29.95;`

   f. `const int max_grade = 100;` or `#define MAX_GRADE 100`

   g. `char first_initial = 'G';`

   h. `float temperature;`

   i. `long net_worth = -30000;`

   j. `double star_distance;`

3. See answer 2.

4. The valid variable names are b, c, e, g, h, i, and j.

   Notice that j is correct; however, it isn't wise to use variable names that are this long. (Besides, who would want to type them?) Most compilers wouldn't look at this entire name. Instead, they would look only at the first 31 characters or so.

   The following are invalid:

   a. You can't start a variable name with a number.

D

d. You can't use a pound sign (#) in a variable name.

e. You can't use a hyphen (-) in a variable name.

Answers for Lesson 4

Quiz

1. It is an assignment statement that instructs the computer to add 5 and 8, assigning the result to the variable x.

2. An expression is anything that evaluates to a numerical value.

3. The relative precedence of the operators.

4. After the first statement, the value of a is 10, and the value of x is 11. After the second statement, both a and x have the value 11. (The statements must be executed separately.)

5. 1

6. 19

7. (5 + 3) * 8 / (2 + 2)

8. 0

9. See the section "Operator Precedence Revisited" near the end of this lesson. It shows the C operators and their precedence.

   a. < has higher precedence than == does.

   b. * has higher precedence than + does.

   c. != and == have the same precedence, so they are evaluated left-to-right.

   d. >= has the same precedence as >. Use parentheses if you need to use more than one relational operator in a single statement or expression.

10. The compound assignment operators enable you to combine a binary mathematical operation with an assignment operation, thus providing a shorthand notation. The compound operators presented in this chapter are +=, -=, /=, *=, and %=.

Exercises

1. This listing should have worked, even though it is poorly structured. The purpose of this listing is to demonstrate that whitespace is irrelevant to how the program runs. You should use whitespace to make your programs readable.

2. The following is a better way to structure the listing from exercise 1:

```
#include <stdio.h>

int x, y;

int main( void )
{
    printf("\nEnter two numbers ");
    scanf( "%d %d",&x,&y);
    printf("\n\n%d is bigger\n",(x>y)?x:y);
    return 0;
}
```

This listing asks for two numbers, x and y, and then prints whichever one is bigger.

3. The only changes needed in Listing 4.1 are the following:

```
16:     printf("\n%d    %d", a++, ++b);
17:     printf("\n%d    %d", a++, ++b);
18:     printf("\n%d    %d", a++, ++b);
19:     printf("\n%d    %d", a++, ++b);
20:     printf("\n%d    %d", a++, ++b);
```

4. The following code fragment is just one of many possible answers. It checks to see if x is greater than or equal to 1 and less than or equal to 20. If these two conditions are met, x is assigned to y. If these conditions are not met, x is not assigned to y; therefore, y remains the same.

```
if ((x >= 1) && (x <= 20))
    y = x;
```

5. The code is as follows:

```
y = ((x >= 1) && (x <= 20)) ? x : y;
```

Again, if the statement is TRUE, x is assigned to y; otherwise, y is assigned to itself, thus having no effect.

6. The code is as follows:

```
if ((x < 1) && (x > 10) )
    statement;
```

7. a. 7

b. 0

c. 9

d. 1 (true)

e. 5

D

8. a. TRUE

b. FALSE

c. TRUE. Notice that there is a single equal sign, making the `if` an assignment instead of a relation.

d. TRUE

9. The following is one possible answer:

```
if( age < 21 )
    printf( "You are not an adult" );
else if( age >= 65 )
        printf( "You are a senior citizen!");
    else
        printf( "You are an adult" );
```

10. This program has four problems. The first is on line 3. The assignment statement should end with a semicolon, not a colon. The second problem is the semicolon at the end of the `if` statement on line 6. The third problem is a common one: The assignment operator (`=`) is used rather than the relational operator (`==`) in the `if` statement. The final problem is the word `otherwise` on line 8. This should be `else`. Here is the corrected code:

```
/* a program with problems... */
#include <stdio.h>
int x = 1;
int main( void )
{
    if( x == 1)
        printf(" x equals 1" );
    else
        printf(" x does not equal 1");
    return 0;
}
```

Answers for Lesson 5

Quiz

1. Yes! (Well, okay; this is a trick question, but you had better answer "yes" if you want to become a good C programmer.)

2. Structured programming takes a complex programming problem and breaks it into a number of simpler tasks that are easier to handle one at a time.

3. After you've broken your program into a number of simpler tasks, you can write a function to perform each task.

4. The first line of a function definition must be the function header. It contains the function's name, its return type, and its parameter list.

5. A function can return either one value or no values. The value can be of any of the C variable types. In Lesson 19, "Getting More from Functions," you can see how to get more values back from a function.

6. A function that returns nothing should be type `void`.

7. A function definition is the complete function, including the header and all the function's statements. The definition determines what actions take place when the function executes. The prototype is a single line, identical to the function header, but it ends with a semicolon. The prototype informs the compiler of the function's name, return type, and parameter list.

8. A local variable is declared within a function.

9. Local variables are independent from other variables in the program.

10. `main()` should be the first function in your listing.

Exercises

1. `float do_it(char a, char b, char c)`

   Add a semicolon to the end, and you have the function prototype. As a function header, it should be followed by the function's statements enclosed in braces.

2. `void print_a_number( int a_number )`

   This is a `void` function. As in exercise 1, to create the prototype, add a semicolon to the end. In an actual program, the header is followed by the function's statements.

3. a. `int`

   b. `long`

4. There are two problems. First, the `print_msg()` function is declared as a `void`; however, it returns a value. The `return` statement should be removed. The second problem is on the fifth line. The call to `print_msg()` passes a parameter (a string). The prototype states that this function has a `void` parameter list and, therefore, shouldn't be passed anything. The following is the corrected listing:

```
#include <stdio.h>
void print_msg (void);
int main( void )
{
    print_msg();
    return 0;
}
```

D

```
void print_msg(void)
{
    puts( "This is a message to print" );
}
```

5. There should not be a semicolon at the end of the function header.

6. Only the `larger_of()` function needs to be changed:

```
21: int larger_of( int a, int b)
22: {
23:     int save;
24:
25:     if (a > b)
26:         save = a;
27:     else
28:         save = b;
29:
30:     return save;
31: }
```

7. The following assumes that the two values are integers and an integer is returned:

```
int product( int x, int y )
{
    return (x * y);
}
```

8. The following listing checks the second value passed to verify that it is not 0. Division by zero causes an error. You should never assume that the values passed are correct. However, this only prevents a division-by-zero error at the function level. It will end up returning 0 to the calling program, because the program needs to always return an integer variable type. To truly avoid division by error, your program should check the value of b before you even call the `divide_em` function.

```
int divide_em( int a, int b )
{
    int answer = 0;

    if( b == 0 )
        answer = 0;
    else
        answer = a/b;

    return answer;
}
```

9. Although the following code uses `main()`, it could use any function. Lines 9, 10, and 11 show the calls to the two functions. Lines 13 through 16 print the values. To run this listing, you need to include the code from exercises 7 and 8 after line 19.

```
1:  #include <stdio.h>
2:
3:  int main( void )
4:  {
5:      int number1 = 10,
6:          number2 = 5;
7:      int x, y, z;
8:
9:      x = product( number1, number2 );
10:     y = divide_em( number1, number2 );
11:     z = divide_em( number1, 0 );
12:
13:      printf( "\nnumber1 is %d and number2 is %d", number1, number2 );
14:      printf( "\nnumber1 * number2 is %d", x );
15:      printf( "\nnumber1 / number2 is %d", y );
16:      printf( "\nnumber1 / 0 is %d", z );
17:
18:      return 0;
19: }
```

10. The code is as follows:

```
/* Averages five float values entered by the user. */

#include <stdio.h>

float v, w, x, y, z, answer;

float average(float a, float b, float c, float d, float e);

int main( void )
{
    puts("Enter five numbers:");
    scanf("%f%f%f%f%f", &v, &w, &x, &y, &z);

    answer = average(v, w, x, y, z);

    printf("The average is %f.\n", answer);

    return 0;
}

float average(float a, float b, float c, float d, float e)
{
    return ((a+b+c+d+e)/5);
}
```

11. The following is the answer using type int variables. It can run only with values less than or equal to 9. To use values larger than 9, you need to change the values to type long.

D

```
/* this is a program with a recursive function */

#include <stdio.h>

int three_powered( int power );

int main( void )
{
    int a = 4;
    int b = 9;

    printf( "\n3 to the power of %d is %d", a,
    three_powered(a) );
    printf( "\n3 to the power of %d is %d\n", b,
    three_powered(b) );

    return 0;
}

int three_powered( int power )
{

    if ( power < 1 )
        return( 1 );
    else
        return( 3 * three_powered( power - 1 ));
}
```

Answers for Lesson 6

Quiz

1. The first index value of an array in C is `0`.

2. A `for` statement contains initializing and increment expressions as parts of the command.

3. A `do...while` contains the `while` statement at the end and always executes the loop at least once.

4. Yes, a `while` statement can accomplish the same task as a `for` statement, but you need to do two additional things. You must initialize any variables before starting the `while` command, and you need to increment any variables as a part of the `while` loop.

5. There is no limit to the number of statements you nest.

6. Yes, a `while` statement can be nested in a `do...while` loop. You can nest any command within any other command.

7. The four parts of a `for` statement are the initializer, the condition, the increment, and the statement(s).

8. The two parts of a `while` statement are the condition and the statement(s).

9. The two parts of a `do...while` statement are the condition and the statement(s).

Exercises

1. `long array[50];`

2. Notice that in the following answer, the 50th element is indexed to `49`. Remember that arrays start at `0`.

   `array[49] = 123.456;`

3. When the statement is complete, x equals `100`.

4. When the statement is complete, `ctr` equals 11. (`ctr` starts at `2` and is incremented by `3` while it is less than `10`.)

5. The inner loop prints five xs. The outer loop prints the inner loop 10 times. This totals 50 xs.

6. The code is as follows:

   ```
   int x;
   for( x = 1; x <= 100; x += 3) ;
   ```

7. The code is as follows:

   ```
   int x = 1;
   while( x <= 100 )
       x += 3;
   ```

   D

8. The code is as follows:

   ```
   int ctr = 1;
   do
   {
       ctr += 3;
   } while( ctr < 100 );
   ```

9. This program never ends. `record` is initialized to `0`. The `while` loop then checks to see whether `record` is less than `100`. `0` is less than `100`, so the loop executes, thus printing the two statements. The loop then checks the condition again. `0` is still, and always will be, less than `100`, so the loop continues. Within the brackets, `record` needs to be incremented. You should add the following line after the second `printf()` function call:

   `record++;`

10. Using a defined constant is common in looping; you can see examples similar to this code fragment in lessons throughout the book. The problem with this fragment is simple. The semicolon doesn't belong at the end of the `for` statement. This is a common bug.

Answers for Lesson 7

Quiz

1. There are two differences between `puts()` and `printf()`:

   `printf()` can print variable parameters.

   `puts()` automatically adds a newline character to the end of the string it prints.

2. You should include the `stdio.h` header file when using `printf()`.

3. a. \\ prints a backslash.

   b. \b prints a backspace.

   c. \n prints a newline.

   d. \t prints a tab.

   e. \a (for "alert") sounds the beep.

4. a. %s for a character string

   b. %d for a signed decimal integer

   c. %f for a decimal floating-point number

5. a. b prints the literal character b.

   b. \b prints a backspace character.

   c. \ looks at the next character to determine an escape character (see Table 7.1).

   d. \\ prints a single backslash.

Exercises

1. `puts()` automatically adds the newline; `printf()` does not. The code is as follows:

   ```
   printf( "\n" );

   puts( "" );
   ```

2. The code is as follows:

   ```
   char c1, c2;
   int d1;
   scanf( "%c %u %c", &c1, &d1, &c2 );
   ```

3. Your answer might vary:

```c
#include <stdio.h>
int x;

int main( void )
{
    puts( "Enter an integer value" );
    scanf( "%d", &x );

    printf( "\nThe value entered is %d\n", x );

    return 0;
}
```

4. It's typical to edit a program to allow only specific values to be accepted. The following is one way to accomplish this exercise:

```c
#include <stdio.h>
int x;

int main( void )
{
    puts( "Enter an even integer value" );
    scanf( "%d", &x );
    while( x % 2 != 0)
    {
        printf( "\n%d is not even, please enter an even \
        number: ", x );
        scanf( "%d", &x );
    }
    printf( "\nThe value entered is %d\n", x );

    return 0;
}
```

D

5. The code is as follows:

```c
#include <stdio.h>
int array[6], x, number;

int main( void )
{
    /* loop 6 times or until the last entered element is 99 */
    for( x = 0; x < 6 && number != 99; x++ )
    {
        puts( "Enter an even integer value, or 99 to quit" );
        scanf( "%d", &number );
        while( number % 2 == 1 && number != 99)
        {
            printf( "\n%d is not even, please enter an even \
                number: ", number);
```

```
            scanf( "%d", &number );
        }
        array[x] = number;
    }
    /* now print them out... */
    for( x = 0; x < 6 && array[x] != 99; x++ )
    {
        printf( "\nThe value entered is %d", array[x] );
    }

    return 0;
}
```

6. The previous answers already are executable programs. The only change that needs to be made is in the final `printf()`. To print each value separated by a tab, change the `printf()` statement to the following:

```
printf( "%d\t", array[x]);
```

7. You can't have quotes within quotes. To print quotes within quotes, you must use the escape character `\"`. In addition, you must include a single slash at the end of the first line to have the text continued to the second line. The following is the corrected version:

```
printf( "Jack said, \"Peter Piper picked a peck of pickled \
peppers.\"");
```

8. This listing has three errors. The first is the lack of quotes in the `printf()` statement. The second is the missing address-of operator in the `answer` variable in the `scanf()`. The final error is also in the `scanf()` statement. Instead of `"%f"`, it should have `"%d"` because `answer` is a type `int` variable, not a type `float`. The following is corrected:

```
int get_1_or_2( void )
{
    int answer = 0;

    while( answer < 1 || answer > 2 )
    {
        printf("Enter 1 for Yes, 2 for No ");      /* corrected */

        scanf( "%d", &answer );                     /* corrected */
    }
    return answer;
}
```

9. Here is the completed `print_report()` function for Listing 7.1:

```
void print_report( void )
{
    printf( "\nSAMPLE REPORT" );
```

```
    printf( "\n\nSequence\tMeaning" );
    printf( "\n=========\t=======" );
    printf( "\n\\a\t\tBell (alert)" );
    printf( "\n\\b\t\tBackspace" );
    printf( "\n\\f\t\tForm feed" );
    printf( "\n\\n\t\tNewline" );
    printf( "\n\\r\t\tCarriage Return" );
    printf( "\n\\t\t\tHorizontal tab" );
    printf( "\n\\v\t\tVertical tab" );
    printf( "\n\\\\\t\tBackslash" );
    printf( "\n\\\?\t\tQuestion mark" );
    printf( "\n\\\'\t\tSingle quote" );
    printf( "\n\\\"\t\tDouble quote" );
    printf( "\n...\t\t...");
}
```

10. The code is as follows:

```
/* Inputs two floating-point values and */
/* displays their product. */

#include <stdio.h>

float x, y;

int main( void )
{
    puts("Enter two values: ");
    scanf("%f %f", &x, &y);
    printf("\nThe product is %f\n", x * y);
    return 0;
}
```

D

11. The following program prompts for 10 integers and displays their sum:

```
/* Input 10 integers and display their sum. */

#include <stdio.h>

int count, temp;
long total = 0;     /* Use type long to ensure we don't */
/* exceed the maximum for type int. */

int main( void )
{
    for (count = 1; count <=10; count++)
    {
        printf("Enter integer # %d: ", count);
        scanf("%d", &temp);
        total += temp;
    }
```

```
    printf("\n\nThe total is %d\n", total);

    return 0;
}
```

12. The code is as follows:

```
/* Inputs integers and stores them in an array, stopping */
/* when a zero is entered. Finds and displays the array's */
/* largest and smallest values */
#include <stdio.h>

#define MAX 100

int array[MAX];
int count = -1, maximum, minimum, num_entered, temp;

int main( void )
{
    puts("Enter integer values one per line.");
    puts("Enter 0 when finished.");

    /* Input the values */

    do
    {
        scanf("%d", &temp);
        array[++count] = temp;
    } while ( count < (MAX-1) && temp != 0 );

    num_entered = count;

    /* Find the largest and smallest. */
    /* First set maximum to a very small value, */
    /* and minimum to a very large value. */

    maximum = -32000;
    minimum = 32000;

    for (count = 0; count <= num_entered && array[count] != 0; count++)
    {
        if (array[count] > maximum)
        maximum = array[count];

        if (array[count] < minimum )
            minimum = array[count];
    }

    printf("\nThe maximum value is %d", maximum);
    printf("\nThe minimum value is %d\n", minimum);

    return 0;
}
```

Answers for Lesson 8

Quiz

1. All of them, but one at a time. A given array can contain only a single data type.

2. 0. Regardless of the size of an array, all C arrays start with subscript 0. (Obviously an array of size 0 would not start with subscript 0, as it has no elements at all.)

3. `n-1`

4. The program compiles and runs, but it produces unpredictable results.

5. In the declaration statement, follow the array name with one set of brackets for each dimension. Each set of brackets contains the number of elements in the corresponding dimension.

6. 240. This is determined by multiplying 2×3×5×8.

7. `array[0][0][1][1]`

Exercises

1. `int one[1000], two[1000], three[1000];`

2. `int array[10] = { 1, 1, 1, 1, 1, 1, 1, 1, 1, 1 };`

3. This exercise can be solved in numerous ways. The first way is to initialize the array when it's declared:

   ```
   int eightyeight[88] = {88,88,88,88,88,88,88,...,88};
   ```

   However, this approach requires you to place 88 `88`s between the braces (instead of using ..., as I did). I don't recommend this method for initializing such a large array. The following is a better method:

   ```
   int eightyeight[88];
   int x;

   for ( x = 0; x < 88; x++ )
       eightyeight[x] = 88;
   ```

4. The code is as follows:

   ```
   int stuff[12][10];
   int sub1, sub2;

   for( sub1 = 0; sub1 < 12; sub1++ )
       for( sub2 = 0; sub2 < 10; sub2++ )
           stuff[sub1][sub2] = 0;
   ```

D

5. Be careful with this fragment. The bug presented here is easy to create. Notice that the array is 10×3 but is initialized as a 3×10 array.

To describe this differently, the left subscript is declared as 10, but the `for` loop uses x as the left subscript. x is incremented with three values. The right subscript is declared as 3, but the second `for` loop uses y as the right subscript. y is incremented with 10 values. This can cause unpredictable results. You can fix this program in one of two ways. The first way is to switch x and y in the line that does the initialization:

```
int x, y;
int array[10][3];
int main( void )
{
    for ( x = 0; x < 3; x++ )
        for ( y = 0; y < 10; y++ )
            array[y][x] = 0;          /* changed */

    return 0;
}
```

The second way (which is recommended) is to switch the values in the `for` loops:

```
int x, y;
int array[10][3];
int main( void )
{
    for ( x = 0; x < 10; x++ )      /* changed */
        for ( y = 0; y < 3; y++ )     /* changed */
            array[x][y] = 0;

    return 0;
}
```

6. This was an easy bug to bust. This program initializes an element in the array that is out of bounds. If you have an array with 10 elements, their subscripts are 0 to 9. This program initializes elements with subscripts 1 through 10. You can't initialize `array[10]` because it doesn't exist. The `for` statement should be changed to one of the following examples:

```
for( x = 1; x <=9; x++ )   /* initializes 9 of the 10 elements */

for( x = 0; x <= 9; x++ )
```

Note that x <= 9 is the same as x < 10. Either is appropriate; x < 10 is more common.

7. The following is one of many possible answers:

```
/* Using two-dimensional arrays and rand() */

#include <stdio.h>
#include <stdlib.h>

/* Declare the array */

int array[5][4];
int a, b;

int main( void )
{
   for ( a = 0; a < 5; a++ )
   {
      for ( b = 0; b < 4; b++ )
      {
         array[a][b] = rand();
      }
   }

   /* Now print the array elements */

   for ( a = 0; a < 5; a++ )
   {
      for ( b = 0; b < 4; b++ )
      {
         printf( "%d\t", array[a][b] );
      }
      printf( "\n" );    /* go to a new line */
   }

   return 0;
}
```

8. The following is one of many possible answers:

```
/* random.c: using a single-dimensional array */

#include <stdio.h>
#include <stdlib.h>
/* Declare a single-dimensional array with 1000 elements */

int randomarray[1000];
int a, b, c;
long total = 0;

int main( void )
{
   /* Fill the array with random numbers. The C library */
   /* function rand() returns a random number. Use one */
```

D

```
/* for loop for each array subscript. */

for (a = 0; a < 1000; a++)
{
   randomarray[a] = rand();
   total += randomarray[a];
}
printf("\n\nAverage is: %ld\n",total/1000);
/* Now display the array elements 10 at a time */

for (a = 0; a < 1000; a++)
{
   printf("\nrandomarray[%d] = ", a);
   printf("%d", randomarray[a]);

   if ( a % 10 == 0 && a > 0 )
   {
       printf("\nPress Enter to continue, Ctrl-C to quit.");
       getchar();
   }
}
   return 0;
}        /* end of main() */
```

9. The following are two solutions. The first initializes the array at the time it is declared, and the second initializes it in a `for` loop.

Answer 1:

```
#include <stdio.h>

/* Declare a single-dimensional array */

int elements[10] = { 0, 1, 2, 3, 4, 5, 6, 7, 8, 9 };
int idx;

int main( void )
{
   for (idx = 0; idx < 10; idx++)
   {
      printf( "\nelements[%d] = %d ", idx, elements[idx] );
   }
   return 0;
}          /* end of main() */
```

Answer 2:

```
#include <stdio.h>

/* Declare a single-dimensional array */

int elements[10];
```

```
    int idx;

    int main( void )
    {
        for (idx = 0; idx < 10; idx++)
            elements[idx] = idx ;

        for (idx = 0; idx < 10; idx++)
            printf( "\nelements[%d] = %d ", idx, elements[idx] );

        return 0;
    }
```

10. The following is one of many possible answers:

```
    #include <stdio.h>
    #define ARRAYSIZE 10

    /* Declare a single-dimensional array */

    int elements[ARRAYSIE] = { 0, 1, 2, 3, 4, 5, 6, 7, 8, 9 };
    int new_array[ARRAYSIZE];
    int idx;

    int main( void )
    {
        for (idx = 0; idx < ARRAYSIZE; idx++)
        {
            new_array[idx] = elements[idx] + 10 ;
        }

        for (idx = 0; idx < ARRAYSIZE; idx++)
        {
            printf( "\nelements[%d] = %d \tnew_array[%d] = %d",
            idx, elements[idx], idx, new_array[idx] );
        }
        return 0;
    }
```

D

Answers for Lesson 9

Quiz

1. The address-of operator is the & sign.

2. The indirection operator * is used. When you precede the name of a pointer by *, it refers to the variable pointed to.

3. A pointer is a variable that contains the address of another variable.

4. Indirection is the act of accessing the contents of a variable by using a pointer to the variable.

5. They are stored in sequential memory locations, with lower array elements at lower addresses.

6. `&data[0]`

   `data`

7. One way is to pass the length of the array as a parameter to the function. The second way is to have a special value in the array, such as NULL, signify the array's end.

8. Assignment, indirection, address-of, incrementing, differencing, and comparison.

9. Differencing two pointers returns the number of elements in between. In this case, the answer is 1. The actual size of the elements in the array is irrelevant.

10. The answer is still 1.

Exercises

1. `char *char_ptr;`

2. The following declares a pointer to `cost` and then assigns the address of `cost` (`&cost`) to it:

   ```
   int *p_cost;
   p_cost = &cost;
   ```

3. Direct access: `cost = 100;`

   Indirect access: `*p_cost = 100;`

4. `printf( "Pointer value: %p, points at value: %d", p_cost, *p_cost);`

5. `float *variable = &radius;`

6. The code is as follows:

   ```
   data[2] = 100;
   *(data + 2) = 100;
   ```

7. This code also includes the answer for exercise 8:

   ```
   #include <stdio.h>

   #define MAX1 5
   #define MAX2 8

   int array1[MAX1] = { 1, 2, 3, 4, 5 };
   int array2[MAX2] = { 1, 2, 3, 4, 5, 6, 7, 8 };
   int total;
   ```

```
int sumarrays(int x1[], int len_x1, int x2[], int len_x2);

int main( void )
{
    total = sumarrays(array1, MAX1, array2, MAX2);
    printf("The total is %d\n", total);

    return 0;
}

int sumarrays(int x1[], int len_x1, int x2[], int len_x2)
{

    int total = 0, count = 0;

    for (count = 0; count < len_x1; count++)
        total += x1[count];

    for (count = 0; count < len_x2; count++)
        total += x2[count];

    return total;
}
```

8. See the answer for exercise 7.

9. The following is just one possible answer:

```
#include <stdio.h>

#define SIZE 10

/* function prototypes */
void addarrays( int [], int []);

int main( void )
{
    int a[SIZE] = {1, 1, 1, 1, 1, 1, 1, 1, 1, 1};
    int b[SIZE] = {9, 8, 7, 6, 5, 4, 3, 2, 1, 0};

    addarrays(a, b);

    return 0;
}

void addarrays( int first[], int second[])
{
    int total[SIZE];
    int *ptr_total = &total[0];
    int ctr = 0;

    for (ctr = 0; ctr < SIZE; ctr ++ )
```

D

```
        {
            total[ctr] = first[ctr] + second[ctr];
            printf("%d + %d = %d\n", first[ctr], second[ctr], total[ctr]);
        }
    }
}
```

Answers for Lesson 10

Quiz

1. The values in the ASCII character set range from 0 to 255. From 0 to 127 is the standard ASCII character set, and 128 to 255 is the extended ASCII character set.

2. As the character's ASCII code.

3. A string is a sequence of characters terminated by the null character.

4. A sequence of one or more characters enclosed in double quotation marks.

5. To hold the string's terminating null character.

6. As a sequence of ASCII values corresponding to the quoted characters, followed by 0 (the ASCII code for the null character).

7. a. 97

   b. 65

   c. 57

   d. 32

   e. 206

   f. 6

8. a. I

   b. a space

   c. c

   d. a

   e. n

   f. NUL

   g. [002]

9. a. 9 bytes. (Actually, the variable is a pointer to a string, and the string requires 9 bytes of memory: 8 for the string and 1 for the null terminator.)

   b. 9 bytes

   c. 1 byte

d. 20 bytes

e. 20 bytes

10. a. A

b. A

c. 0 (NULL)

d. This is beyond the end of the string, so it could have any value.

e. 73

f. This contains the address of the first element of the string.

Exercises

1. `char letter = '$';`

2. `char array[] = "Pointers are fun!";`

3. `char *array = "Pointers are fun!";`

4. The code is as follows:

```
char *ptr;
ptr = malloc(81);
gets(ptr);
```

5. The following is just one possible answer. A complete program is provided:

```
#include <stdio.h>

#define SIZE 10

/* function prototypes */
void copyarrays( int [], int []);

int main( void )
{
    int ctr=0;
    int a[SIZE] = {1, 2, 3, 4, 5, 6, 7, 8, 9, 10};
    int b[SIZE];

    /* values before copy */
    for (ctr = 0; ctr < SIZE; ctr ++ )
    {
        printf( "a[%d] = %d, b[%d] = %d\n",
                ctr, a[ctr], ctr, b[ctr]);
    }

    copyarrays(a, b);

    /* values after copy */
```

D

```
        for (ctr = 0; ctr < SIZE; ctr ++ )
        {
            printf( "a[%d] = %d, b[%d] = %d\n",
                        ctr, a[ctr], ctr, b[ctr]);
        }

        return 0;
    }

    void copyarrays( int orig[], int newone[])
    {
        int ctr = 0;

        for (ctr = 0; ctr < SIZE; ctr ++ )
        {
            newone[ctr] = orig[ctr];
        }
    }
```

6. The following is one of many possible answers:

```
    #include <stdio.h>
    #include <string.h>

    /* function prototypes */
    char * compare_strings( char *, char *);

    int main( void )
    {
        char *a = "Hello";
        char *b = "World!";
        char *longer;

        longer = compare_strings(a, b);

        printf( "The longer string is: %s\n", longer );

        return 0;
    }

    char * compare_strings( char * first, char * second)
    {
        int x, y;

        x = strlen(first);
        y = strlen(second);

        if( x > y)
            return(first);
        else
            return(second);
    }
```

7. This exercise was on your own!

8. `a_string` is declared as an array of 10 characters, but it's initialized with a string larger than 10 characters. `a_string` needs to be bigger.

9. If the intent of this line of code is to initialize a string, it is wrong. You should use either `char *quote` or `char quote[100]`.

10. No.

11. Yes. Although you can assign one pointer to another, you can't assign one array to another. You should change the assignment to a string-copying command such as `strcpy()`.

Answers for Lesson 11

Quiz

1. The data items in an array must all be of the same type. A structure can contain data items of different types.

2. The structure member operator is a period. It is used to access members of a structure.

3. `struct`

4. A structure tag is tied to a template of a structure and is not an actual variable. A structure instance is an allocated structure that can hold data.

5. These statements define a structure and declare an instance called `myaddress`. This instance is then initialized. The structure member `myaddress.name` is initialized to the string `"Bradley Jones"`, `myaddress.add1` is initialized to `"RTSoftware"`, `myaddress.add2` is initialized to `"P.O. Box 1213"`, `myaddress.city` is initialized to `"Carmel"`, `myaddress.state` is initialized to `"IN"`, and `myaddress.zip` is initialized to `"46032-1213"`.

6. `word myWord;`

7. The following statement changes `ptr` to point to the second array element:
   `ptr++;`

Exercises

1. The code is as follows:
```
struct time {
    int hours;
    int minutes;
    int seconds;
} ;
```

D

2. The code is as follows:
```
struct data {
    int value1;
    float value2;
    float value3;

} info ;
```

3. `info.value1 = 100;`

4. The code is as follows:
```
struct data *ptr;
ptr = &info;
```

5. The code is as follows:
```
ptr->value2 = 5.5;
(*ptr).value2 = 5.5;
```

6. The code is as follows:
```
struct data {
    char name[21];

};
```

7. The code is as follows:
```
typedef struct {
    char address1[31];
    char address2[31];
    char city[11];
    char state[3];
    char zip[11];
} RECORD;
```

8. The following uses the values from quiz question 5 for the initialization:
```
RECORD myaddress = {"RTSoftware",
                    "P.O. Box 1213",
                    "Carmel", "IN", "46032-1213" };
```

9. This code fragment has two problems. The first is that the structure should contain a tag. The second is the way `sign` is initialized. The initialization values should be in braces. Here is the corrected code:
```
struct zodiac {
    char zodiac_sign[21];
    int month;
} sign = {"Leo", 8};
```

10. The `union` declaration has only one problem. Only one variable in a union can be used at a time. This is also true of initializing the union. Only the first member of the union can be initialized. Here is the correct initialization:

```
/* setting up a union */
union data{
    char a_word[4];
    long a_number;
}generic_variable = { "WOW" };
```

Answers for Lesson 12

Quiz

1. The scope of a variable refers to the extent to which different parts of a program have access to the variable, or where the variable is visible.

2. A variable with local storage class is visible only in the function where it is defined. A variable with external storage class is visible throughout the program.

3. Defining a variable in a function makes it local; defining a variable outside of any function makes it external.

4. Automatic (the default) or static. An automatic variable is created each time the function is called and is destroyed when the function ends. A static local variable persists and retains its value between calls to the function.

5. An automatic variable is initialized every time the function is called. A static variable is initialized only the first time the function is called.

6. False. When declaring register variables, you're making a request. There is no guarantee that the compiler will honor the request.

7. An uninitialized global variable is automatically initialized to `0`; however, it's best to initialize variables explicitly.

8. An uninitialized local variable isn't automatically initialized; it could contain anything. You should never use an uninitialized local variable.

9. Because the variable `count` is now local to the block, the `printf()` no longer has access to a variable called `count`. The compiler gives you an error.

10. If the value needs to be remembered, it should be declared as static. For example, if the variable were called `vari`, the declaration would be
    ```
    static int vari;
    ```

11. The `extern` keyword is used as a storage-class modifier. It indicates that the variable has been defined somewhere else in the program.

D

12. The `static` keyword is used as a storage-class modifier. It tells the compiler to retain the value of a variable or function for the duration of a program. Within a function, the variable keeps its value between function calls. Outside a function, the keyword tells the computer to limit the scope of the modified to just the single file.

Exercises

1. `register int x = 0;`

2. The code is as follows:

```
/* Illustrates variable scope. */
#include <stdio.h>

void print_value(int x);

int main( void )
{
    int x = 999;

    printf("%d", x);
    print_value( x );

    return 0;
}

void print_value( int x)
{
    printf("%d", x);
}
```

3. Because you're declaring `var` as a global, you don't need to pass it as a parameter.

```
/* Using a global variable */
#include <stdio.h>

int var = 99;

void print_value(void);

int main( void )
{
    print_value();
    return 0;
}

void print_value(void)
{
    printf( "The value is %d\n", var );
}
```

4. Yes, you need to pass the variable `var` to print it in a different function.

```
/* Using a local variable */
#include <stdio.h>

void print_value(int var);

int main( void )
{
    int var = 99;
    print_value(  var );

    return 0;
}

void print_value(int var)
{
    printf( "The value is %d\n", var );
}
```

5. Yes, a program can have a local and global variable with the same name. In such cases, active local variables take precedence.

```
/* Using a global */
#include <stdio.h>

int var = 99;

void print_func(void);

int main( void )
{
    int var = 77;
    printf( "Printing in function with local and global:");
    printf( "\nThe value of var is %d", var );
    print_func( );

    return 0;
}
void print_func( void )
{
    printf( "\nPrinting in function  only global:");
    printf( "\nThe value of var is %d\n", var );
}
```

D

6. There is only one problem with `a_sample_function()`. Variables can be declared at the beginning of any block, so the declarations of `crt1` and `star` are fine. The other variable, `ctr2`, is not declared at the beginning of a block; it needs to be. The following is the corrected function within a complete program.

Note: If you use a C++ compiler instead of a C compiler, the listing with a bug might run and compile. C++ has different rules concerning where variables can be declared. However, you should still follow the rules for C, even if your compiler lets you get away with something different.

```c
#include <stdio.h>

void a_sample_function( );
int main( void )
{
    a_sample_function();
    return 0;
}

void a_sample_function( void )
{
    int ctr1;

    for ( ctr1 = 0; ctr1 < 25; ctr1++ )
        printf( "*" );

    puts( "\nThis is a sample function" );
    {
        char star = '*';
        int ctr2;        /* fix */
        puts( "\nIt has a problem\n" );
        for ( ctr2 = 0; ctr2 < 25; ctr2++ )
        {
            printf( "%c", star);
        }
    }
}
```

7. This program actually works properly, but it could be better. First, there is no need to initialize the variable x to 1 because it's initialized to 0 in the for statement. Also, declaring the variable tally to be static is pointless because within the main() function, static keywords have no effect.

8. What is the value of star? What is the value of dash? These two variables are never initialized. Because they are both local variables, each could contain any value. Note that, although this program compiles with no errors or warnings, there is still a problem.

There is a second issue that should be brought up about this program. The variable ctr is declared as global, but it's used only in print_function(). This isn't a good assignment. The program would be better if ctr were a local variable in print_function().

9. This program prints the following pattern forever. See exercise 10.

```
X==X==X==X==X==X==X==X==X==X==X==X==X==X==X==X==X==...
```

10. This program poses a problem because of the global scope of `ctr`. Both `main()` and `print_letter2()` use `ctr` in loops at the same time. Because `print_letter2()` changes the value, the `for` loop in `main()` never completes. This could be fixed in a number of ways. One way is to use two different counter variables. A second way is to change the scope of the counter variable `ctr`. It could be declared in both `main()` and `print_letter2()` as a local variable.

An additional comment on `letter1` and `letter2`: Because each of these is used in only one function, they should be declared as local. Here is the corrected listing:

```c
#include <stdio.h>
void print_letter2(void);            /* function prototype */

int main( void )
{
    char letter1 = 'X';
    int ctr;

    for( ctr = 0; ctr < 10; ctr++ )
    {
        printf( "%c", letter1 );
        print_letter2();
    }
    return 0;
}

void print_letter2(void)
{
    char letter2 = '=';
    int ctr;                /* this is a local variable */
                            /* it is different from ctr in main() */
    for( ctr = 0; ctr < 2; ctr++ )
        printf( "%c", letter2 );
}
```

D

Answers for Lesson 13

Quiz

1. Never. (Unless you are very careful.)

2. When a `break` statement is encountered, execution immediately exits the `for`, `do...while`, or `while` loop that contains the `break`. When a `continue` statement is encountered, the next iteration of the enclosing loop begins immediately.

3. An infinite loop executes forever. You create one by writing a `for`, `do...while`, or `while` loop with a test condition that is always true.

4. Execution terminates when the program reaches the end of `main()` or the `exit()` function is called.

5. The expression in a `switch` statement can evaluate to a `long`, `int`, or `char` value.

6. The `default` statement is a case in a `switch` statement. When the expression in the `switch` statement evaluates to a value that doesn't have a matching case, control goes to the default case.

7. The `exit()` function causes the program to end. A value can be passed to the `exit()` function. This value is returned to the operating system.

Exercises

1. `continue;`

2. `break;`

3. This code fragment is correct. You don't need a `break` statement after the `printf()` for `'N'`, because the `switch` statement ends anyway.

4. You might think that the `default` needs to go at the bottom of the `switch` statement, but this isn't true. The `default` can go anywhere. There is a problem, however. There should be a `break` statement at the end of the `default` case.

5. The code is as follows:
```
if( choice == 1 )
    printf("You answered 1");
else if( choice == 2 )
        printf( "You answered 2");
    else
        printf( "You did not choose 1 or 2");
```

6. The code is as follows:
```
do {
    /* any C statements */
} while ( 1 );
```

Answers for Lesson 14

Quiz

1. A stream is a sequence of bytes. A C program uses streams for all input and output.

2. a. A printer is an output device.

b. A keyboard is an input device.

c. A modem is both an input and an output device.

d. A monitor is an output device. (Although a touch screen would be an input device and an output device.)

e. A flash drive can be both an input and an output device.

3. All C compilers support three predefined streams: `stdin` (the keyboard), `stdout` (the screen), and `stderr` (the screen).

4. a. `stdout`

b. `stdout`

c. `stdin`

d. `stdin`

c. `fprintf()` can use any output stream. Of the three universal streams, it can use `stdout` and `stderr`.

5. Buffered input is sent to the program only when the user presses Enter. Unbuffered input is sent one character at a time, as soon as each key is pressed.

6. Echoed input automatically sends each character to `stdout` as it is received; unechoed input does not.

7. You can "unget" only one character between reads. The EOF character can't be put back into the input stream with `ungetc()`.

8. With the newline character, which corresponds to the user pressing Enter.

9. a. Valid

b. Valid

c. Valid

d. Not valid. There is not an identifier of q.

e. Valid

f. Valid

10. `stderr` shouldn't be redirected; it should always print to the screen. `stdout` can be redirected to somewhere other than the screen.

Exercises

1. `printf( "Hello World" );`

2. `fprintf( stdout, "Hello World" );`

`puts( "Hello World");`

D

3. The code is as follows:

```
char buffer[31];
scanf( "%30[^*]", buffer );
```

4. The code is as follows:

```
printf( "Jack asked, \"What is a backslash\?\"\nJill said, \
\"It is \'\\\'\"");
```

Answers for Lesson 15

Quiz

1. The code is as follows:

```
float x;
float *px = &x;
float **ppx = &px;
```

2. The error is that the statement uses a single indirection operator and, as a result, assigns the value 100 to px instead of to x. The statement should be written with a double indirection operator:

```
**ppx = 100;
```

3. array is a 3-D array with two elements. Each of these elements is itself an array that contains three elements. Each of these elements is an array that contains four type int variables.

4. array[0][0] is a pointer to the first four-element array of type int.

5. The first and third comparisons are true; the second is not true.

6. void func1(char *p[]);

7. It has no way of knowing. This value must be passed to the function as another argument.

8. a. var1 is a pointer to an integer.

b. var2 is an integer.

c. var3 is a pointer to a pointer to an integer.

9. a. a is an array of 36 (3×12) integers.

b. b is a pointer to an array of 12 integers.

c. c is an array of 12 pointers to integers.

Exercises

1. `char *ptrs[10];`

2. `ptr` is declared as an array of 12 pointers to integers, not a pointer to an array of 12 integers. The correct code is

```
int x[3][12];
int (*ptr)[12];

ptr = x;
```

Answers for Lesson 16

Quiz

1. A pointer to a function is a variable that holds the address where the function is stored in memory.

2. `char (*ptr)(char *x[]);`

3. If you omit the parentheses surrounding `*ptr`, the line is a prototype of a function that returns a pointer to type `char`.

4. The structure must contain a pointer to the same type of structure.

5. It means that the linked list is empty.

6. Each element in the list contains a pointer that identifies the next element in the list. The first element in the list is identified by the head pointer.

7. a. `z` is an array of 10 pointers to characters.

   b. `y` is a function that takes an integer (`field`) as an argument and returns a pointer to a character.

   c. `x` is a pointer to a function that takes an integer (`field`) as an argument and returns a character.

Exercises

1. `float (*func)(int field);`

2. `int (*menu_option[10])(char *title);`

   An array of function pointers can be used with a menuing system. The number selected from a menu could correspond to the array index for the function pointer. For example, the function pointed to by the fifth element of the array would be executed if item 5 were selected from the menu.

D

3. The following is one of many possible solutions:

```
struct friend {
    char name[35+1];
    char street1[30+1];
    char street2[30+1];
    char city[15+1];
    char state[2+1];
    char zipcode[9+1];
    struct friend *next;
}
```

Answers for Lesson 17

Quiz

1. A text-mode stream automatically performs translation between the newline character (\n), which C uses to mark the end of a line, and the carriage-return linefeed character pair that Windows uses to mark the end of a line. In contrast, a binary-mode stream performs no translations. All bytes are input and output without modification.

2. Open the file using the fopen() library function.

3. When using fopen(), you must specify the name of the disk file to open and the mode to open it in. The function fopen() returns a pointer to type FILE; this pointer is used in subsequent file access functions to refer to the specific file.

4. Formatted, character, and direct.

5. Sequential and random.

6. EOF is the end-of-file flag. It is a symbolic constant equal to -1.

7. EOF is used with text files to determine when the end of the file has been reached.

8. In binary mode, you must use the feof() function. In text mode, you can look for the EOF character or use feof().

9. The file position indicator indicates the position in a given file where the next read or write operation will occur. You can modify the file position indicator with rewind() and fseek().

10. The file position indicator points to the first character of the file, or offset 0. The one exception is if you open an existing file in append mode, in which case the position indicator points to the end of the file.

Exercises

1. `fcloseall();`

2. `rewind(fp);` and `fseek(fp, 0, SEEK_SET);`

3. You can't use the EOF check with a binary file. You should use the `feof()` function instead.

Answers for Lesson 18

Quiz

1. The length of a string is the number of characters between the start of the string and the terminating null character (not counting the null character). You can determine the length of a string using the `strlen()` function.

2. You must be sure to allocate sufficient storage space for the new string.

3. *Concatenate* means to join two strings, appending one string to the end of another.

4. When you compare strings, "greater than" means that one string's ASCII values are larger than the other string's ASCII values.

5. `strcmp()` compares two entire strings. `strncmp()` compares only a specified number of characters within the string.

6. `isascii()` checks the value passed to see whether it's a standard ASCII character between 0 and 127. It doesn't check for extended ASCII characters.

7. `isascii()` and `iscntrl()` both return TRUE; all others return FALSE. Remember, these macros look at the character value.

8. 65 is equivalent to the ASCII character A. The following macros return TRUE: `isalnum()`, `isalpha()`, `isascii()`, `isgraph()`, `isprint()`, and `isupper()`.

9. The character-test functions determine whether a particular character meets a certain condition, such as whether it is a letter, punctuation mark, or something else.

D

Exercises

1. TRUE (1) or FALSE (0)

2. a. 65

   b. 81

   c. −34

   d. 0

   e. 12

   f. 0

3. a. 65.000000

b. 81.230000

c. –34.200000

d. 0.000000

e. 12.000000

f. 1000.000000

4. string2 should be a character pointer, and it wasn't allocated space before it was used. There is no way to know where strcpy() copies the value of string1.

Answers for Lesson 19

Quiz

1. Passing by value means that the function receives a copy of the value of the argument variable. Passing by reference means that the function receives the address of the argument variable. The difference is that passing by reference allows the function to modify the original variable, whereas passing by value does not.

2. A type void pointer can point to any type of C data object. (In other words, it's a generic pointer.)

3. By using a void pointer, you can create a generic pointer that can point to any object. The most common use of a void pointer is to declare function parameters. You can create a function that can handle different types of arguments.

4. A typecast provides information about the type of the data object that the void pointer is pointing to at the moment. You must typecast a void pointer before dereferencing it.

5. A function that takes a variable argument list must be passed at least one fixed argument. This is done to inform the function of the number of arguments being passed each time it is called.

6. va_start() should be used to initialize the argument list. va_arg() should be used to retrieve the arguments. va_end() should be used to clean up after all the arguments have been retrieved.

7. Trick question! void pointers can't be incremented because the compiler wouldn't know what value to add.

8. A function can return a pointer to any of the C variable types. A function can also return a pointer to such storage areas as arrays, structures, and unions.

9. `va_arg()`

10. The elements are `va_list`, `va_start()`, `va_arg()`, and `va_end()`.

Exercises

1. `int function( char array[] );`

2. `int numbers( int *nbr1, int *nbr2, int *nbr3);`

3. The code is as follows:

   ```
   int number1 = 1, number2 = 2, number3 = 3;
   numbers( &number1, &number2, &number3);
   ```

4. Although the code might look confusing, it is correct. This function takes the value being pointed to by `nbr` and multiplies it by itself.

5. When using variable parameter lists, you should use all the macro tools. This includes `va_list`, `va_start()`, `va_arg()`, and `va_end()`. See Listing 19.3 for the correct way to use variable parameter lists.

Answers for Lesson 20

Quiz

1. Type `double`.

2. On most compilers, it's equivalent to a `long`; however, this isn't guaranteed. Check the TIME.H file with your compiler or your reference manual to find out what variable type your compiler uses.

3. The `time()` function returns the number of seconds that have elapsed since midnight, January 1, 1970. The `clock()` function returns the number of 1/100 seconds that have elapsed since the program began execution.

4. Nothing. It simply displays a message that describes the error.

5. Sort the array into ascending order.

6. 14

7. 4

8. 21

9. `0` if the values are equal, `>0` if the value of element 1 is greater than element 2, and `<0` if the value of element 1 is less than element 2.

10. `NULL`

D

Exercises

1. The code is as follows:

```
bsearch( myname, names, (sizeof(names)/sizeof(names[0])),
sizeof(names[0]), comp_names);
```

2. There are three problems. First, the field width isn't provided in the call to `qsort()`. Second, the parentheses shouldn't be added to the end of the function name in the call to `qsort()`. Third, the program is missing its comparison function. `qsort()` uses `compare_function()`, which isn't defined in the program.

3. The compare function returns the wrong values. It should return a positive number if `element1` is greater than `element2` and a negative number if `element1` is less than `element2`.

Answers for Lesson 21

Quiz

1. `malloc()` allocates a specified number of bytes of memory, whereas `calloc()` allocates sufficient memory for a specified number of data objects of a certain size. `calloc()` also sets the bytes of memory to `0`, whereas `malloc()` doesn't initialize them to any specific value.

2. To preserve the fractional part of the answer when dividing one integer by another and assigning the result to a floating-point variable.

3. a. `long`

   b. `int`

   c. `char`

   d. `float`

   e. `float`

4. Dynamically allocated memory is allocated at runtime—while the program executes. Dynamic memory allocation enables you to allocate exactly as much memory as is needed, only when it is needed.

5. `memmove()` works properly when the source and destination memory regions overlap, whereas `memcpy()` does not. If the source and destination regions don't overlap, the two functions are identical.

6. By defining a bit field member with a size of 3 bits. Because 2^3 equals 8, such a field is sufficient to hold values `1` through `7`.

7. 2 bytes. Using bit fields, you could declare a structure as follows:

```
struct date
{
    unsigned month : 4;
    unsigned day   : 5;
    unsigned year  : 7;
}
```

This structure stores the date in 2 bytes (16 bits). The 4-bit `month` field can hold values from 0 to 15, sufficient for holding 12 months. Likewise, the 5-bit `day` field can hold values from 0 to 31, and the 7-bit `year` field can hold values from 0 to 127. You can assume that the year value will be added to 1900 to allow year values from 1900 to 2027.

8. 00100000

9. 00001001

10. These two expressions evaluate to the same result. Using exclusive OR with 11111111 is the same as using the complement operator: Each bit in the original value is reversed.

Exercises

1. The code is as follows:

```
long *ptr;
ptr = malloc( 1000 * sizeof(long));
```

2. The code is as follows:

```
long *ptr;
ptr = calloc( 1000, sizeof(long));
```

D

3. Using a loop and assignment statement:

```
int count;
for (count = 0; count < 1000; count++)
data[count] = 0;
```

Using the `memset()` function:

```
memset(data, 0, 1000 * sizeof(float));
```

4. This code compiles and runs without error; however, the result is incorrect. Because `number1` and `number2` are both integers, the result of their division is an integer, thus losing any fractional part of the answer. To get the correct answer, you need to cast the expression to type `float`:

```
answer = (float) number1/number2;
```

5. Because `p` is a type `void` pointer, it must be cast to the proper type before being used in an assignment statement. The third line should be as follows:

```
*(float*)p = 1.23;
```

6. No. When using bit fields, you must place them within a structure first. The following is correct:

```
struct quiz_answers
{
  unsigned answer1   : 1;
  unsigned answer2   : 1;
  unsigned answer3   : 1;
  unsigned answer4   : 1;
  unsigned answer5   : 1;
  char student_name[15];
-Dean}
```

Answers for Lesson 22

Quiz

1. *Modular programming* refers to the program development method that breaks a program into multiple source-code files.

2. The main module contains the `main()` function.

3. To avoid unwanted side effects by ensuring that complex expressions passed as arguments to the macro are fully evaluated first.

4. Compared to a function, a macro results in faster program execution but larger program size.

5. The `defined()` operator tests to see whether a particular name is defined, returning TRUE if the name is defined and FALSE if it isn't.

6. You must use `#endif`.

7. Compiled source files become object files with an .OBJ extension.

8. `#include` copies the contents of another file into the current file.

9. An `#include` statement with double quotes looks in the current directory for the include file. An `include` statement with `<>` searches the standard directory for the include file.

10. `__DATE__` is used to place into the program the date that the program was compiled.

11. A string containing the name of the current program, including path information.

Index

How can we make this index more useful? Email us at indexes@samspublishing.com

I

IDE (Integrated Development Environments), 14, 579

if, 590

if loops, perror() function and error-handling, 521

if statements, 71-77, 111

illustrated functions, 92-93

Imaginary, 591

implicit conversions, 534

include files. *See* header files

increment operators, 62

incrementing
  counter variables, 124
  expressions, 122
  for statements, 122, 126
  pointers, 198-200, 264-266

indenting styles, nesting loops, 141

independent functions, 282

indexes, 120

indirect access, 191

indirect membership operator (->), 263, 268

indirect recursion, 112

indirection operator (*), 189-191, 259, 262, 362
  functions returning pointers, 499
  passing by reference, 492
  precedence, 386

infinite loops, 307-310

initial expressions, 121, 126

initializing
  arrays, 178
    character arrays, 219
    multidimensional, 179-182
    of pointers, 374
    of structures, 257-258
  character variables, 215

memory, memset() function, 545-548

pointers, 190, 261-262, 400

pointers to functions, 387-396

structures, 256-258

unions, 269

variables, 45-46, 215

inline functions, 115, 590

input
  defining, 326
  device independent programming, 326
  keyboard input, 329
    fflush() function, 344
    fgetc() function, 335
    fgets() function, 336-338
    getc() function, 335
    getchar() function, 330-332
    getche() function, 334
    getch() function, 332-334
    gets() function, 336
    line-input functions, 336
    putchar() function, 333
    scanf() function, 156-161, 338-347
    ungetc() function, 335
  standard input/output files. *See* predefined streams
  streams
    binary streams, 327
    defining, 326
    equivalence of streams, 329
    files, 326
    input/output functions, 328-329
    predefined streams, 327-328
    text streams, 327

strings
  gets() function, 228-232
  printf() function, 227-228
  puts() function, 226-227
  scanf() function, 232-235

input fields, 339

instances, defining, 245

int, 590

intcmp() function, 526

integers, converting strings to, 475

integer variables, 41, 156

I/O. *See* input; output

isxxxx() macros, 477-480

iteration, 114

J - K

Java, 7

key arguments, 521

keyboard
  character input functions
    buffered, 330
    echoing, 330
    fgetc() function, 335
    fgets() function, 336-338
    getc() function, 335
    getchar(), 330-332
    getche() function, 334
    getch() function, 332-334
    gets() function, 336
    line-input, 336
    putchar() function, 333
    unbuffered, 330
    ungetc() function, 335
  formatted input functions
    fflush() function, 344

How can we make this index more useful? Email us at indexes@samspublishing.com

Sams Teach Yourself C Programming in One Hour a Day

SEVENTH EDITION
Covers C11

FREE
Online Edition

Safari
Books Online

Your purchase of *Sams Teach Yourself, C Programming in One Hour a Day* includes access to a free online edition for 45 days through the **Safari Books Online** subscription service. Nearly every Sams book is available online through **Safari Books Online**, along with thousands of books and videos from publishers such as Addison-Wesley Professional, Cisco Press, Exam Cram, IBM Press, O'Reilly Media, Prentice Hall, Que, and VMware Press.

Safari Books Online is a digital library providing searchable, on-demand access to thousands of technology, digital media, and professional development books and videos from leading publishers. With one monthly or yearly subscription price, you get unlimited access to learning tools and information on topics including mobile app and software development, tips and tricks on using your favorite gadgets, networking, project management, graphic design, and much more.

Activate your FREE Online Edition at
informit.com/safarifree

STEP 1: Enter the coupon code: JXRIEBI.

STEP 2: New Safari users, complete the brief registration form.
Safari subscribers, just log in.

If you have difficulty registering on Safari or accessing the online edition,
please e-mail customer-service@safaribooksonline.com